MW01625856

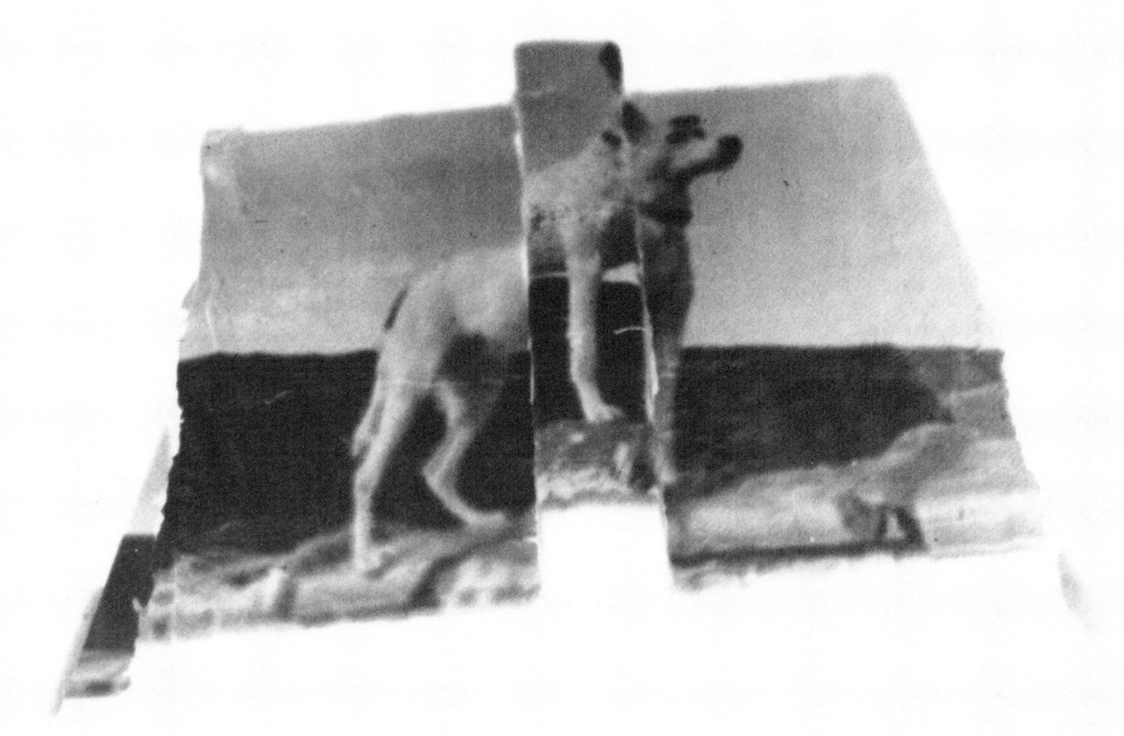

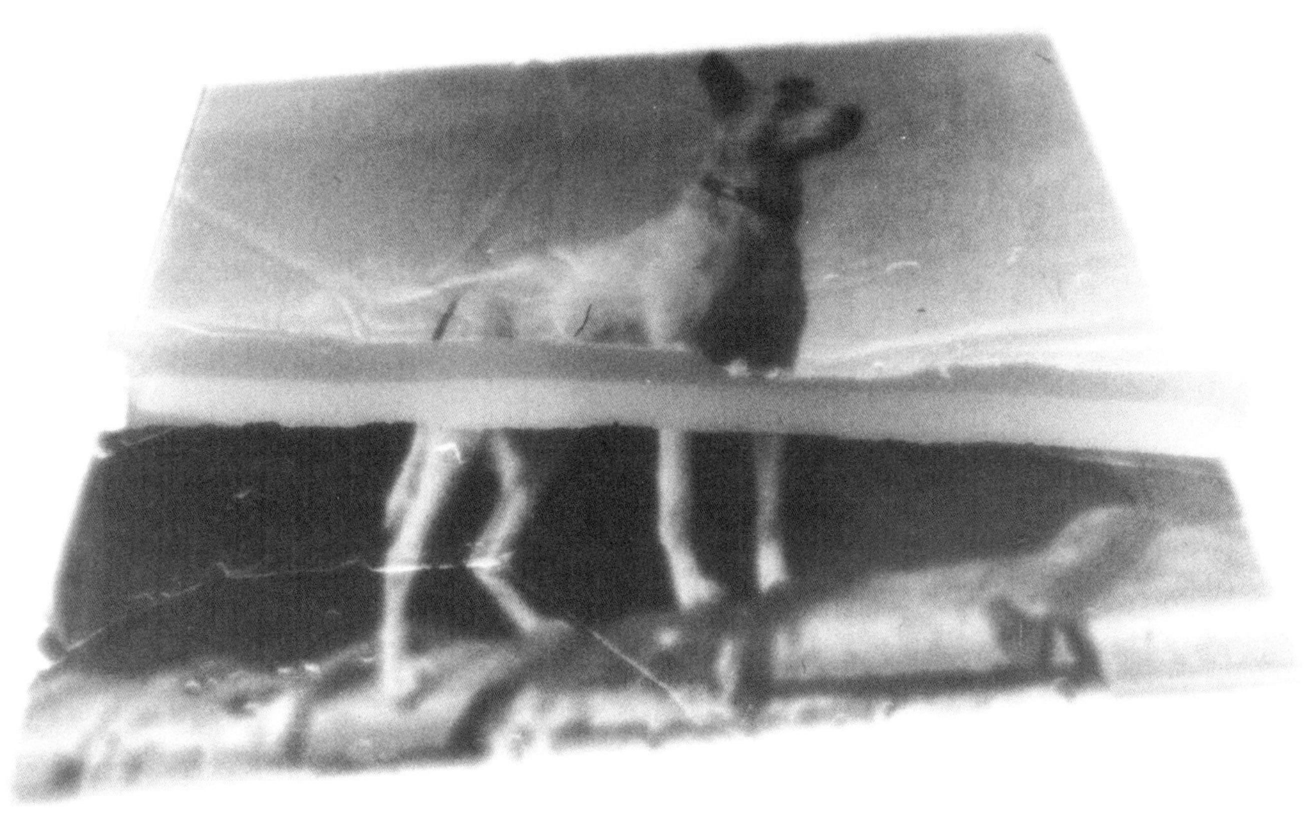

previous page
*Untitled (Dog)*, ca. 1987–91
Gelatin silver print
8 × 10 in.

*Untitled (Dog)*, ca. 1987–91
Gelatin silver print
16 × 20 in.

*Untitled (Dog)*, ca. 1987–91
Gelatin silver print
16 × 20 in.

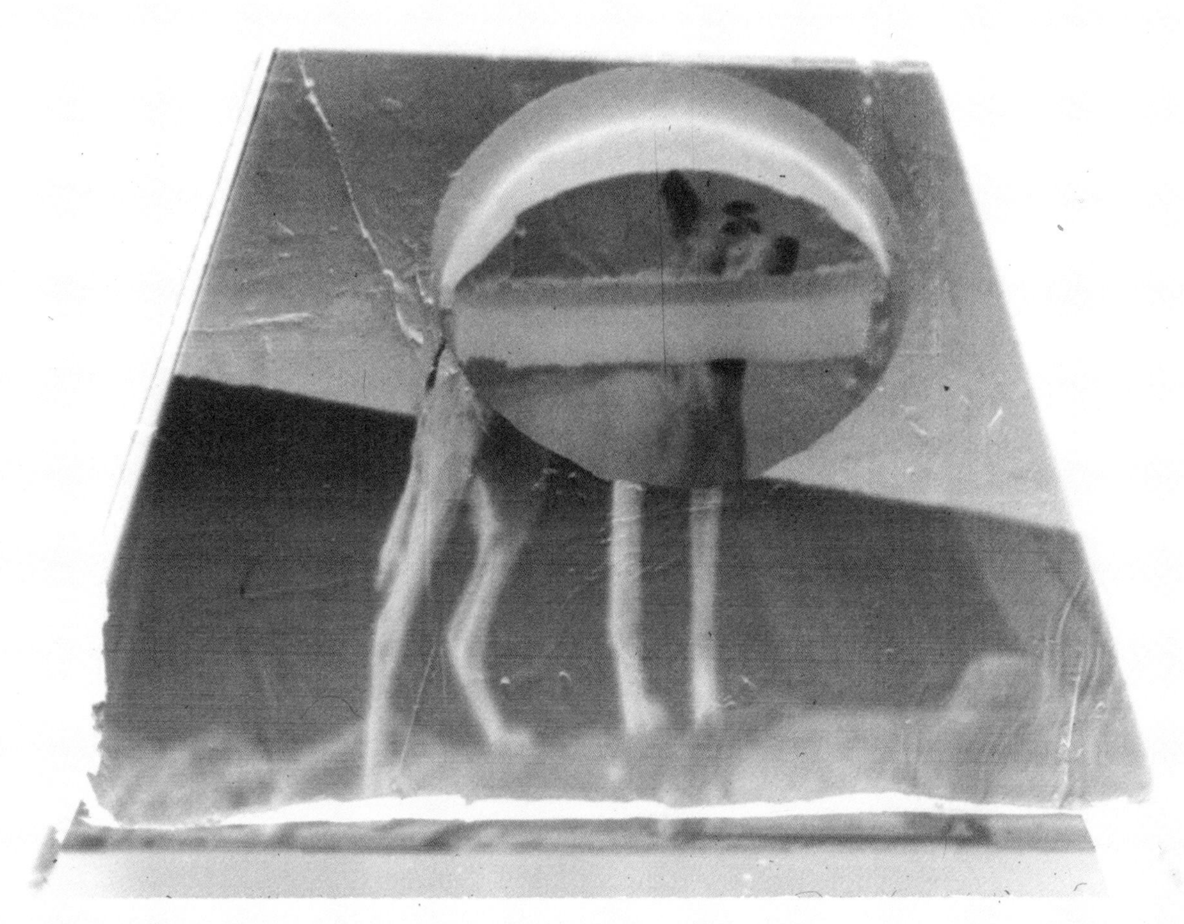

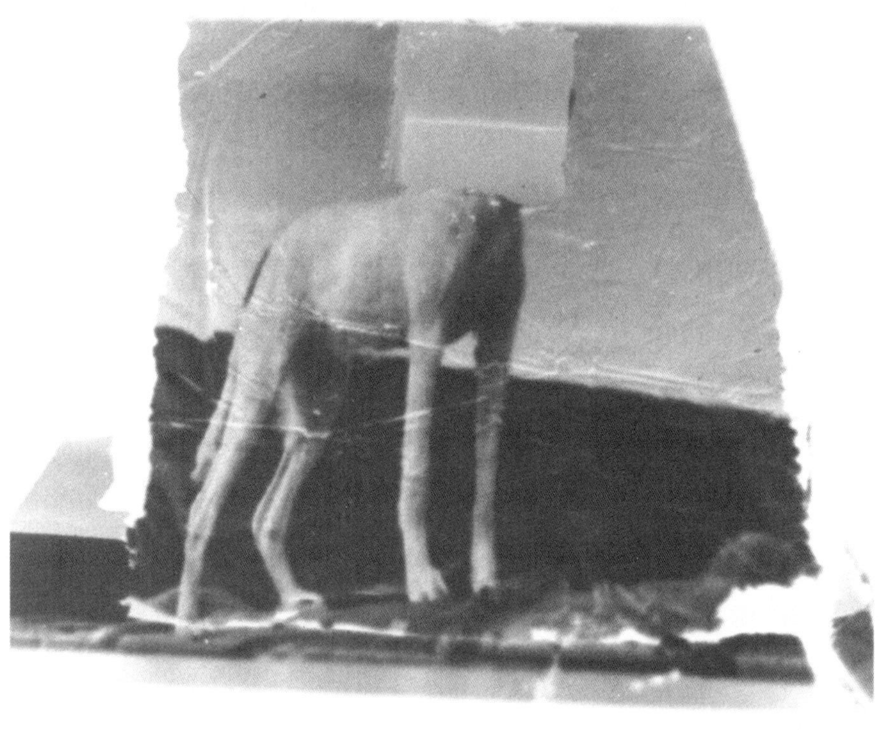

*Untitled (Dog)*, ca. 1987–91
Gelatin silver print
10 × 8 in.

*Untitled (Dog)*, ca. 1987–91
Gelatin silver print with pen and brush
and colored inks
10 × 8 in.

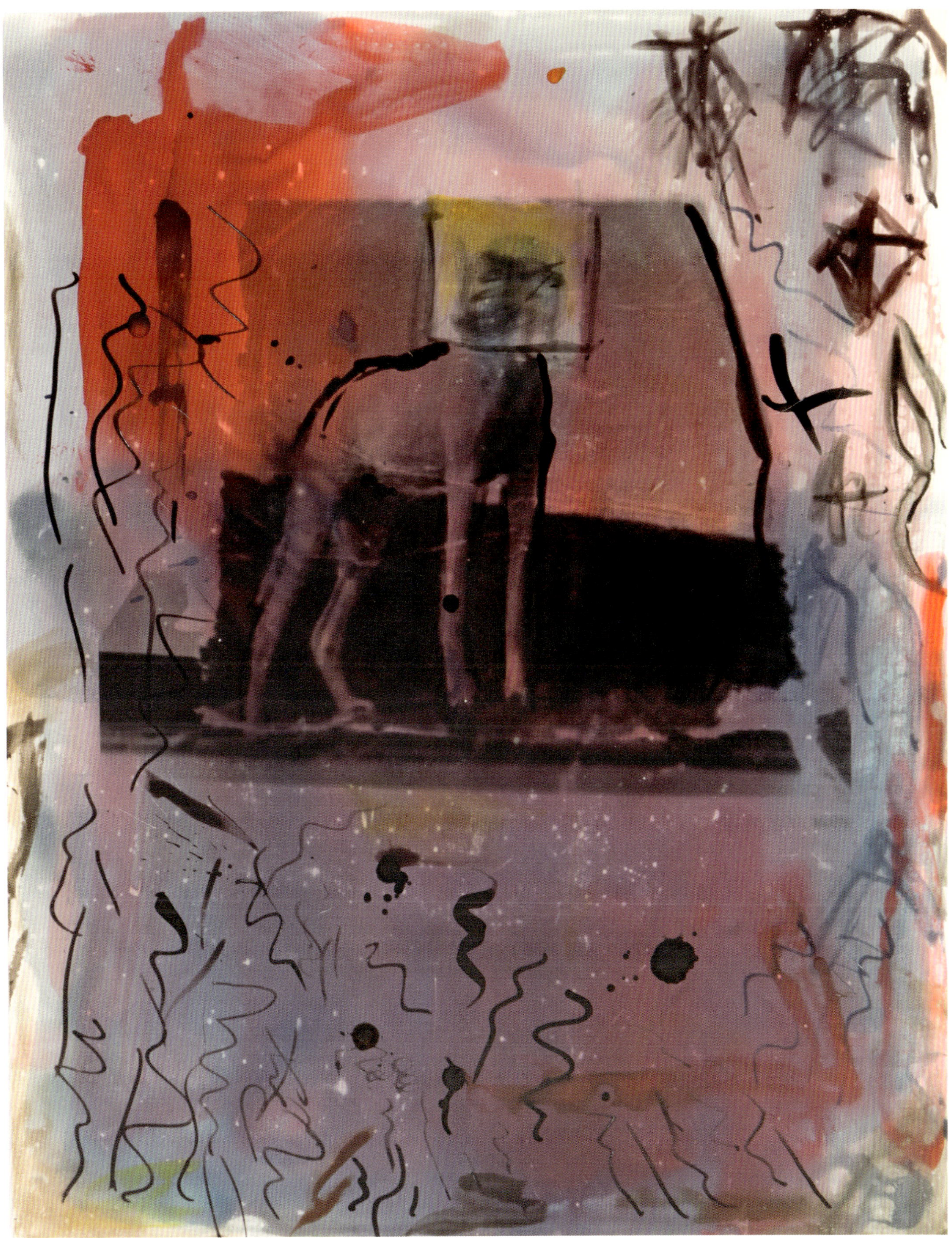

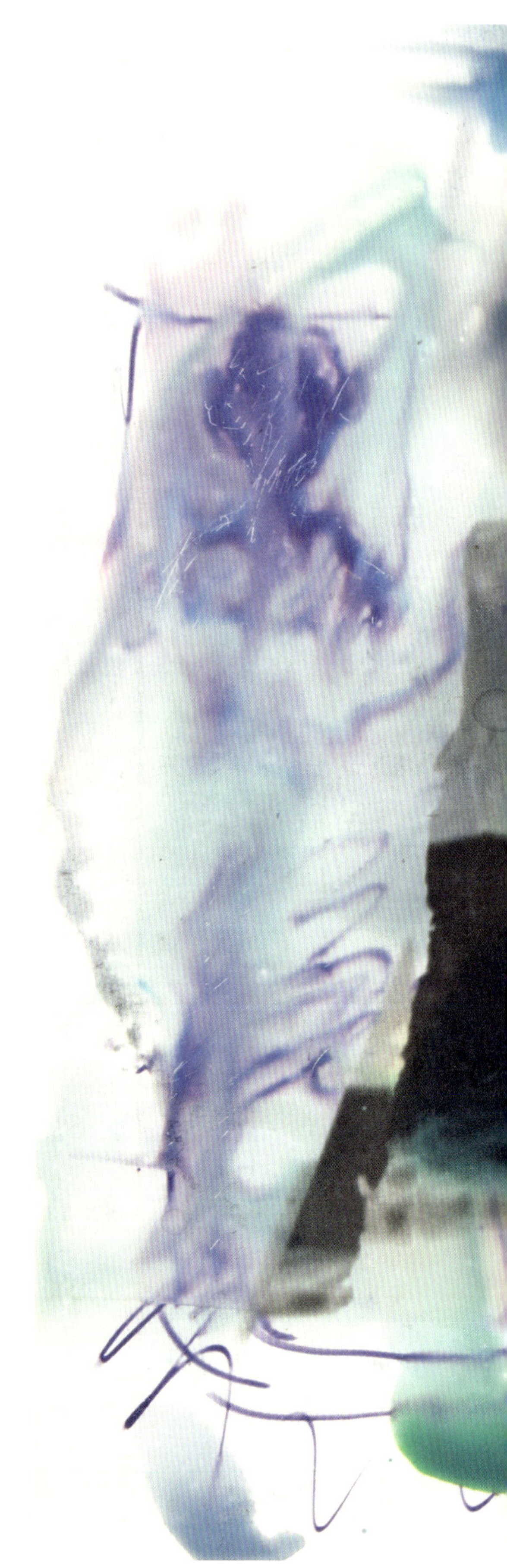

*Untitled (Dog)*, ca. 1987–91
Gelatin silver print with pen and brush
and colored inks
8 × 10 in.

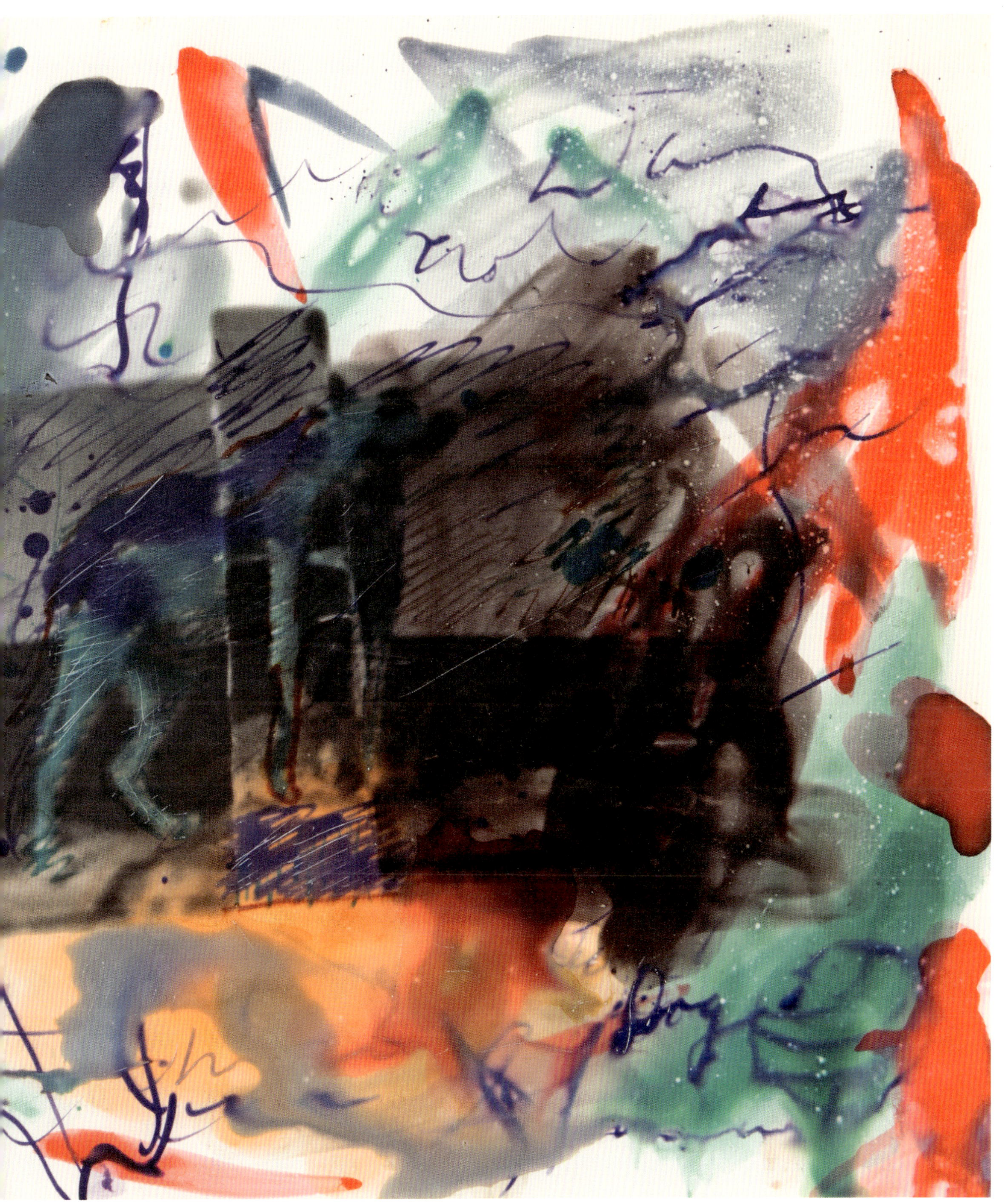

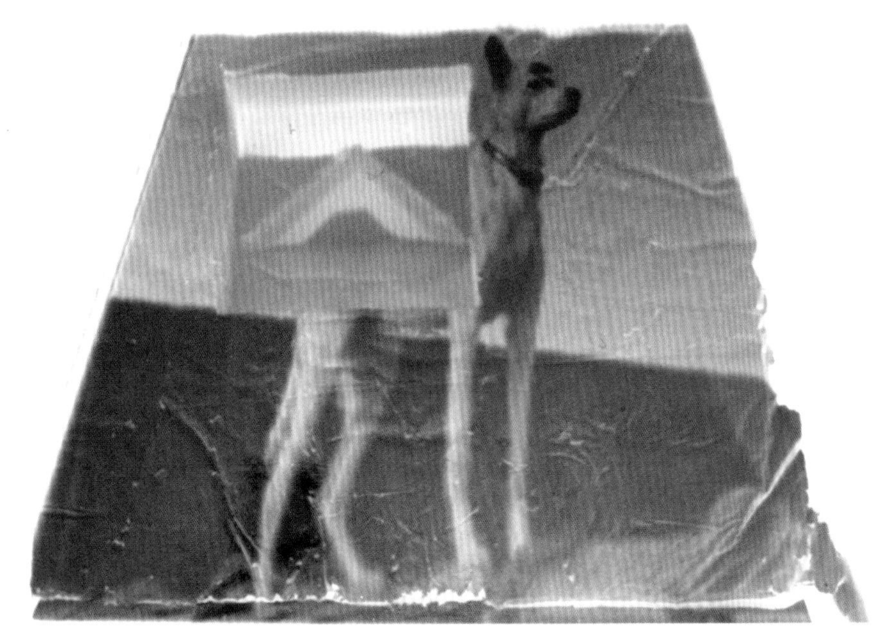

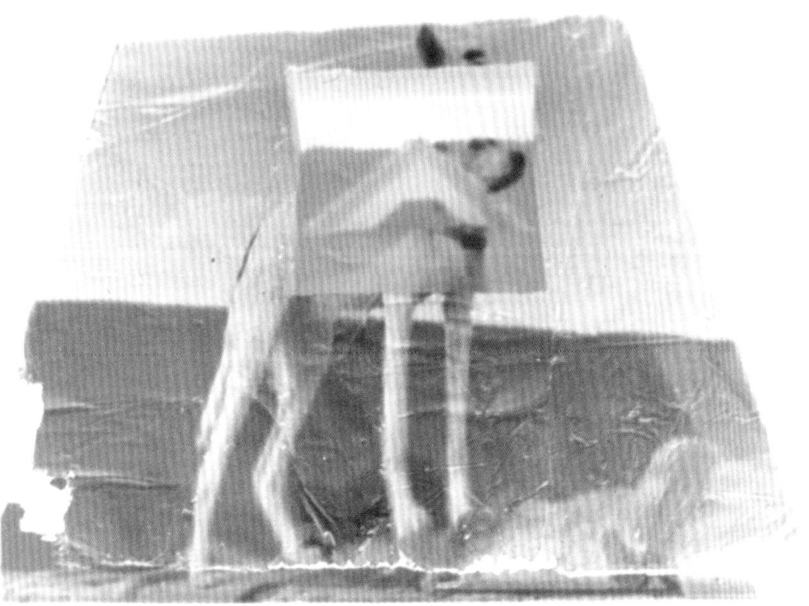

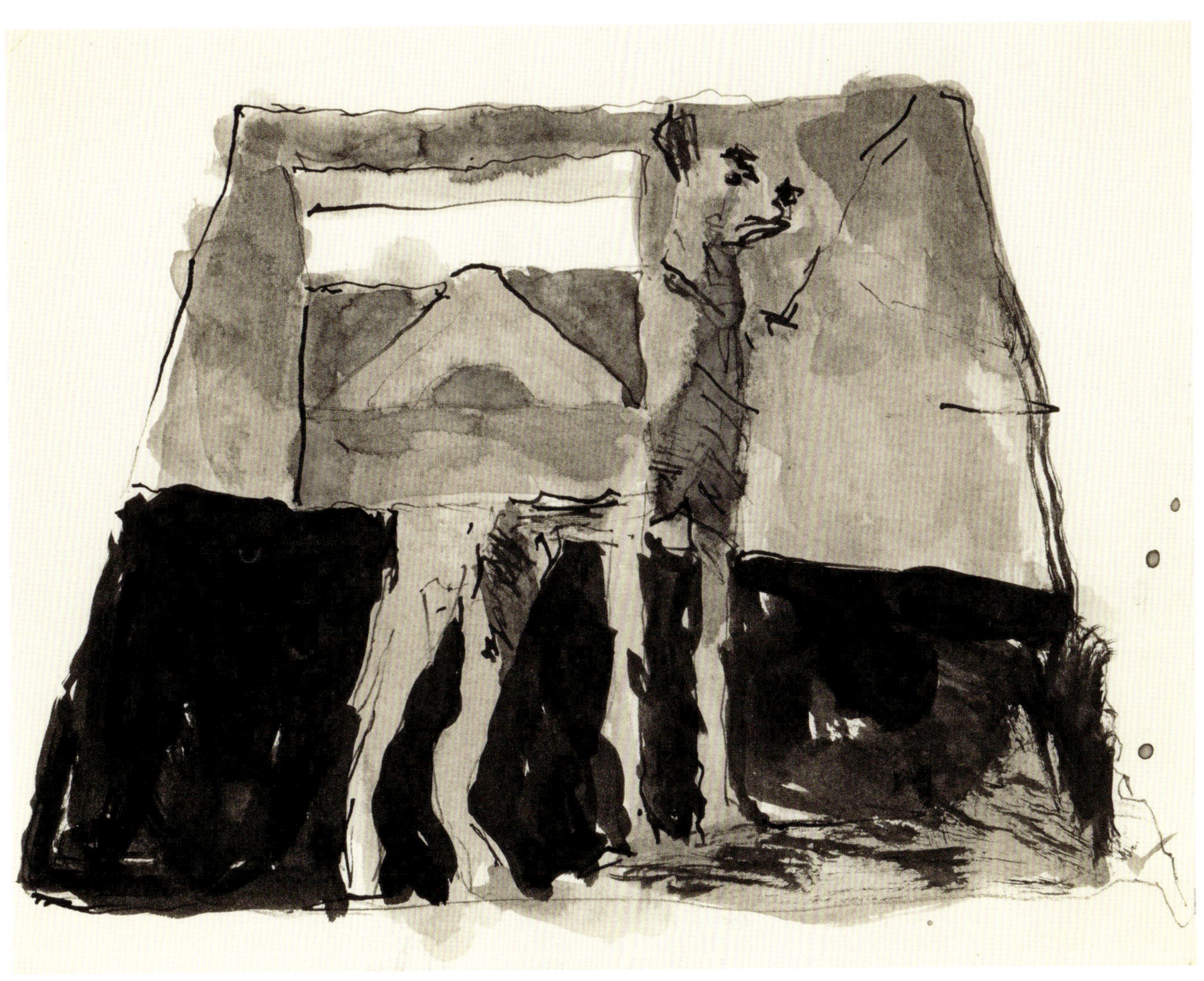

*Untitled (Dog)*, ca. 1987–91
Gelatin silver print
8 × 10 in.

*Untitled (Dog)*, ca. 1987–91
Gelatin silver print
16 × 20 in.

*Untitled (Dog)*, ca. 1987–91
Pen and brush and black ink, wash,
and graphite on paper
11 × 14 in.

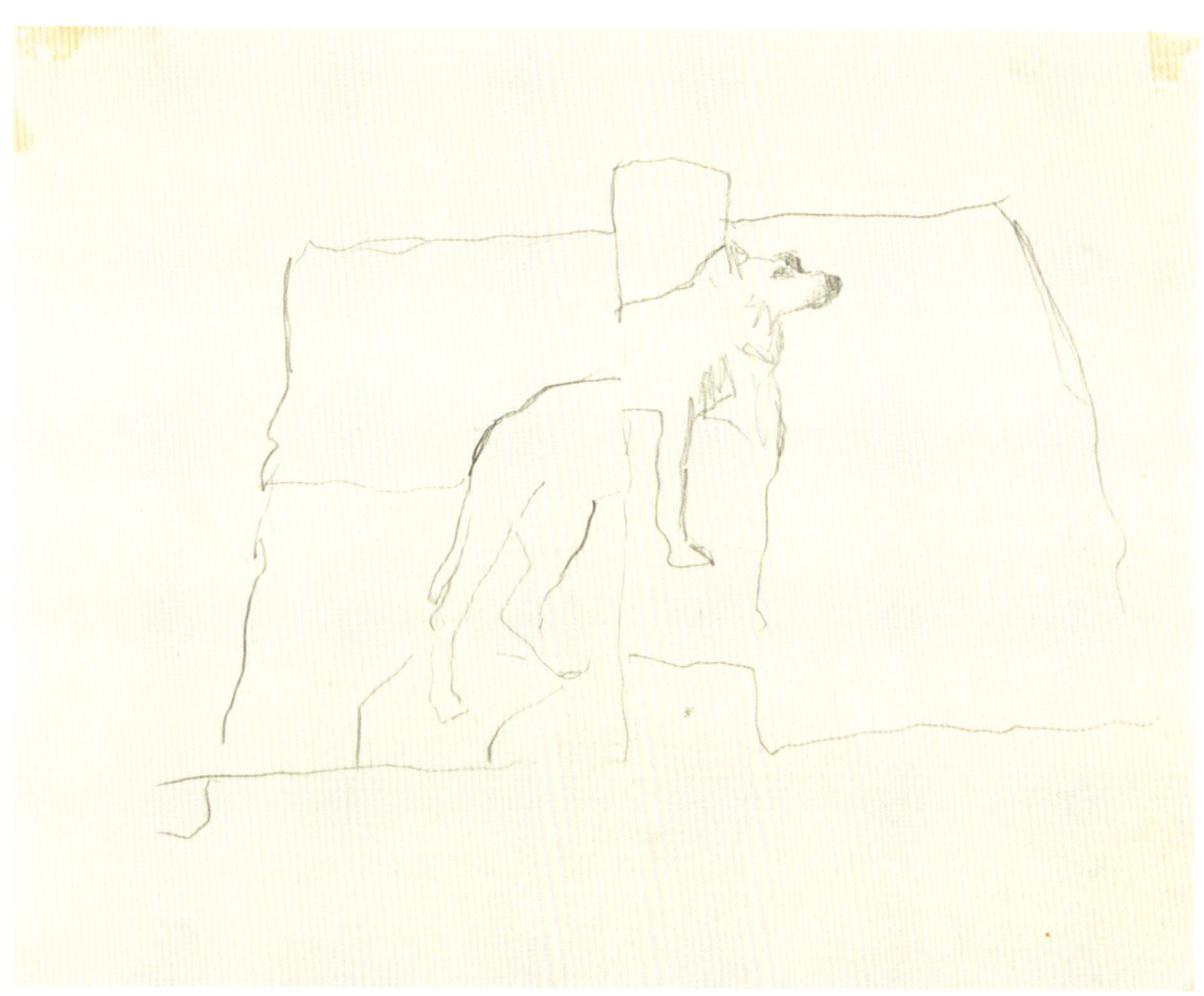

*Untitled (Dog)*, ca. 1987–91
Graphite on paper
11 × 14 in.

*Untitled (Dog)*, ca. 1987–91
Gelatin silver print
20 × 16 in.

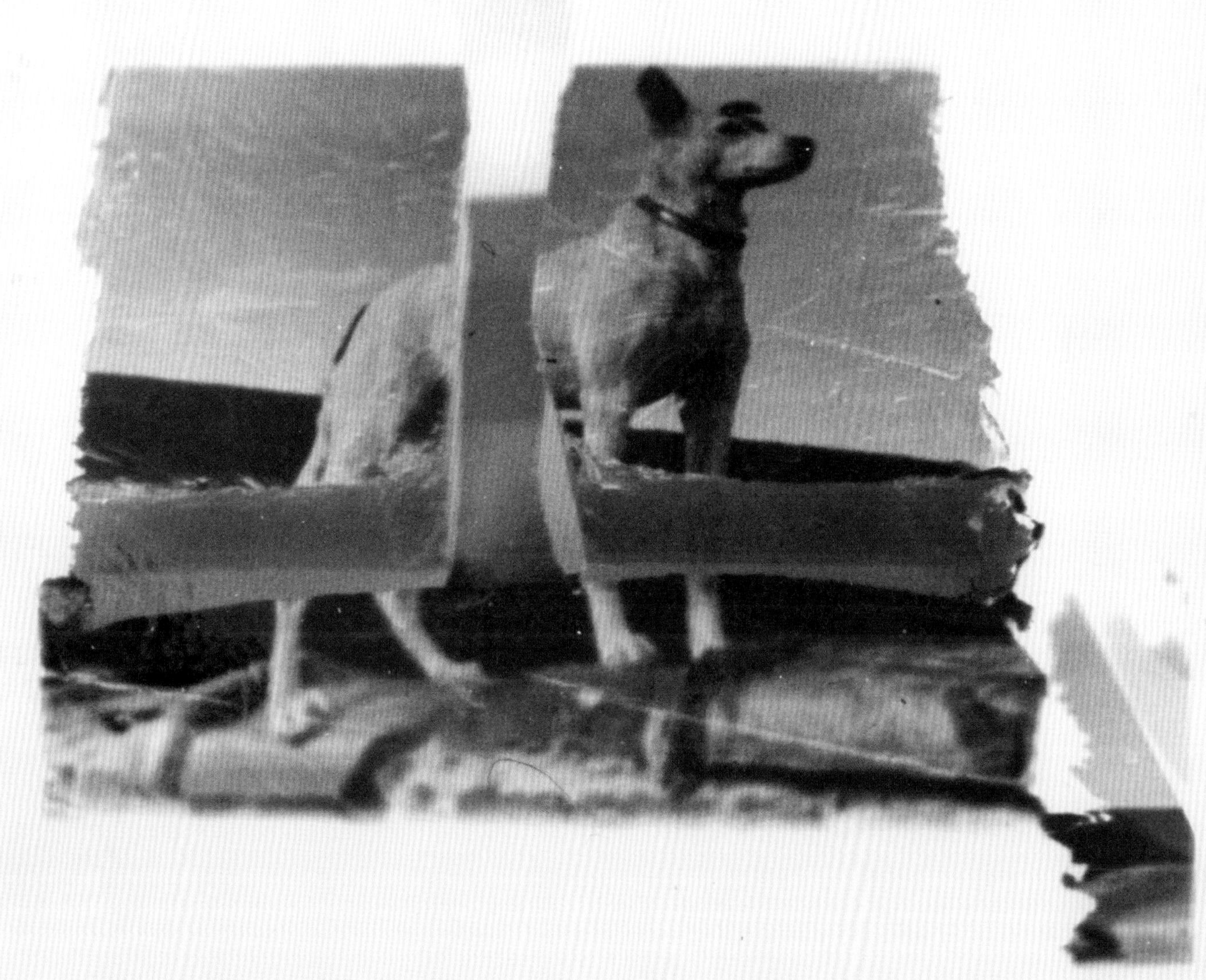

# DARREL ELLIS Regeneration

Antonio Sergio Bessa | Leslie Cozzi

With essays by Makeda Best, Allen Frame,
Linda Owen and Scott Homolka, Kyle Croft

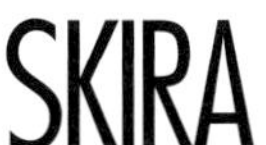

*Cover*
*Untitled (Laure on Easter Sunday)*,
ca. 1989–91
(p. 118)

*Back Cover*
*Self-Portrait after Photograph by Peter Hujar*, 1989
The Baltimore Museum of Art
(p. 139)

*Design*
Anna Cattaneo

*Editorial Coordination*
Eva Vanzella

*Copy Editor*
Doriana Comerlati

*Layout*
Evelina Laviano

First published in Italy in 2022 by
Skira editore S.p.A.
Palazzo Casati Stampa
via Torino 61
20123 Milano
Italy
www.skira.net



Printed and bound in Italy. First edition

ISBN: 978-88-572-4687-1

Distributed in USA, Canada, Central & South America by
ARTBOOK | D.A.P., 75 Broad Street, Suite 630, New York, NY 10004, USA.
Distributed elsewhere in the world by Thames and Hudson Ltd., 181A High Holborn, London WC1V 7QX, United Kingdom.

**Darrel Ellis: Regeneration**

The Baltimore Museum of Art
Baltimore, Maryland
November 20, 2022 to April 23, 2023

The Bronx Museum of the Arts
Bronx, New York
May 24, 2023 to August 27, 2023

Columbia Museum of Art
Columbia, South Carolina
February 17, 2024 to May 12, 2024

*Darrel Ellis: Regeneration* is co-organized by The Bronx Museum of the Arts and The Baltimore Museum of Art

# Contents


17 Foreword
*Asma Naeem and Klaudio Rodriguez*

21 Darrel Ellis: The Haunting
*Leslie Cozzi*

43 Touch, Feel: Darrel Ellis's Regenerative Photography
*Makeda Best*

105 "A Hole in the Picture": Darrel Ellis Was Here
*Antonio Sergio Bessa*

129 Uptown/Downtown: A Remembrance of Darrel Ellis
*Allen Frame*

147 Observations on Darrel Ellis's Materials and Process
*Linda Owen and Scott Homolka*

153 The Notebooks of Darrel Ellis
*Kyle Croft*

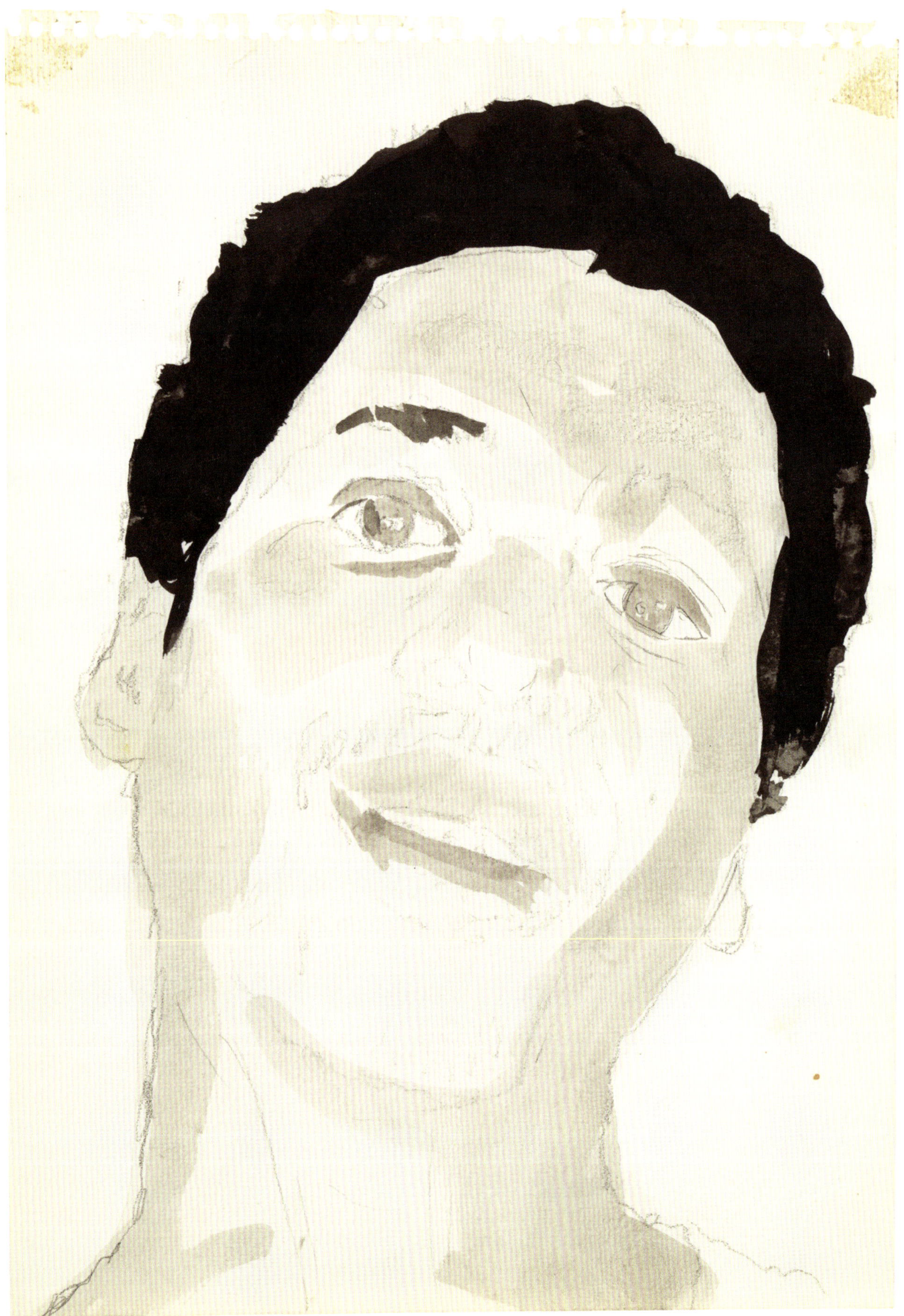

# Foreword

*We're embodied souls. We are connected to some infinite intangible source of life, of creation.*
*Darrel Ellis*

The Baltimore Museum of Art and the Bronx Museum of the Arts are proud to co-publish this illuminating volume on Darrel Ellis on the occasion of the long overdue presentation of this pioneering artist's work. The exhibition *Darrel Ellis: Regeneration* is the first comprehensive survey of Ellis's oeuvre. His highly original and visionary style layered and merged photography, painting, and printmaking—foreseeing the artistic interest in archives, appropriation, and personal narrative that is prevalent today. In 1992, Ellis died from AIDS-related causes. Only thirty-three when he passed, he was unable to fully explore his unique technique that combined his years of sketching with the distorting and rephotographing of his father's photographs. However, Ellis left behind a treasure trove of documentation through notebooks that he maintained from his high school years until his untimely death delineating his artistic impulses and explorations. Based on this important archival material as well as extant works, this exhibition and catalogue are the first thoroughly researched assessment of Ellis's oeuvre, a mapping of his evocative and complex artmaking onto the 1980s art movement in the Bronx where he grew up; in the downtown New York scene which he was a part of along with fellow artists such as Nan Goldin, Allen Frame, Robert Mapplethorpe, and Peter Hujar; and today's contemporary art world. To share Ellis's art and life with our audiences reflects the commitment of the Baltimore Museum of Art and the Bronx Museum of the Arts to pursuing social justice and artistic excellence, as well as our drive to expand our work beyond the dominant histories of contemporary art.

Darrel Ellis was gripped by the past, whether he was sketching the old masters at the Metropolitan Museum of Art, studying traditional Eastern religions, or repurposing and distorting his father's faded, old photos into brilliant new work. He was constantly in search of the concrete and the intangible, exploring his personal history through the lens of his father Thomas, a photographer who died at the hands of police weeks before Ellis was born. In a wrenching twist of fate, Ellis died at the same age as his father before him, and much like his father's images, his works were largely undiscovered and remained relatively obscure for many years. During his brief career he mounted just a handful of exhibitions. While he was on the cusp of major recognition, he gained his only glimpse of wider notoriety as a participant in Nan Goldin's controversial group exhibition about the AIDS crisis, *Witnesses: Against Our Vanishing*, in 1989. In 1996, future Bronx Museum Director Holly Block oversaw a retrospective of Ellis's work at Art in General, curated by Allen Frame, which traveled to five institutions. In 1999, his work entered the Bronx Museum's collection and was featured in the groundbreaking exhibition *Urban Mythologies*, organized by Lydia Yee and Betti-Sue Hertz. In 2016 a second work was donated to the

page 16
*Untitled (Self-Portrait)*, ca. 1990–92
Pen and brush and black ink and wash on paper, 11 ½ × 8 ¼ in.
The Neal Baer Collection

Bronx Museum collection. This exhibition and catalogue were conceptualized beginning in 2019 when the Baltimore Museum of Art acquired its first works by the artist.

Indeed, *Darrel Ellis: Regeneration* is the result of a rich collaboration between the dedicated staffs of the Bronx Museum and the Baltimore Museum of Art, and we are thankful for their individual contributions. The exhibition was organized by Antonio Sergio Bessa, Chief Curator Emeritus at the Bronx Museum, and Leslie Cozzi, Curator of Prints, Drawings and Photographs at the Baltimore Museum of Art. The curators are especially grateful for the tremendous insight and scholarly generosity Cecilia Wichmann, Associate Curator of Contemporary Art at the Baltimore Museum of Art, lent as a collaborator on the initial stages of this project. The curators would also like to thank Baltimore Museum of Art colleagues Linda Owen, Paper Conservator, and Scott Homolka, Director of Conservation, for the technical expertise they lent this research and for their insightful commentary about Ellis's work in this volume. We also thank Dr. Makeda Best, Richard L. Menschel Curator of Photography, Harvard Art Museums, whose phenomenological appraisal of Ellis's intervention in the genre of family photography is an important addition to the scholarship on this understudied artist.

We are deeply indebted to the many individuals who have collaborated with us in this project. Major thanks go to Candice Madey for her unstinting generosity without which this exhibition would not have come to fruition. She provided much needed logistical and material support for this exhibition, and we thank gallery assistants Bella Anastasio and Diego Olveda for their assistance with our research as well. We would also like to acknowledge Allen Frame, not only for his contribution to this volume which situates Ellis's work within its historical milieu, but also for his decades-long stewardship of the Ellis estate. His dedication and foresight have made Ellis's accomplishments available for today's audiences and preserved the artist's considerable legacy despite widespread institutional neglect. We also thank Ellis's friends and collaborators who generously shared their reflections and archives with us: John Ahearn, Joe Lewis, Liora Mondlak, Clarissa Sligh, and James Wentzy. Finally, we extend our thanks to the artist's family, who have welcomed our enthusiasm with considerable trust and openness.

At multiple points throughout this catalogue, the authors reference Ellis's notebooks, which are part of a trove of uncatalogued archival material maintained by the artist's estate. We are deeply grateful to our colleagues at Visual AIDS, Kyle Croft and Esther McGowan, for initially making this archival material accessible. We would also like to acknowledge the work of Rebecca Pollak and Dr. Jennifer Mass at Scientific Analysis of Fine Art LLC, for their analysis of Ellis's materials. Many other individuals assisted with our research, including Sarah Dansberger, Head Librarian and Archivist at the Baltimore Museum of Art, Tara Hart and Michael Beiser at the Whitney Museum's Library and Archives, Matthew Higgs and Brittany Adeline King at White Columns, Leslie Tonkonow, Mark Baron and Elise Boisanté, Hedi Sorger at The Peter Hujar Archive, Monica Smith, Dalila Scruggs at the Schomburg Center, Erin Zona at Women's Studio Workshop, Luke Batten of the Robert Heinecken Trust, and Chris Rawson at David Zwirner.

We salute our many colleagues at the Baltimore Museum of Art whose dedication and professionalism have elevated all aspects of this endeavor. Sincere thanks go to Steven Mann, Senior Director of Exhibitions and Program Alignment, whose efforts have been integral to the administration of this partnership. The Baltimore Museum of Art's installation relied on the hard work of many colleagues, particularly Caitlin Perry-Vogelhut, Registrar, Database Administration and Exhibitions; David Zimmerman, Exhibition Designer; and Hannah Ziesmann, Curatorial Assistant. The sustained efforts of Christine Dietze, Chief Operating Officer and Interim Co-Director, make all our work possible. We are grateful to our colleagues in Advancement for supporting the financial needs of the exhibition; particular thanks are due to Elizabeth Courtemanche, Senior Director and Department Head of Advancement. This endeavor would not have been possible without the support of the Baltimore Museum of Art Board of Trustees. We are particularly grateful to former Board Chair Clair Zamoiski Segal, former Dorothy Wagner Wallis Director Christopher Bedford, and current Board Chair Jim Thornton for their resolute support of the Museum and its exhibition program. Their generosity enabled us to undertake the scholarship and planning required to bring this ambitious project to fruition.

At the Bronx Museum, we are deeply grateful for the institutional support provided by our Deputy Director Shirley Solomon, and our colleagues in development, Yvonne Garcia and Elizabeth Grady. As this project evolved we were able to welcome our new Director of Curatorial Programs Eileen Jeng Lynch, and we thank her for overseeing the coordination of the details related to the installation. For the catalogue production and coordination, we were fortunate to count on Kyle Croft as this year's Curatorial Fellow. His previous work transcribing and cataloguing Ellis's notebooks provided a wealth of valuable information for the curators and guest essayists. In addition, his knowledge of the material has been a great asset in translating the original checklist for our Bronx audiences. We thank our exhibition designer Guy Willey for helping us articulate how Ellis had originally envisioned his work to be presented. We are deeply thankful to our colleagues who work tirelessly with our visitors and student program, including Patrick Rowe, Director of Education and Public Engagement; Nell Klugman, Education Programs Manager; and Angelica Pomar, Education and Public Programs Coordinator. Last but not least, we thank Moises Rivera, Director of Safety and Security, who over the past twenty year has personally greeted our visitors, adding a friendly note to their museum experience. *Darrel Ellis: Regeneration* would not be possible without the lead sponsorship of an anonymous patron and support from the Bronx Museum's Director's Circle. Their generosity has afforded the opportunity for Ellis's work to find a home in the Bronx.

Asma Naeem
*Interim Co-Director and Eddie C. and C. Sylvia Brown Chief Curator, The Baltimore Museum of Art*

Klaudio Rodriguez
*Executive Director, The Bronx Museum of the Arts*

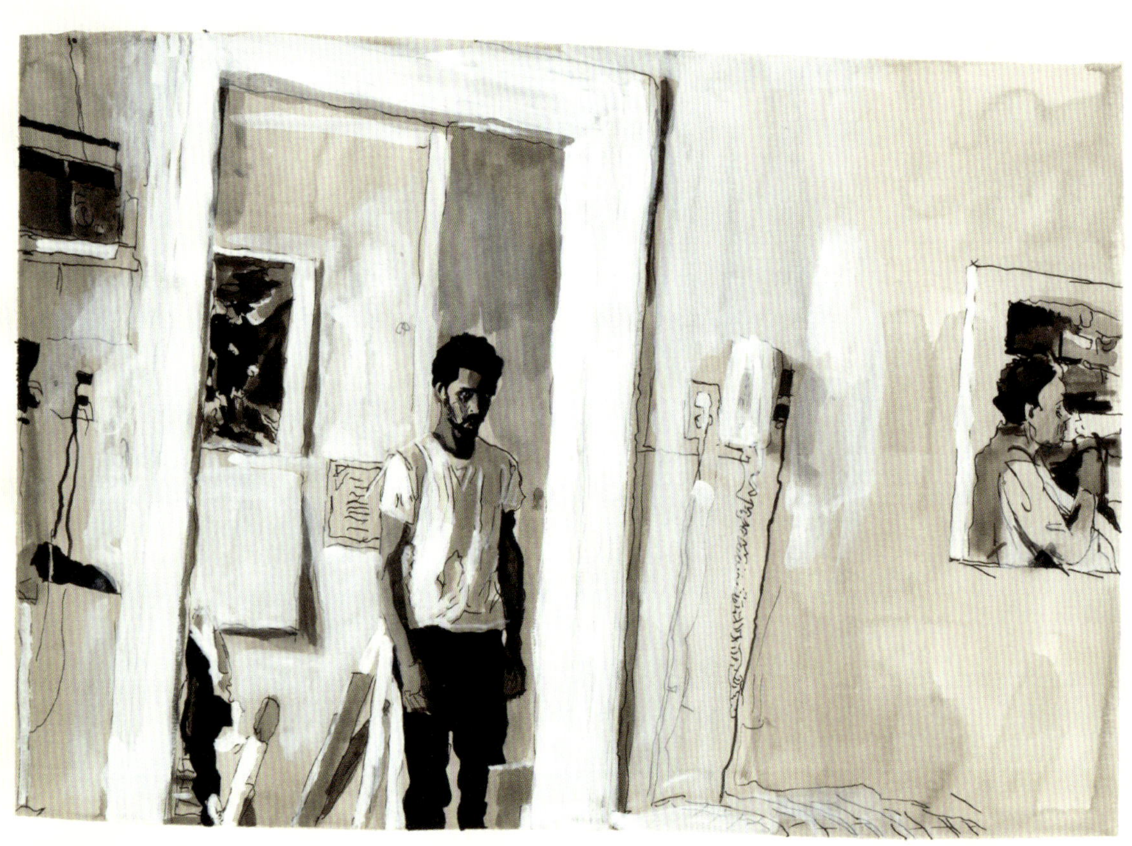

Leslie Cozzi

# Darrel Ellis: The Haunting

*I want to capture the ethereal,*
*ghostly image life. . .*[1]

In the 1860s, in an America haunted by the trauma of civil war, William H. Mumler became the first photographer to claim to capture the spirit of the dead. Mumler reported that this "ghost" manifested while he was alone in the studio attempting to make a self-portrait, and his discovery quickly sparked a craze for posthumous portraits of dead relatives that made Mumler's abilities as a photographic spirit medium a *cause célèbre*.[2] A hundred years later, fueled by a different kind of trauma entirely, Darrel Ellis would practice his own form of photographic necromancy. Ellis, whose father was killed by the police before he was born, would go on to develop a profoundly moving oeuvre using the work of Bronx studio photographer Thomas Ellis as source material and subject matter. Moving from drawn variations on existing photographs and reprints to manipulations of his father's original negatives using inventive techniques that merged photography, printmaking and sculpture, Ellis's practice was predicated on constant technical exploration and self-questioning quite distinct from Mumler's maudlin sensationalism. Yet Ellis too would claim to be haunted by the spirit of the dead.[3] Art and its histories became the medium through which he negotiated both the terrors of an uncertain present—a precarity that his status as a young gay HIV-positive man of color exacerbated—and his tenuous connection to an occluded past.

Ellis's work mediated not only the lost social world of his father, but also a canon that both attracted and alienated him. The literature on the artist already includes important observations on this score. Former friends have noted Ellis's fascination with a panoply of European modern artists, including Edgar Degas, Pablo Picasso, Claude Monet, Paul Klee, and Edvard Munch, while in recorded interviews Ellis himself also cited Alberto Giacometti, Lucian Freud, and Frank Auerbach as points of departure.[4] His library included tomes on Honoré Daumier, Rembrandt van Rijn, Jean-Antoine Watteau, and Nicolas Poussin, among others. Ellis not only immersed himself in the literature, but also studied particular techniques and genres, including grisaille, anamorphic perspective, and portraiture.[5] A black and white illustration from a particularly well-loved copy of Jean Cassou's 1947 monograph on Eugène Delacroix would serve as the basis for his undated copy of *Hamlet and Horatio in the Graveyard*. This image of a man contemplating the specter of death in the wake of his father's passing encapsulates the prevailing narrative of Ellis's career. His connection to the nineteenth century was particularly marked, and it comes as no surprise that much of his work is situated in the same spaces of modernity that formed the backdrop for the art of that period—the park, the family parlor, and the studio. Ellis's engagement with history fueled his formal evolution. The artist's journals, from which this study is drawn, provide a detailed synthesis of past and present.

While Ellis would prove an avid gallery goer throughout his adult life, his early

[1] Darrel Ellis, Notebook 1988.1. Citations throughout this book refer to catalogue numbers given to the notebooks in 2022. For more information, see Kyle Croft, "The Notebooks of Darrel Ellis," p. 153.
[2] Pierre Apraxine and Sophie Schmit, "Photography and the Occult," 12–15, and Christa Cloutier, "Mumler's Ghosts," 20–21, in Clément Chéroux et al., *The Perfect Medium: Photography and the Occult* (New Haven: Yale University Press, 2005).
[3] Susan Spencer Crowe, "Memories of Darrel," in Allen Frame, ed., *Darrel Ellis* (New York: Art in General, 1996), 32, 36.
[4] Ibid., 50.
[5] Lara Mimosa Montes and Kyle Croft, eds., *Darrel Ellis* (New York: Visual AIDS, 2021), 171, 177.

page 20
*Untitled (Self-Portrait after Allen Frame Photograph)*, ca. 1990
Brush and black ink, wash, opaque watercolor, and pen and black ink on paper, 22 ½ × 30 in.
Collection of Spaghetti Western

William H. Mumler, *Mr. Brown and His Spirit Sister Recognized*, 1862–75
Albumen silver print, 3 ⅞ × 2 ⁹⁄₁₆ in.
The J. Paul Getty Museum, Los Angeles

Auguste Rodin, *Eternal Spring*, 1907
Marble, 28 × 29 × 18 in.
Museum of Metropolitan Art, New York

exposure to art was triangulated between three venerable, and historically white, New York institutions: the Metropolitan Museum of Art, the Museum of Modern Art, and the Whitney Museum. Ellis's self-guided itinerary as an aspiring artist began at the Met. His early sketchbooks are full of precociously sophisticated drawings from life and from an array of ancient and modern sources. He sketched Greek sculpture and suits of armor. He studied Renaissance and Baroque examples to familiarize himself with classical proportion, including Cristoforo Stati's serpentine *Orpheus* (1600–01) and Tullio Lombardo's more static *Adam* (ca. 1490–95). Looking to turn-of-the-century sculpture as well, he copied Gaston Lachaise's monumental *Standing Woman* (1912–15, cast 1930), as well as Auguste Rodin's *Eternal Spring* (modeled ca. 1881, carved 1907), whose performative embrace would prove an enduring leitmotif in his subsequent work (see pp. 88, 142).

In a 1976 sketchbook, Ellis jots down a reference to works in an exhibition at MoMA, *European Master Paintings from Swiss Collections: Post-Impressionism to World War II*, that would have a profound impact on his subsequent development.[6] The work of Edouard Vuillard would prove a particularly enduring frame of reference.[7] In it, Ellis would find a source for his own intense receptivity to, even love for, his own environment.[8] The French artist's work centered on family subjects, in particular the relationships between his widowed mother and his sister, a comparable situation within his own family that Ellis returned to frequently.[9] Yet Vuillard offered Ellis a vehicle to visualize the familiar while preserving the spatial and psychological remove that expressed his own feelings of alienation. He made evident that "the look of things and of people has a thousand ways of defeating expectation."[10] For Vuillard, this would be expressed through the perspectival distortion of his pictorial construction, which avoided neat symmetry and clear sightlines, and did not locate the viewer centrally within the composition. In his work, depicted space,

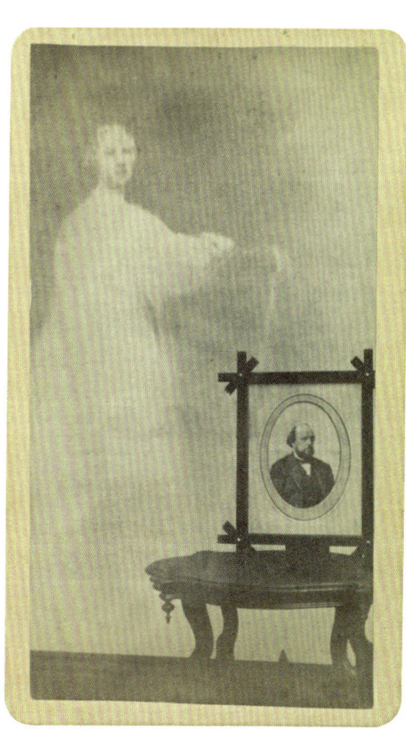

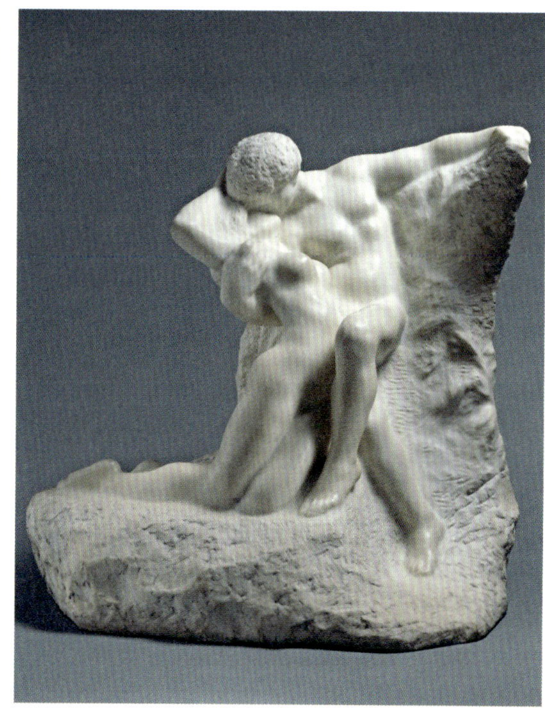

[6] Darrel Ellis, Notebook 1976.2.
[7] In a recent interview with Allen Frame, Susan Spencer Crowe recalled that Ellis was ecstatic to see the Brooklyn Museum's 1990 Vuillard exhibition.
[8] John Elderfield, *European Master Paintings from Swiss Collections: Post-Impressionism to World War II* (New York: The Museum of Modern Art, 1976), 64.
[9] William Kelly Simpson, "On Vuillard," in Elizabeth Easton, *The Intimate Eye of Edouard Vuillard* (Katonah, NY: Katonah Gallery, 1989), 9.
[10] Elderfield, *European Master Paintings*, 64.

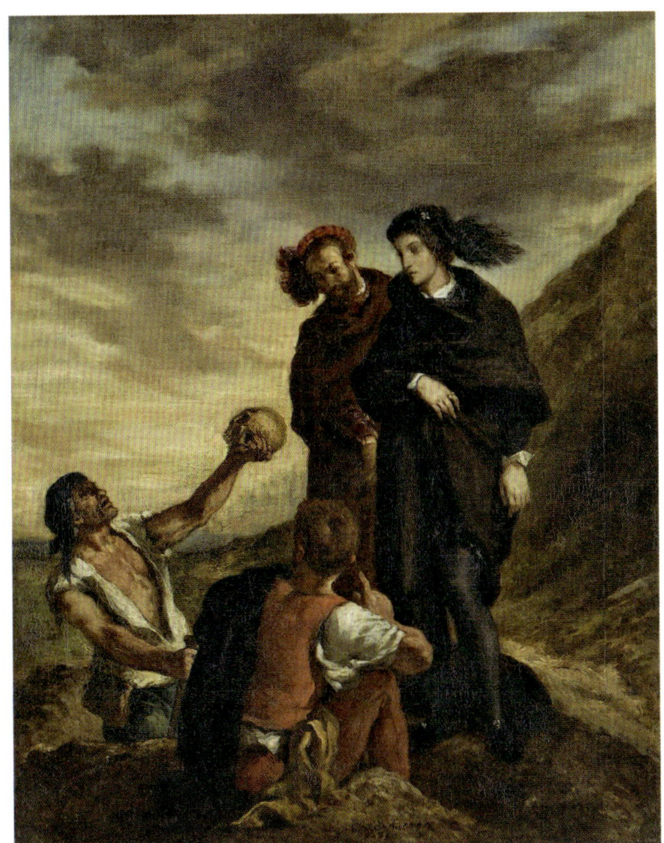

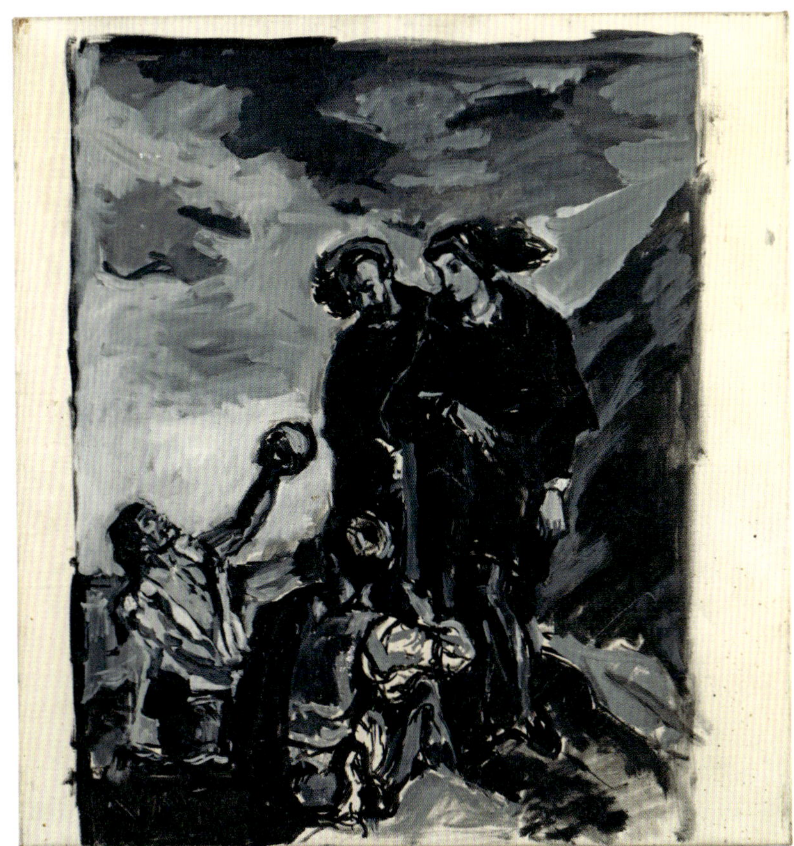

Eugène Delacroix, *Hamlet and Horatio in the Graveyard*, 1839
Oil on canvas, 32 ¼ × 25 ½ in.
Musée du Louvre, Paris

*Untitled (After Delacroix)*, ca. 1980–90
Acrylic on canvas, 25 × 24 in.
Collection of Katrina Stewart

sometimes too low for the figures to stand up within it, expands and compresses, cutting off walls, windows and furniture at unexpected angles. Ellis took these lessons of painterly construction to heart. In the late 1980s, next to a preparatory sketch for a painting made after a photo he took of a figure standing at his mother's bedroom window (see pp. 171, 150), Ellis would remind himself to stretch his smaller canvases to the size of the Vuillard at MoMA. In the realized painting, Ellis would translate the skewed perspective characteristic of Vuillard into the trapezoidal shape of the canvas itself. Ellis effaces the detail from his interior, preserving only the outlines of drapery, bedding and furniture that anchor the composition. This grim, dislocated atmosphere enables the interiors to "become images of supplication, embarrassment, or hurt feelings."[11] Ellis would render the interior of his mother's bedroom in multiple iterations whose inherent sense of psychological scrutiny would offer, like Vuillard's *intimiste* environments, a metaphor for the self—"an inner space self-controlled and cut off from the world, but rife with possibilities."[12]

The other references Ellis made to the MoMA *European Master Paintings* exhibition are also to works which thematize the psychology of the artist. Ellis's reminder to study the history of the Harlequin, though perhaps related to his own bourgeoning interest in scenic design, also recalls Picasso's understanding of the clown as an artistic alter ego, a motif that he employed to lend personal expressiveness to his art.[13] Two 1914 portraits by Marc Chagall, the *Jew in Red* and *Jew in Green*, are mentioned specifically, and both use color to enhance the psychological estrangement of their subjects. Later, when experimenting with rephotographed likenesses, Ellis would adapt Chagall's expressionistic use of color to veil

[11] Elizabeth Wynne Easton, *The Intimate Interiors of Edouard Vuillard* (Houston: The Museum of Fine Arts; Washington: The Smithsonian Institute Press, 1989), 58.
[12] Ibid., 4.
[13] Elderfield, *European Master Paintings*, 86.

Edouard Vuillard, *Interior, Mother and Sister of the Artist*, 1893
Oil on canvas, 18 ¼ × 22 ¼ in.
The Museum of Modern Art, New York
Gift of Mrs. Saidie A. May

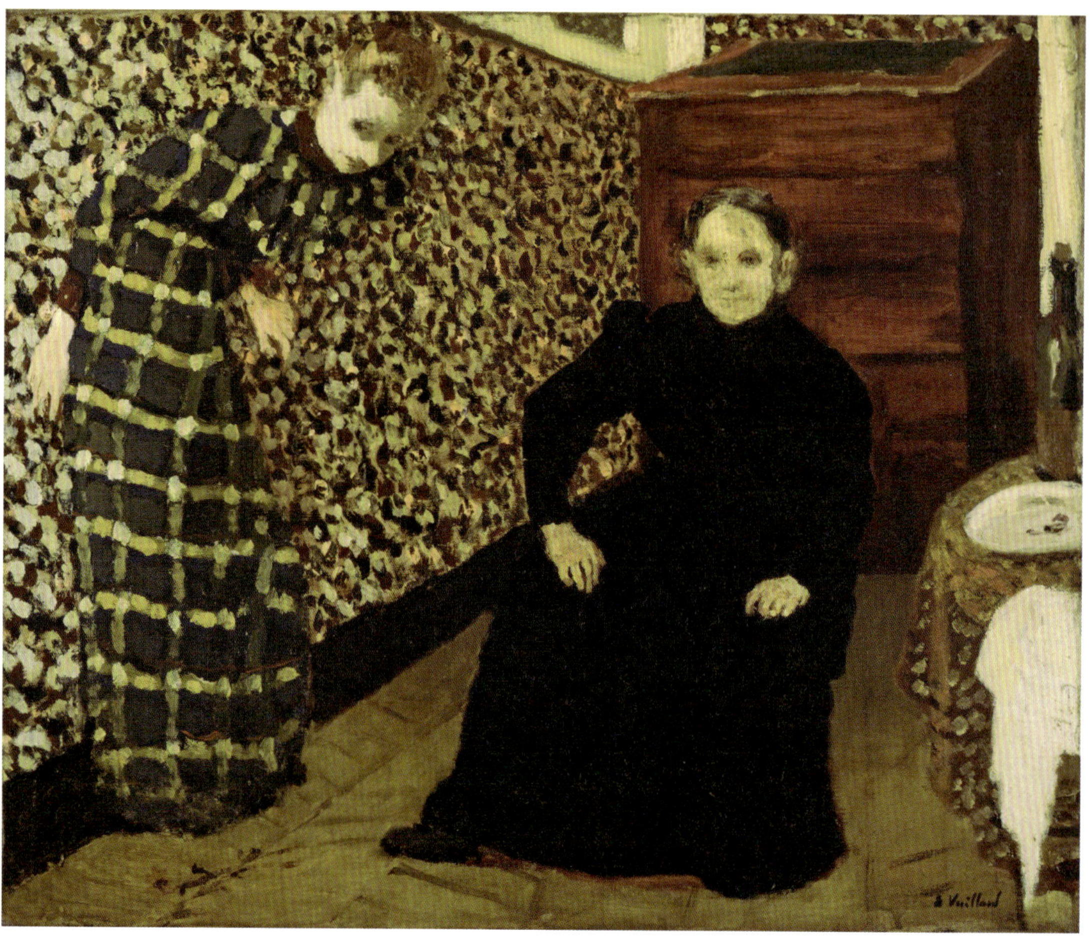


people's visages, including his own, in washes of pigmented ink that partially or entirely obliterate their features (see p. 117). These obstructions exemplify the dialectic of intimacy and estrangement that characterizes Ellis's entire oeuvre. Always attuned to the psychological impact of plastic elements, Ellis would also make several reminders to study Expressionism—via Egon Schiele and Larry Rivers—for what he referred to as its superimposition of body and emotion.

As the 1970s progress, Ellis's tone becomes more confident and self-assured about his artistic practice, despite frequent emotional distress and constant financial insecurity. He continues his art historical education, referencing Peter de Hooch, Alberto Giacometti, and Aristide Maillol, and begins to explore a range of literary source materials, from nineteenth-century Symbolist authors to the poetry of Anne Sexton.
The paintings in a 1977 exhibition of Pierre Bonnard's work at Aquavella Galleries left an indelible impression on the budding artist, impacting the palette, composition, and brushwork of youthful images of himself and his family. He reminds himself to "analize western painting, Piero, Ucello [*sic*], etc. portraits."[14] His lingering fascination with Balthus, a modern exponent of Piero della Francesca who anticipated Ellis's interest in the depiction of children and interiors, also begins in this moment. In his studies, Ellis plays with the cropping and viewpoint of his living spaces and begins to model with color rather than with graphite alone. He also devotes more obvious attention to his family as a subject, making a drawing that he labels "my stepfather from memory."[15] Progressing from his previous study of sculpture in the

[14] Darrel Ellis, Notebook 1977.2.
[15] Darrel Ellis, Notebook 1977.5.

round, he begins to cut and silhouette drawings against the page and starts thinking about film as a vehicle to capture depth. In both domestic interiors as well as nude figure studies in academic poses, Ellis uses planes rendered in vigorously hatched lines to demarcate space, and his engagement with Paul Cézanne is evident. Over the next decade, he would continue to muse over Cézanne in communion with other artists, like Malcolm Morley, for whom the post-Impressionist's sense of natural order, solidity and balance remained a touchstone.[16]

Ellis's consuming passion for drawing is captured in one of his journal entries, "Centurys [*sic*] of drawing I'm talking about drawings, Drawing Drawing."[17] Dubbed a "latter-day Toulouse-Lautrec," Ellis drew constantly as a way of understanding the world and his position within it.[18] Drawing followed the unceasing motion of the artist's thoughts. As if responding to Robert Frank's belief that "the subway is pure theater," his early sketchbooks are filled with sketches of other passengers crowded into subway cars, some hastily executed, others more concerted and detailed.[19] For Ellis, drawing was both therapeutic pastime ("I draw because that's what I can do to get me by the hard moments in life") and art historical necessity. Ellis's investment in technique developed as his theory of art became more concrete, and he not only begins listing specific media, like water-soluble black pencil, but names draftsmen of particular interest including Henri Matisse, Willem de Kooning, and Philip Guston. Ellis emphasizes the need to draw from life, disputing Piet Mondrian's belief that figuration had come to an end and instead aligning himself with Giacometti in pursuing "the great rebirth of self in imagery." He also speculates about using

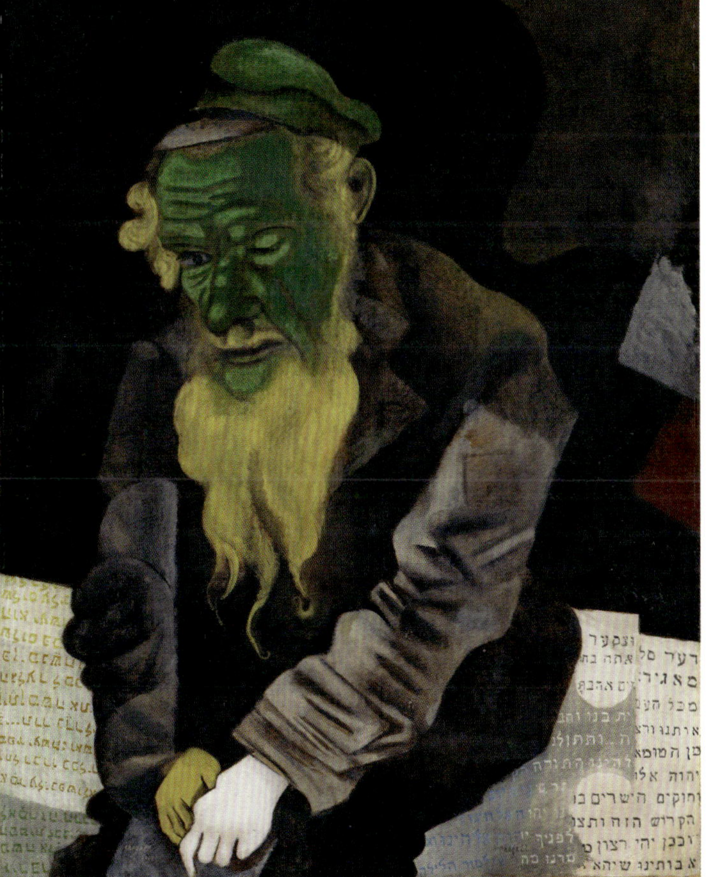

Marc Chagall, *Jew in Green*, 1914
Oil on paper, mounted on composition board, 39 ⅜ × 31 ½ in.
Collection Jürg Im Obersteg, Basel

[16] "I feel New York has betrayed Cézanne. . . . Cézanne would be horrified by the idea of flatness. The idea is to represent three-dimensional sensations on a two-dimensional plane." "A Conversation: Malcolm Morley and Arnold Glimcher," in *Malcolm Morley* (New York: Pace Gallery, 1988), unpaginated. See also Darrel Ellis, Notebook 1978.5.
[17] Darrel Ellis, Notebook 1978.5.
[18] Allen Frame, "One Family Legacy: Variations in Black and White," in Frame, *Darrel Ellis*, 14.
[19] https://time.com/3776275/underneath-beijing-in-transit/.

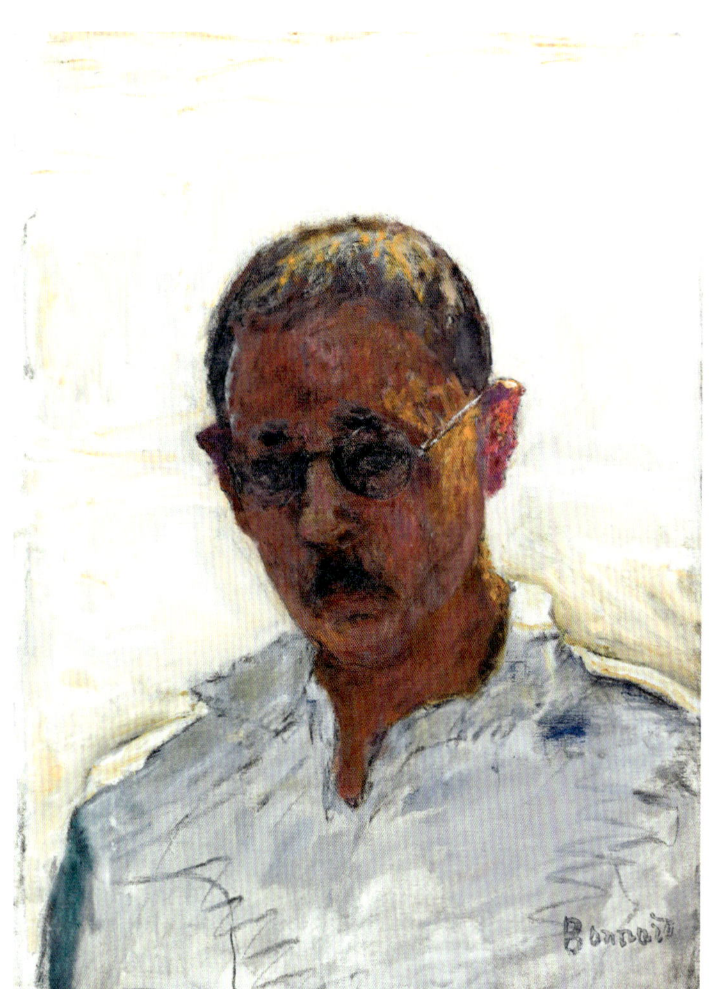

Pierre Bonnard, *Self-Portrait on White Background*, 1930
Oil on canvas, 20 ¾ × 15 in.
Fondation Bemberg, Toulouse

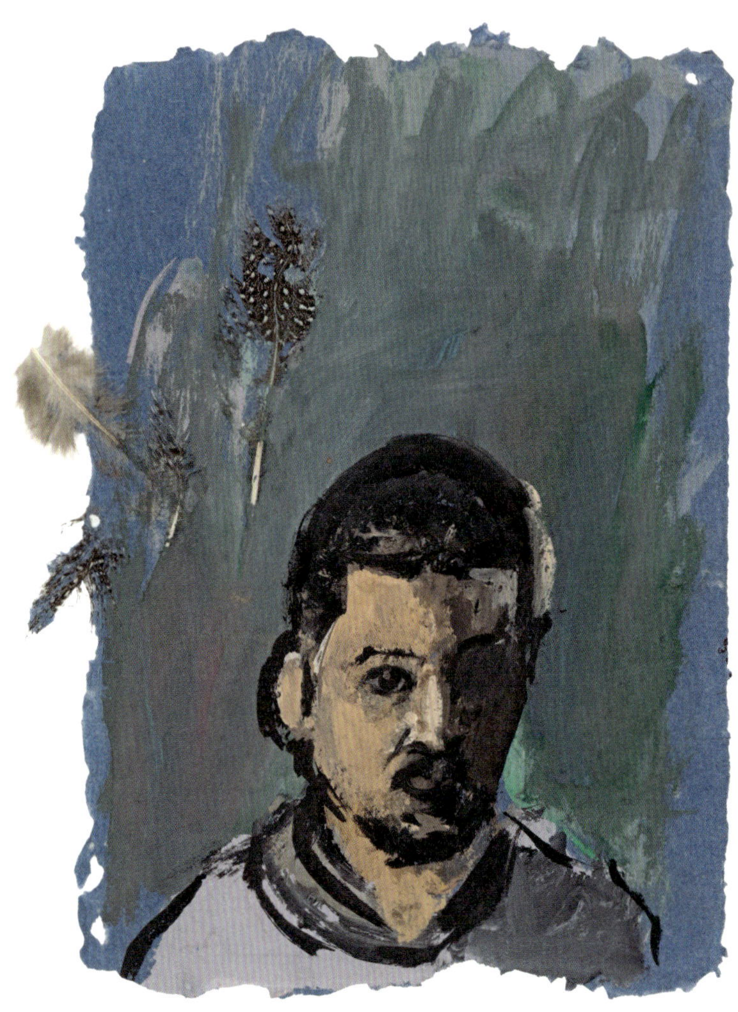

*Untitled (Self-Portrait with Feather)*, ca. 1981
Opaque watercolor, brush and black ink, and feathers on paper, 10 ¼ × 8 in.
Collection of Michael Sherman and Carrie Tivador

dark paper prepared with white ground so that he can control the lights himself and "liberate the drawing from [the] page."[20] This attention to the hierarchy of light and dark, and its cultural ramifications, would receive increasing scrutiny in subsequent meditations.

A current of fervid technical and philosophical speculation runs throughout Ellis's journals. Among the many ruminations regarding new theoretical systems and procedures to attempt, none would be more transformative than his turn, in 1979, to photography. Three artists—Ellis's PS1 studio-mate James Wentzy, the photographer Dan Rodan, and the sculptor Suzanne Harris—shaped Ellis's emerging photo practice as he experimented with the visual properties of varying f-stops, apertures, and depths of field.[21] His attempt to master the technical aspects of photography would strain against the historical associations of the medium with naturalism, and to that end Ellis insists that the goal of his work is not to provide a narrative framework but to highlight the movement and space between figures—thereby positioning his practice as relational rather than purely objective. It is in this moment that he starts to invoke the term "generations" to describe the interplay of images from related negatives and positives. Ellis thinks through the possible use of 3-D screens, holographic or unfixed film, camera movement, and building up projection surfaces that would mimic the curves of the human body with different materials including polyurethane, cast plastic, or fiberglass. Sketches and negatives inserted between leaves of the notebooks of the period show Ellis workshopping a photograph created with Wentzy of both artists near a window in their studio, where Ellis notes, "lines important in giving feeling of air to photo as form." Photography remained imbricated in the artist's mind with the legacy of his father, whose negatives he inherited from his mother in 1981. Ellis would also make drawings experimenting with the camera as a physical object with a distinctive vocabulary of shapes—circles, squares, and rectangles—and pleated recessions. The essential symbolic geometry of these forms would be translated into the sculpted projection process he elaborated years later.

1983 proved a transformative year for Ellis both physically and mentally, and it inaugurated a period of increasing scrutiny of the art historical nexus of race, viewpoint, and privilege, in tandem with a growing fascination with his father's oeuvre. The enigmatic statement "no race-color separation" appears at the beginning of one of his journals from that moment, followed by mentions of the Harlem museum (likely the Studio Museum) and the Afro-American bookstore.[22] Ellis admonishes himself for holding up the values of the white art world, declaring instead "blacks have to be the center of work."[23]

The polyvalence of that statement—which is preceded by a list of colors (including ultramarine, cobalt, cadmium red, and chrome yellow)—is fascinating, because it bespeaks not just a new cultural awareness, but also an understanding of persistent formalist debates over the uses and value of color (as opposed to line). A developing interest in Honoré Daumier, Edouard Manet, Jasper Johns, R. B. Kitaj, and Alice Neel, as well as the work of Black American photographers, informed Ellis's sensibility towards color as both a visual and social construct. When Ellis became an instructor in the Whitney ArtReach program, he made a point of updating their curriculum to showcase important Black artists, from Benny Andrews to James Van Der Zee. The filiation between Ellis and Van Der Zee is particularly striking. Van Der Zee's collaborative photobook, *The Harlem Book of the Dead*, was published in 1978, at a formative moment for Ellis.[24] Beyond the technical similarities—Van Der Zee routinely retouched his images with oils and transparent watercolors, a technique Ellis would adapt in applying ink to his own

[20] Darrel Ellis, Notebook 1978.5.
[21] For more on Ellis's formative collaboration with James Wentzy, see the chronology of his work in Mimosa Montes and Croft, *Darrel Ellis*. Ellis's journals include contact information and several references to Rodan, including a note regarding a 1986 exhibition of his photographs at Leo Castelli Gallery. While noting that the exhibition made him feel uneasy, Ellis states that nevertheless he loves the work and the manner in which Rodan uses painter's techniques to get across his humanity (Notebook 1979.1). Ellis also invokes Harris at several points in his notes, pasting a brief obituary into one of his journals from 1979 (Notebook 1979.4) and subsequently praising her use of pyramids as related to strength, weakness, and what lies between (Notebook 1980.1).
[22] Darrel Ellis, Notebook 1983.4.
[23] Darrel Ellis, Notebook 1983.1.
[24] James Van Der Zee, Owen Dodson and Camille Billops, *The Harlem Book of the Dead*, with an introduction by Toni Morrison (Dobbs Ferry, NY: Morgan & Morgan, Inc., 1978).

hand-painted prints—both artists routinely thematized loss. Van Der Zee's joy in photographing children was counterbalanced by the mortuary portraits he created of them.[25] Ellis's numerous images of his sister Laure with a bunny (see pp. 117–27) recall the props Van Der Zee included to make difficult images more palatable. In Ellis's oeuvre, the stuffed animal serves as a reminder of lost youth.

Ellis once postulated, "god was a . . . handsome young well dressed Black man."[26] Such a heroically melancholy view of black masculinity informed his profoundly moving self-portraits. In a written statement, he describes how his approach to portraiture evolved from his engagement with his father's photographs through the work made after photographs of him by Mapplethorpe and Hujar. Ellis, interpreting Marx, would come to understand that everyone is an object outside themselves, and his portraits enabled him to critically embody that notion while pushing back against received stereotypes of black masculinity.[27] Responding to the photographic portraits created by two white male artists, he would again invoke the paranormal: "I struggle to resist the frozen images of myself taken by Robert Mapplethorpe and Peter Hujar. They haunt me."[28] The drawings Ellis created after these originals (see pp. 104, 139) depart from the languid sexuality that those artists invested in Ellis's image. Instead, their subtle chiaroscuro emphasizes a Baroque sense of psychological intensity. "I am Curious George," Ellis states at one point, after wondering why the character was a monkey from Africa.[29] This declaration problematized the fetishized and hyper-sexual representations of black masculinity against which his self-images contend. Ellis's speculation on his father's work would feed this concern. He makes notes regarding the role public housing played in the assimilation of black America into post-war culture, and notes that his rephotography of his father's images was a means of exploring the impact of this economic boom on people's self-image.[30]

For an artist who continually returned to Eurocentric traditions, the question of how to represent black subjectivity as somehow distinct from the history of portraiture of largely white subjects was a continual problem. In a notebook dated to 1989, Ellis would contemplate making work based on negative media portrayals of Black subjects, but would soon discard the idea. In that same diary, he calls his own work Eurocentric and writes that he is "disgusted with the white picture" while wondering how to distinguish his representations of black subjects to harness both anger and realism.[31] Ellis ultimately found that authenticity lay in the connections between photography and drawing, and not within specific disciplines. Ellis posited that drawing from photos enables you to use the context as well as the image. In understanding this claim, and the connection he forged between observational drawing and the lens, it is interesting to consider another reference embedded in his journals—to Svetlana Alpers's work on seventeenth-century Dutch painting.[32] Ellis's image practice lends an entirely different valence to her claim regarding images that "do not disguise meaning or hide it beneath the surface but rather show that meaning by its very nature is lodged in what the eye can take in—however deceptive that might be."[33] The lens is the mediator of the known world—producing an image of life itself that at once confirms what we thought we knew, while also casting doubt onto that knowledge. This is because the lens calls into question any fixed sense of scale and proportion. The lens affirms and undermines the truth of vision, and drawing registers the ambivalence instantiated by the lens. Thus Ellis's rephotographed images of his family with their faces distorted and obscured unite both empiricism and doubt in the reality his father had previously captured on film. Ellis's exploration of sequenced positive and negative images embodies what Alpers describes as the "falsifying" paradox of the

[25] *James Van Der Zee: Harlem Guaranteed* (New York: Michael Rosenfeld Gallery, 2002), 12–14.
[26] Darrel Ellis, Notebook 1989.1.
[27] Darrel Ellis, Notebook 1980.1.
[28] Darrel Ellis, quoted in Nan Goldin, *Witnesses: Against Our Vanishing* (New York: Artists Space, 1989), 20.
[29] See p. 154. Darrel Ellis, Notebook 1980.1.
[30] Darrel Ellis, Notebook 1984.1.
[31] Darrel Ellis, Notebook 1989.1.
[32] Darrel Ellis, Notebook 1984.1.
[33] Svetlana Alpers, *The Art of Describing: Dutch Art in the Seventeenth Century* (Chicago: The University of Chicago Press, 1983), xxiv.

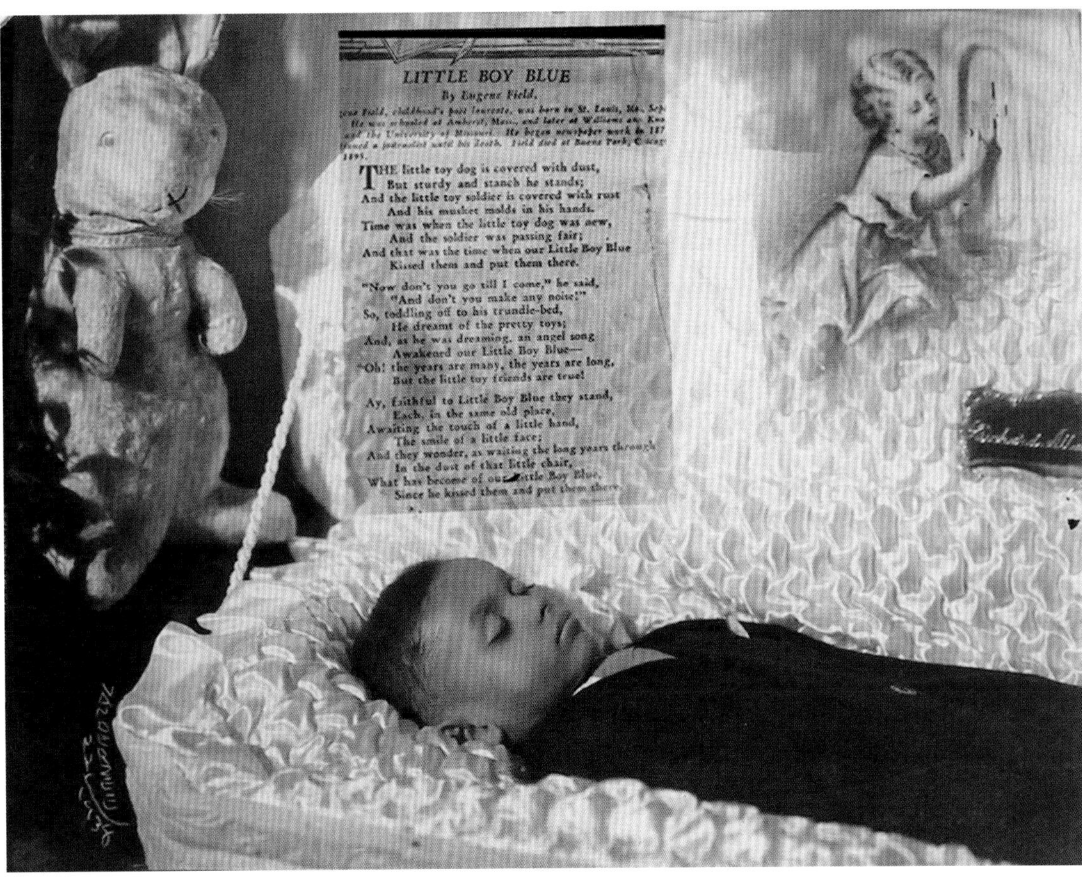


James Van Der Zee, *Untitled (Boy in Coffin)*, 1938
Gelatin silver print, 8 × 10 in.
James Van Der Zee Archive

camera obscura which "upends" the world it captures.[34]

In diagrams from the mid to late 1980s, Ellis would map out the notion of a succession of images from a single source, with variations made in different media, as he ruminated over using drawing, offset, and photostat to capture the unseen reality beyond the physical.[35] How to capture depth became a particular concern—one with literal and figurative implications. Ellis was as obsessed with sculpture and the process of 3-D casting as he was with drawing and photographic projection, and he speculates on multiple techniques, including making resin castings from plaster, modeling with clay directly on the surface of the enlarger, or cast paper. A diagram shows Ellis embedding various shaped objects into the surface to create the negative recessions that would distort the resulting photographs (see pp. 154–57). He also makes notes on the relationship between the scale of his sculpted recessions and the effects it produces on the projected negative. He even speculates on the possibility of casting people's heads—as if searching for a vehicle appropriate to bear the distorted effects of memory his photographs would produce. It is interesting to note that this fascination with the negative and positive surfaces of his sculpted reliefs coincides with mentions of Julian Schnabel, Juan Gris, Cubist relief, African art, and twentieth-century "negro" sculpture—artists and movements for whom the dialectic of illusionistic versus actual depth would be paramount. At one point, the artist mentions going to the Met to see sculpture and "primitive" art for inspiration for his shapes.[36]

An inexhaustible fascination with process, self, and history drove Ellis's constant formal and technical experimentation. He offers a lengthy meditation on his relationship to surface, which he describes wanting to

[34] Ibid., xxiii.
[35] Darrel Ellis, Notebook n.d. 6.
[36] Darrel Ellis, Notebook 1984.1.

Henry Ossawa Tanner, *Jessie Olssen Tanner and Jesse Ossawa Tanner posing for the painting "Christ and His Mother Studying the Scriptures,"* not after 1910
Photographic print, 4 ¾ × 3 ½ in.
Archives of American Art, Smithsonian Institution

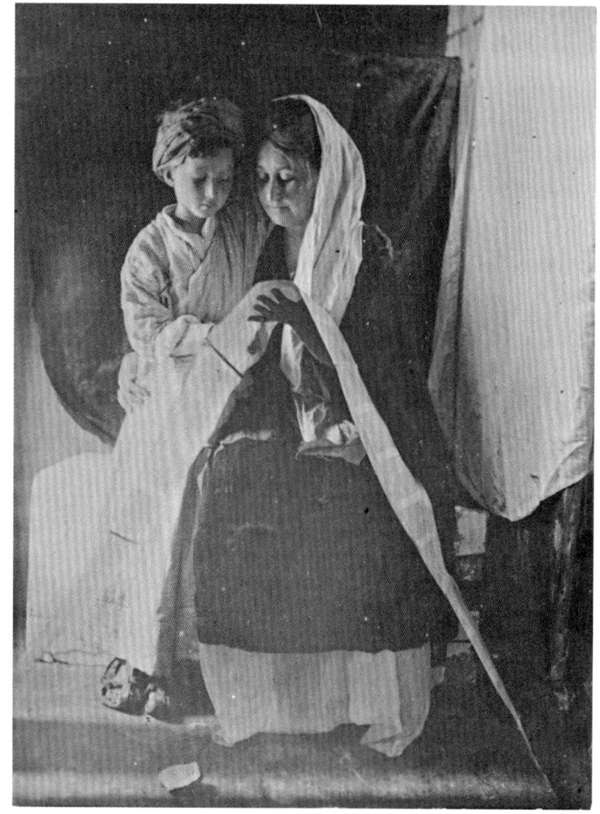

punch holes in and expose in order to give full life to his humanity. Ever the consummate art historian, Ellis notes that he is in effect undoing the history of sculpture in the round through his composite sculptural photographic projections: "Before sculpture was 3-D it was attached to architecture. These photographs use the reverse approach. The photograph and the sculpture attached to a flat ground."[37] Drawings from that moment also show Ellis developing the characteristic square-within-trapezoid shape that he would use to organize both photographs as well as paintings and drawings. The conjunction enabled the artist to think through perspective (a trapezoid is a square seen in recession) as a form of self-projection, and as a metaphor for the passage of time (see p. 164).

Shape would increasingly take on symbolic import for Ellis, serving variously as a metaphor for the family, the home, and the earth itself. Shape, he acknowledged, was also gendered. "Nature geometrizes," he writes, and "nature is female."[38] Ellis's journal references to Yvonne Rainer and Carolee Schneemann from the early 1980s demonstrate an engagement with feminist art practices at a moment when the mainstream art world was theorizing feminist art, particularly women artists practicing rephotography, as a genre of post-modernism.[39] While Ellis shared the interest in domesticity so often associated with feminist work, his treatment of the bedroom scene as a site of self-production would appear to be governed by a sense of restraint and estrangement more native to the nineteenth century than his own present.

Perhaps the ultimate irony of Ellis the historian was that the more enmeshed he became in the metaphysical and theoretical aspects of art history, the more tied to objective reality he strove for his work to be. He began to study artists who invested figurative motifs with abstract significance and attempted to see beyond apparent physical reality, including Chaïm Soutine, André Derain, and Marsden Hartley, and would declare his art a manifestation of a unifying spirit. Hence statements such as, "It is through the surface (medium) of the work that the soul 'voice' speaks."[40] Around 1987, his sketchbooks become less a series of technical "what ifs," and we see more evident connections between the instructions and diagrams and existing works. He also begins to think more deeply about the material support as the matrix where past and present, spirit and matter meet, making notes about different types of paper, pigments, and the succession of black and white in his drawings. As he was riddling over the material realities of his work, concern for his own mortality grew.

Approaching the end of the twentieth century, Ellis brought the long-standing artistic fascination with the unknown and the unseen to fruition.[41] Steven G. Fullwood describes the artist's challenge to the temporal authority of his father's photographs

[37] See p. 159. Darrel Ellis, Notebook 1980.1.
[38] Darrel Ellis, Notebook 1987.1.
[39] See Darrel Ellis, Notebook 1980.1 and Craig Owens, "The Discourse of Others: Feminists and Postmodernism," in Hal Foster, ed., *The Anti-Aesthetic: Essays on Post-Modern Culture* (Port Townsend, WA: Bay Press, 1983), 75–82.
[40] Darrel Ellis, Notebook 1988.1.
[41] See Ellis's comments on Surrealism in Darrel Ellis, Notebook 1988.1.

as a process of queering them, but it was also a form of visual transcendentalism.[42] Although he did not articulate this connection himself among the manifold references he pursued in his journals, we can locate Ellis's work in a lineage that yokes the black academic figurative tradition to modern mysticism, as exemplified by Henry Ossawa Tanner, Charles White, and Robert Pruitt. Ellis shared their concerns around "portraiture's capacity for the dignified individuation of black subjects."[43] Furthermore, Tanner's Marian imagery—which often relied his wife and son as models—provides a corollary for Ellis's continual reinterpretation of the mother and child theme. The connection Ellis's work forged with these diverse art histories finds its own afterlife in the photography of Albert Chong, Todd Gray, and Lyle Ashton Harris, all of whom have similarly questioned the complex interplay of race, sexuality and family history in the formation of the self. A unique and important contribution to these discourses, the work of Darrel Ellis embodies a metaphysical history of art—a connection across space and time where the spirit of the past continually inhabits the material reality of the present.

[42] Steven G. Fullwood, "The Case of the Artist's Archive," in Mimosa Montes and Croft, *Darrel Ellis*, 154.
[43] Connie H. Choi, *Black Refractions: Highlights from The Studio Museum in Harlem* (New York: The American Federation of the Arts, The Studio Museum in Harlem, Rizzoli Electa, 2019), 164 (Jared Richardson entry on Pruitt).

*Untitled (Grandmother Lilian Ellis)*, ca. 1981–85
Brush and black ink, wash, and graphite
on paper
12 ½ × 10 ½ in.

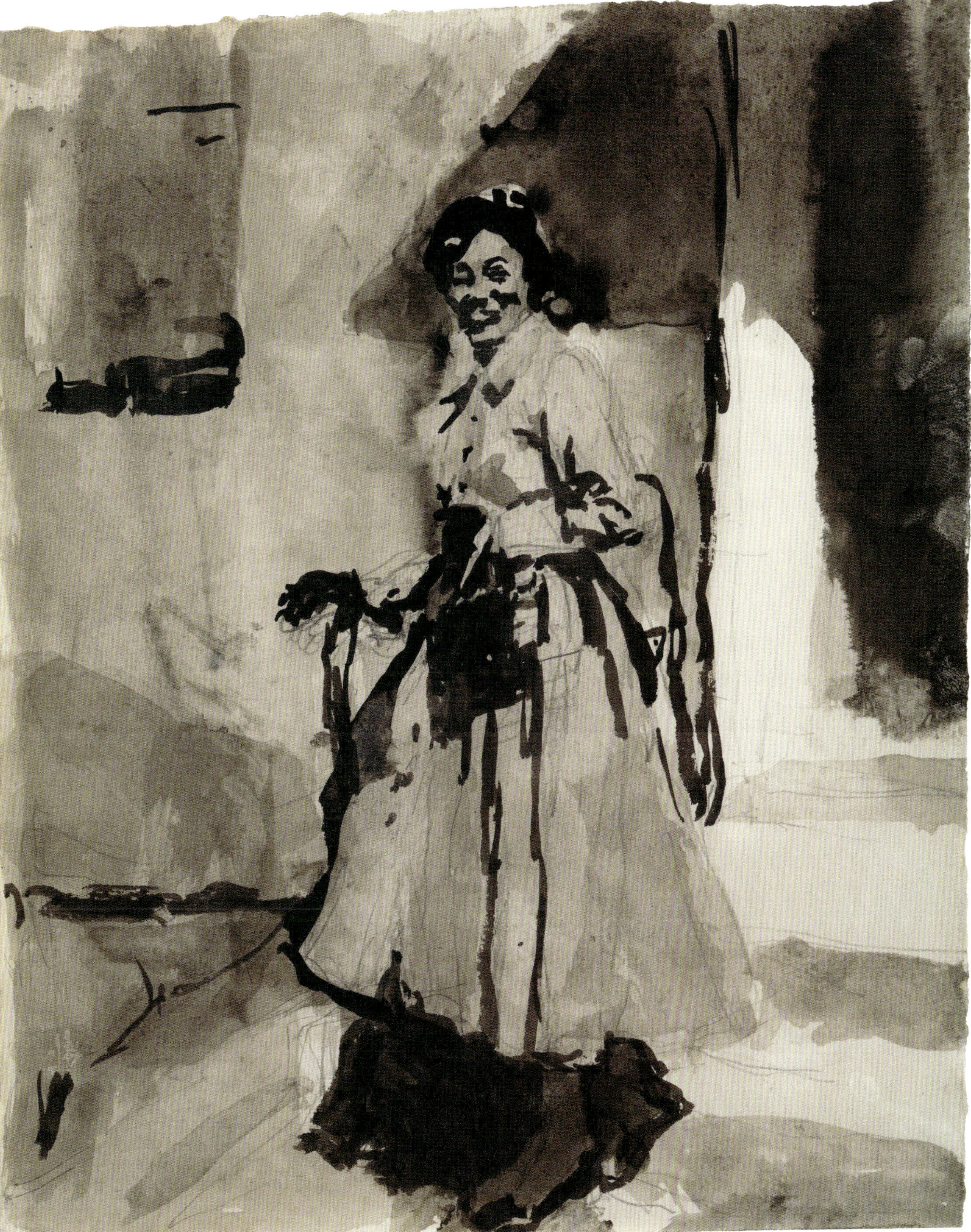

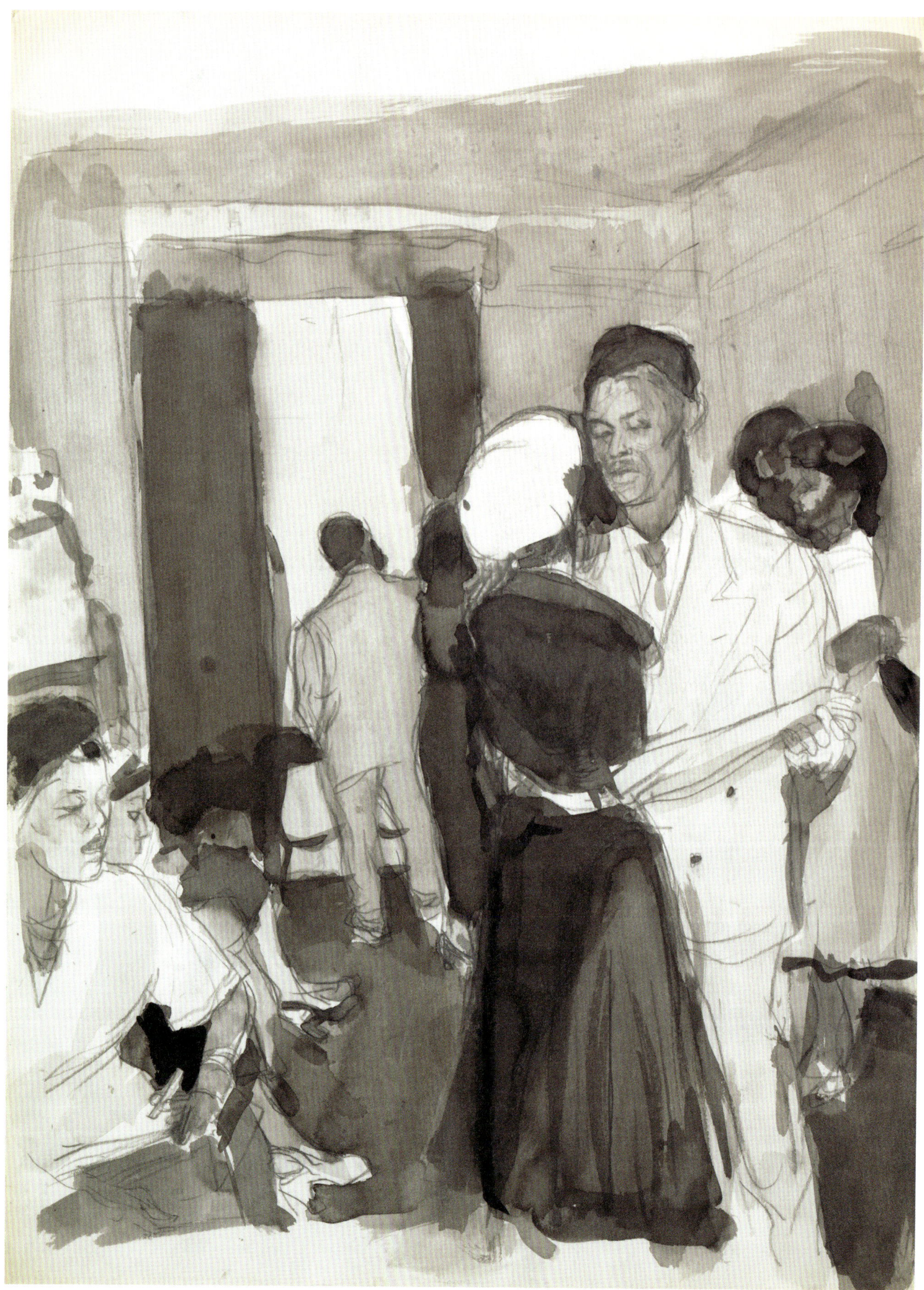

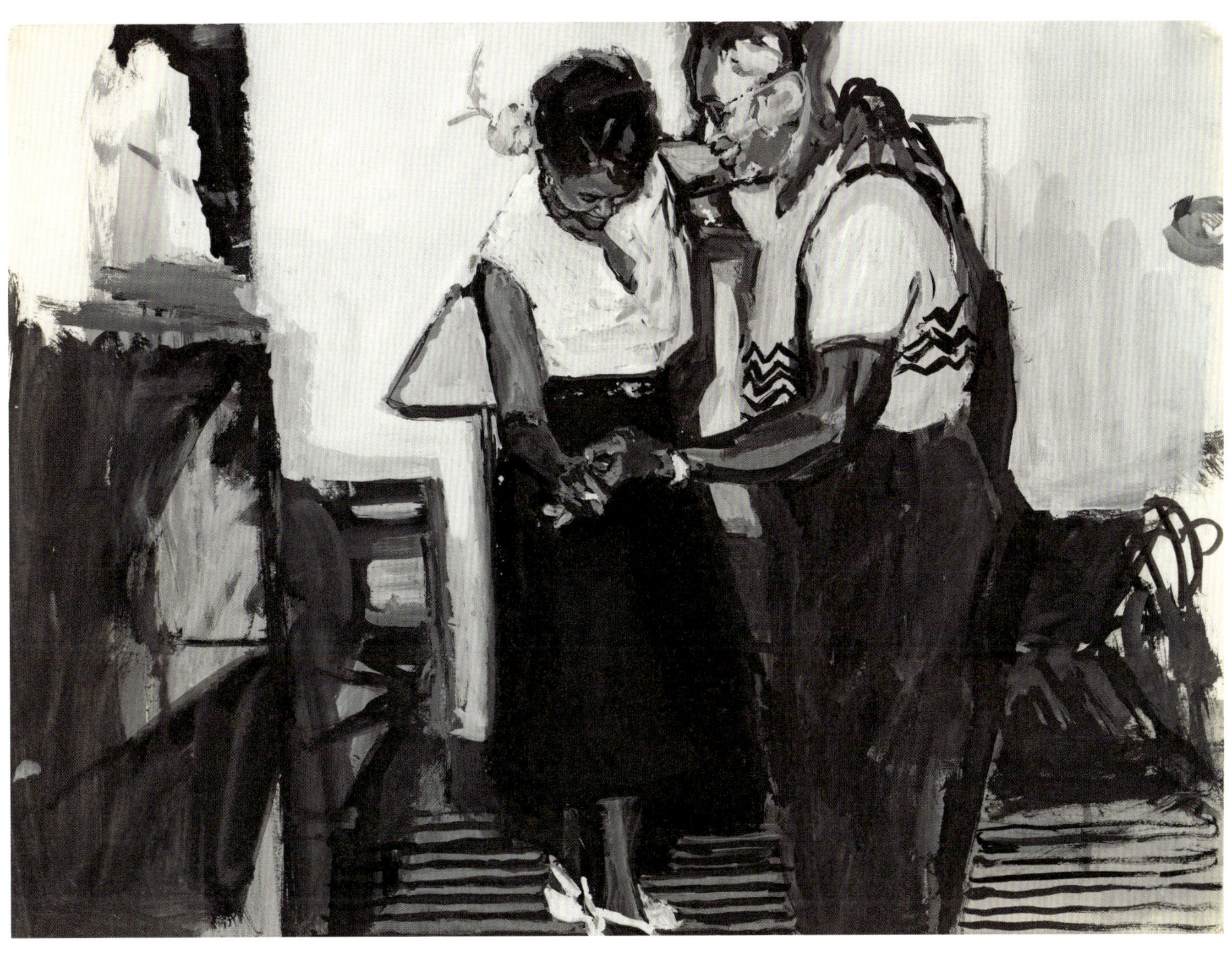

*Untitled (Dancing Couple)*, ca. 1981–85
Pen and brush and black ink, wash, and graphite on paper
30 × 21 in.
Dr. Kenneth Montague / The Wedge Collection

*Untitled (Grandparents Dancing)*, ca. 1981–85
Opaque watercolor and brush and black ink on paper
22 × 30 in.
Collection of Aime van Heddeghem

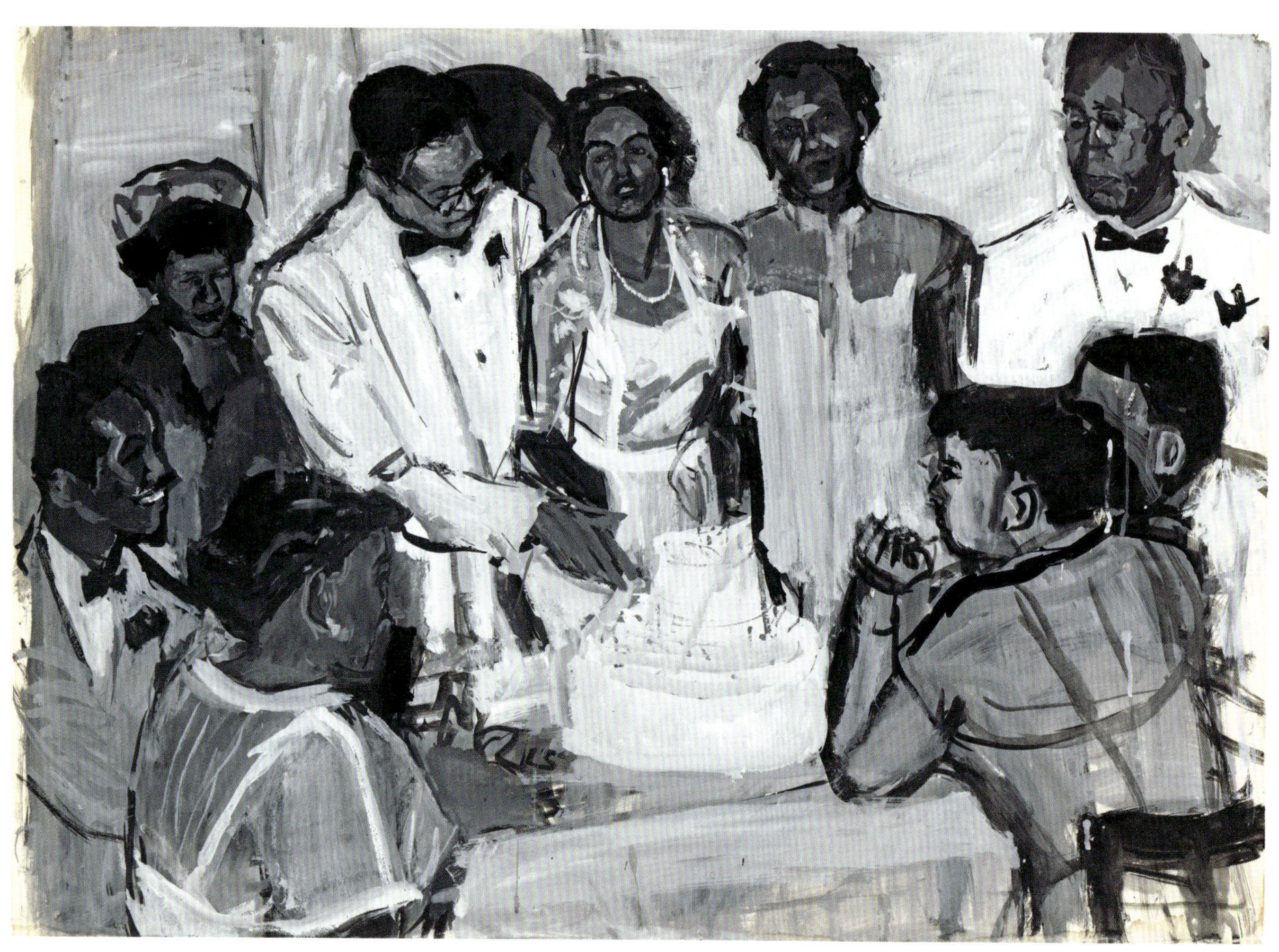

*Untitled (Group at Aunt Lena's Wedding)*,
ca. 1981–85
Opaque watercolor and brush
and black ink on paper
30 × 43 in.
Private collection

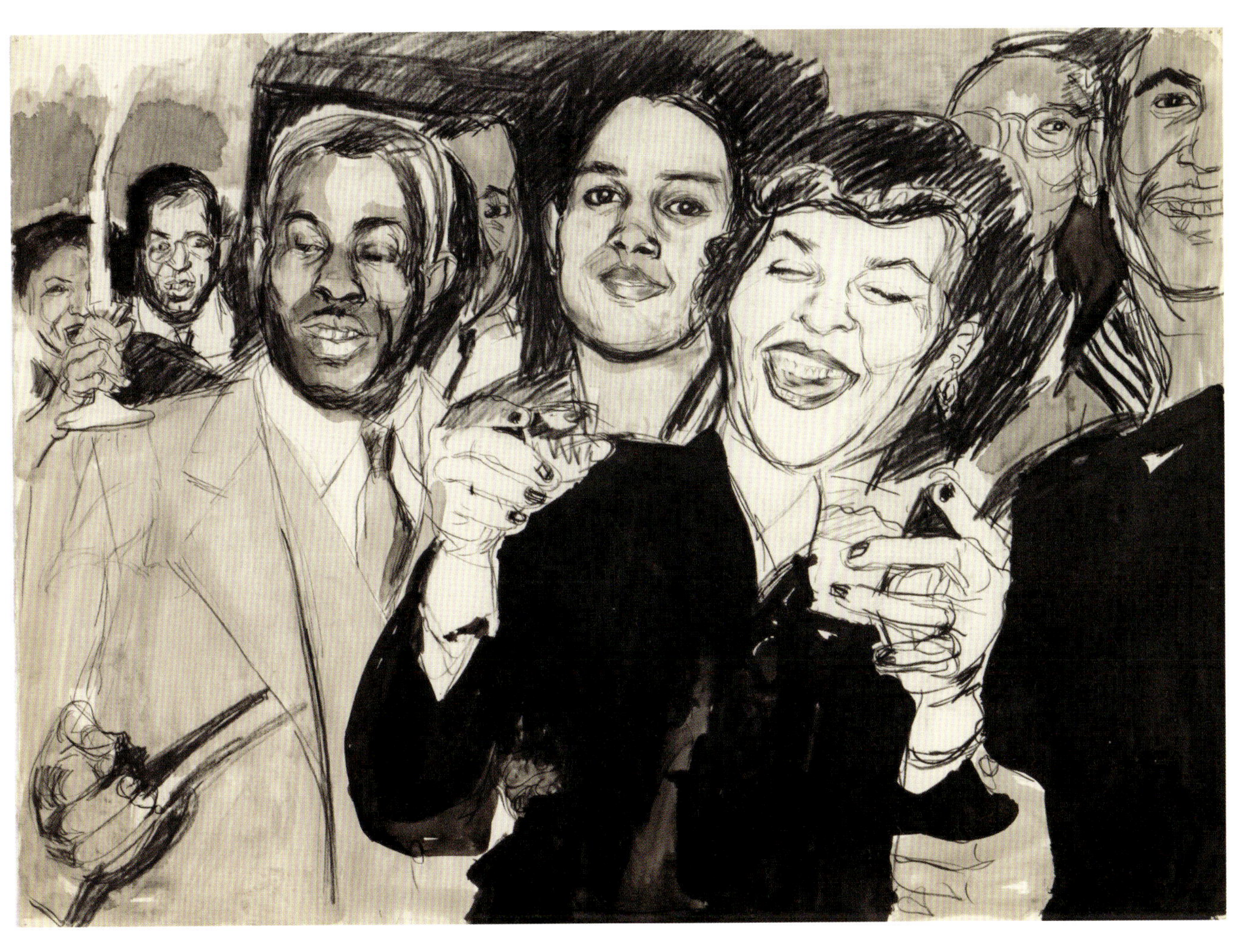

*Family Party*, 1983
Pen and brush and black ink, wash,
and charcoal on paper
30 ½ × 40 in.

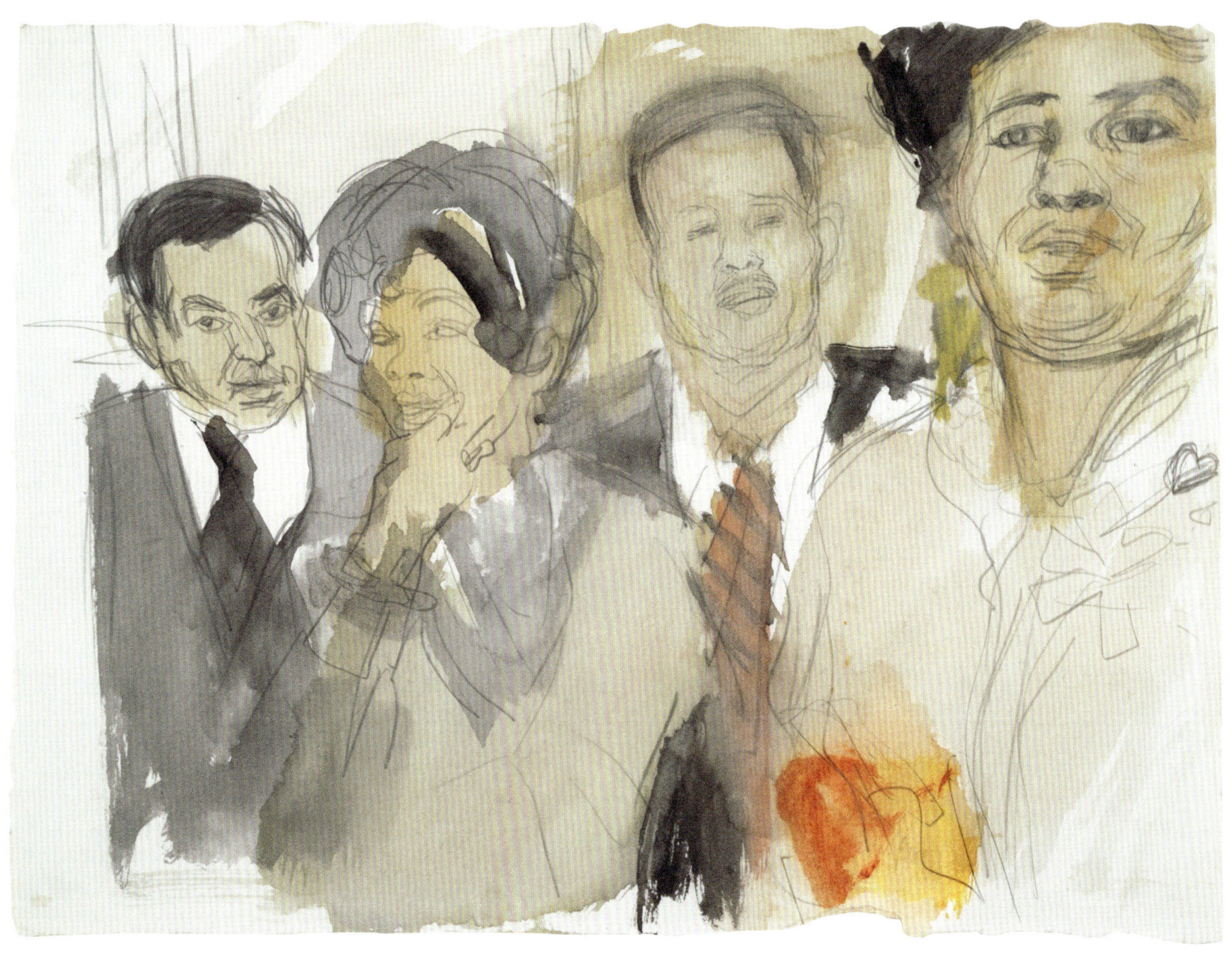

*Untitled (Four Figures)*, ca. 1981–85
Watercolor and graphite on paper
11 × 15 in.

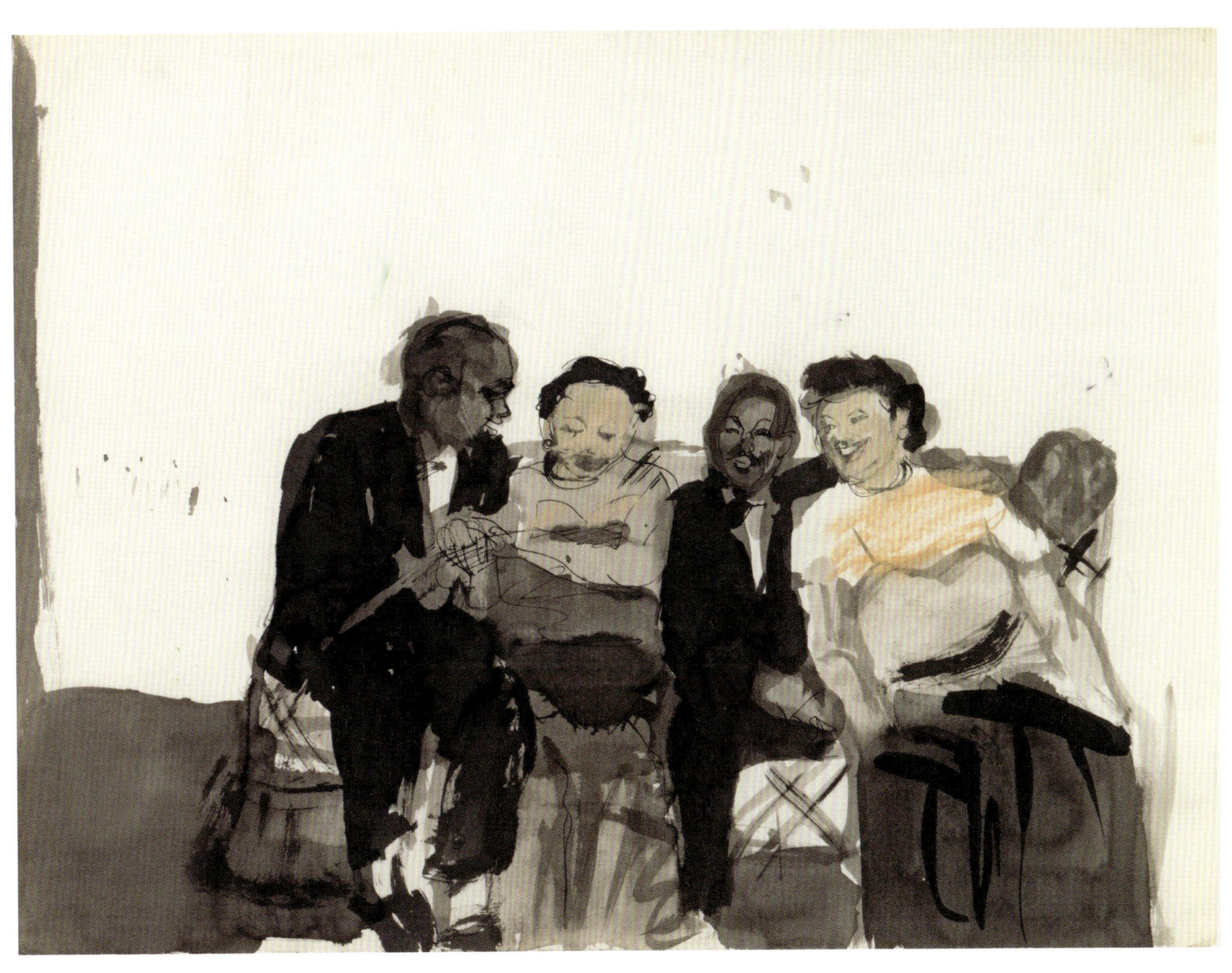

*Untitled (Four People Sitting)*, ca. 1981–95
Pen and brush and black ink, wash,
and pastel on paper
22 × 30 in.
Collection of Candice Madey
and Thomas Lewis

*Untitled (Katrina Styling Susan's Hair)*,
ca. 1985–88
Brush and black ink, wash, and charcoal
on two sheets of paper
55 × 39 ½ in.

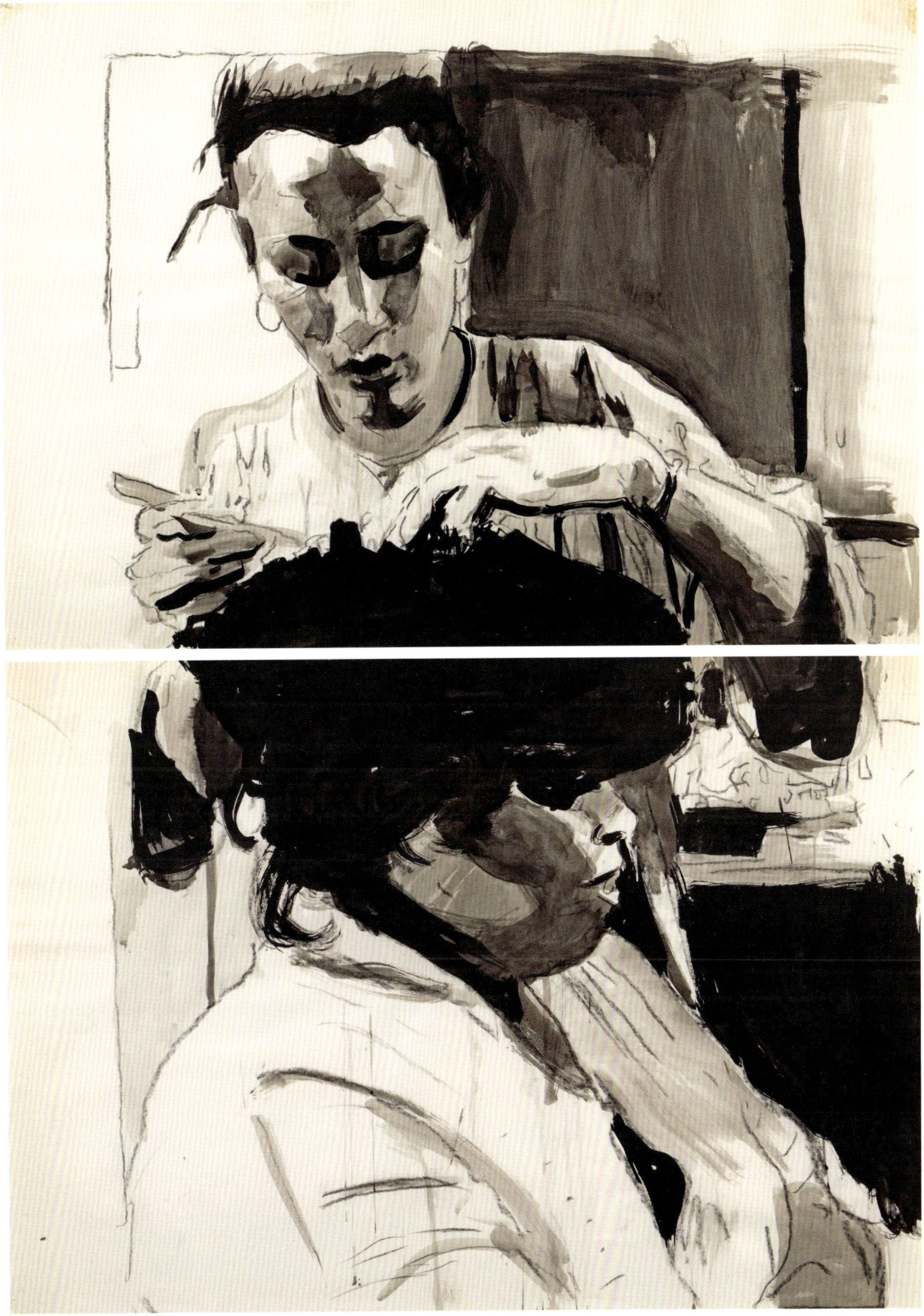

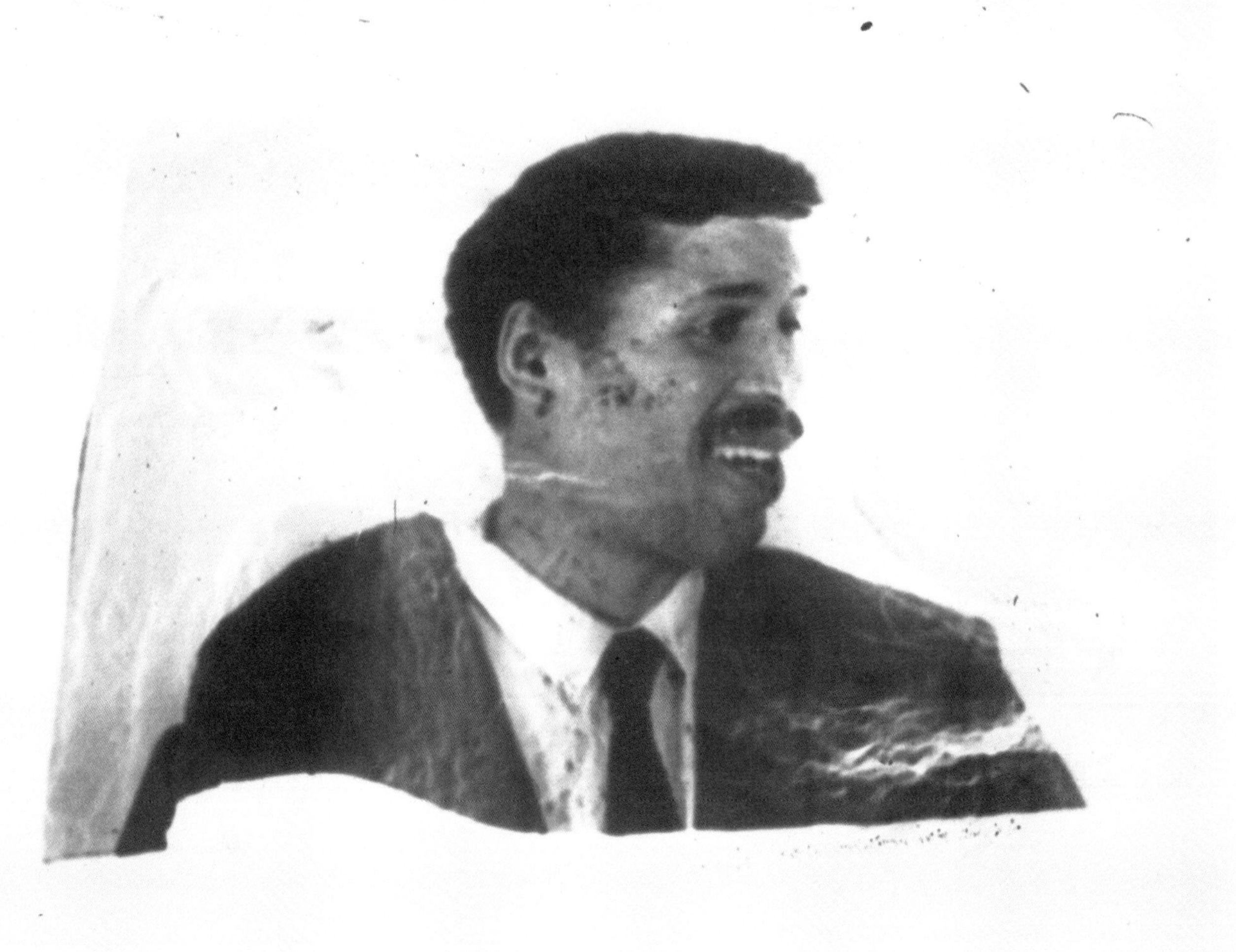

Makeda Best

# Touch, Feel: Darrel Ellis's Regenerative Photography

In 1988, Darrel Ellis commented in one of his sketchbooks on the relationship between sculpture and photography in his work: "The geometric shape introduces the element of touch, feel—the basic element of photography. By rephotographing the photograph with a sculpture form I emphasize the materiality of physical reality."[1]

Sometimes he uses a singular shape, or pairs of different ones. The edges of the objects are not necessarily smooth. Jagged edges remind the viewer of the hand that cut and shaped them. There are rectangles repeated in a ladder-like way. When positioned horizontally, the repetition of rectangles has the effect of making the image feel as if it is both moving together and apart. Ellis's shapes declare their existence as both mysterious voids and recognizably basic elementary forms. Meddling into the family photograph's representational work of optical description, and personal and cultural memory, the shapes render the supposedly familiar space of the photographic as new terrain. The smoothness and regularity of the shapes seem at odds with the emotional nuance and temporal specificity of the photographic. Boldly placed at focal points in the images—such as a subject's face—the shapes are familiar, but their presence is jarring. Within the pictorial field, Ellis's shapes frustrate our access to the informational syntax we expect to encounter and to the details and cues we need access to in order to read the faces and bodies. The works are presented as photographs, but Ellis also translated them into heavily worked paintings. These interventions juxtapose the indexical function of the photograph with its multivalent promise as a medium of gesture, presence and absence, past and present. Ellis described the effect to arts writer David Hirsh in this way: "the whole process is very ephemeral; the images are very ephemeral."[2]

Another technique Ellis uses makes the images appear even more fragile, as if they have gotten wet. Again, the artist manipulates our material understanding of the three-dimensional information captured and contained by the camera. Like submerged fabric, the images appear wavy, the emulsion seemingly disintegrated in parts. The slippery surfaces in which the image threatens to dissolve refer to the primal crisis of the photographic process: fixing the captured image. Surfaces look wrinkled, puckered, and shrunken. Scenes are also dreamlike and diffuse, like mirages in the bright sun. Evoking the metaphysical and otherworldly interested Ellis. The images are ephemeral and "they're in line with my beliefs, inasmuch I feel that, even though we live a in a physical world—we live in a real world and we're made of flesh and blood and everything—deeper down, the reality of human beings is that we are in fact spiritual beings," he explained to Hirsh. "We're connected to some source, some infinite, intangible source of life and creation."[3]

As he acknowledges in his reflection on photography and sculpture, Ellis's voids and forms allow him to bring together the different syntaxes of each practice. The perceptual disturbance generated by the simultaneous presentation of material loss and material presence is facilitated by forms that encourage two different kinds of viewership.

[1] See p. 162. Darrel Ellis, Notebook 1988.1.
[2] David Hirsh, "A New Sensibility: Interview with Darrel Ellis," in Lara Mimosa Montes and Kyle Croft, eds., *Darrel Ellis* (New York: Visual AIDS, 2021), 33.
[3] Ibid.

page 42
*Untitled (Self-Portrait after Museum Guard Photograph)*, ca. 1989–90
Gelatin silver print, 8 × 10 in.
Whitney Museum of American Art, New York

*Untitled (Mother, Father, Laure)*, ca. 1990
Gelatin silver print, 11 × 14 in.
Whitney Museum of American Art, New York

Robert Heinecken, *Fractured Figure Sections*, 1967
Gelatin silver prints on wood blocks, 10 3/16 × 3 3/4 × 3 3/4 in.
Princeton University Art Museum

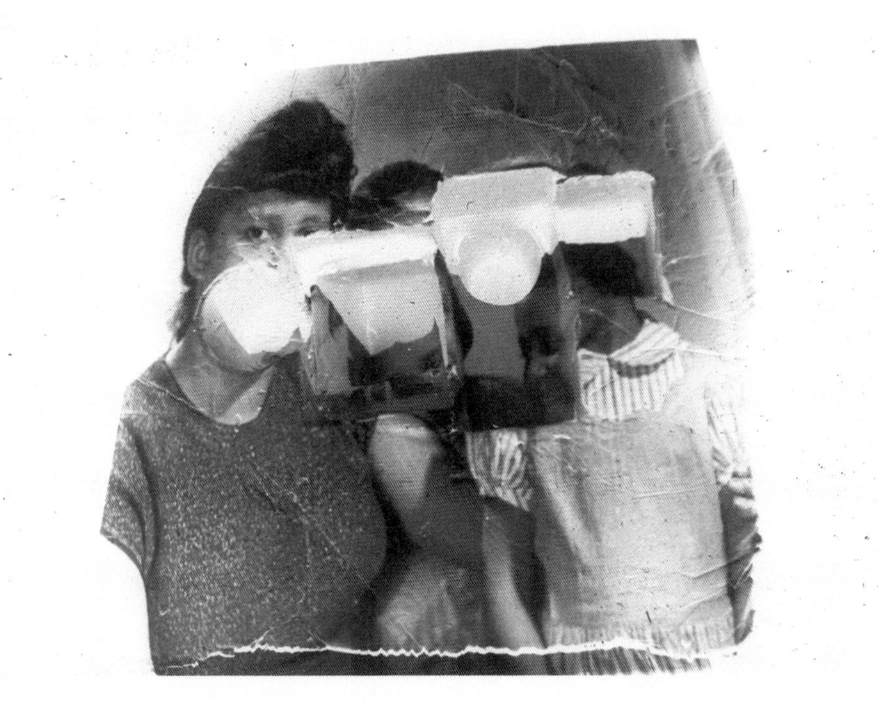

One viewing practice is usually performed at a distance and in relation to the body, whereas the family photograph in particular is typically read close-up and in an intimate way. As viewers, our perception is thrown askew by the pairing of what theorist D. N. Rodowick describes as the historic distinction between photography and sculpture, or two different "regimes of visibility: the former as a representation deployed in two dimensions and limited by a frame, a transcription of past presence in space and time now given to perception as absence; the latter, a presentation in three dimensions, occupying space materially and volumetrically in direct confrontation with vision at variable distances."[4] The conflict of perception within Ellis's images is further deepened through the visible presence of the photographic enlarger—the trapezoidal shape of the pictorial space—as an additional level of mediation. Rephotographing the photograph as distorted projection forces an awareness of the image on the paper—indeed, an awareness of paper, and thus of representation. With their slanted shapes, the images almost seem to be slipping away down off of the page. Renouncing his control over the images and upending the convention of a crisp border and the definitive line between the representational "living" zone and the non-representational "dead" zone, Ellis's images appear to be shifting within the physical space of the paper as a substrate for the image. Without an understanding of the function of the white "border," all of a sudden, the typically blank zone has the potential to absorb the representation while at the same time calling attention to the photograph as just a piece of paper. Hovering uncomfortably in the border space, the photographic representation appears unbound materially as well as from its position in space and time.

The conceptual and formal inquiries of Ellis's practice evince the ongoing currency of a number of trends in American photography in the late twentieth century. Critics and scholars have suggested his connection to his 1980s and 1990s contemporaries, but there are other connections as well. One less

[4] D. N. Rodowick, "A Virtual Presence in Space," in Sarah Hamill and Megan R. Luke, eds., *Photography and Sculpture: The Art Object in Reproduction* (Los Angeles: The Getty Research Institute, 2017), 212.

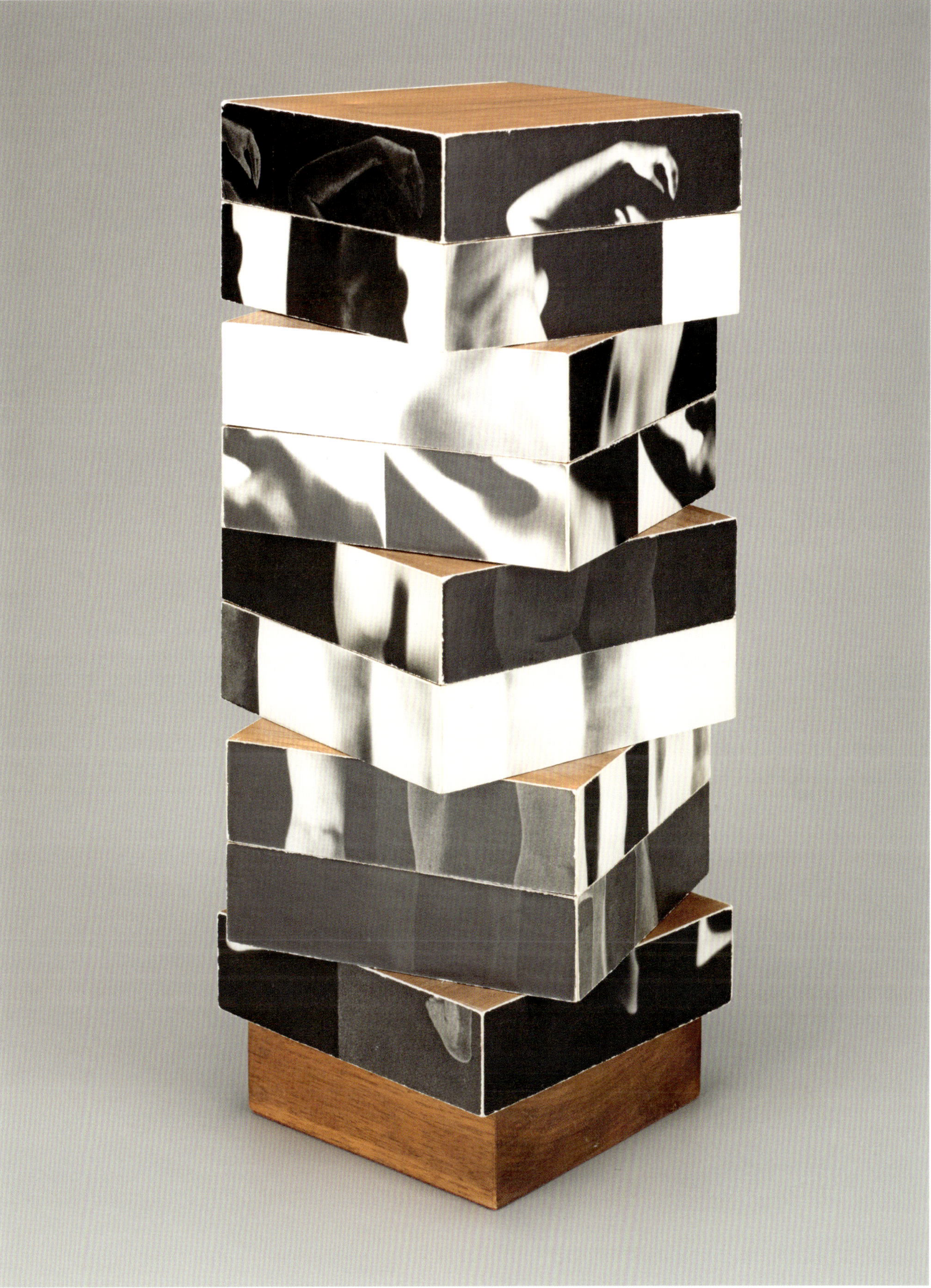

Nathan Lyons, *Untitled*, 1959
Gelatin silver print, 7 11⁄16 × 9 3⁄4 in.
George Eastman Museum,
Rochester, NY

acknowledged context is the legacy of curator and historian Peter Bunnell's pioneering 1970 Museum of Modern Art exhibition *Photography into Sculpture*—recognized as a turning point in the broader acceptance of practices that combined the two mediums. Historian Mary Statzer summarizes the theoretical arguments of Bunnell and artist Robert Heinecken, writing that Bunnell and Heinecken "dislocated 'straight' photography's reliance on the image and optical description as its primary source of meaning."[5] These *objects* (as opposed to photographs) were dedicated to the interplay between the image, materials, and the sculptural form.[6] In their interactivity, the objects puzzled the boundaries of both sculpture and photography. Artists featured in *Photography into Sculpture*, Bunnell states in the press release, "are seeking a new intricacy of meaning analogous to the complexity of our senses. They are moving from internal meaning or iconography—of sex, the environment, war—to a visual duality in which materials are also incorporated as content and at the same time are used as a way of conceiving actual space."[7] Statzer argues the artists featured disrupted the foundations of the medium by asking: what is a photograph? And how does photography convey meaning?[8] For Ellis, the incorporated materials displace notions of internal meaning in photography, and the limits of the photograph as a structure to contain meaning.

What Ellis furthers in his practice is not the externalization of the interrupted form, but the internalization of the experience of interplay between seriality, materials, and the sculptural form. He was clear about his desire to maintain the integrity of the photograph: ". . . my work looks like it's collaged or cut up, but it's only an illusion—nothing is destroyed. The photos, the negatives, are perfectly intact. I only project the image, I don't touch the negative, and the surfaces I use, they're all intact. Everything is intact. It's just that they come together and they marry for a while, then they split up, but they're still intact."[9] The "found" image still retains its presence,

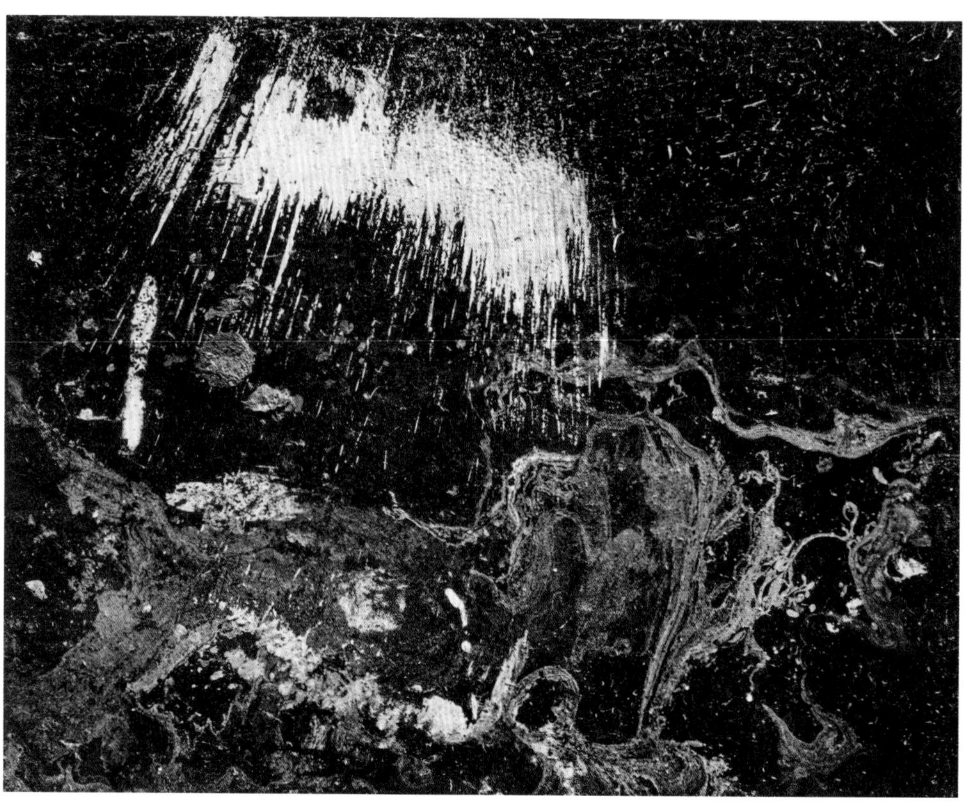

[5] Mary Statzer, "'Photography into Sculpture': Peter Bunnell, Robert Heinecken and Experimental Forms of Photography Circa 1970," Ph.D. dissertation (Tucson, The University of Arizona, 2015), 6.
[6] Ibid., 15.
[7] *Photography into Sculpture* press release. Press release, no. 36. April 8, 1970. The Museum of Modern Art, New York, NY. https://www.moma.org/momaorg/shared/pdfs/docs/press_archives/4438/releases/MOMA_1970_Jan-June_0035_36.pdf. Accessed December 29, 2020.
[8] Statzer, "Photography into Sculpture," 32.
[9] Hirsh, "A New Sensibility," 33.

Thomas Ellis with his wife, Jean,
and daughter Laure, ca. 1953
Photographs by Thomas Ellis
Estate of Darrel Ellis

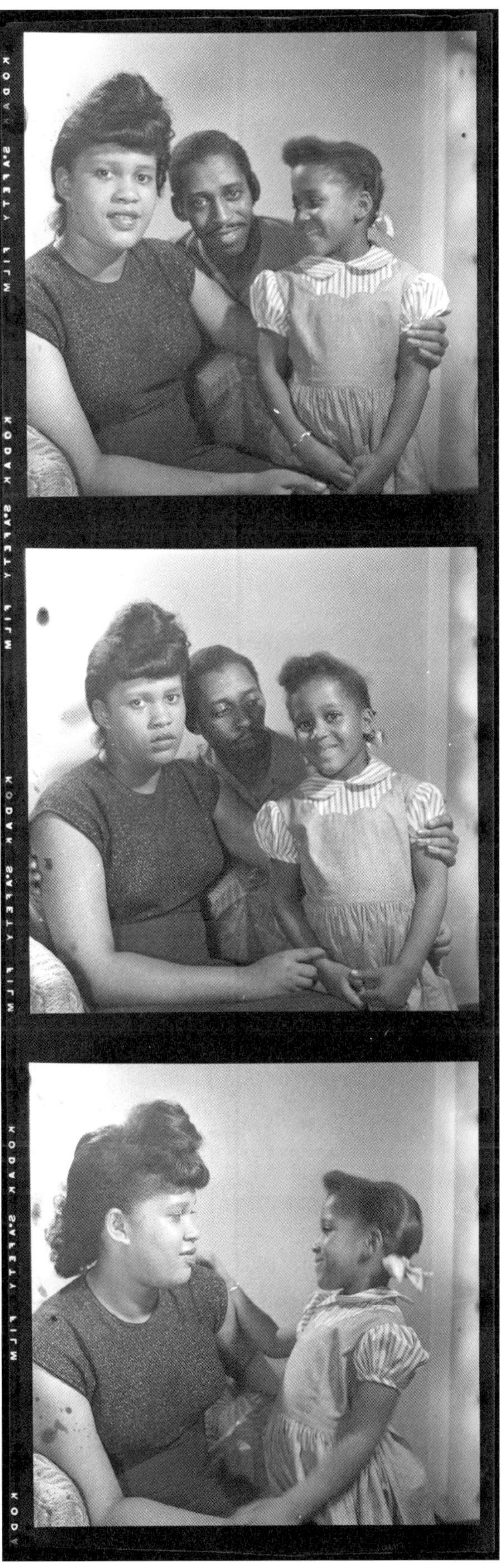

Clarissa Sligh, *What's Happening with Momma?*, 1988
Artist book, 11 × 6 × 1 ½ in.
Women's Studio Workshop

Thomas Ellis, *Untitled*, ca. 1953–54
Mounted silver gelatin print, 20 × 16 in.
Estate of Darrel Ellis

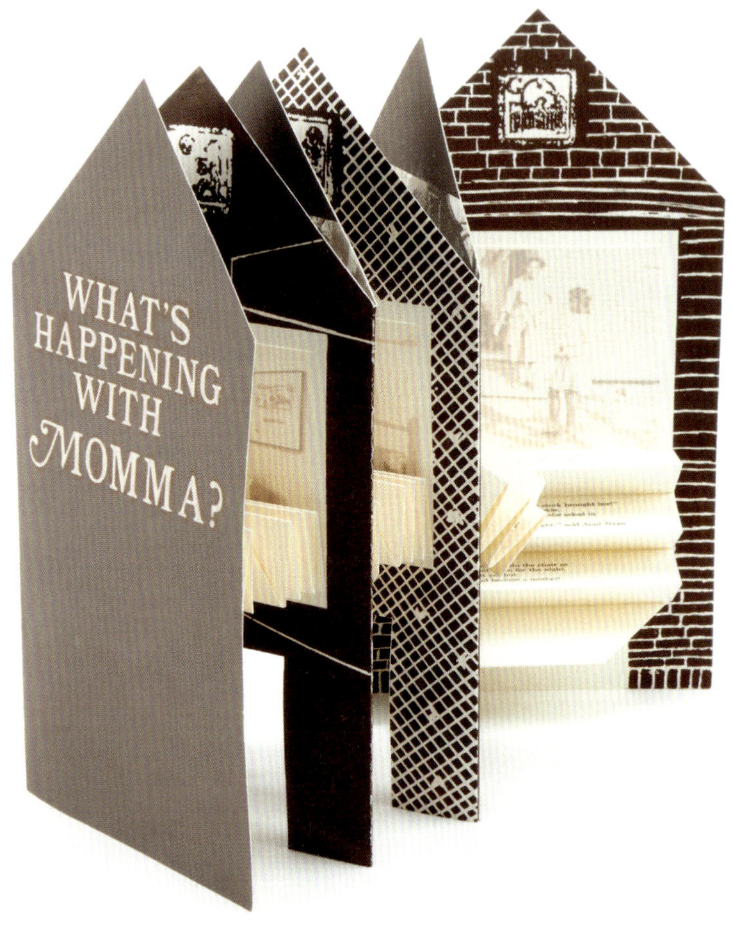


but the viewer becomes aware of its qualities as an object. Ellis is able to dislocate photography's optical representational function through his interventions, and to activate the senses—what Bunnell called a "new intricacy of meaning." The photographic, he communicates, is not just representation, but it is the sensed, the material, and felt world. He articulated his commitment to both deconstruction and reconstruction: "I've always tried—to make the family to my liking somehow. In order to do that, you really look into it, deeply. I feel strongly that deconstructing is all right. But what's more important is reconstruction. It's very cerebral work, very mental work, and in a way, very soulful work."[10] His use of concrete metaphors is notable. His making, he underscores, requires a looking into something with a physical presence. One can imagine that when he projected the photographs in order to create his works, the world within them was briefly resurrected through the illusion of the projector. Inserting the objects into specific spaces, he captures the memory as material form.

Ellis belongs to a generation of artists that arose following the institutional recognition of formal experimentation in photography which went beyond the *Photography into Sculpture* exhibition. Photographer, author, and educator Nathan Lyons discussed hybrid practices that could "make visible imaginative preoccupations which go beyond the technical event."[11] *Photography into Sculpture* and Nathan Lyons's theories (which led to the University of Rochester's Visual Studies Workshop) took place against the backdrop of

[10] Ibid.
[11] Nathan Lyons, "To the Spirit of a Time IN CONSIDERATION," *Aperture* 8, no. 2 [30], 1960, 119.

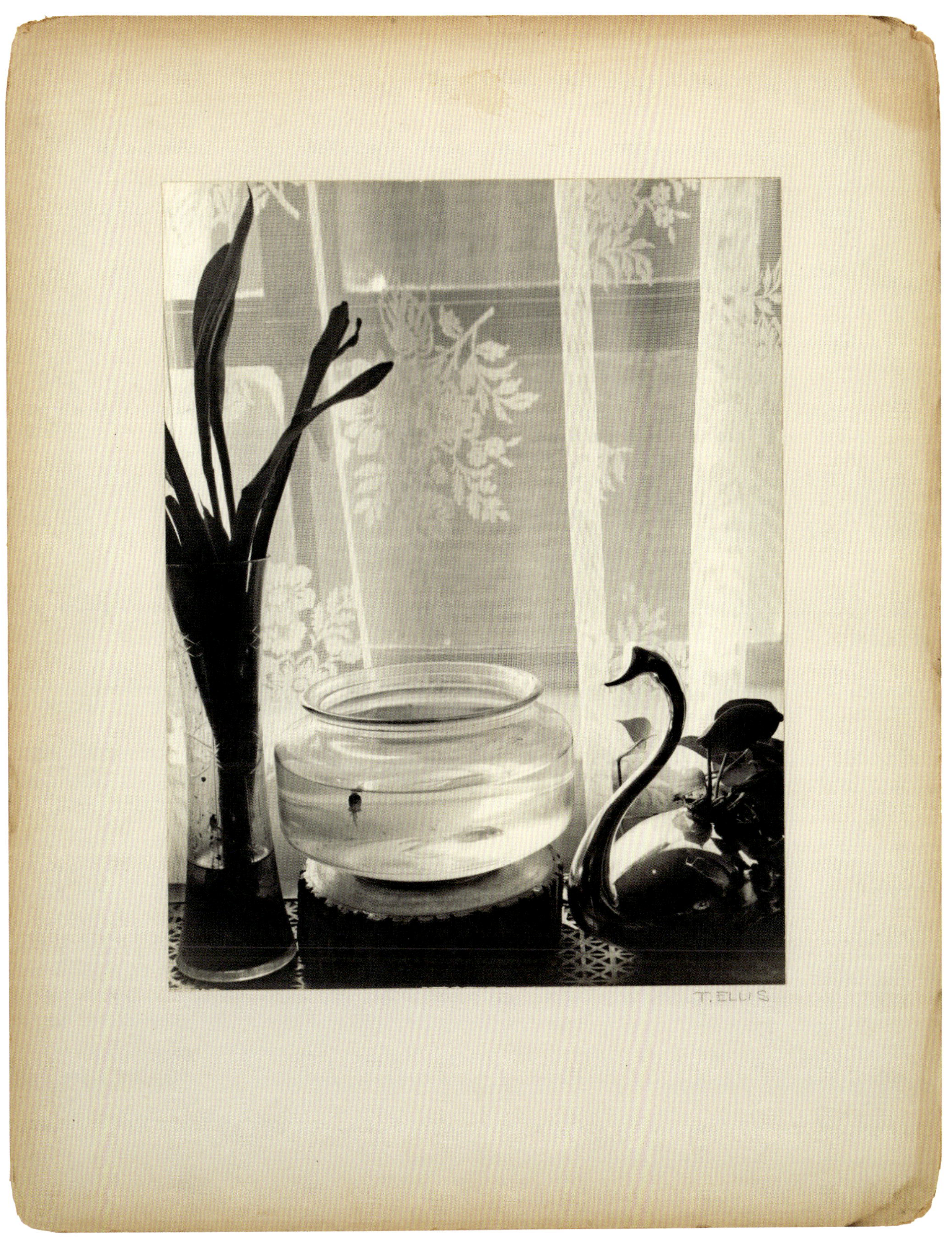
T. ELLIS

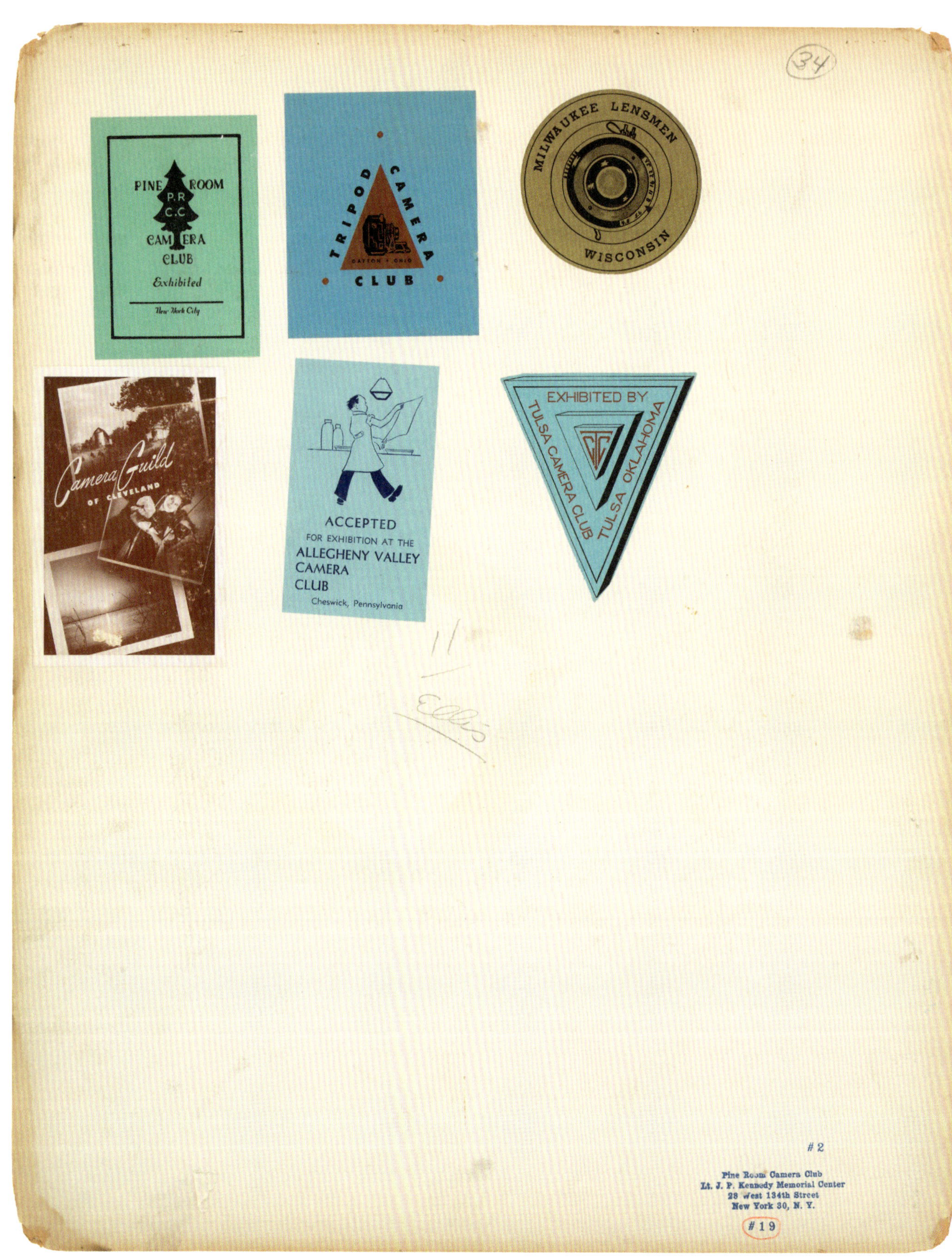
34
PINE ROOM
P.R.
C.C.
CAMERA
CLUB
Exhibited
New York City
TRIPOD CAMERA CLUB
DAYTON • OHIO
MILWAUKEE LENSMEN
WISCONSIN
Camera Guild
OF CLEVELAND
ACCEPTED
FOR EXHIBITION AT THE
ALLEGHENY VALLEY
CAMERA
CLUB
Cheswick, Pennsylvania
EXHIBITED BY
TULSA CAMERA CLUB
TULSA OKLAHOMA
TCC
11
Ellis
# 2
Pine Room Camera Club
Lt. J. P. Kennedy Memorial Center
28 West 134th Street
New York 30, N. Y.
# 19

The verso of the Thomas Ellis print includes stickers from various camera clubs where the photograph was exhibited

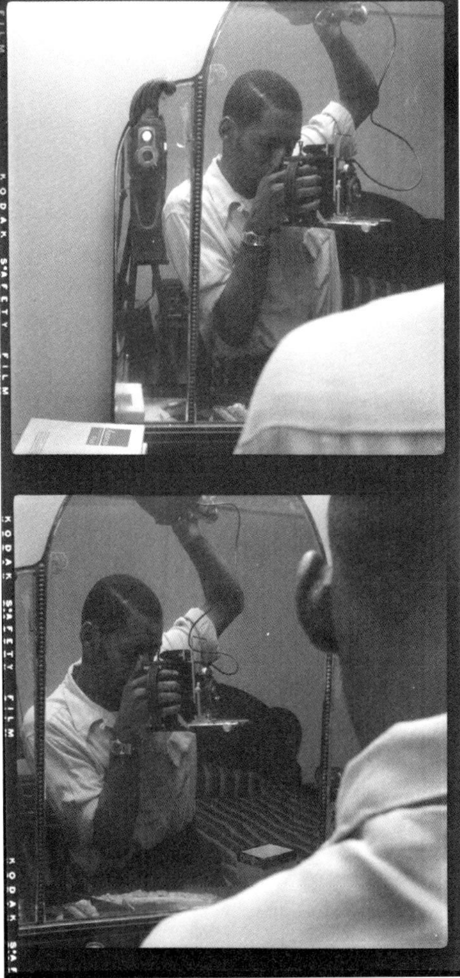


Self-portraits by Thomas Ellis, ca. 1950s
Estate of Darrel Ellis

a society inundated with images, the founding of academic programs dedicated to photographic practice, and a new generation more responsive to the unconventional. Unlike the works that were multimedia and three-dimensional, a clear tension in Ellis's work is that he maintains the wholeness of the paper form, acting within the space of photographic representation, and in so doing he combines a critique of the internal meaning while constructing a space that fosters both a process of reflection and remembrance, through the senses.

While his contemporaries were preoccupied with mass media images, Ellis attends to a specific kind of subject, representational schema and material object: family photographs. Turning to family and community is something Ellis shared with other African American artists using photography at this time.[12] Adding his shapes and voids, Ellis interrogates the gaze as a core relational aspect of the family photograph genre. Historian Marianne Hirsch summarizes the circuit of looking inherent to this genre. She writes: "The photograph is the site at which numerous looks and gazes intersect: the look exchanged between the photographer/camera and the subject; the looks between the subjects within the image; the look of the viewer, which often exceeds and complicates that of the camera and which, in itself, is an infinitely multiple and contradictory series of looks; and the external institutional and ideological gazes in relation to the which the act of taking pictures defines itself."[13] Ultimately, this looking serves as a means to create and enforce relationships. Hirsch explains further: ". . . each picture is also the product of other looks and gazes as family members define themselves in relation to each other in the roles they occupy as mother, father, daughter, son, husband, or lover. That process of definition—that familial act of looking—is also recorded visually in photographs."[14]

In family photographs, looking, knowing, and understanding is facilitated not just through the eyes, but crucially, through touch. Family photographs are intimately touched, kept, held, and shared. New contexts of belonging are created or remembered. Touch offers another way to re-negotiate relationships and reinterpret events. This is also the means by which the relationship of the family photograph to collective and individual memory deepens. Through the process of direct interaction, memory, to borrow Ellis's words, is deconstructed and reconstructed. He describes his use of his father's photographs as a way to create distance: "As for using my father's pictures specifically, it helps me to keep a certain amount of distance and detachment from the reality I know, growing up after my father's death. The world he photographed was one I didn't know, because I wasn't born yet. . .

[12] Deborah Willis, "An Overview: African American Photographers 1839–1989," *The International Review of African American Art*, Summer 1989, 16.
[13] Marianne Hirsch, *The Familial Gaze* (Hanover, NH: Dartmouth College, published by University Press of New England, 1999), xvi.
[14] Ibid.

Photographs of the Ellis family by Thomas Ellis, ca. 1950s
Estate of Darrel Ellis

I don't know any life from the forties and fifties with their picnics and their beautiful clothes and everything is so nice and perfect and wholesome."[15] In speaking of using the photographs, he demonstrates how the handling of the family photograph can aid in facilitating the working through of trauma and loss. In this way, the shapes function as material emblems and manifestations of his sense of estrangement. When Ellis speaks of not knowing the life depicted in the photographs, he seems to refer to more than just what it looks like, but to the experience of that world and of the moments depicted in the photographs. The shapes he integrates into the artistic space offer material to grasp, a connection to hold onto and a link to that world. At the same time, they hold space for the lack of knowing and trauma.

Ellis's experience of his region of the world was far different from his father's. Born in 1958, he did not migrate to New York, but was born there. He straddles two historical eras of hope and disillusionment. Ellis reached adolescence as the Great Migration of African Americans from places like Louisiana and Georgia (where Thomas Ellis's family had roots) was coming to an end. The elder Ellis witnessed Harlem as the spiritual capital of black America, as it came to be known. "It's close-to-war America and my work is something else," Ellis said of his father's work.[16] He described the person he sees in the body of work left behind as a "good, honest, hardworking, responsible, idealistic, optimistic war veteran."[17] The younger Ellis's sense of uncertainty is profound. Marked first by the murder of his own father, his was an era that struggled with a vision of black identity that had become politically, economically, and socially difficult to maintain.

Thomas Ellis belonged to another era, and so did the aesthetic of his photographs. In addition to working as a postal clerk, he briefly ran a photography studio and was active making photographs commercially in Harlem and the South Bronx. He participated in camera club activities, which included juried exhibitions. Camera clubs originally emerged in cities like Boston and New York in the late nineteenth century as an alternative to the broader commercialization that took place following Kodak's introduction of mass-market cameras. Serious practitioners like Thomas Ellis utilized clubs as resources for networking and sharing, and as a forum for supporting their belief in photography as a fine art form. The clubs offered those who were working commercially a space for dialogue about creative work and the opportunity for recognition of their own non-commercial production. African Americans created their own camera clubs, as did other ethnic groups. Thomas Ellis was, according to his son, "very involved with photography. He knew the history and he had an enormous amount of equipment. He left literally hundreds and hundreds of negatives and pictures behind . . . [he] devoted a whole lot of time to photographing. He had a huge encyclopedia of photography, the most up to date volumes on the history of photography, all the best cameras."[18]

There is a sense of clarity in the aesthetic of the photographs of the elder Ellis that reflects a shared vision of the era about African American identity and promise. This clarity comes from the detail offered by the medium format camera, but also from the deliberation the process of making photographs required. The sitters would have watched him as he composed the photograph, perhaps making a few images before deciding to add a handheld flash. The square frame of the pictorial space provides a neat container. Sitters are generally fixed in the middle ground of the composition and centered in the frame. The indoor spaces are comfortably furnished, and Ellis is careful to include some of this context. Different photographs of people in various settings indicate Ellis brought out the camera with intention. It also suggests the ways the subjects responded to the process of having their picture made. Even as they sit or lean into one another, the subjects comport

[15] Hirsh, "A New Sensibility," 33.
[16] Ibid.
[17] Ibid., 31.
[18] Ibid., 31 and 33.

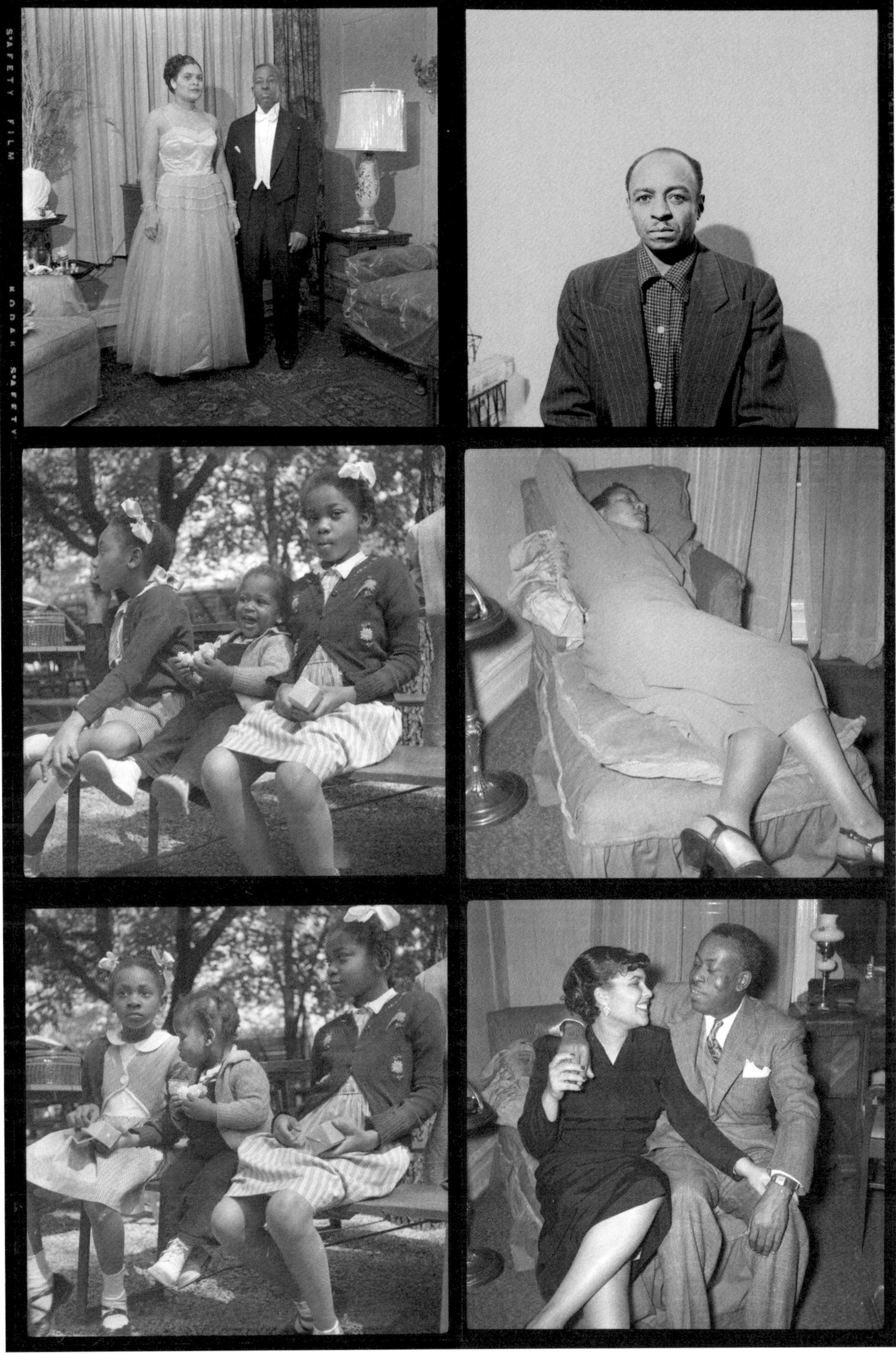

Marvin and Morgan Smith, *Marvin and Morgan Smith setting up for a photography session with model Sara Lou Harris Carter*, 1942
Gelatin silver print, 10 ¼ × 8 ¼ in.
Schomburg Center for Research in Black Culture, New York

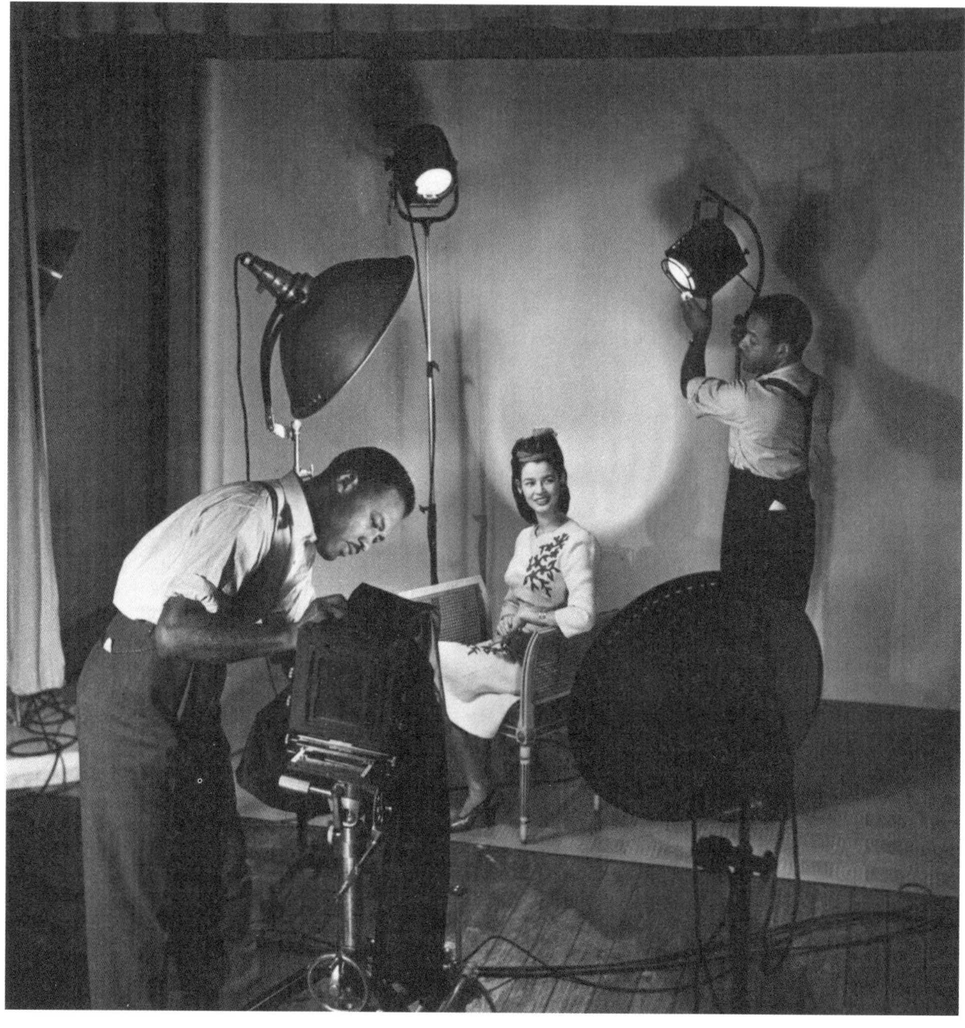

themselves expectantly, even in the more candid scenes. From the way he worked at his still life scenes, we see Ellis striving for an aesthetic of the everyday that is elegant, composed, proud, and yet natural. Plain or graphically simple backgrounds allow for the human form—the poses, clothing and accessories—to be the central focus of attention. Lighting is always considered, and we see Ellis working with different forms of natural and artificial illumination. Someone who studied photography would have understood this—the ways small adjustments in light can dramatically change how we see the subject. We also see Ellis trying to both take advantage of and minimize dramatic shadows. The right amount of dark space can frame the subject, but too much shadow, even in just a portion of a photograph, can be distracting. Just as the images evince a clarity in technique and mood, there is a confidence in Thomas Ellis's approach. The vantage points, lighting, and positioning of subjects demonstrate an understanding of what he is trying to produce and a knowledge of which techniques create desired effects.

In addition to camera clubs, Thomas Ellis's aesthetic would have been influenced by celebrated contemporaries. One of the most well-known studios was the Smith Studio of Harlem, owned by twins Marvin and Morgan Smith, which opened next door the Apollo Theater in 1939, and which they ran until 1969. In photographing the political and cultural leaders of the era, the Smiths, curator and scholar Brian Piper writes, "prioritized images of African Americans that were polished, glamorous, and performative."[19] Their work telegraphed messages of respectability and uplift. Not all their sitters were famous. They also catered to a middle-class clientele eager to be associated with this vision of black life. These studios played an influential role in the visual culture of the era. Their photographs decorated people's homes and regularly appeared in the black press. Beyond the well-known Smith brothers, local photographers could find work photographing social clubs, churches, fraternal groups, and events. Photography of this era was about more than just human subjects, but also about the spaces they occupy—black space where they felt comfortable and safe. Piper explains that "photography studios shared similarities to the barber shop, the beauty salon, the Church, the law office, and even the corner bar as important spaces where African Americans gathered to express themselves in relative freedom and safety."[20] Piper's reference to space is important here. Ellis explains he is interested in the materiality of reality. The found images do more than just represent what a space looks like, they embody a world and the feeling of that world, and this space was equally as unfamiliar to Ellis.

Ironically, the addition of the sculptural form and the manipulation of the image bring Ellis closer to a reality that felt distant. Through the introduction of the sense of touch, he gains access to the world that was lost to him. The forms are not voids after all, they are foundations. Ellis said, "They're all different, the photos: they're like regeneration, regenerated. From one you get many. And that works as a metaphor for the family."[21] Deliberately contrasting the different formal syntaxes of photography and sculpture while disrupting conventions allows him to call into being a new aesthetic language for his time. In place of doubt and suspicion of the medium, he proposes a closer relation to it by returning to its basic elements of touch and feeling. Historian of African American photography Deborah Willis calls artists working with photography at this time "interpreters" who feel charged to address broader human as well as internal struggles.[22] Ellis ponders not just what photographic meaning is, but the function of the space of the photographic. He suggests an answer: "I want the work I make to affect people, which seems to be getting harder and harder, to really affect many people anymore, with images, with pictures. Who knows? But I would like to affect people, as an artist."[23]

[19] Brian Piper, "Cameras at Work: African American Studio Photographers and the Business of Everyday Life, 1900–1970", Ph.D. dissertation (Williamsburg, VA, College of William and Mary, 2016), 12.
[20] Ibid., 8.
[21] Hirsh, "A New Sensibility," 33.
[22] Willis, "An Overview," 16.
[23] Hirsh, "A New Sensibility," 34.

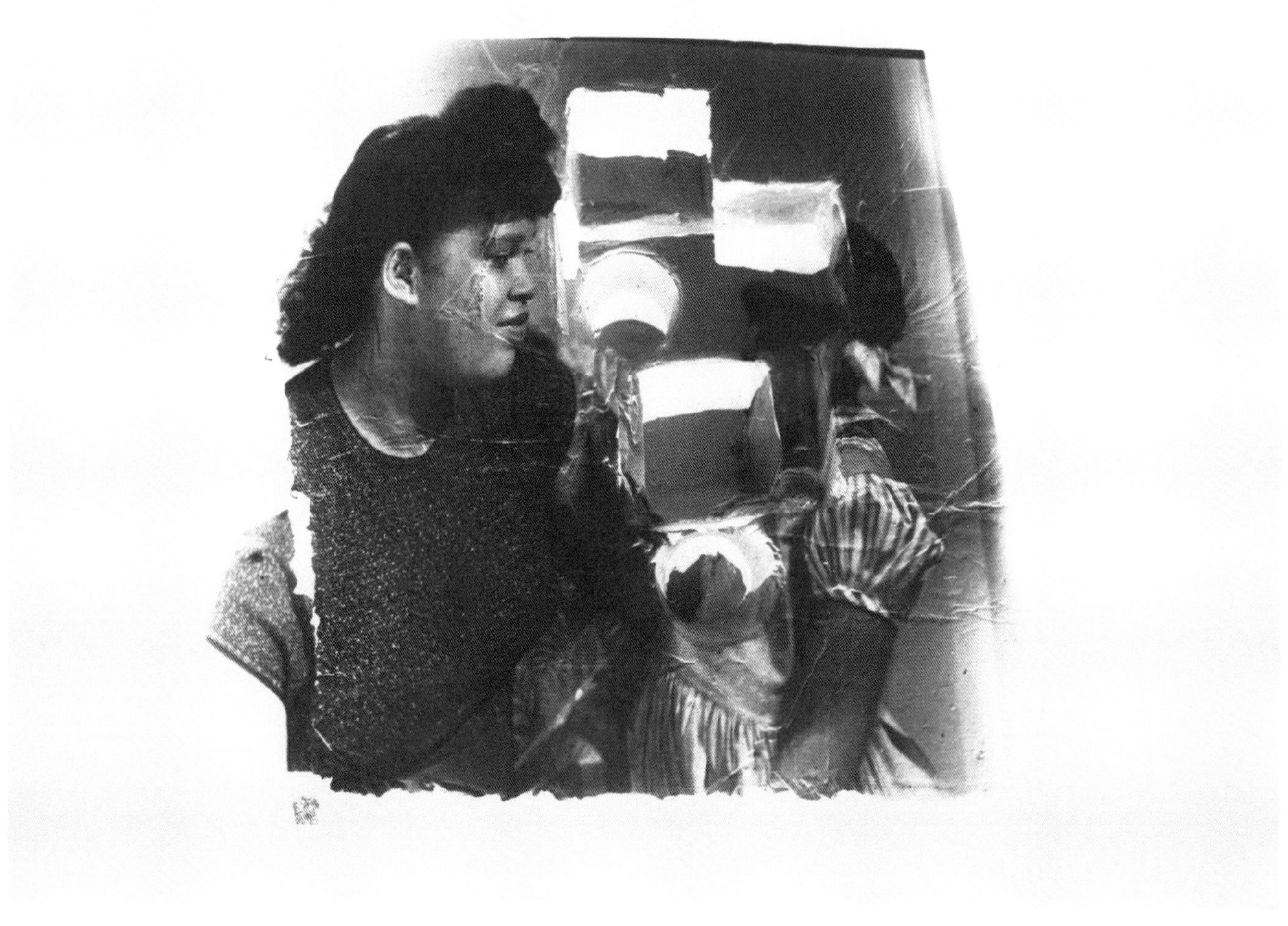

*Untitled (Mother and Laure)*, 1990
Gelatin silver print
10 ½ × 13 ½ in.

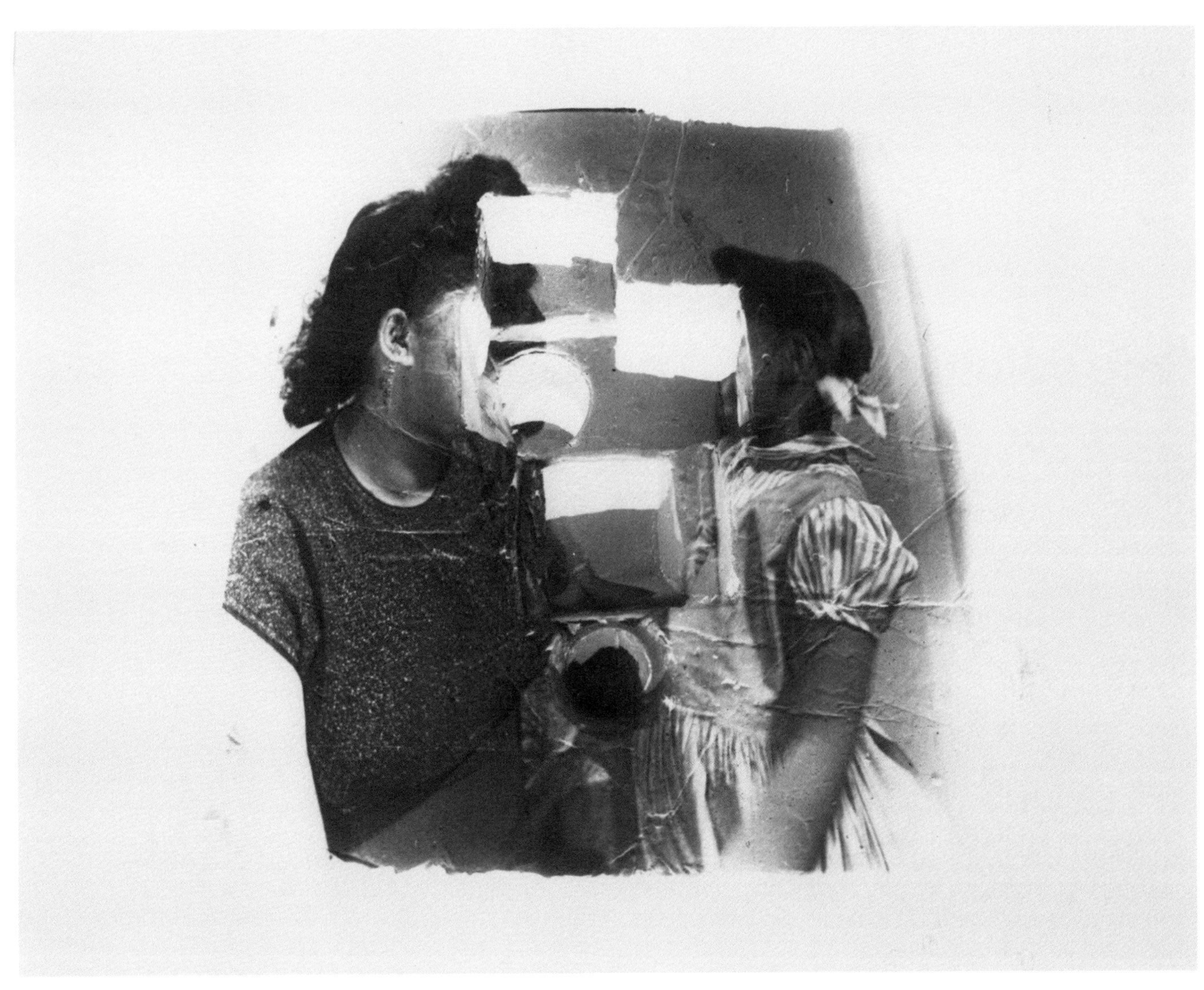

*Untitled (Mother and Laure)*, 1990
Gelatin silver print
11 × 14 in.
Private collection

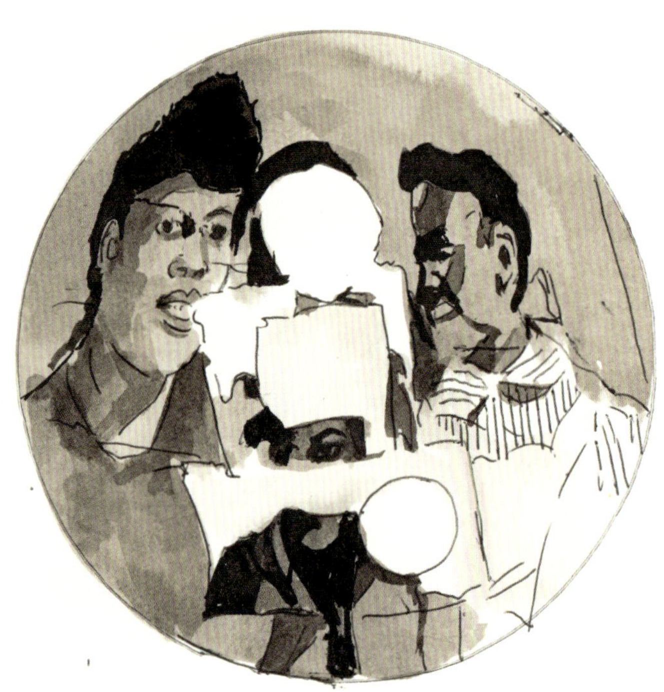

*Untitled (Mother, Father, and Laure)*,
ca. 1990
Pen and brush and black ink and wash
on paper
9 × 10 in.

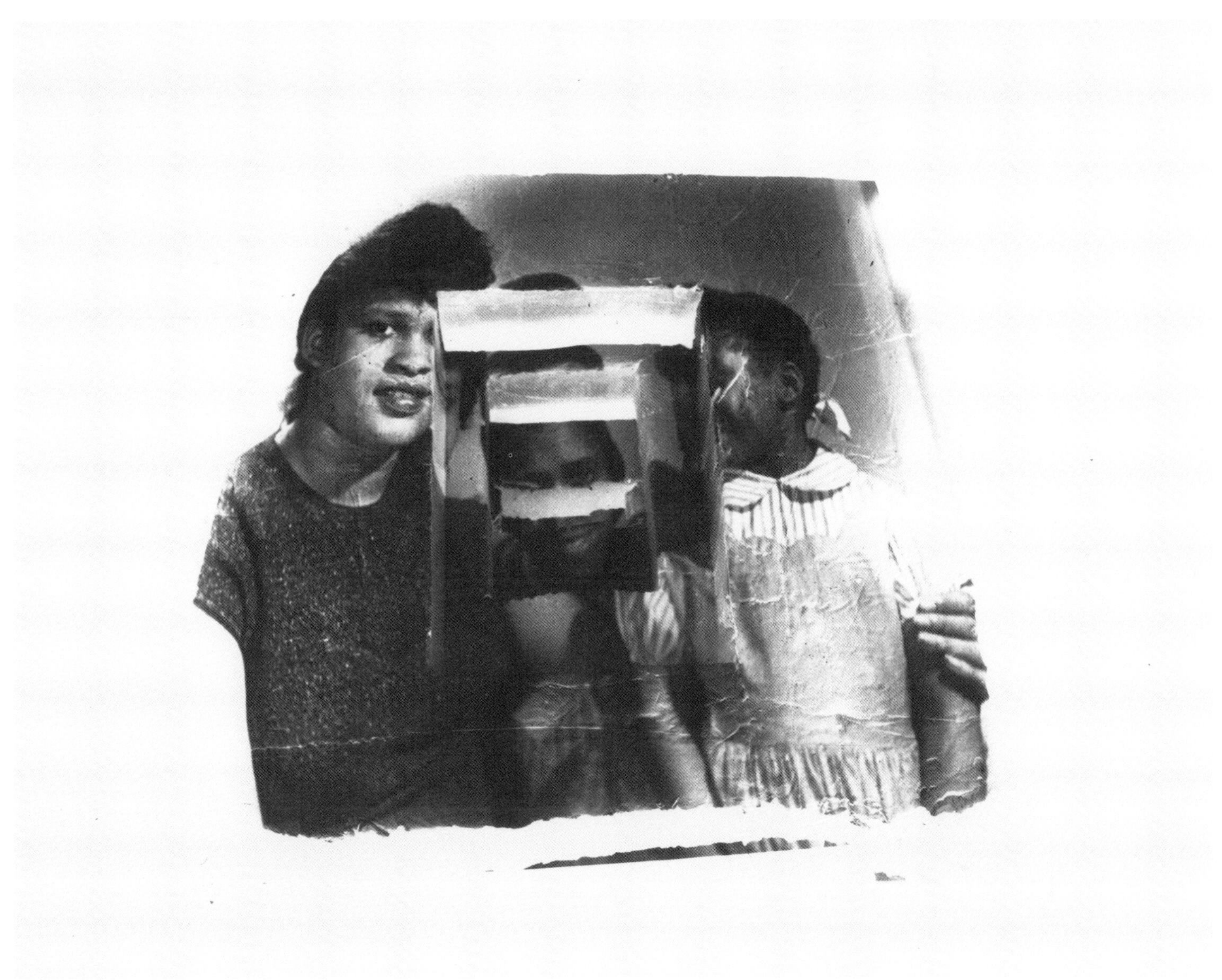

*Untitled (Mother, Father, and Laure)*, 1990
Gelatin silver print
11 × 14 in.
Private collection

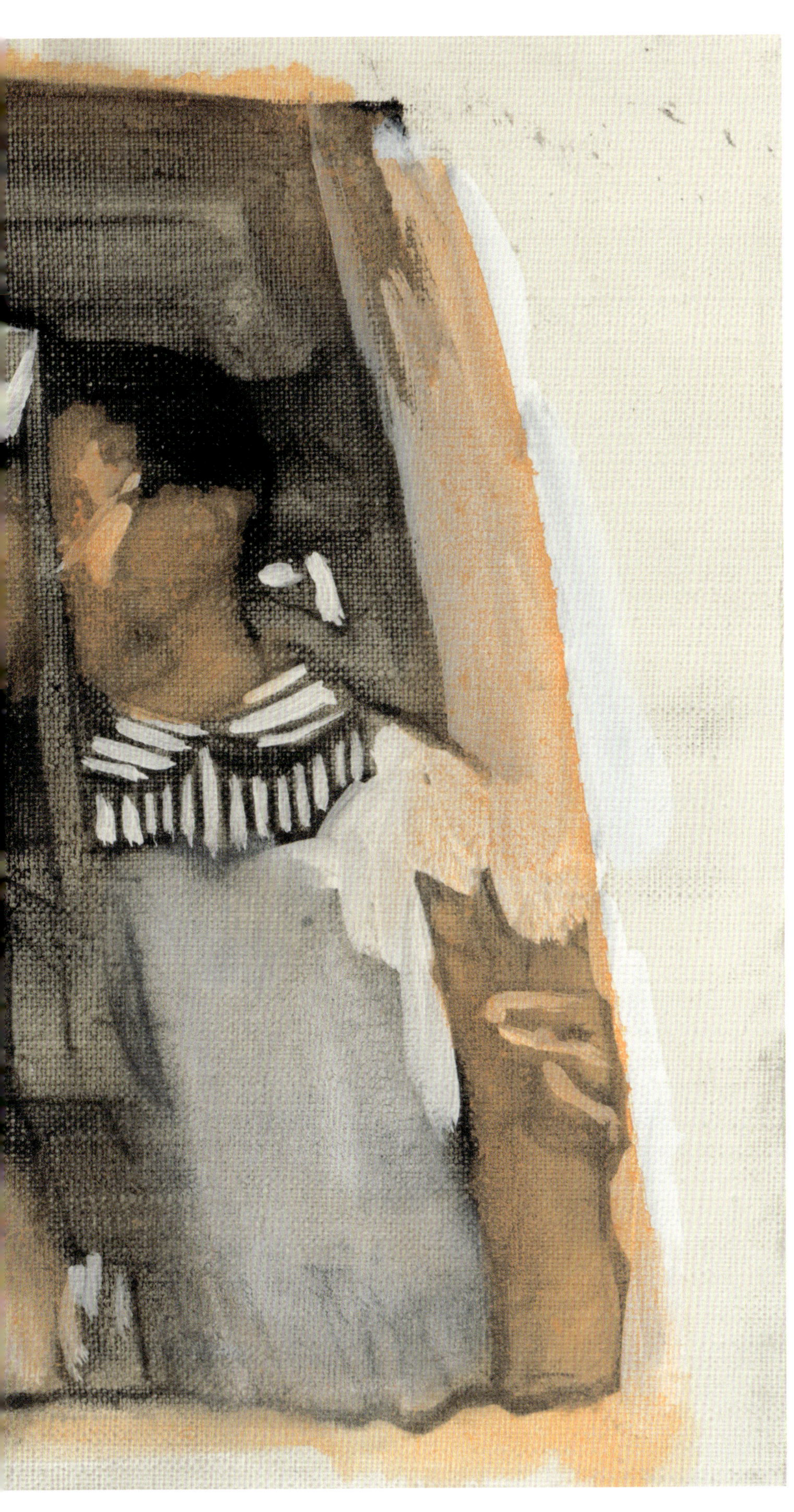

*Untitled (Mother, Father, and Laure)*,
ca. 1990
Acrylic and charcoal on canvas
10 ¼ × 13 ¼ in.
Collection of Martin Weinstein
and Teresa Liszka

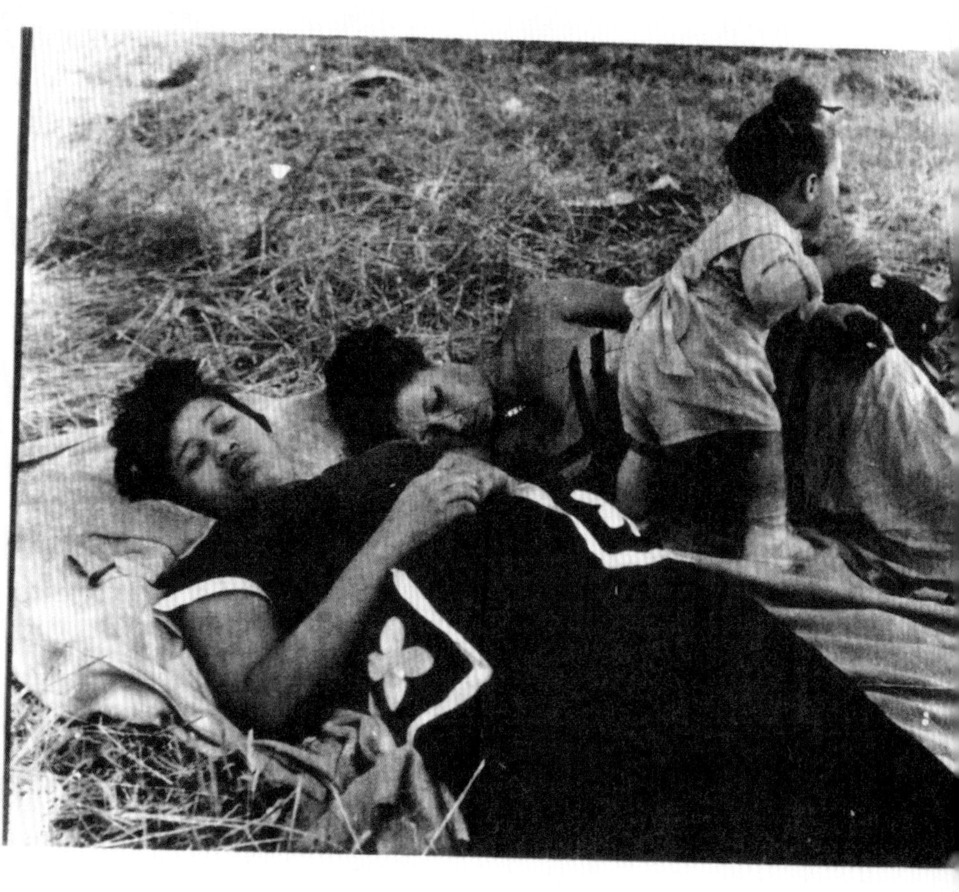

*Untitled (Laure and Mother in the Grass)*,
ca. 1985–87
Screenprint, brush and black ink,
and graphite on paper
19 × 32 in.
The Neal Baer Collection

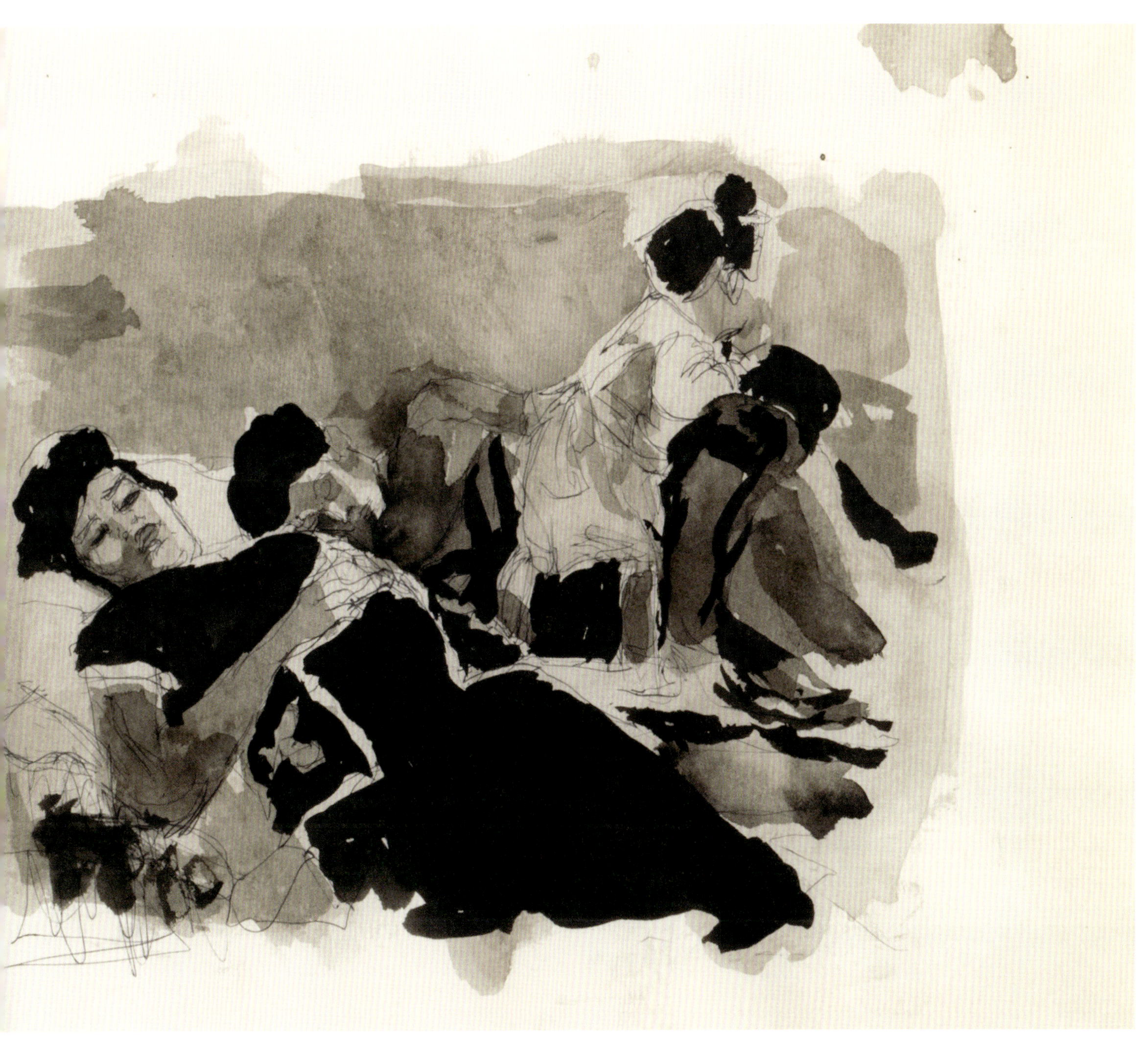

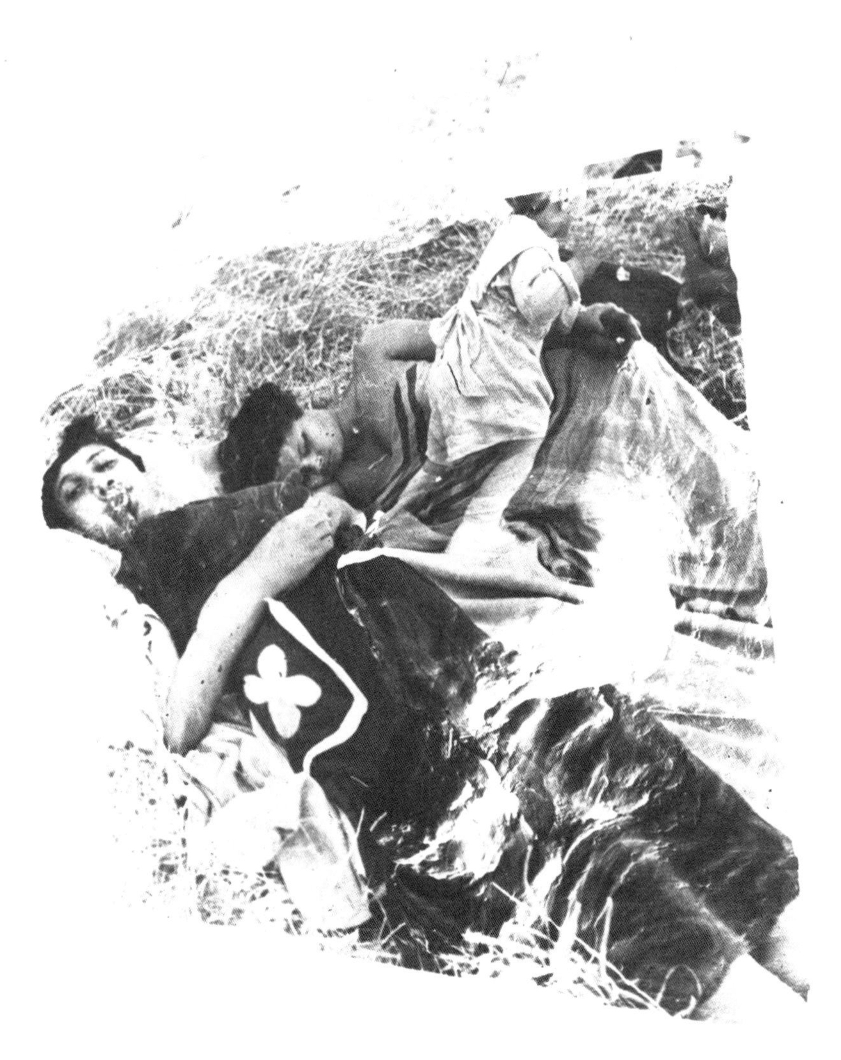

*Untitled (Laure and Mother in the Grass)*,
ca. 1988–91
Gelatin silver print
16 × 20 in.

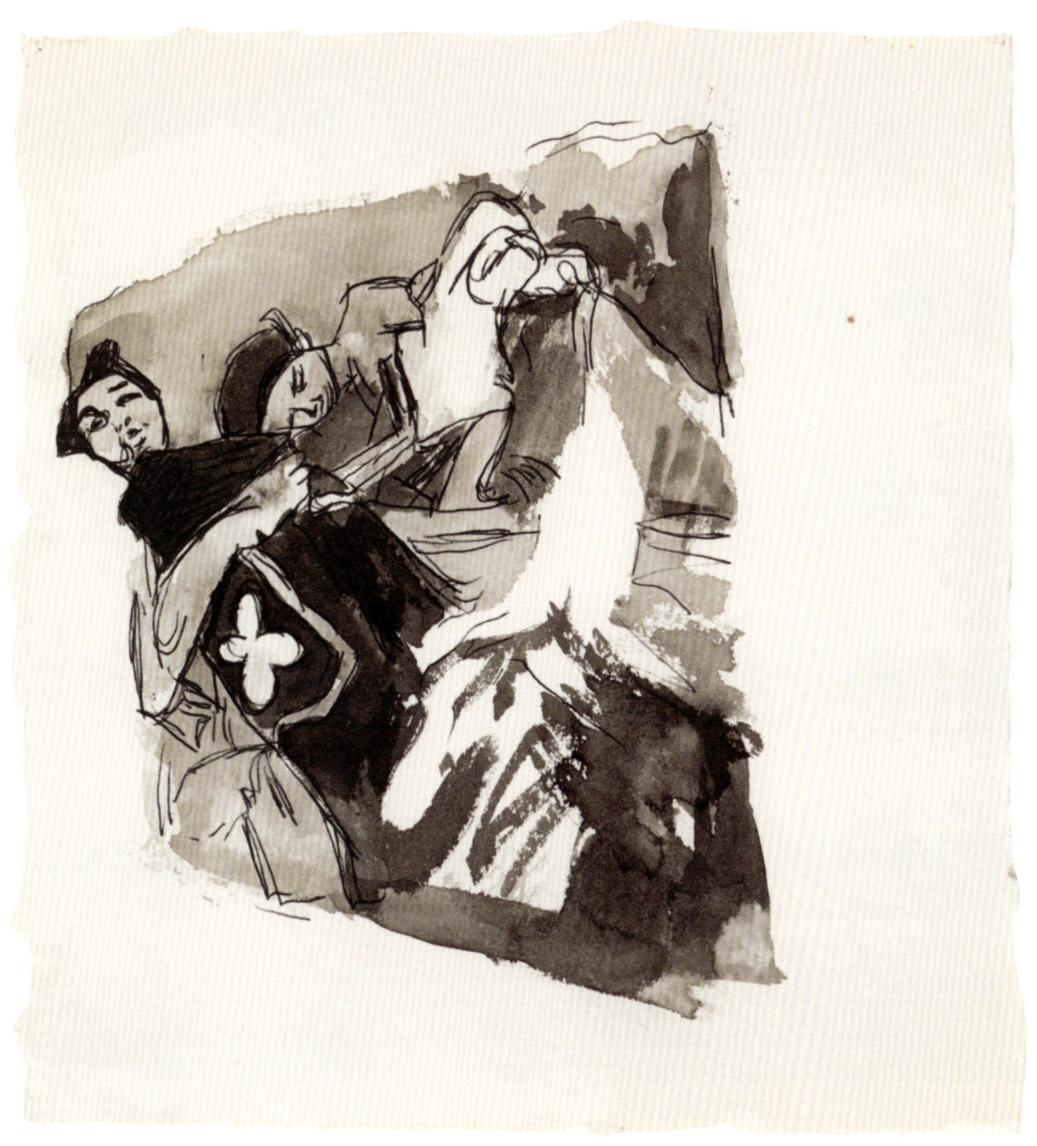

*Untitled (Laure and Mother in the Grass)*,
ca. 1989–91
Pen and brush and black ink and wash
on paper
12 ¼ × 11 ½ in.

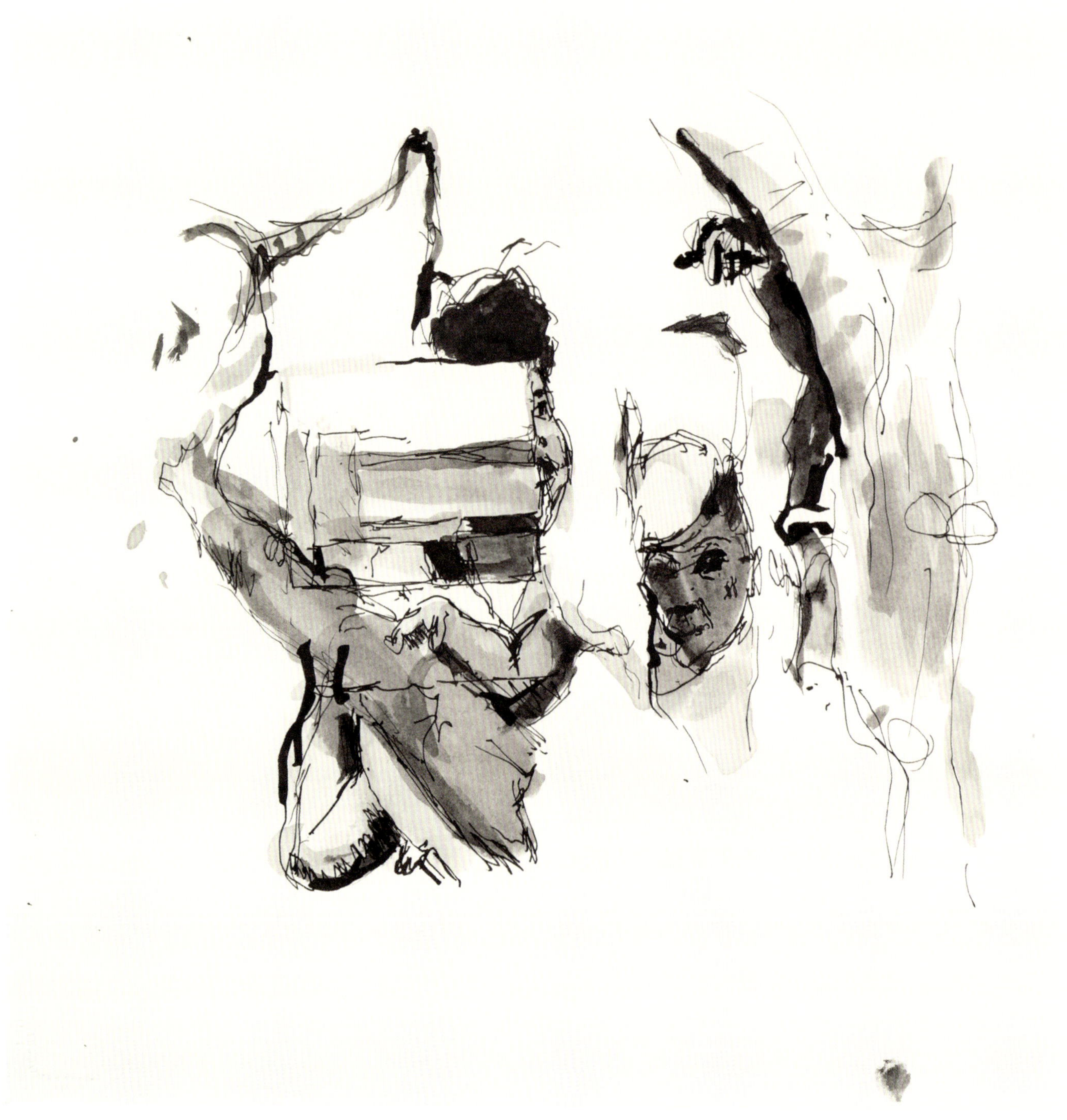

*Untitled (Mother and Laure in Tree, Crotona Park)*, ca. 1990
Pen and brush and black ink and wash on paper
17 ¼ × 16 ¾ in.

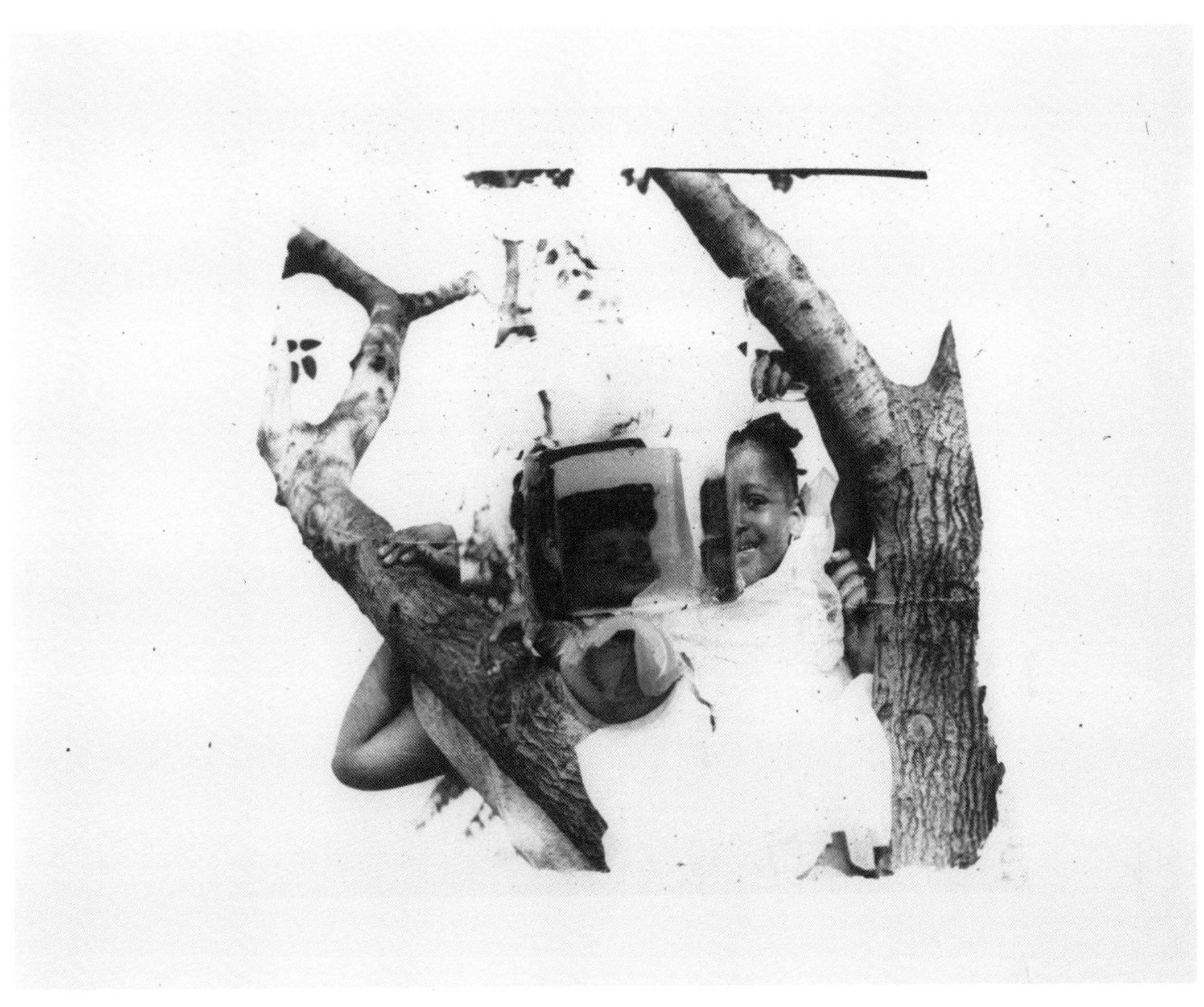

*Untitled (Mother and Laure in Tree, Crotona Park)*, 1990
Gelatin silver print
11 × 14 in.

*Untitled (Mother, diptych)*, ca. 1985–87
Screenprint and acrylic on canvas
14 × 25 in.

*Untitled (Mother, diptych)*, ca. 1985–87
Brush and black ink, wash,
and screenprint on paper
17 × 25 in.
Collection of Rosemary Moore

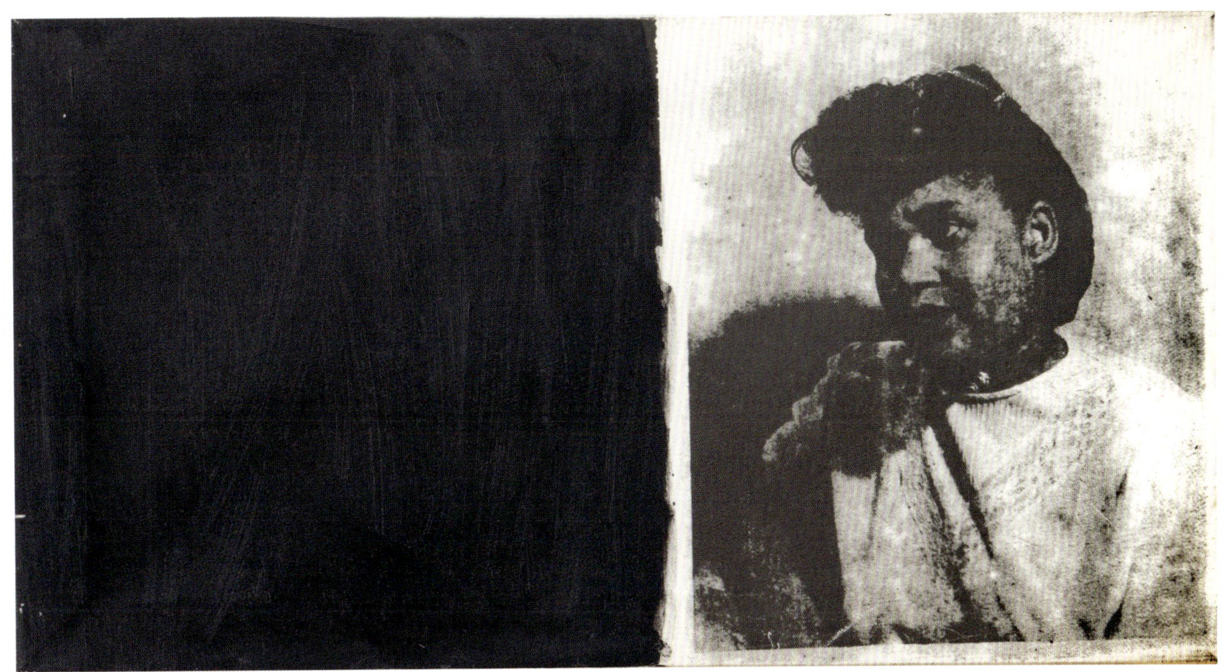

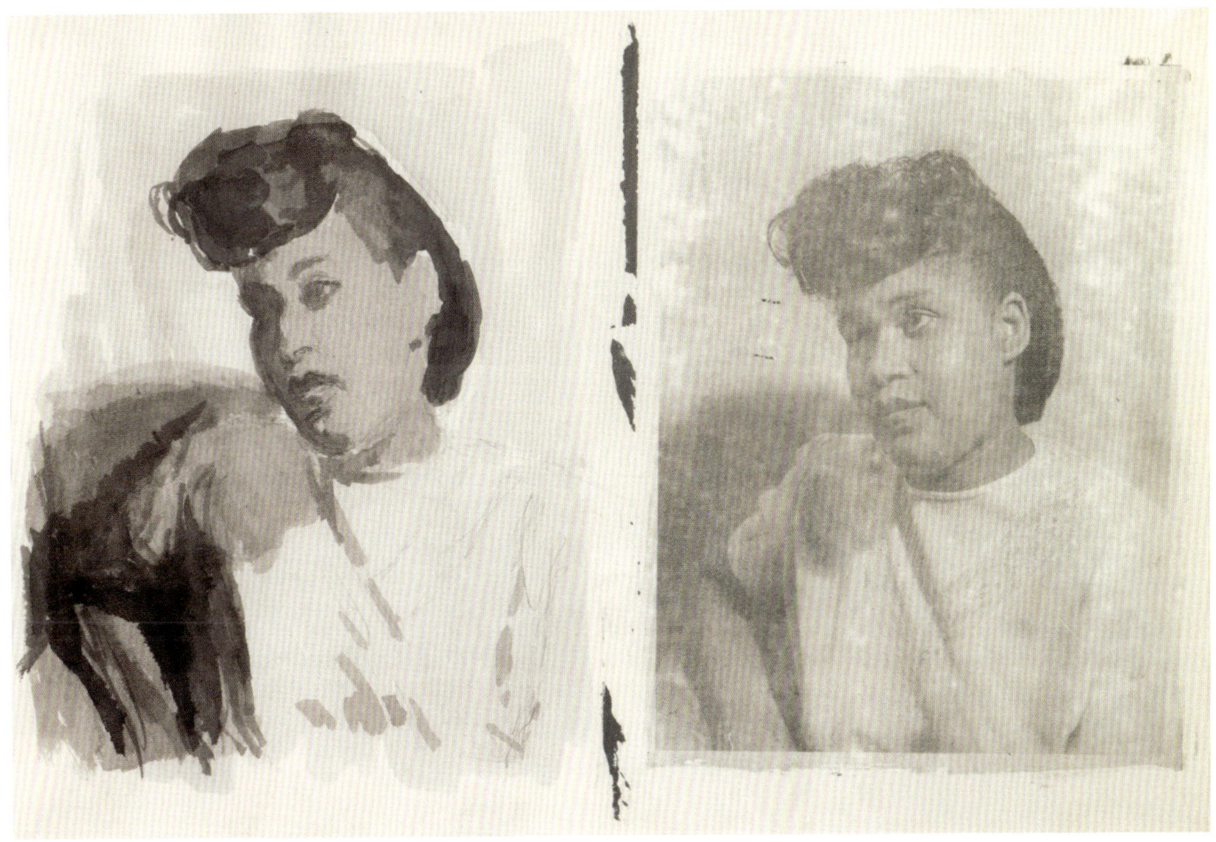

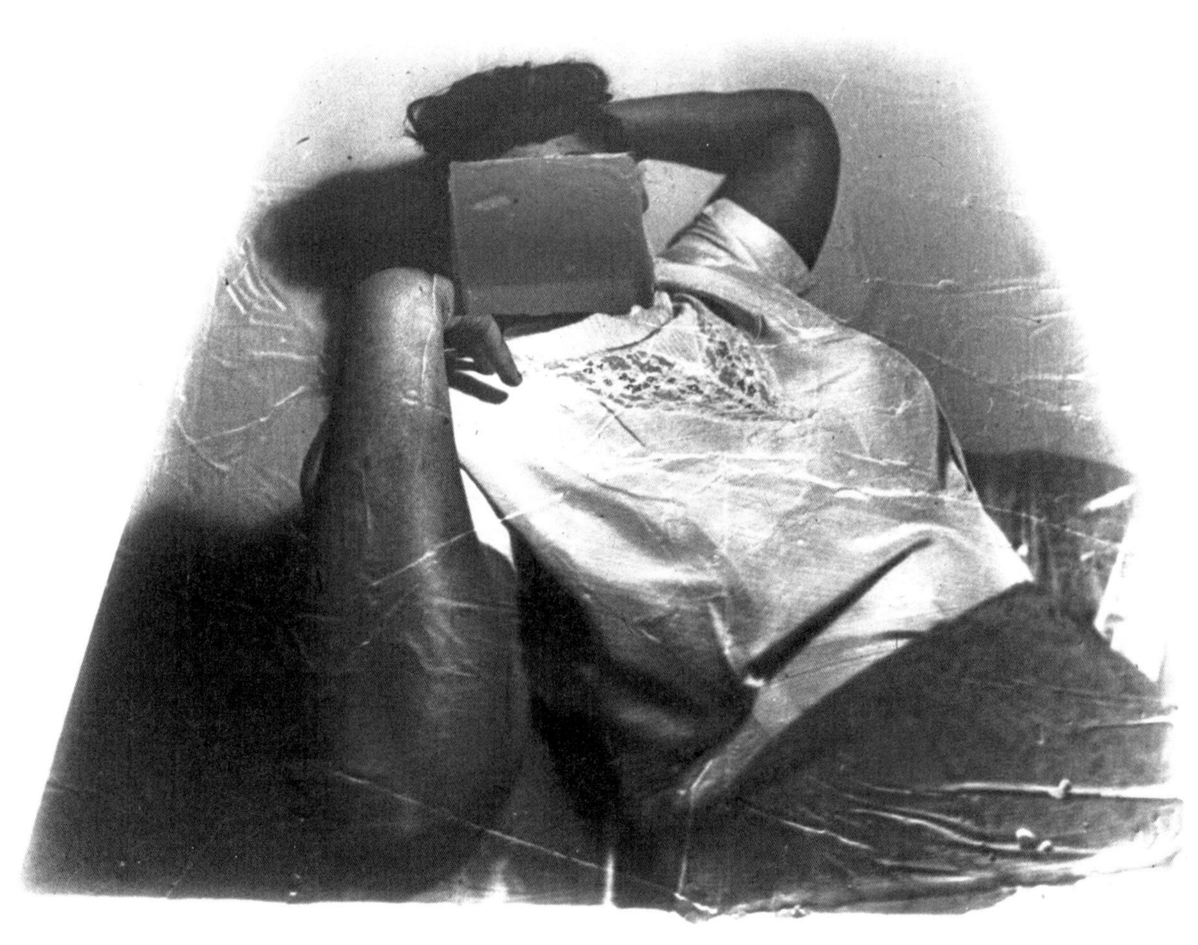

*Untitled (Mother)*, ca. 1989–90
Gelatin silver print
11 × 14 in.
Collection of Butch Walker

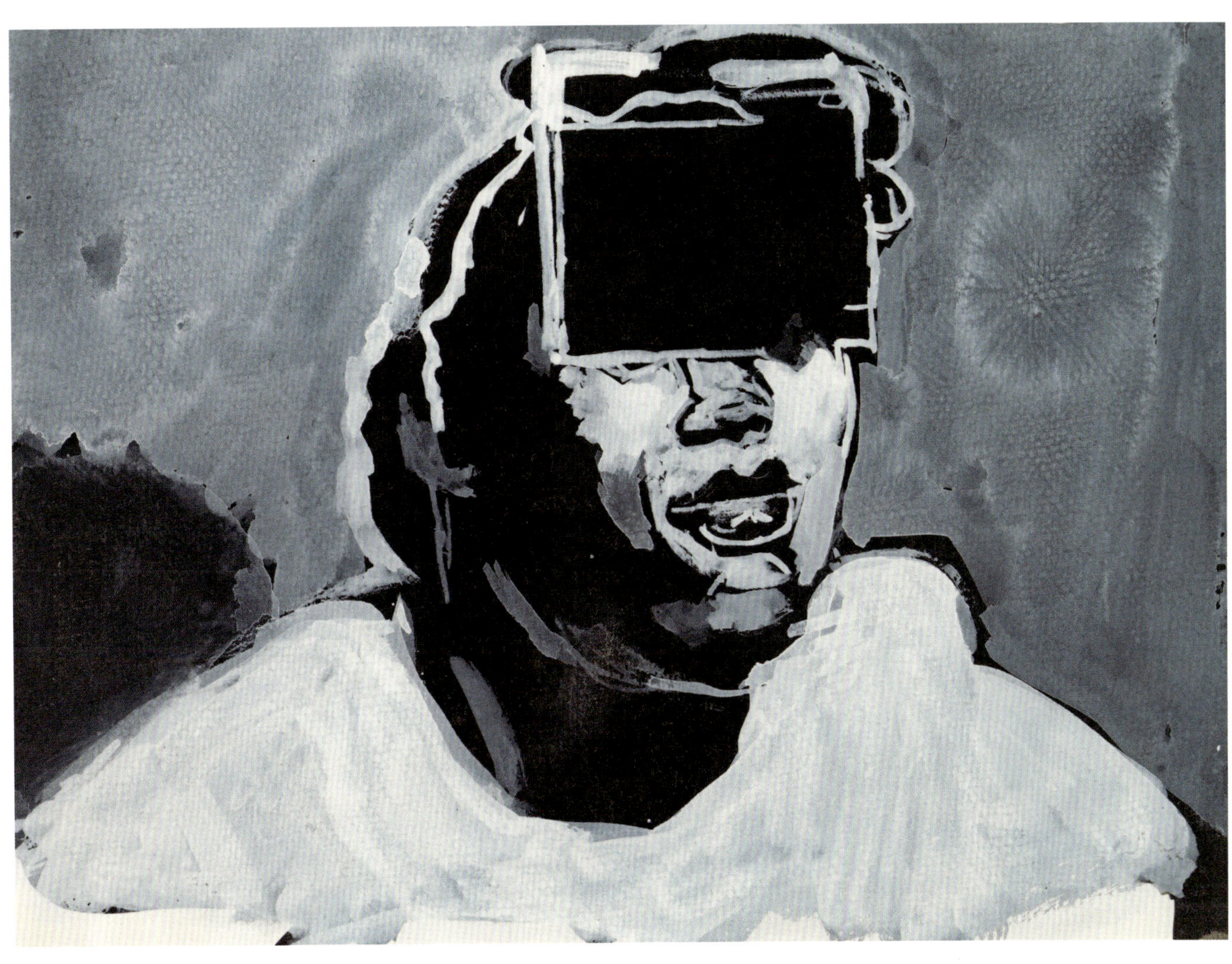

*Untitled (Mother)*, ca. 1989–90
Opaque watercolor and brush
and black ink on paper
8 ¾ × 11 ¾ in.
Collection of Burt Aaron

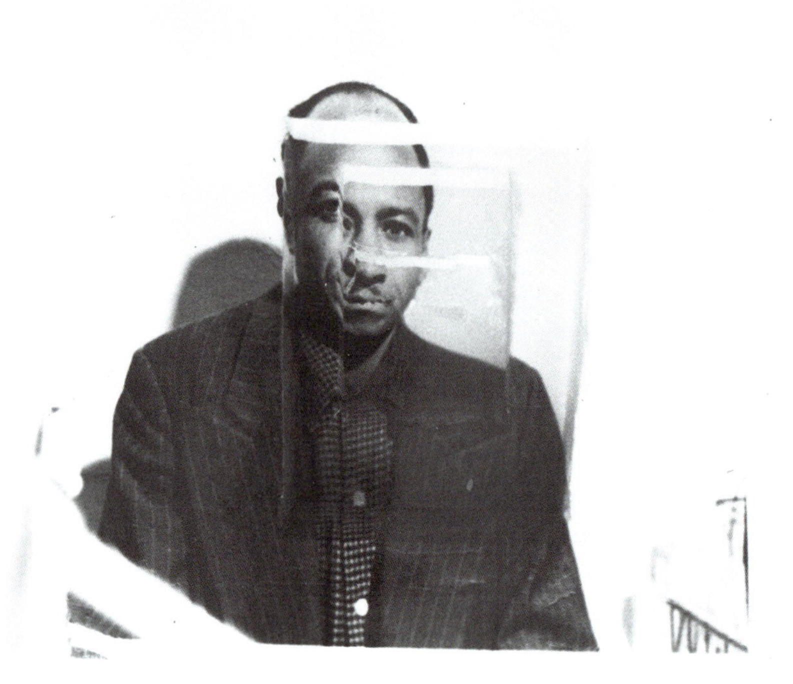

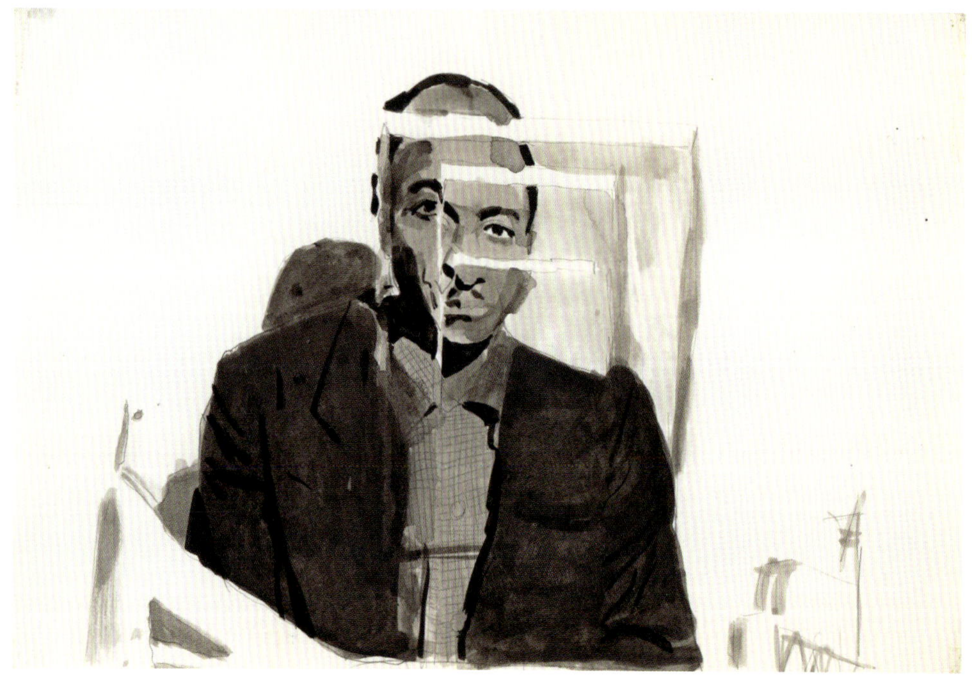

*Untitled (Great Uncle Joseph Tansle)*,
ca. 1988–91
Gelatin silver print
11 × 14 in.
Collection of Marcos Chaves,
Rio de Janeiro

*Untitled (Great Uncle Joseph Tansle)*,
ca. 1988–91
Pen and brush and black ink and wash
on paper
14 ½ × 22 in.
Private collection

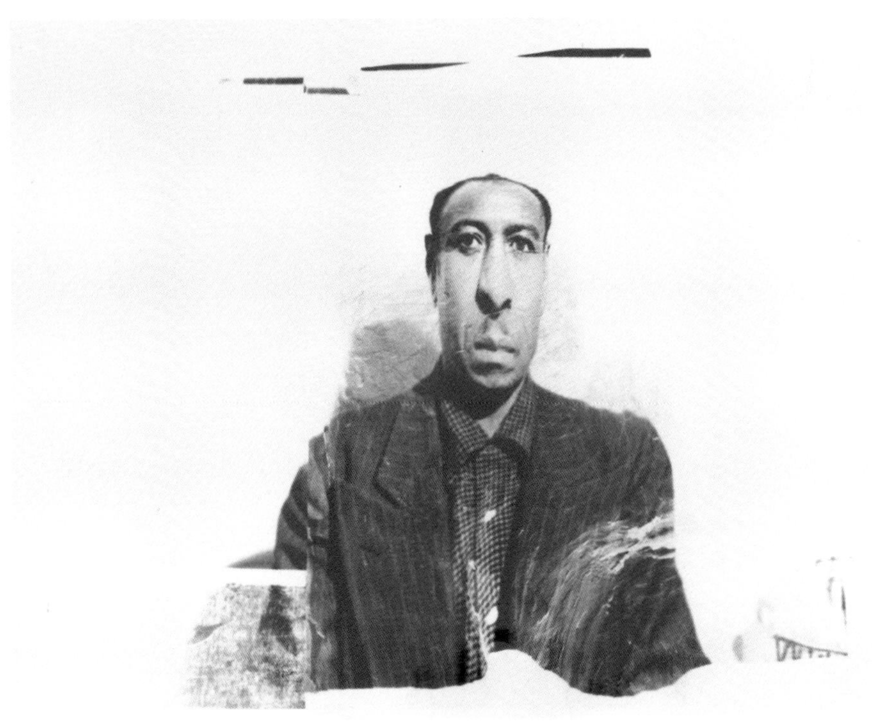

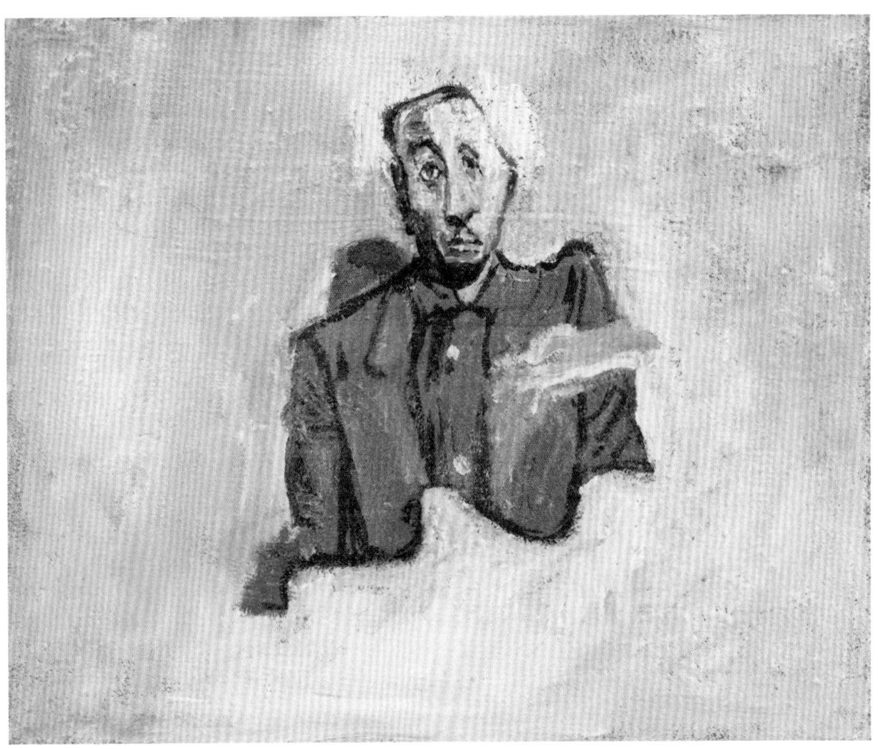

*Untitled (Great Uncle Joseph Tansle)*,
ca. 1988–91
Gelatin silver print
11 × 14 in.

*Untitled (Great Uncle Joseph Tansle)*,
ca. 1988–91
Oil on canvas prepared with textured sand ground
17 × 21 in.

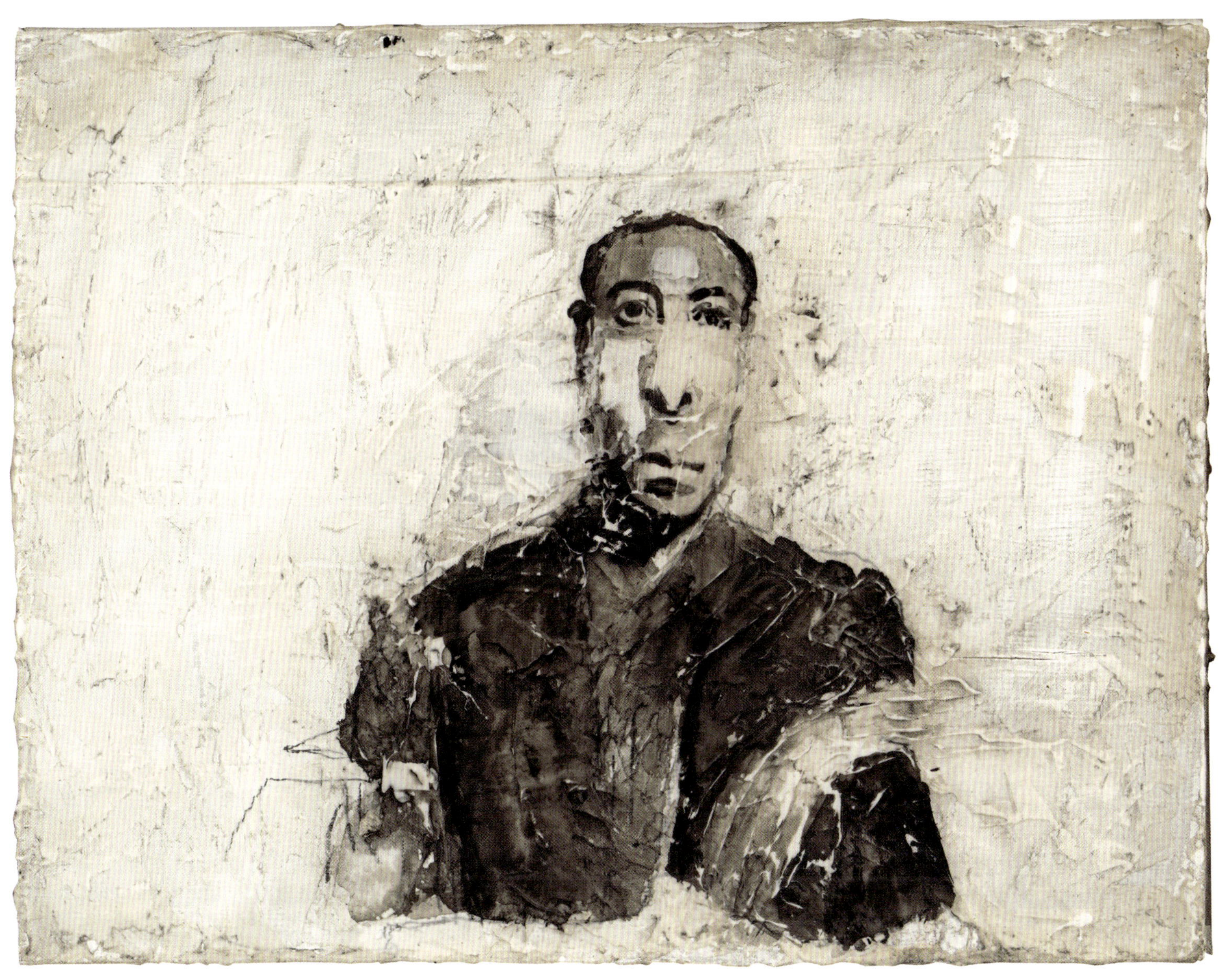

*Untitled (Great Uncle Joseph Tansle)*,
ca. 1988–91
Brush and black ink, wash, graphite, and acrylic modeling paste on wood panel
12 ½ × 16 in.
Collection of Butch Walker

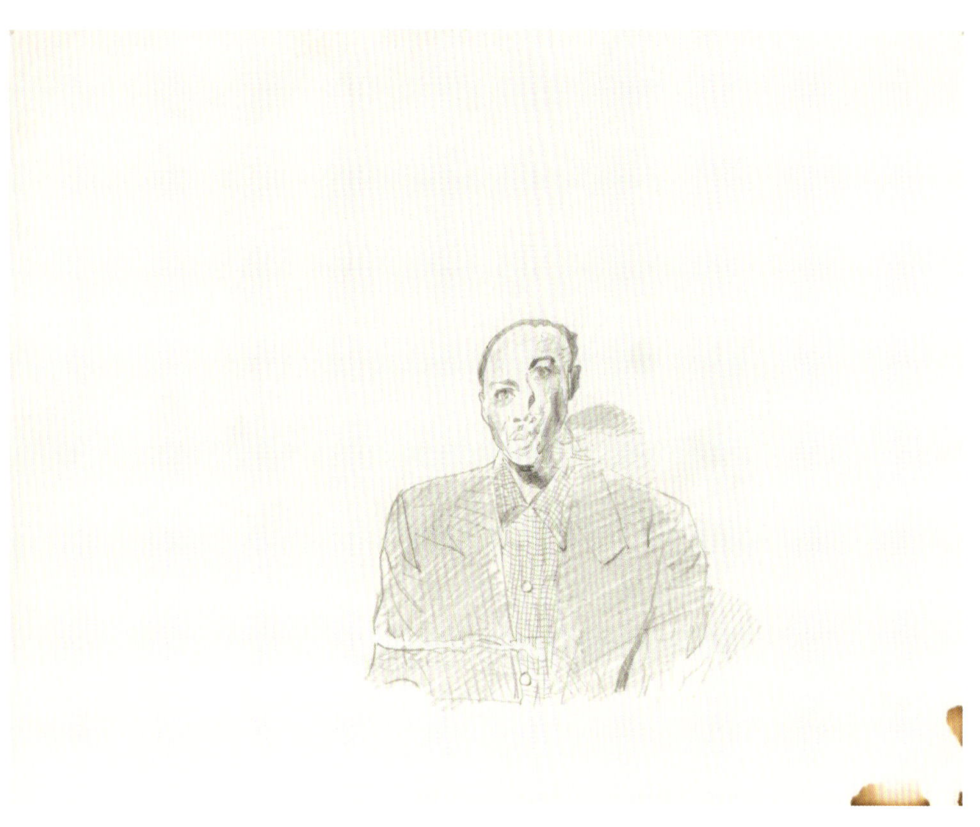

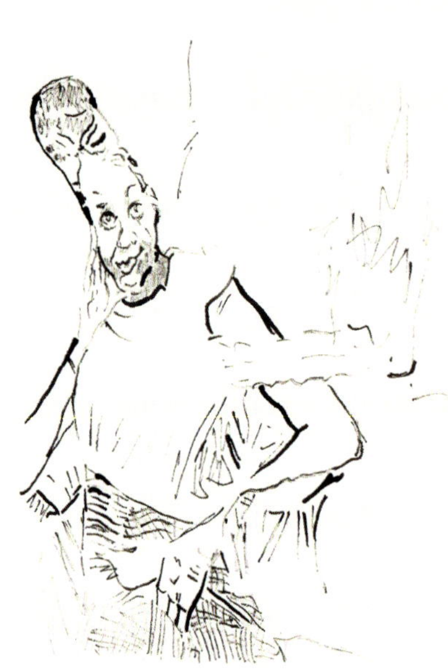

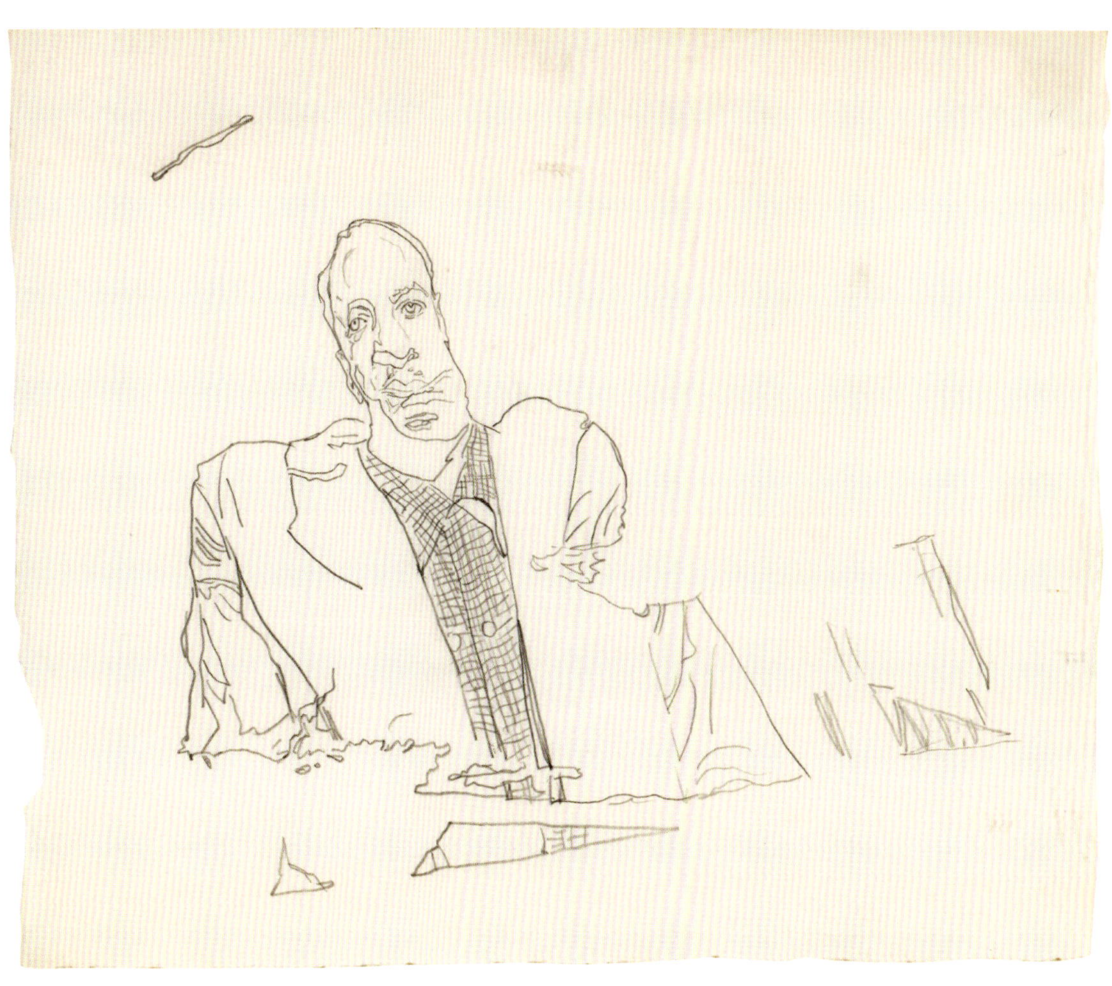

*Untitled (Great Uncle Joseph Tansle)*,
ca. 1988–91
Graphite on paper
11 × 14 ⅜ in.

*Untitled (Birdie Seated)*, ca. 1988–91
Pen and black ink on paper
11 × 14 in.

*Untitled (Great Uncle Joseph Tansle)*,
ca. 1988–91
Graphite on paper
11 ½ × 14 in.

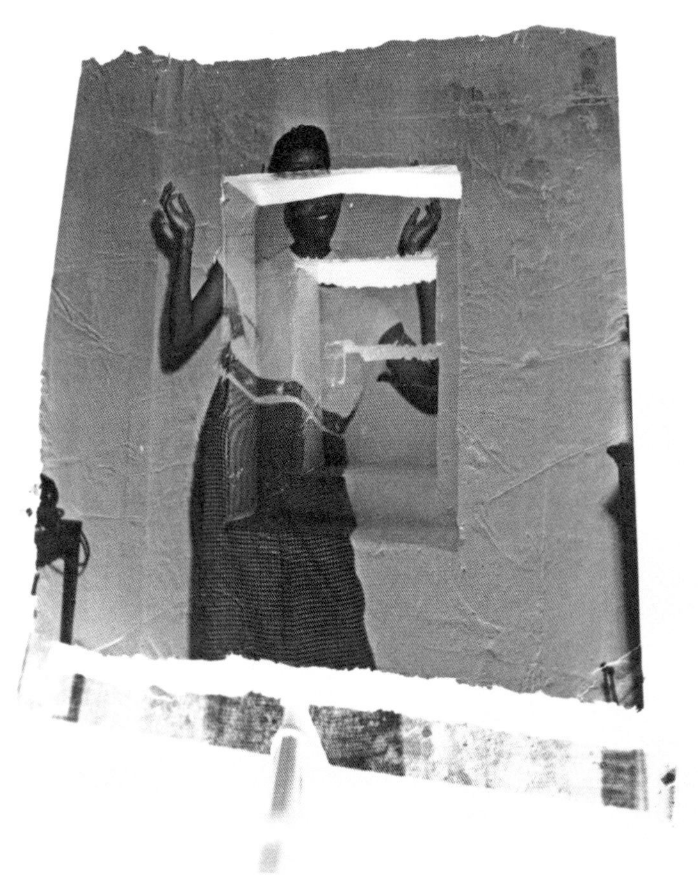

*Untitled (Woman Posing)*, ca. 1988–91
Gelatin silver print
11 × 14 in.
Collection of Shelly and Phil Aarons

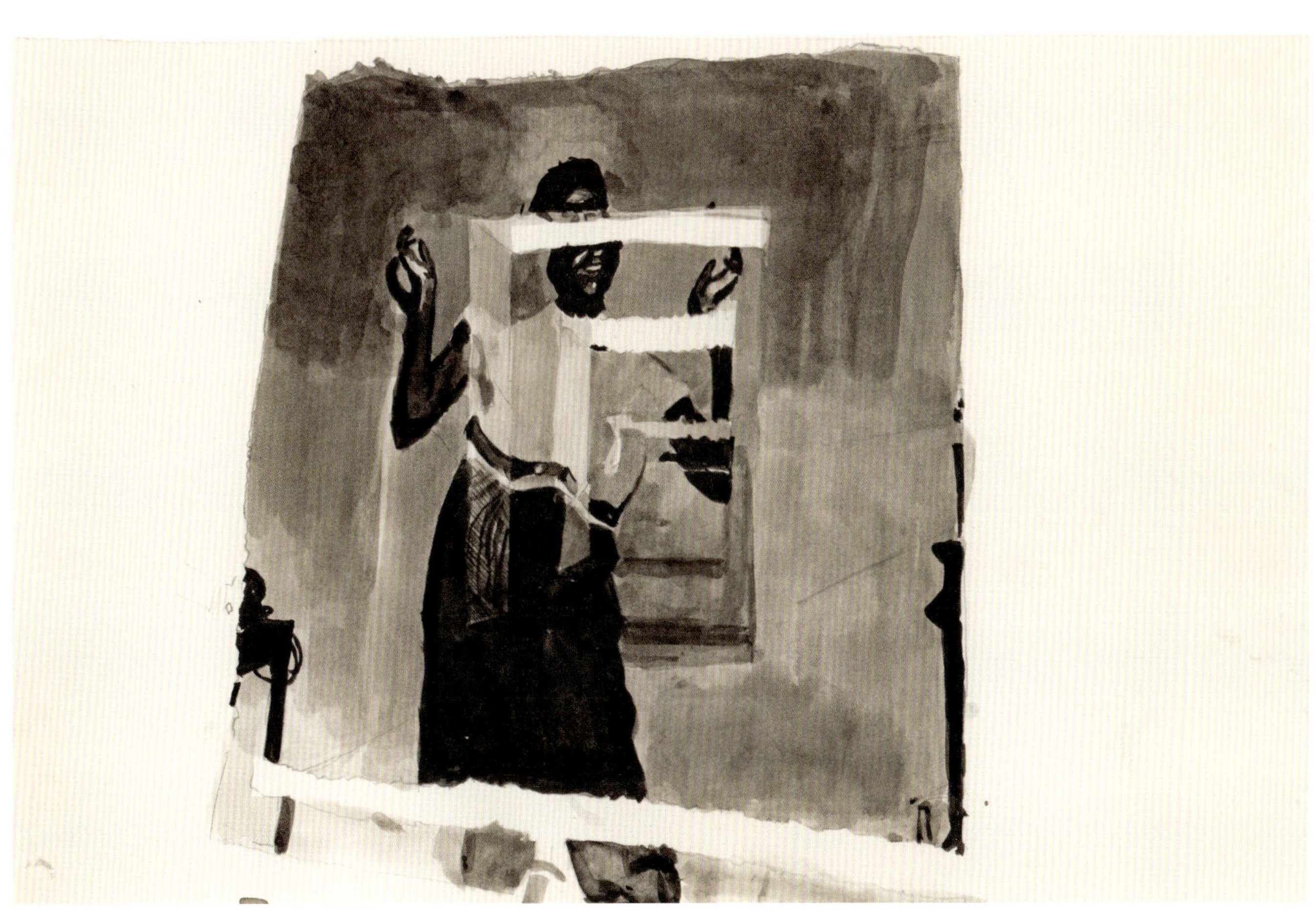

*Untitled (Woman Posing)*, ca. 1988–91
Brush and black ink, wash,
and graphite on paper
15 × 22 ½ in.

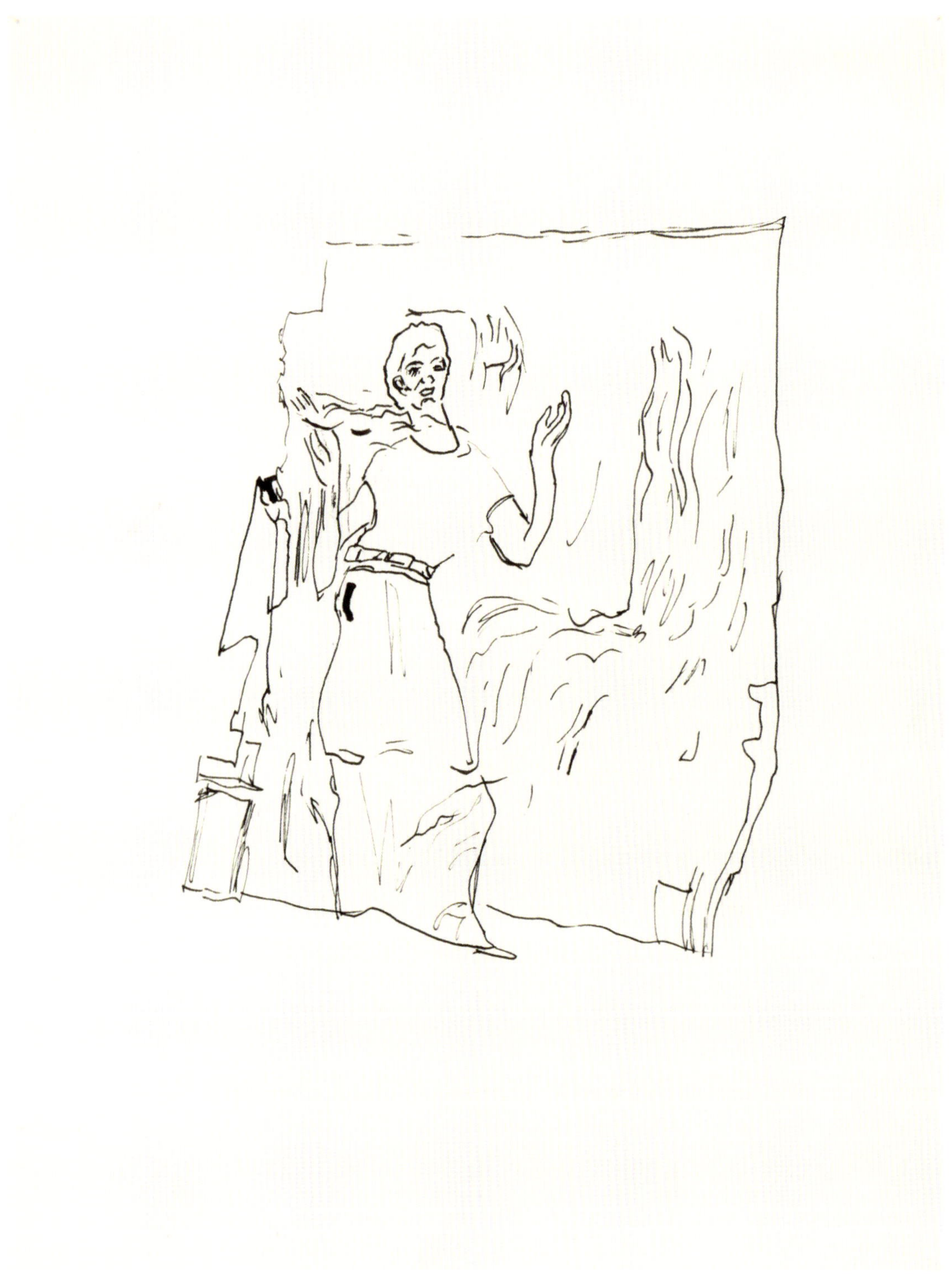

*Untitled (Woman Posing)*, ca. 1988–91
Pen and black ink on paper
14 × 11 in.

*Untitled (Woman Posing)*, ca. 1988–91
Brush and black ink, wash, and graphite on paper
22 ½ × 15 in.
Collection of Stephanie Serino and David Jarrett

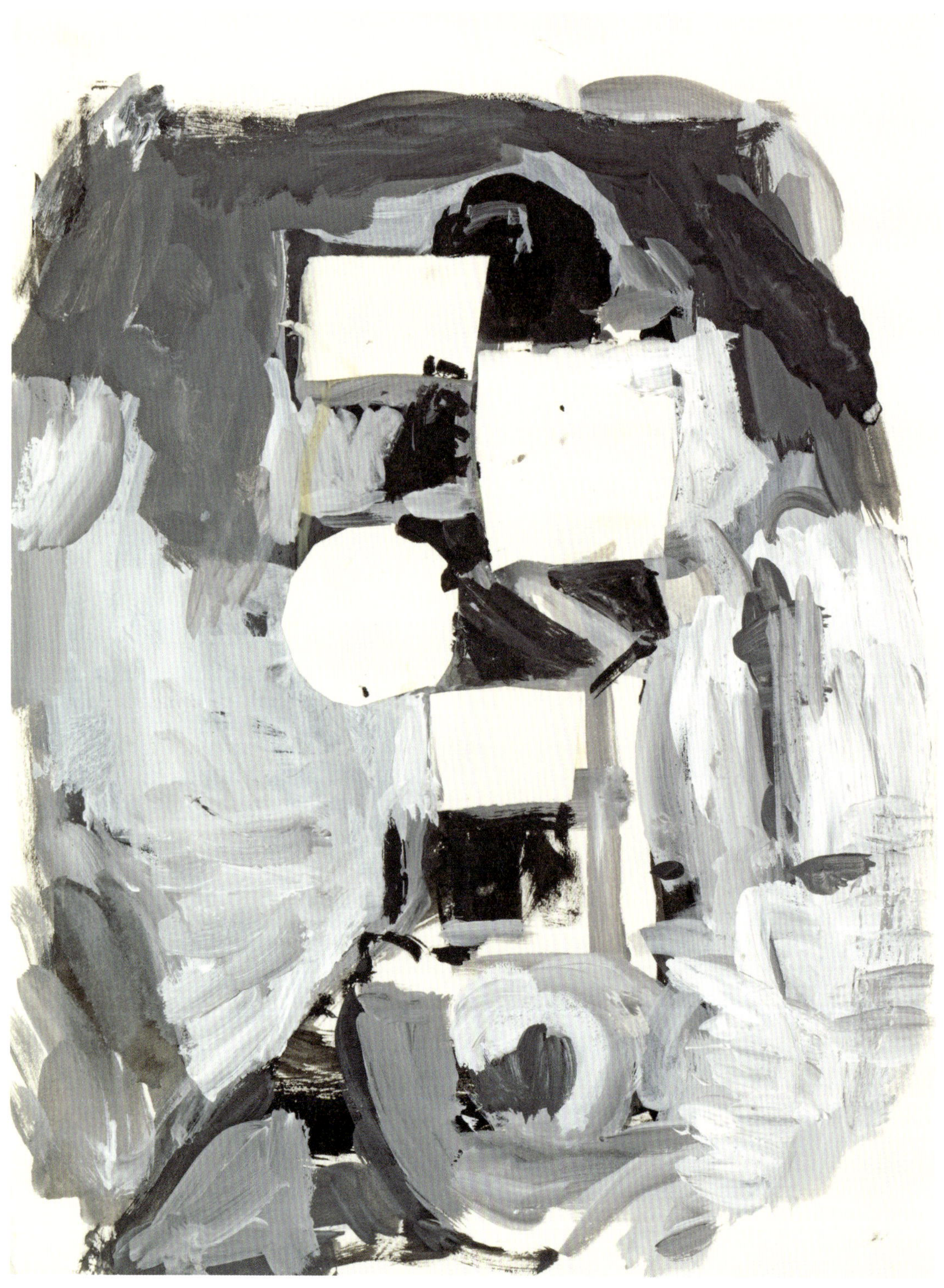

*Untitled (Bathing Beauty)*, ca. 1987–89
Acrylic paint and collage of cut paper on paper
13 × 10 in.

*Untitled (Bathing Beauty)*, ca. 1987–89
Gelatin silver print
14 × 11 in.

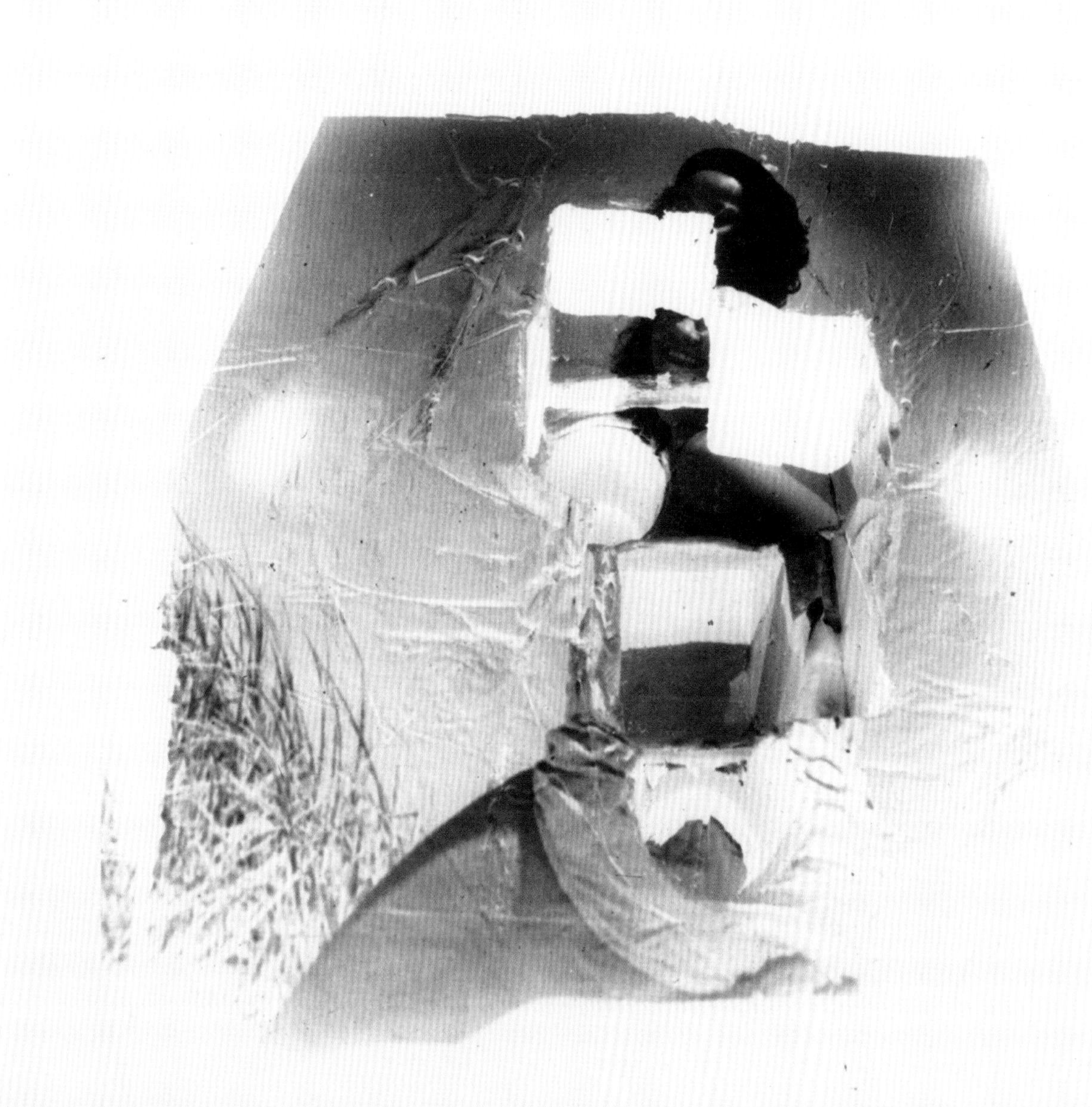

*Untitled (Aunt Lena and Grandmother Lilian Ellis)*, ca. 1983–88
Charcoal, black ink wash, acrylic paint, and graphite on paper
11 × 15 in.

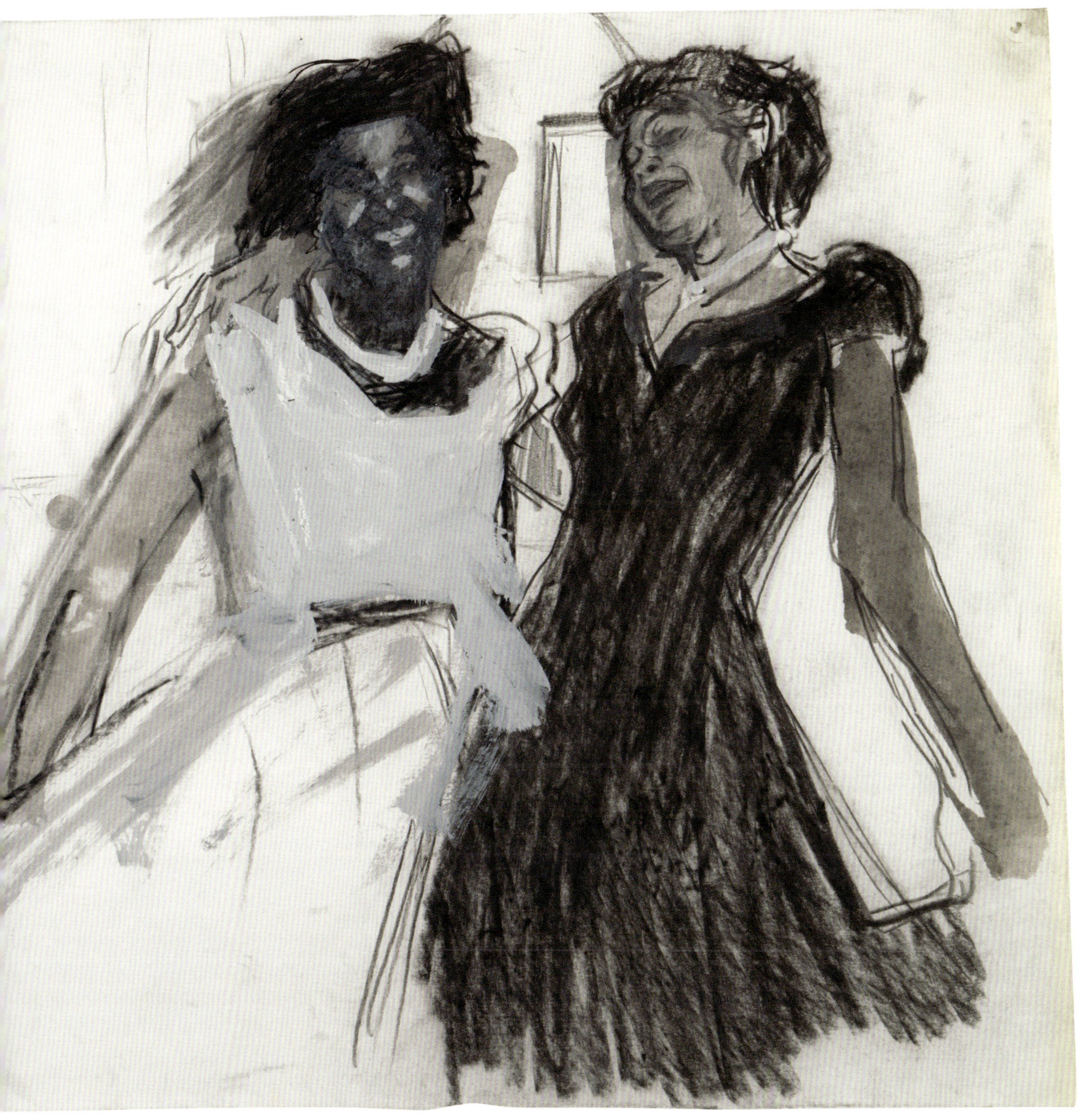

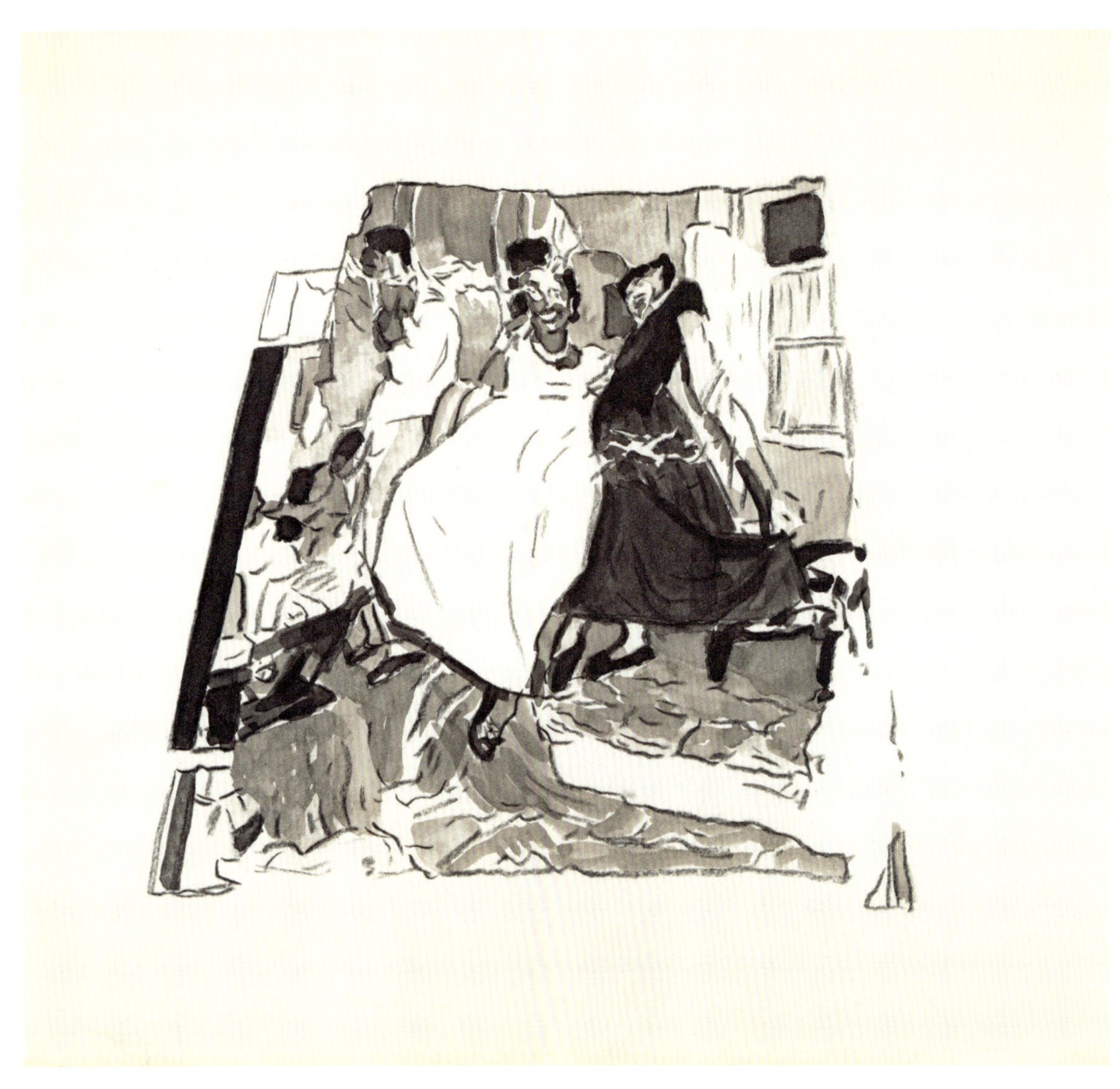

*Untitled (Aunt Lena and Grandmother Lilian Ellis)*, ca. 1988–91
Brush and black ink, wash, and graphite on paper
11 × 15 in.

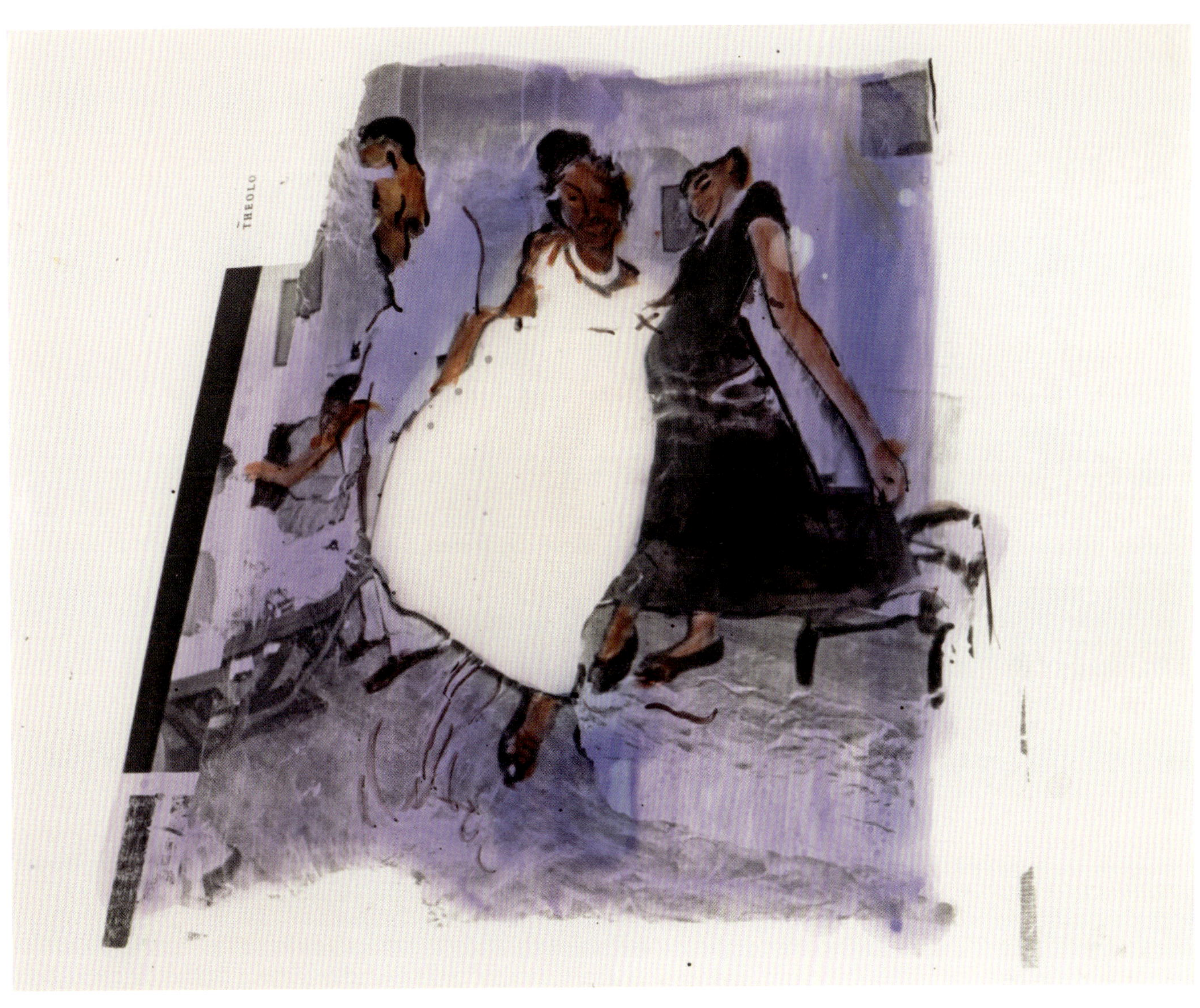


*Untitled (Aunt Lena and Grandmother Lilian Ellis)*, ca. 1990
Gelatin silver print with colored ink
11 × 14 in.
Collection of Frank Franca

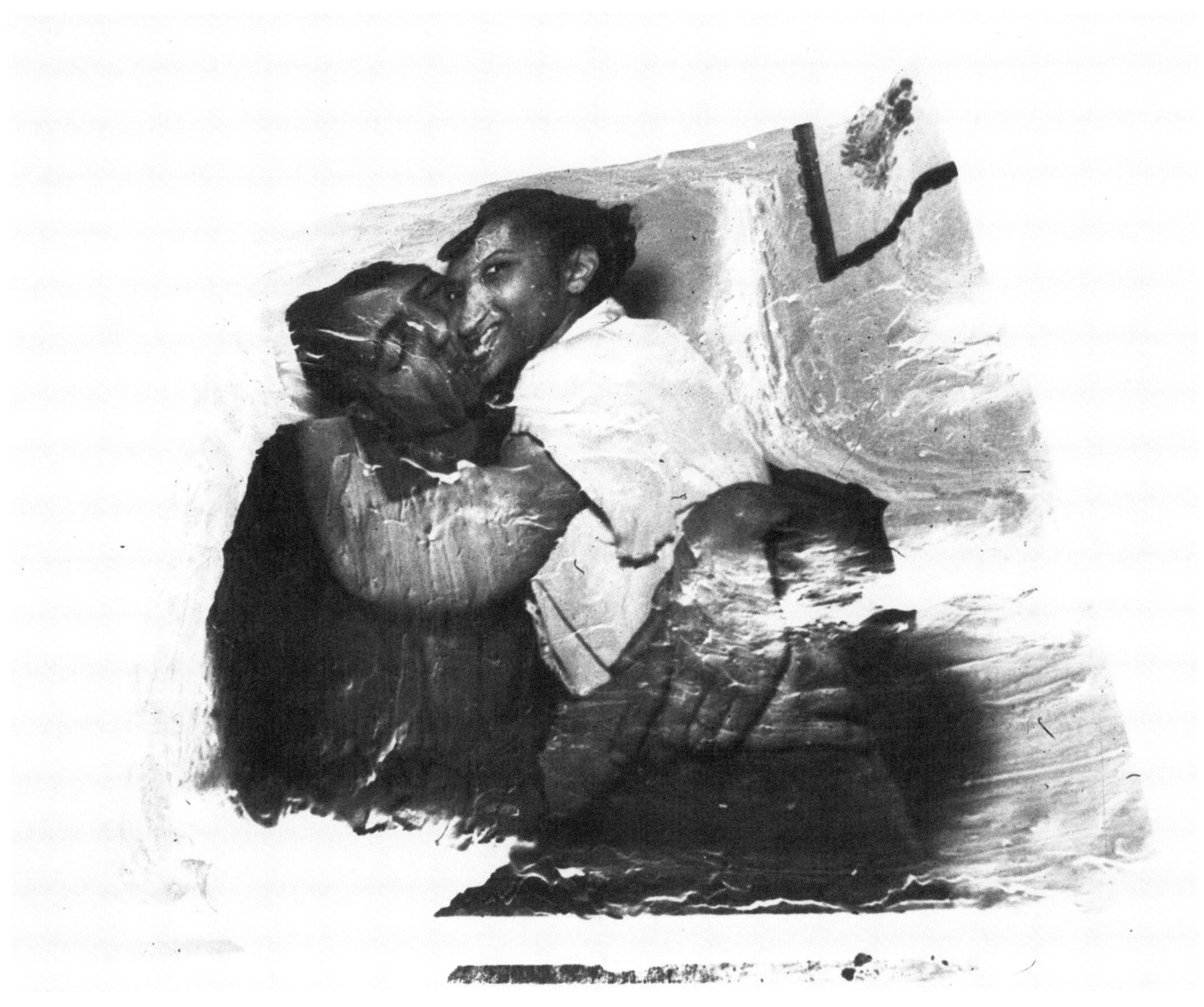

*Untitled (Aunt Connie and Uncle Richard)*, ca. 1989–91
Gelatin silver print
15 ¾ × 19 ¼ in.
Collection of Ebony G. Patterson

*The Kiss*, 1990
Gelatin silver print
20 × 16 in.
Harvard Art Museums

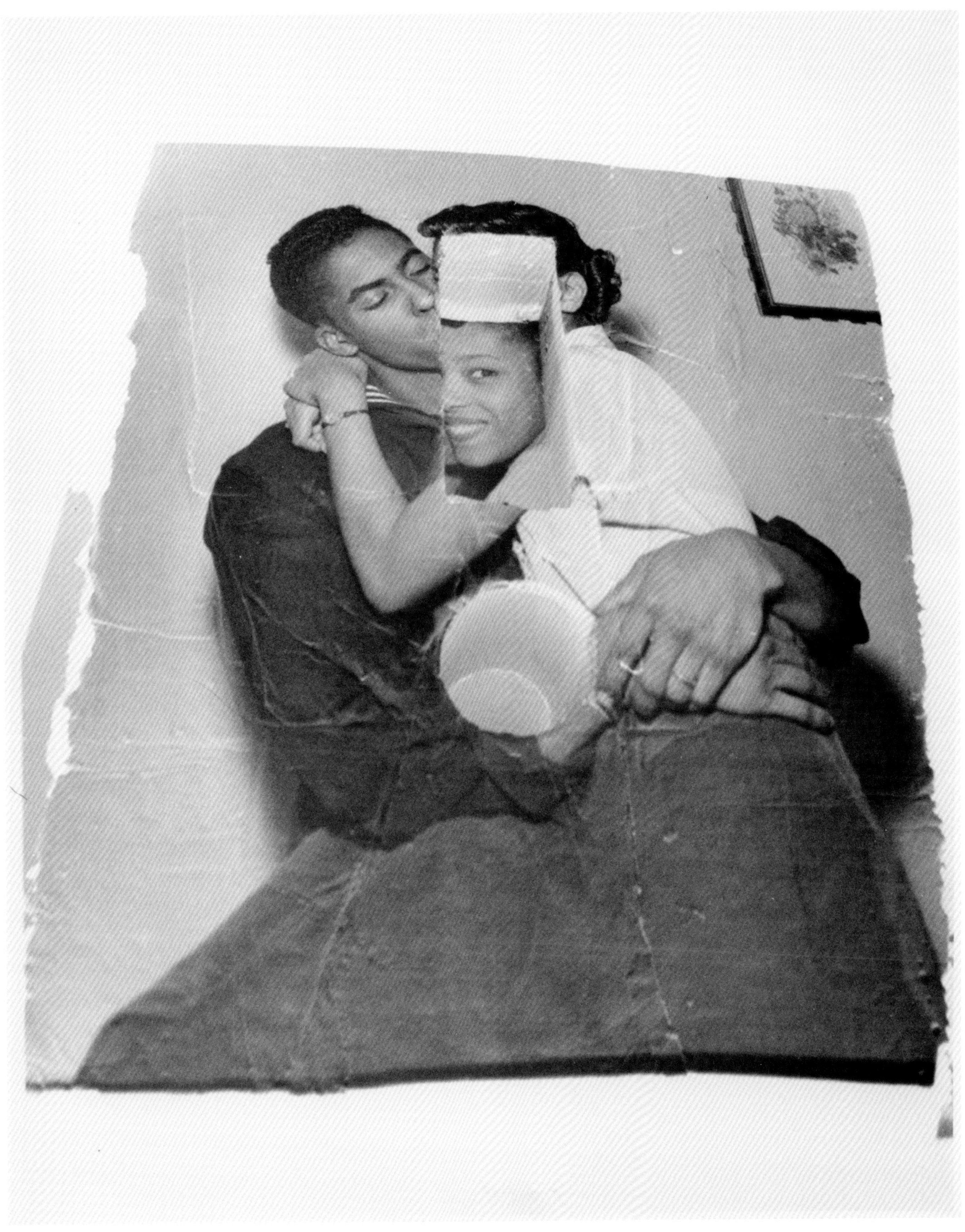

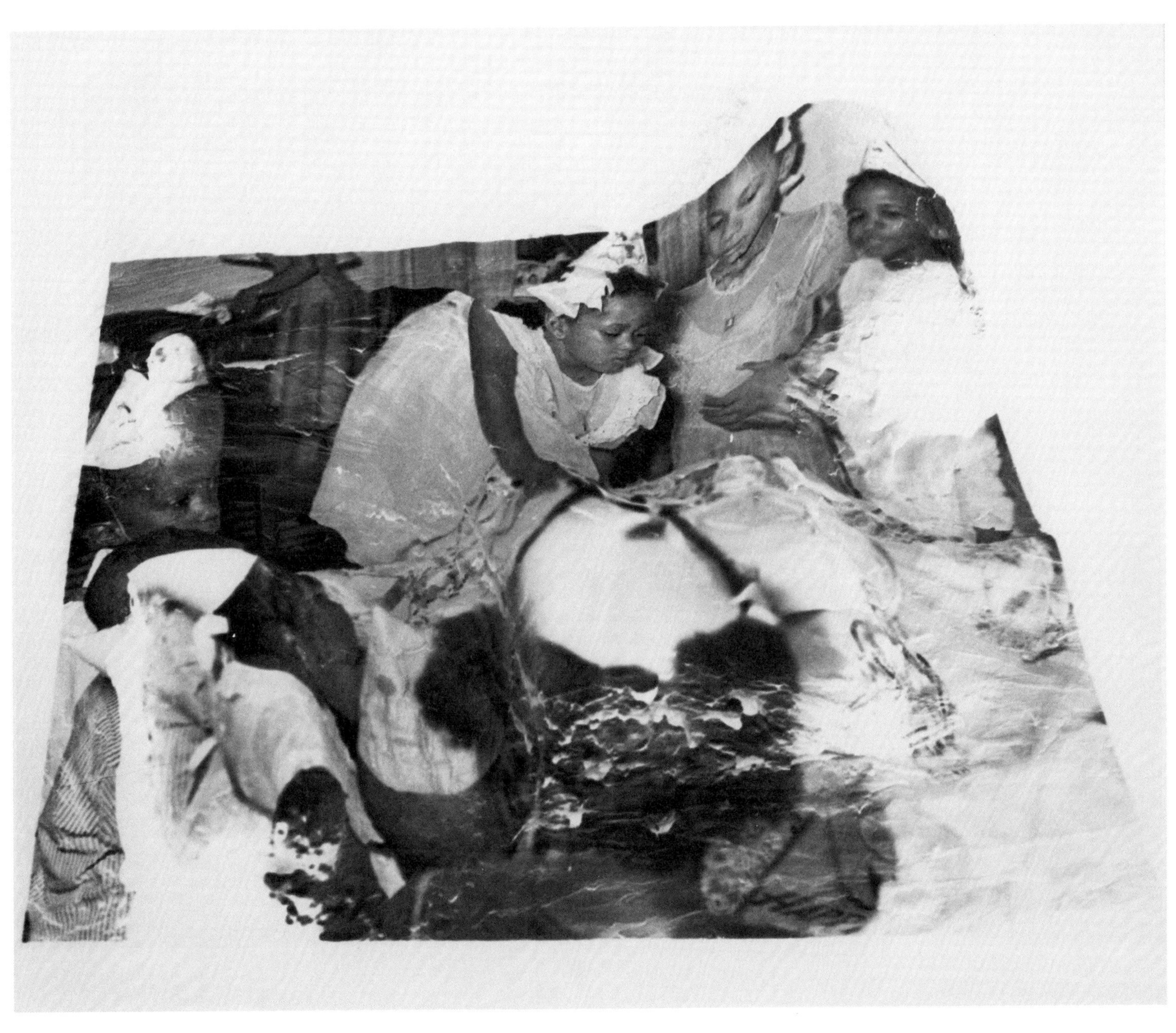

*Untitled (Birthday Party)*, 1990
Gelatin silver print
25 × 29 in.
Collection of Hendrik Vermeire
and Arne Notebaert

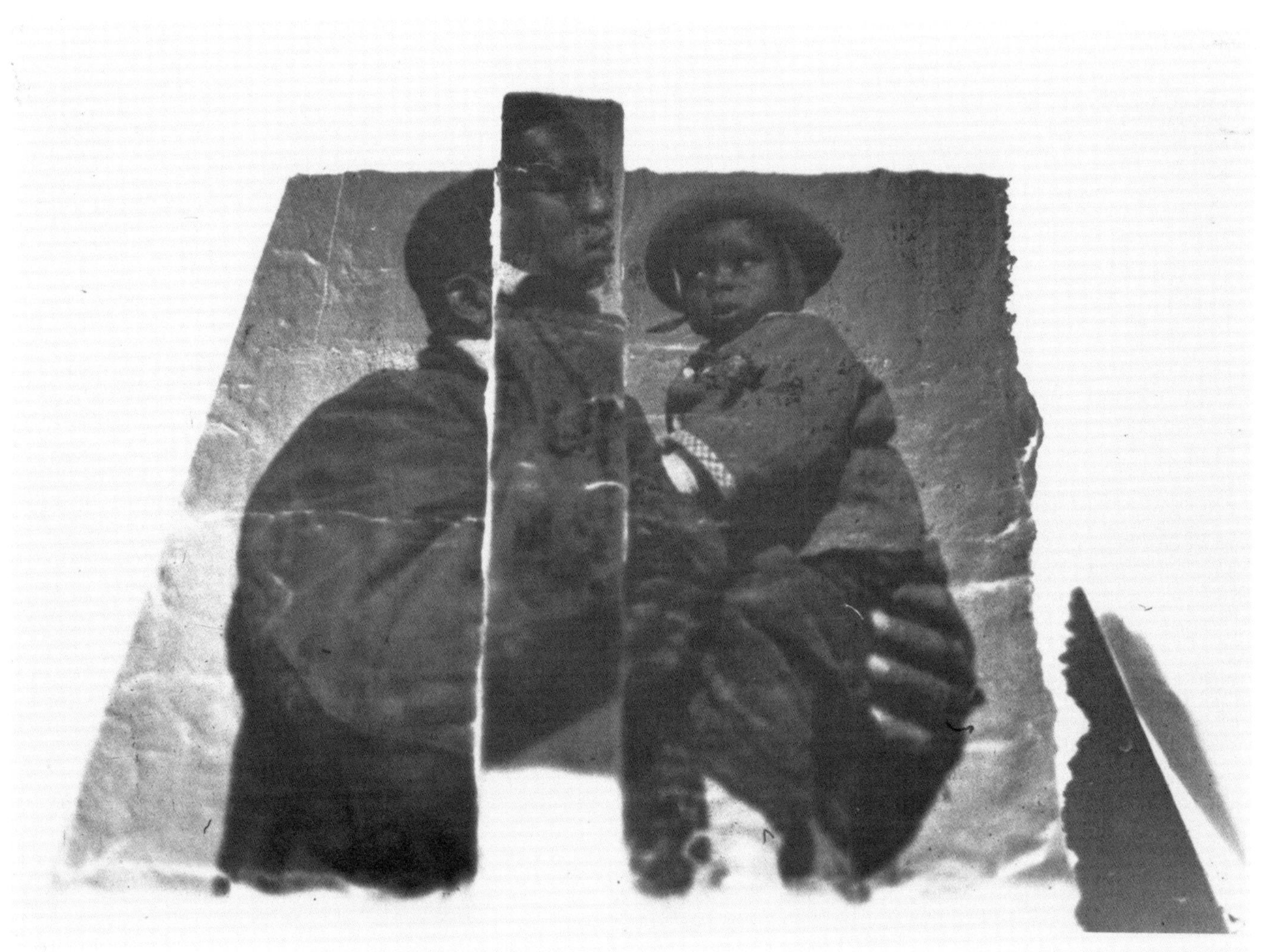

*Untitled (Grandfather Thomas and Cousin Irving)*, ca. 1990
Gelatin silver print
7 ½ × 9 ½ in.
The Baltimore Museum of Art;
The William G. Baker, Jr. Memorial Fund

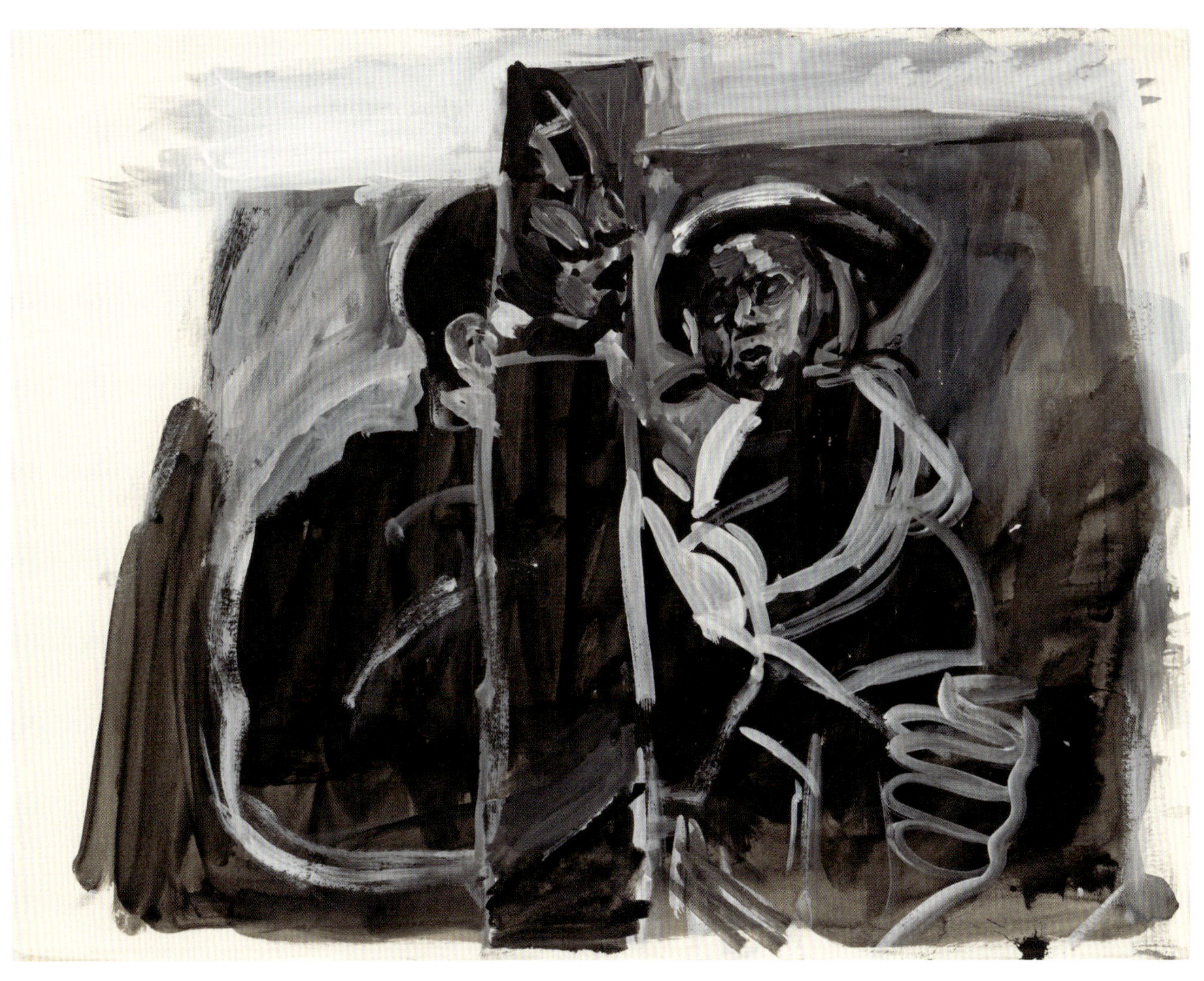

*Untitled (Grandfather Thomas and Cousin Irving)*, ca. 1988–91
Brush and black ink and acrylic paint on paper
23 × 30 in.

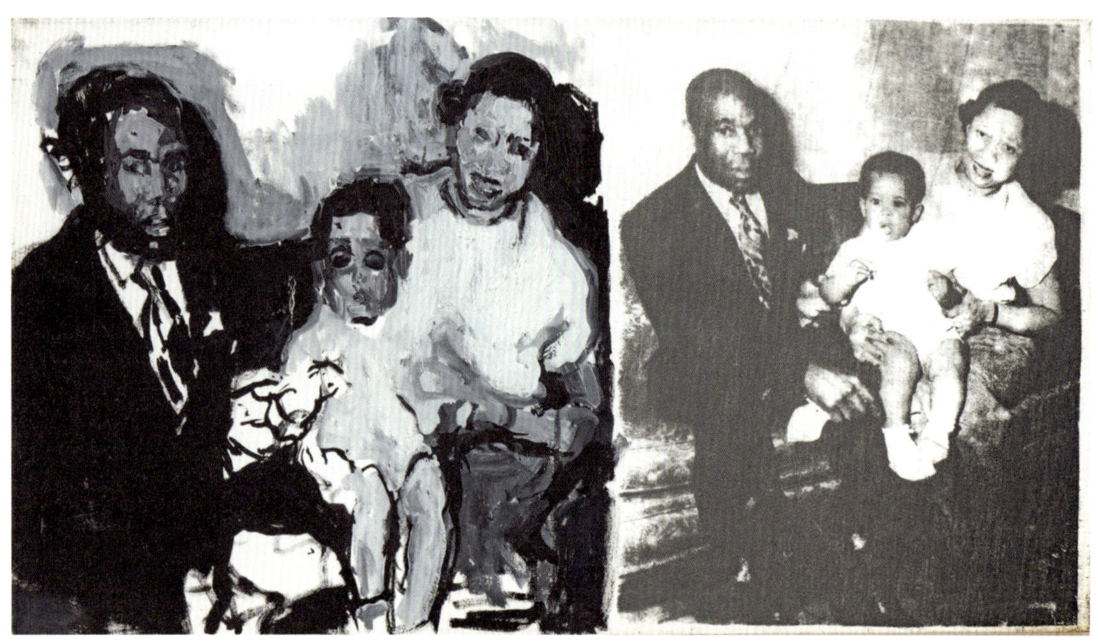

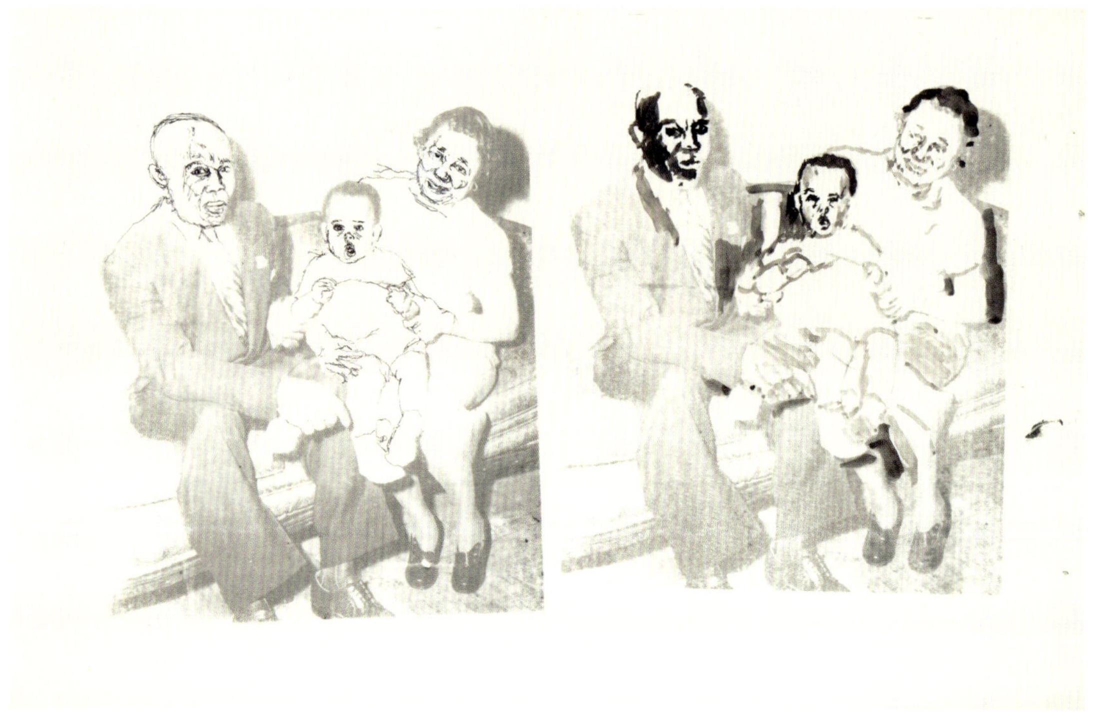

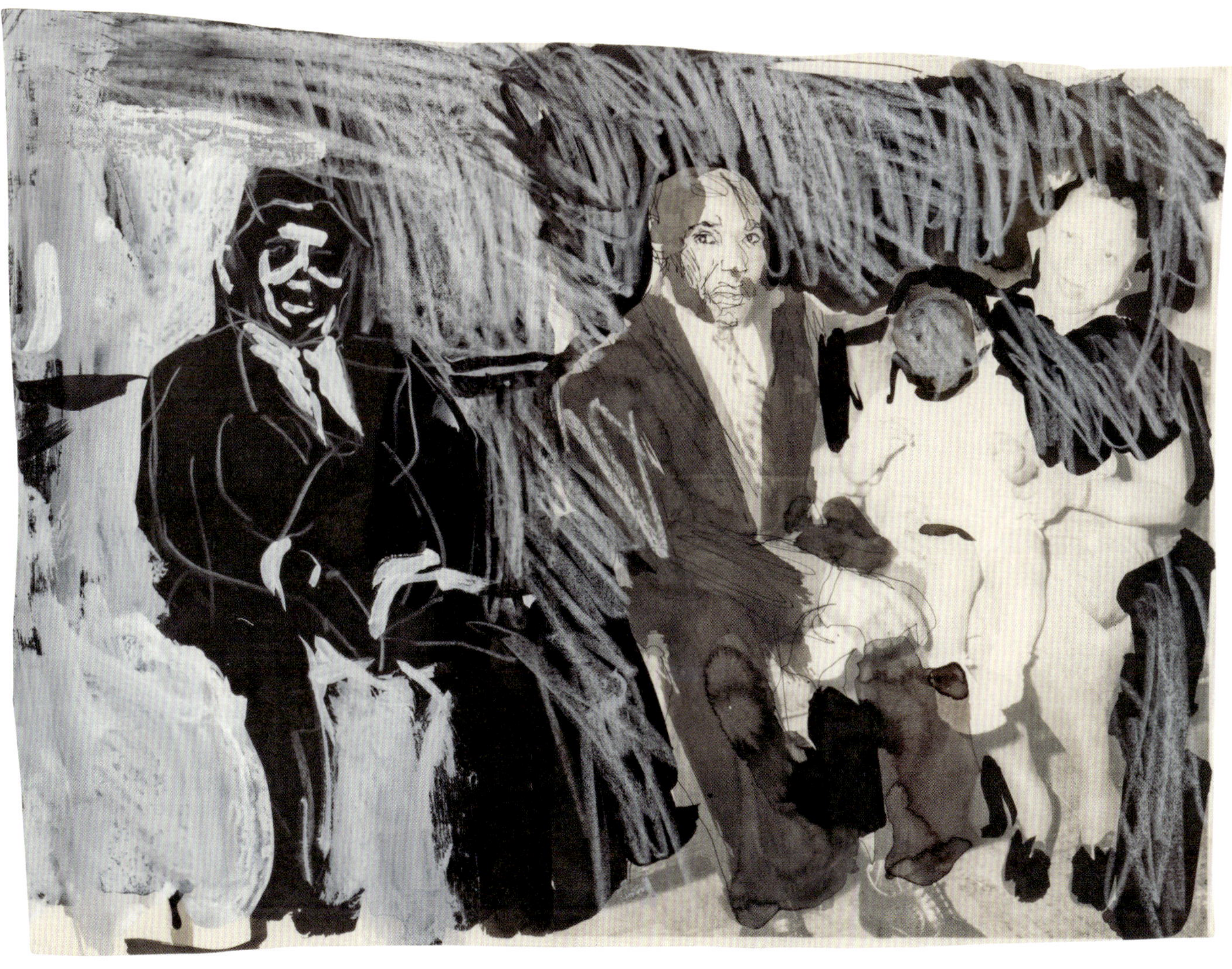

*Untitled (Grandparents with Laure)*, ca. 1985–87
Brush and black ink, acrylic paint, and screenprint on canvas
14 × 25 in.
Private collection, New York

*Untitled (Grandparents with Laure)*, ca. 1985–87
Pen and brush and black ink, wash, and opaque watercolor over screenprint on paper
17 ¼ × 26 ¼ in.

*Untitled (Grandparents with Laure)*, 1984
Screenprint, brush and black ink, opaque watercolor, ballpoint pen, and pastel on paper
22 × 26 in.
Collection of Cher Lewis

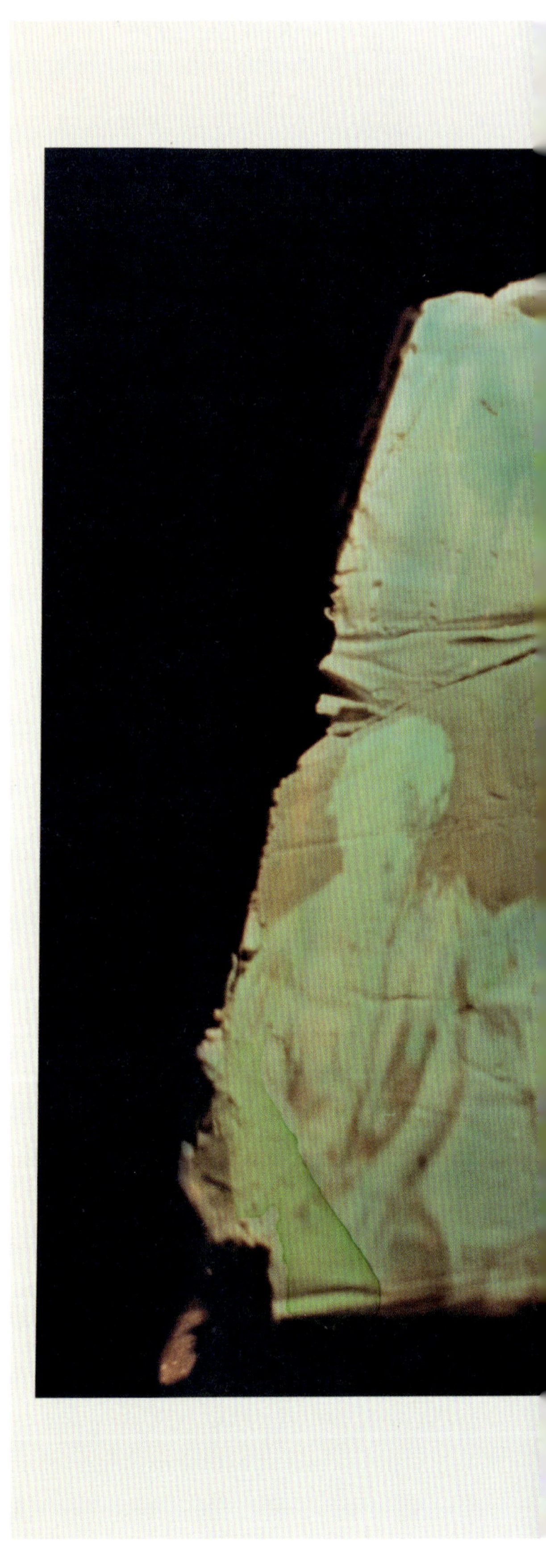

*Untitled (Figures in Bedroom)*, ca. 1988–91
Chromogenic print
11 × 14 in.
Collection of Candice Madey
and Thomas Lewis

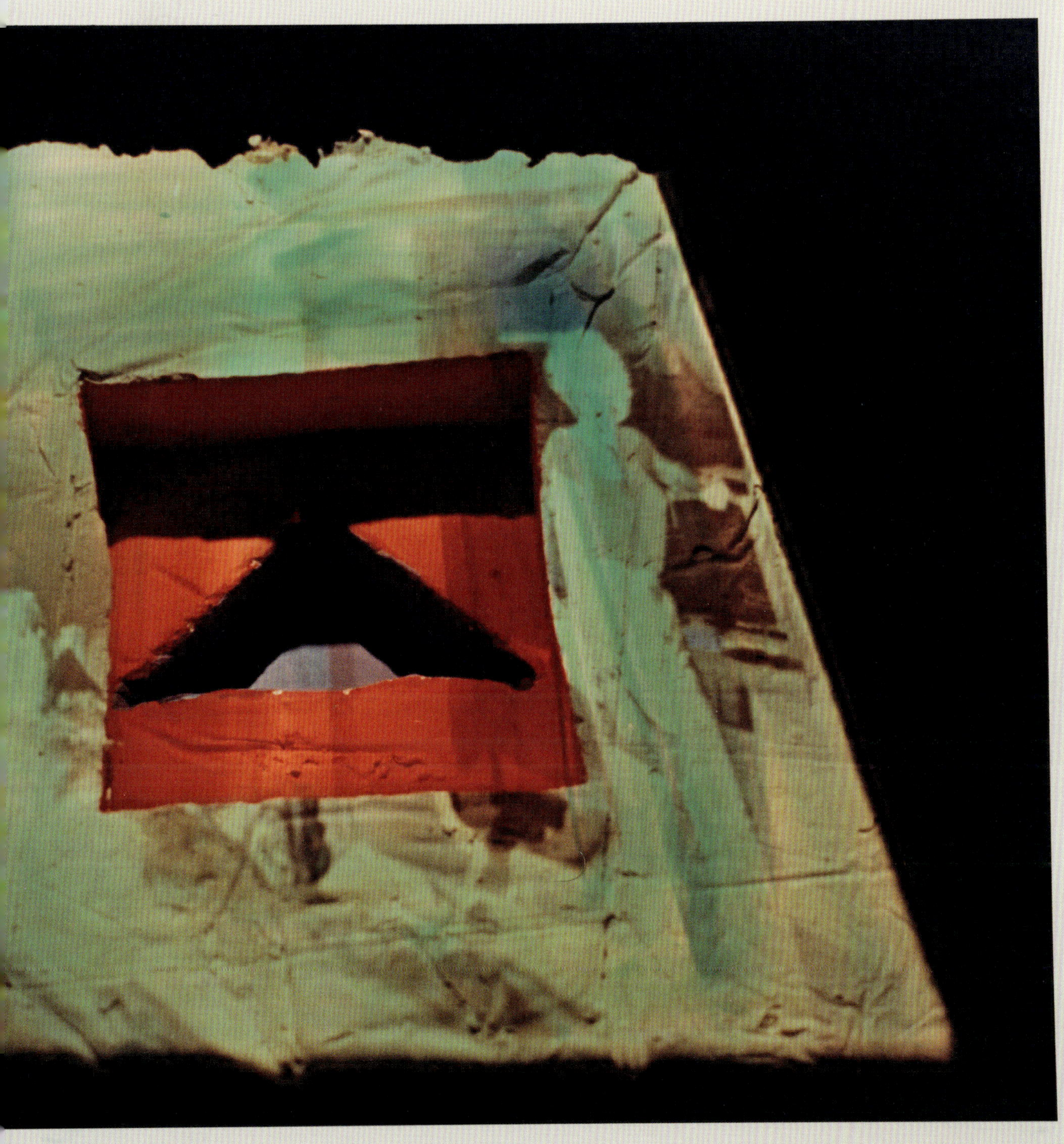

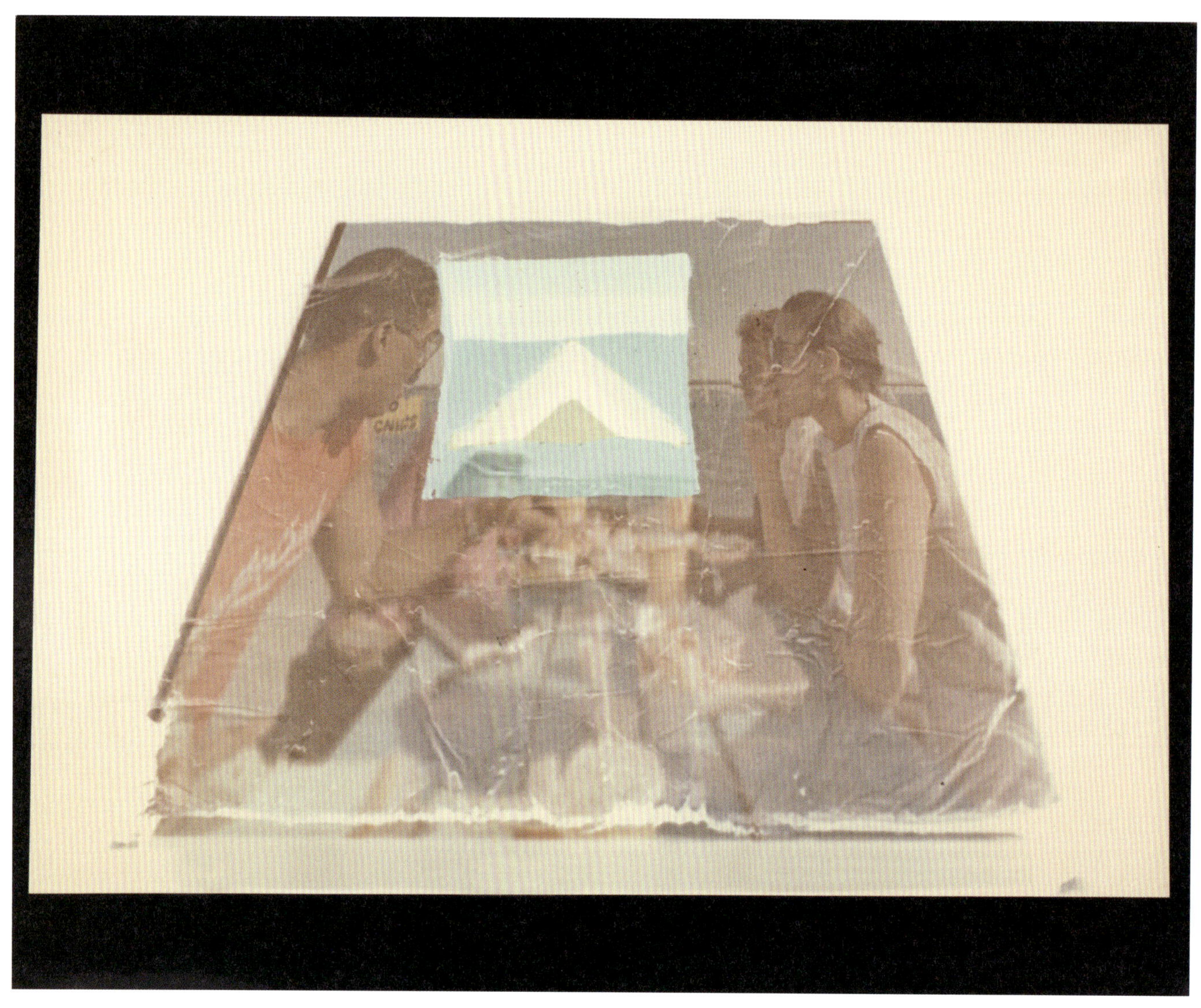

*Untitled (Picnic Scene)*, ca. 1988–91
Chromogenic print
16 × 20 in.

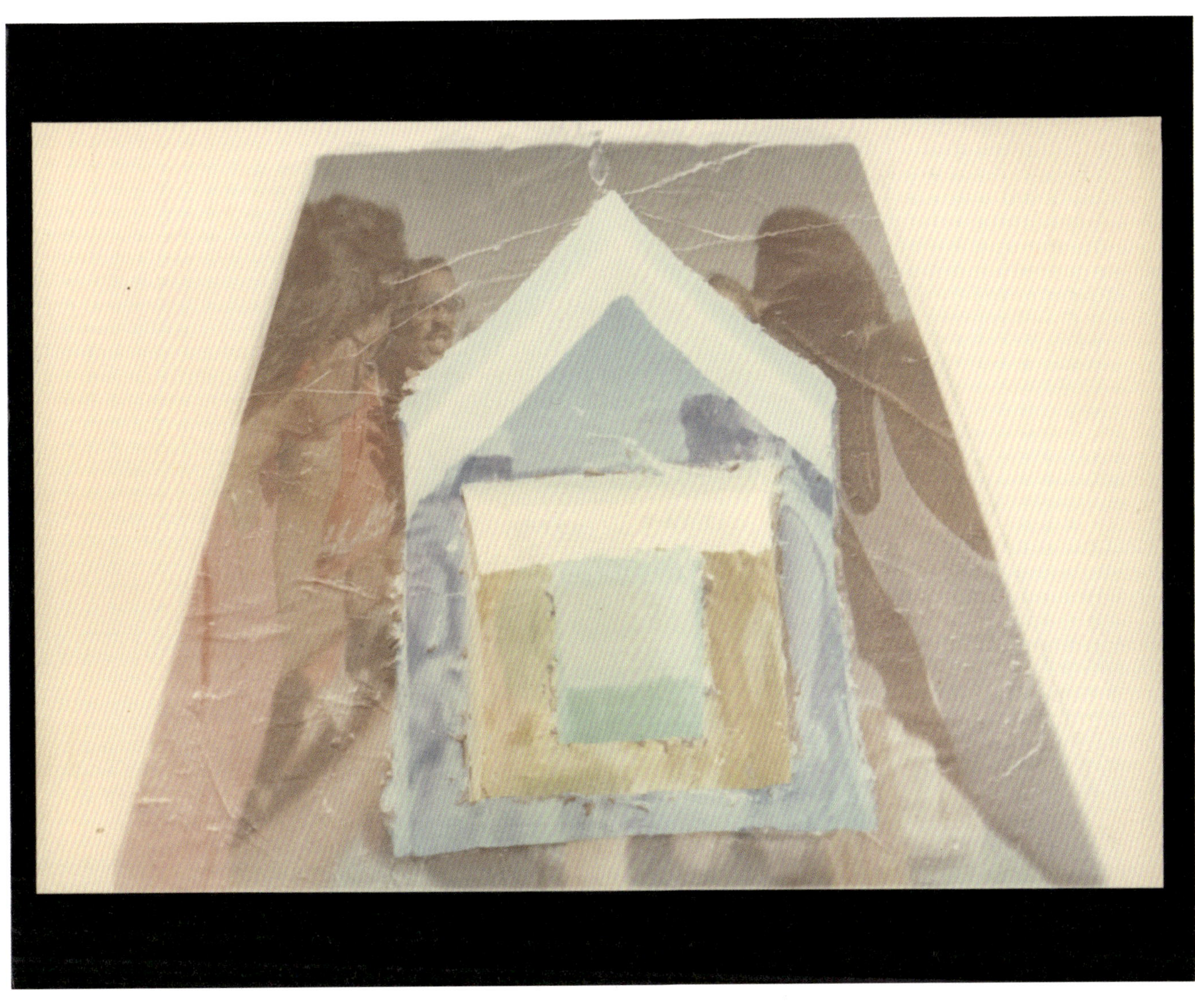

*Untitled (Picnic Scene)*, ca. 1988–91
Chromogenic print
8 × 10 in.

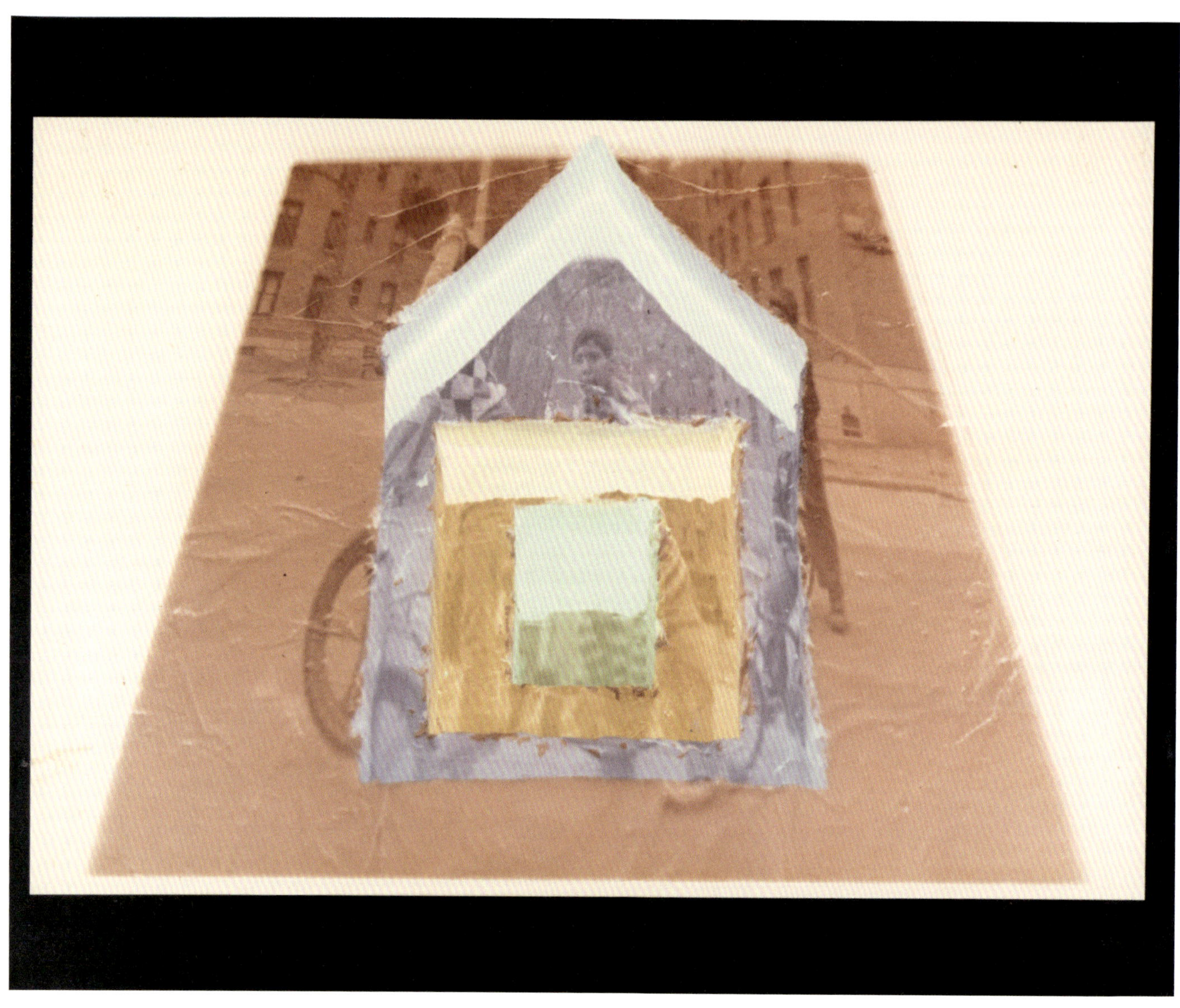

*Untitled (Boy with Bicycle)*, ca. 1988–91
Chromogenic print
8 × 10 in.

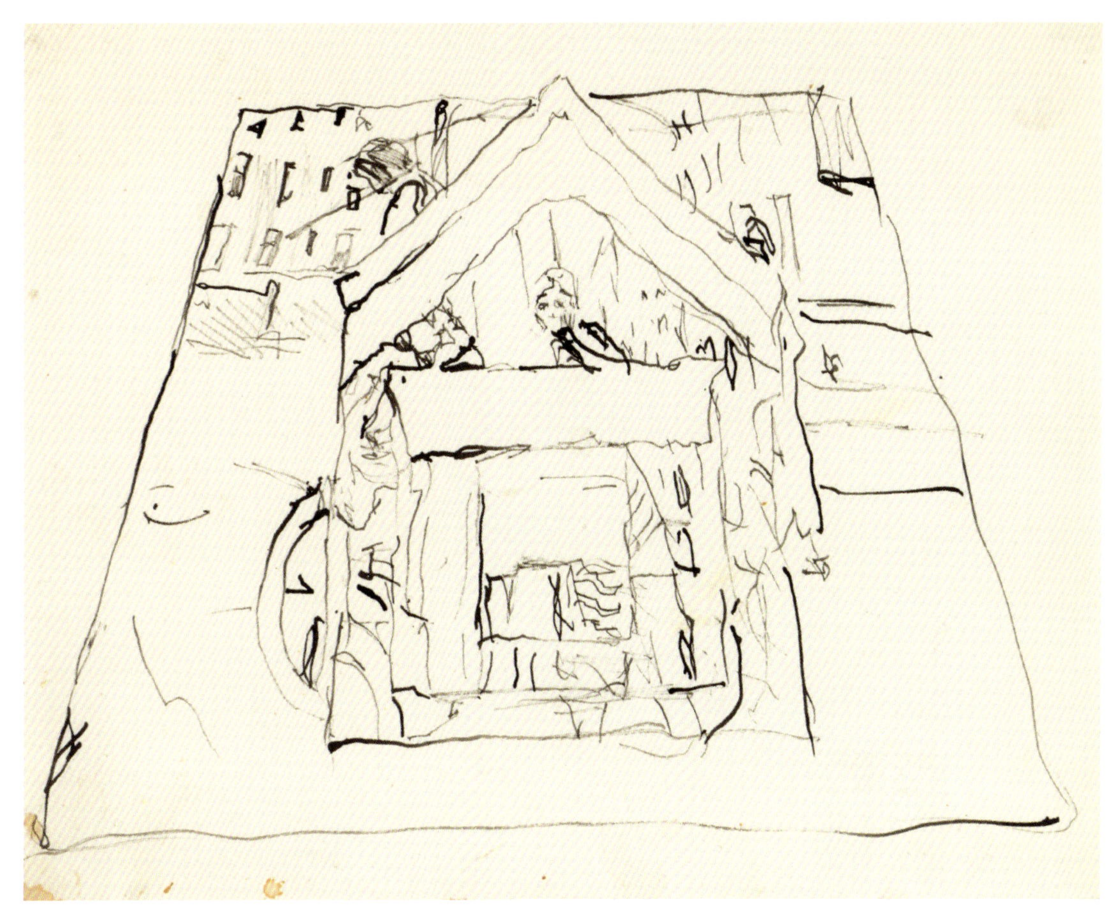

*Untitled (Boy with Bicycle)*, ca. 1988–91
Pen and black ink on paper
11 × 14 in.

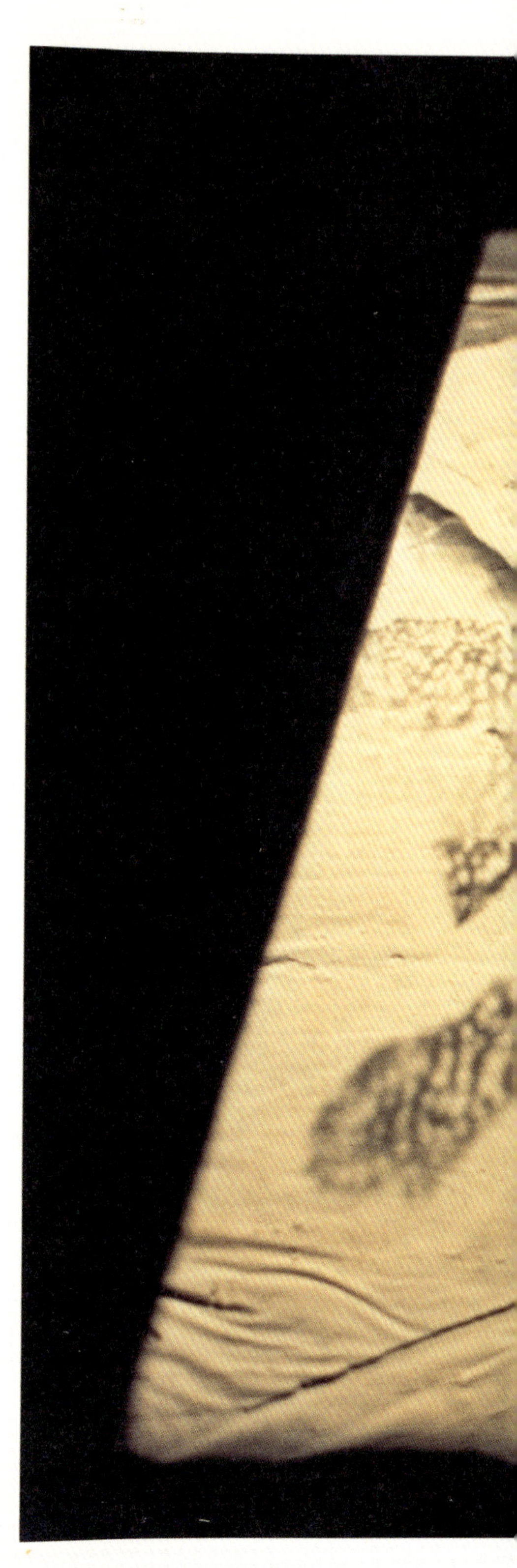

*Untitled (Woman with Leopard Skin)*,
ca. 1988–91
Chromogenic print
16 × 20 in.

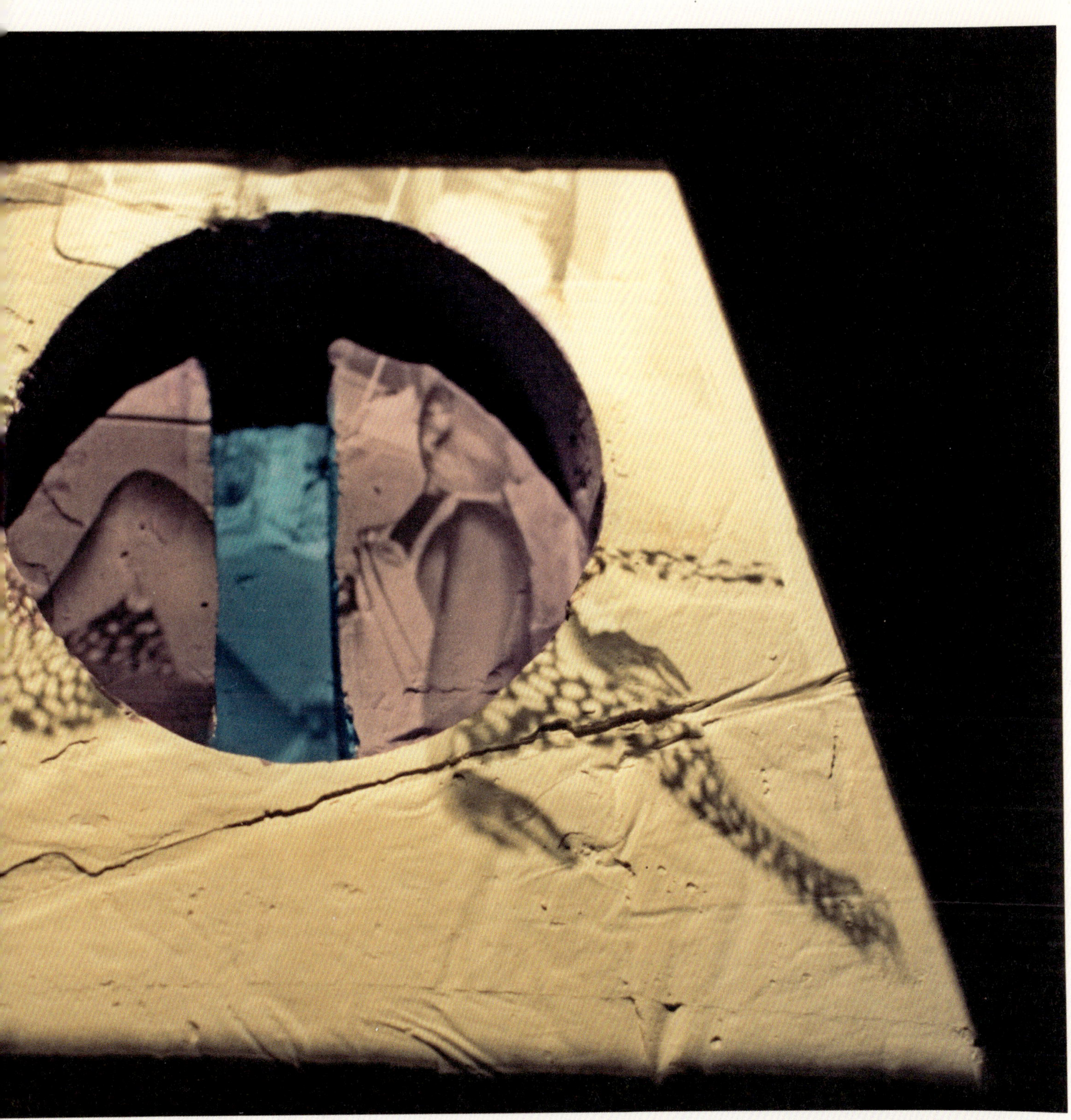

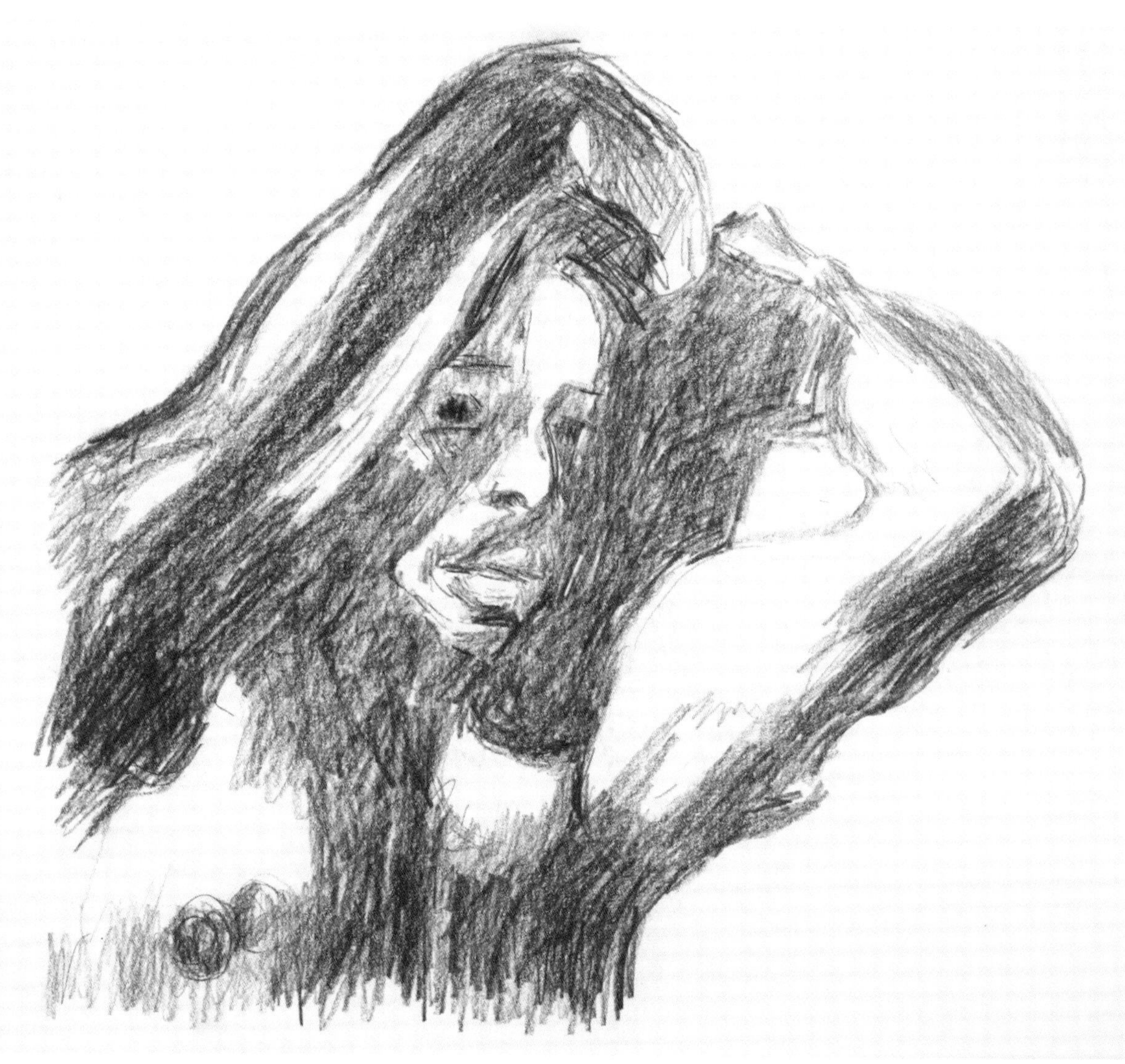

Antonio Sergio Bessa

# "A Hole in the Picture": Darrel Ellis Was Here

A central argument in Douglas Crimp's introduction to *Pictures*—the exhibition that championed a new brand of conceptualism based on image appropriation—was the notion that we experience reality through mediated images, that is, images disseminated through mass media (newspaper, magazines, television, cinema) rather than the product of firsthand experience such as family snapshots. The complexity Crimp envisioned in picture-making—"The actual event and the fictional event, the benign and the horrific, the mundane and the exotic, the possible and the fantastic: all are fused into the all-embracing similitude of the picture"[1]—makes for a compelling subject despite obscure references to topics such as "sensory experience" and "psychological images." Drawn from an essay by Rosalind Krauss,[2] the latter concept seemed particularly irrelevant when applied to the five artists[3] featured in *Pictures*, who purposefully pursued representation "freed from the tyranny of the represented." Issued two years after the end of the Vietnam War—when the United States grappled with unemployment, homelessness, drug addiction, and the imminent spread of HIV infection—Crimp's call for an art infected by memory could have more poignantly referred to the work of other contemporaneous artists who eschewed theory to produce highly personal records of the life they were experiencing at the time.[4] A careful review of *Pictures* in the broader context of the decade it aimed to represent inevitably exposes the art world mechanics of privileging theory-sanctioned art at the expense of works informed by personal experience. In this context, the work of Darrel Ellis is of particular relevance, not only because of its timeline but also because it too embodied the clash between tradition and the experimental that was at the core of Crimp's argument. The fact that Ellis managed to construct a highly personal, quasi-biographical work while also incorporating procedures related to "quotation, excerption, framing, and staging" seems to indicate that theory and firsthand experience do not necessarily imply a dichotomy.

Indeed, the task that Ellis took on involved rescuing the formidable archive left by a father he did not have a chance to meet. As he told David Hirsh: "I use images of my family because they affect me so strongly; they're just something I know extremely well, very deeply. As for using my father's pictures specifically, it helps me to keep a certain amount of distance and detachment from the reality I know, growing up after my father's death."[5] Ellis was nineteen years old when *Pictures* opened at Artists Space in 1977, and although there is no mention of the exhibition in the notebooks he laboriously kept starting as early as 1976, it is not implausible to assume that he visited the exhibition. Born and raised in the South Bronx, Ellis became acquainted with the downtown Manhattan art scene as a student at the High School of Fashion Industries from which he graduated in 1976. Records indicate that on Monday, April 9, 1979, he participated in one of Helène Aylon's *Formations Breaking* performances at 112 Workshop; and two months later, with a

[1] Douglas Crimp, "Pictures," in *Pictures* (New York: Artists Space, 1977), 3.
[2] For an informed discussion on the process of "converting the complex data of sensory experience into a schematic representation" cited by Crimp, see J. L. Austin's *Sense and Sensibilia* (New York: Oxford University Press, 1964). The term "psychological images," I assume, is Krauss's concept based on psychoanalytical notions by Jacques Lacan. Crimp's source is to be found in Krauss's essay "Objecthood," in *Critical Perspectives in American Art* (Amherst: Fine Arts Center Gallery, University of Massachusetts, 1976), 25–27.
[3] The five artists featured in *Pictures* were Troy Brauntuch, Jack Goldstein, Sherrie Levine, Robert Longo, and Philip Smith.
[4] In his review of *The Pictures Generation: 1974–1984*, organized by the Metropolitan Museum of Art in 2009, Holland Cotter addressed the "disturbing sight" of history being written through exhibitions that present art in "epochal terms, as defining not styles or trends but generations," and he criticized Crimp's (and the Met's) exhibition as being "based on several broader exclusions." See Holland Cotter, "Framing the Message of a Generation," *New York Times*, May 29, 2009.
[5] David Hirsh, "Family Photos," *New York Native*, no. 408 (February 11, 1991). Hirsh's review of Ellis solo exhibition at Baron/Boisanté Gallery was accompanied by excerpts from an interview. This unpublished excerpt was taken from the interview's complete transcript. An account of Thomas Ellis's death was given by Laure J. Banks, Darrel Ellis's older sister, in a March 7, 2021, email exchange with Allen Frame: "The circumstances surrounding my father's death is painful. A car had my father double parked after leaving his mother's house. Two men jumped out did not identify themselves as police officers. Words and fists were exchanged. They then identified who they were and placed him under arrest. My uncle watched from my grandmothers and came downstairs. My father did not to go but my uncle

page 104
*Untitled (Self-Portrait after Peter Hujar Photograph)*, ca. 1981–90
Conte crayon on paper, 12 ¾ × 16 in.
Private collection

Documentation of Helène Aylon, *Formations Breaking* at 112 Workshop (325 Spring Street, New York), 1979
Photograph by Pat Craig

Program for Helène Aylon, *Formations Breaking* at 112 Workshop
(325 Spring Street, New York), 1979

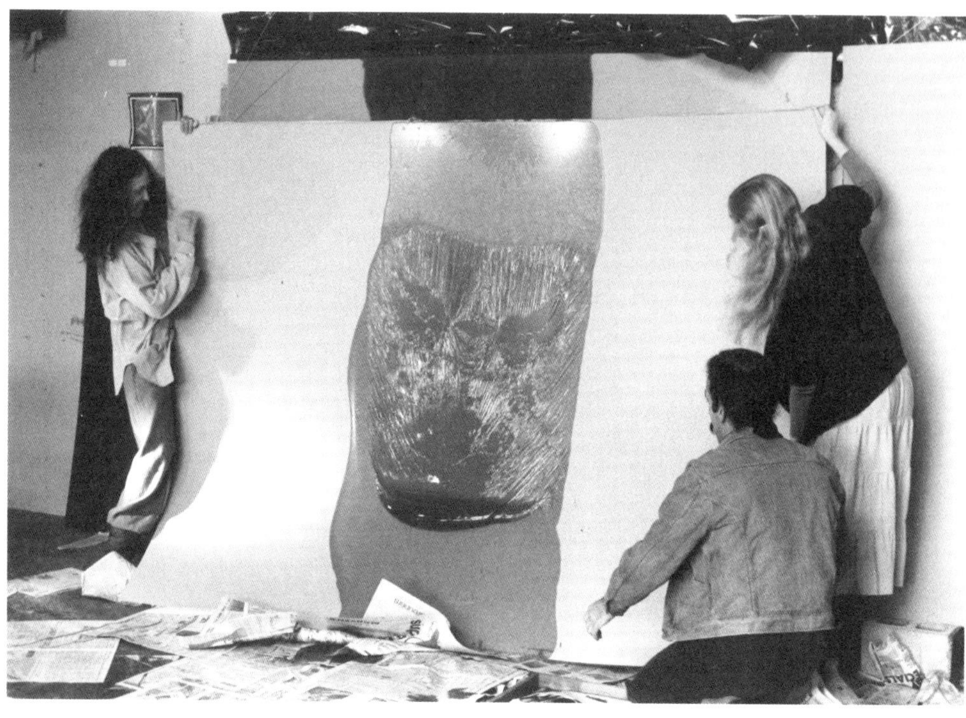

convinced him. Yes, he followed them, but he was beaten in the patrol car. The undertaker informed my mother that the back of his skull was smashed. He was not handcuffed. The two arresting officers were bragging at the precinct that they had just killed a nigger when my uncle Richard who at the time was a police officer informed them that the man they killed was his brother-in-law. Darrel was born 2 months after my father's death."

[6] John D. Abbott Jr. (1966–2000) was the founding director of 112 Work Shop Inc., the organization that served as the pioneer alternate space at 112 Greene Street and which was renamed White Columns in 1979.

[7] Located on the northwest corner of Broadway and 67th Street, Casa du Monde was the overflow room for a restaurant open to the public in the evening that lasted for just a few months. Following the advice of Joe Lewis, Mondlak organized a joint exhibition of Ellis and Jules Allen in 1985. Other artists featured in the gallery included Gerald Jackson, David Kapp, Victor Kerpel, and William Hellerman.

[8] Douglas Crimp, "Controlling Pictures," in *Jack Goldstein × 10,000* (Newport Beach, CA: Orange County Museum, 2012), 44–53.

[9] Meg Cranston, "Over Here: Interview with Jack Goldstein," in *Jack Goldstein × 10,000*, 203–12.

recommendation letter from John Abbott,[6] he applied for studio space at then emerging PS1. The 1982 Bulletin of the Whitney Museum of American Art lists Ellis as a participant in the 1981–82 Independent Study Program; the bulletin also indicates that Crimp was one of the seminar's guest critics that year.

After graduating from high school, Ellis led a bohemian life, split between short stays at his family's home in the South Bronx and sharing apartments with friends and lovers in Lower Manhattan. He also lived for a brief period in his studio at PS1 in Long Island City. An assiduous visitor of alternative art spaces such as the Clocktower Gallery in Downtown Manhattan and Fashion Moda in the South Bronx, Ellis tapped into a remarkable network that conveys a more complex picture of the late 1970s and 1980s in New York and included artists such as James Wentzy, Miguel Ferrando, Wendell Headley, Clarissa Sligh, and Liora Mondlak, who in 1983 offered him an exhibition at Casa du Monde.[7] Joe Lewis, cofounder of Fashion Moda, Malcolm Morley, Not Vital, Richard Brintzenhofe, and John Ahearn, among others, would become strong supporters by collecting Ellis's work or offering opportunities to exhibit. Particularly significant are the acquaintances he made with Allen Frame, Peter Hujar, Robert Mapplethorpe, and Nan Goldin—photographers who, like Ellis, reflected their personal experiences in their work.

In 2012, on the occasion of a retrospective of Jack Goldstein's career, Crimp considered the "psychological affect in the work of the *Pictures* artists," hinting at topics related to narcissism and childhood memory.[8] In the context of that catalogue, however, Crimp's understanding of *psychological affect* seems at odds with Goldstein's own view of art as biography, a theme he explored to some extent in an interview with Meg Cranston in which Goldstein discussed his deep psychological fear of disappearing and confessed that his drive as an artist was "to prove that I exist."[9] For Goldstein, who would commit suicide in 2003, *picture*, as verb or noun, was not merely an exploration of theories and art historical tropes but an effort to assert presence and a right to belong.

It is thus in the archetype of the artist as a tragic figure that the highly personal work

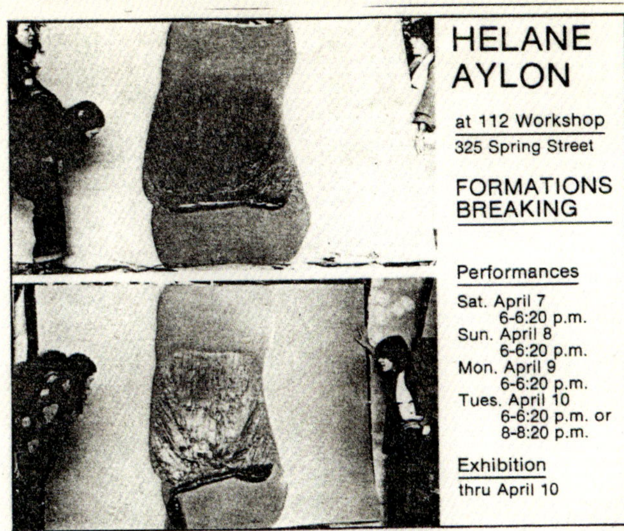


Participants:

Sat. 6 p.m.

Mya Hay Bannard
Brenda Dixon
Mark Elliot
Frieda Gorewitz
Suzanne Harris
Judy Hudson
Arlene Ladden
Sylvia Sleigh

Sun. 6 p.m.

Dottie Attie
Nancy Azara
Robyn Brentano
Vivian Eversman
Flora Irving
Howardina Pindell
Linda Scheinberg
Elke Solomon

Mon. 6 p.m.

Darrel Ellis
April Kingsley
Mary Lucier
Betty Parsons
Liz Phillips
Christian Moon

Tues. 6 P.m. & 8 p.m.

Leslie Cohen
Jane deLynn
Donna'Dennis
Harmony Hammond
Layne Redmond
John Ellis

Renee Emuna
Nathaniel Fisch
Joyce Kozloff
Ruth Shuman
May Stevens

"participants will initiate the breaking;"
Helane Aylon "will accept the pouring and resolution."

James Welling, *Jack Goldstein*, 1977
Inkjet print, 13 ¼ × 16 ¾ in.
Collection of the artist

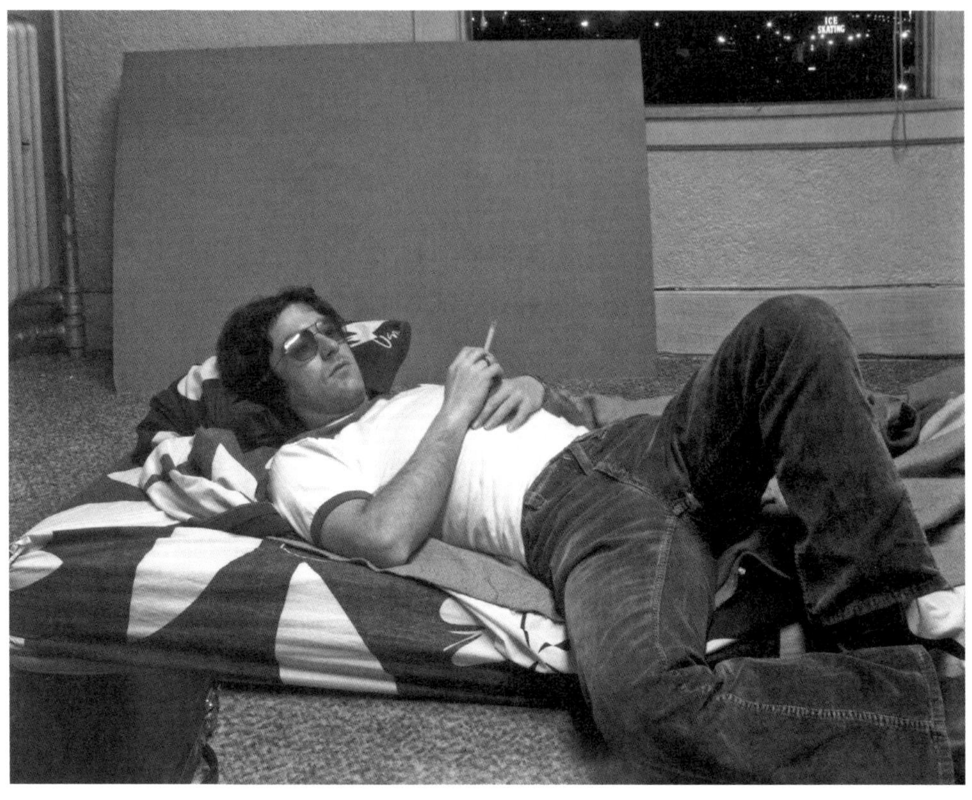


Darrel Ellis set himself to do converges with the cool, theory-laden approach embraced by Jack Goldstein and other artists of the Pictures Generation. It is to his credit that Ellis valued craft and direct observation as opposed to appropriating images from the media. As he commented to David Hirsh: ". . . deconstructing is all right. But what's more important is reconstruction."[10] In contrast to Goldstein, who produced his films with the help of able technicians, Ellis honed his craft as a draftsman through persistently sketching at the Metropolitan Museum, and later, working closely with James Wentzy, he developed a highly sophisticated and personal understanding of photography. The most remarkable contrast, however, relates to their relationship to writing, which pits once again Goldstein's conceptual approach against Ellis's more confessional tone. Goldstein's interest in writing dated back to 1977 with the production of *Aphorisms* and resurged again in the last decade of his life in *Selected Writings 1994–2000*, "an autobiography constructed of scraps of other authors' writings."[11] Ellis, in contrast, kept from 1976 until 1992 a series of notebooks that offers a consistent record of his life and work process, mixing sketches and grocery lists with terse thoughts about his psychological state. Often combining emotional observations about personal relationships, dreams, states of mind, and health concerns, these notebooks are an essential source to understanding the evolution of his experiments using his father's archives replete with detailed sketches and diagrams of solutions he meant to incorporate.

Entries in Ellis's notebooks become noticeably more pointed and charged with emotion shortly after his mother bestowed him his father's archives of prints and negatives in 1981. Through his father's photographs he recovered a blissful moment in his family history that also helped him understand the struggles faced by black families to assimilate into post-war American culture. As we gather from his notebooks,

[10] David Hirsh, "A New Sensibility: Interview with Darrel Ellis," in Lara Mimosa Montes and Kyle Croft, eds., *Darrel Ellis* (New York: Visual AIDS, 2021), 33.
[11] See Carol Cheh, "Jack Goldstein: The Subject Vanishes," *Art 21 Magazine*, August 20, 2012, https://magazine.art21.org/2012/08/20/word-is-a-virus-jack-goldstein-the-subject-vanishes.

Poster for *Drawings from My Father's Photographs* at Fashion Moda, 1983–84
The Bronx Museum of the Arts, New York

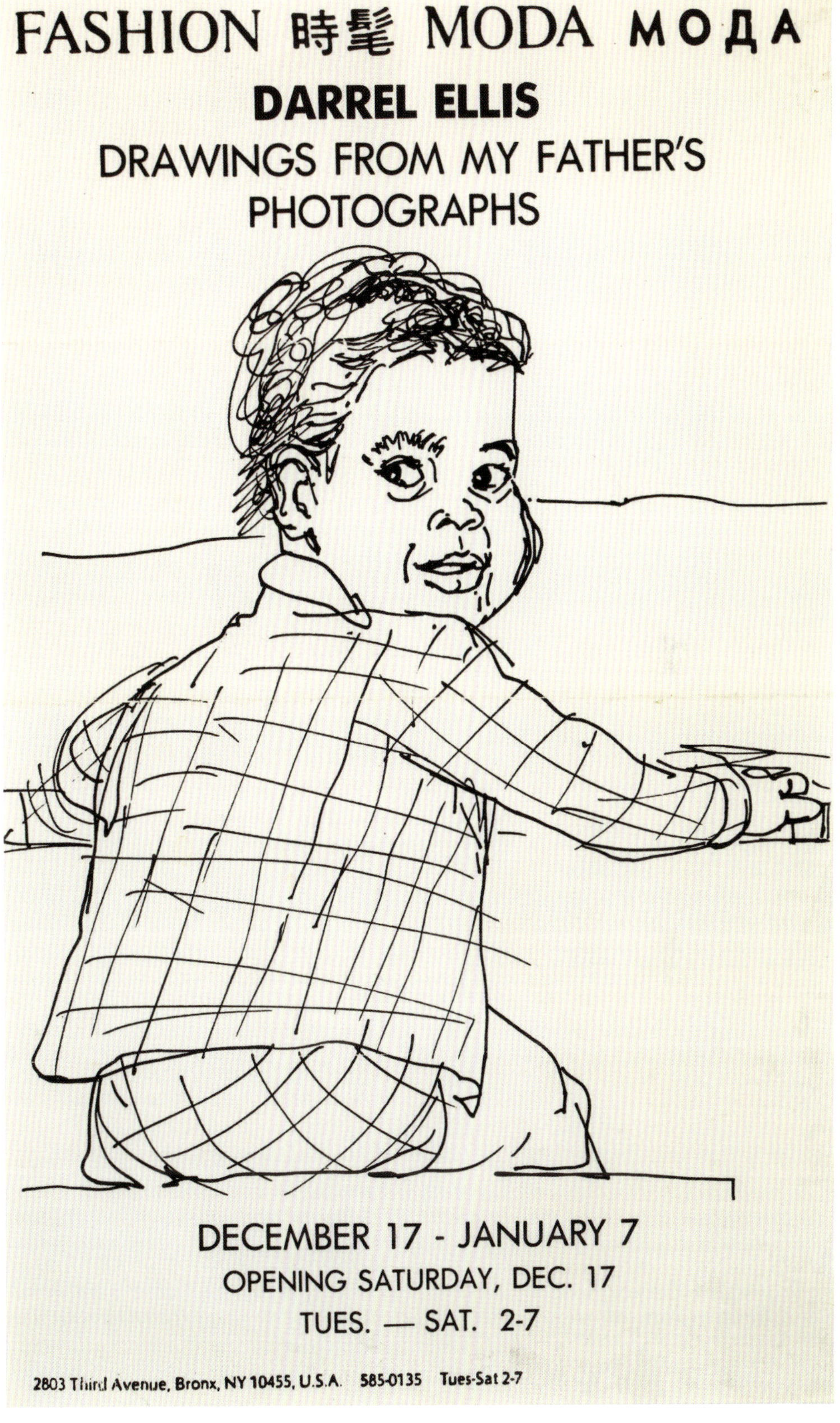

the stakes for Ellis throughout his brief career were not only personal but also of great social import. In embracing his father's legacy, he was led on a path that was part self-discovery, part awareness of the societal constrictions affecting African Americans. In the 1990 draft of a letter to be sent to art dealers, he wrote: "When I worked from those photographs, I was investigating the sensibility of a man who was lost to me. And in that work my visual sense was informed by years of looking at those same people, my father's subjects, in the years since his death."[12]

It would not be too farfetched to consider the work produced by Ellis based on his father's archive as "psychological images." As it happened, the appropriation is not entirely reverential as Ellis rephotographs his father's negatives by projecting them onto irregular surfaces. Often, faces are obliterated through holes on the projection surface, thus complicating the original image. He seemed aware of the symbolism the operation entailed, as he wrote in an entry from 1987: "The hole is there instead of a normal whole image of family to signify the present condition of the family (fragmented). Not whole. It is impossible presently to try to show a whole—a 'normal' reality, since it does not exist."[13] Most remarkably, he conveyed his vision with an apt play of language:

> What can be made of the relationship between the words *whole* and *hole*. The whole represents totality—completeness—self-existence. A hole signifies a break in the whole—a part—being taken from something. This symbol acts in both ways as a hole in the picture—and being a circle, located with the image symbolizes the whole in the part. The circle represents wholeness rather than painting the photo exactly, the addition of the circle in the picture signifies the wholeness of the subject, without the details of the whole picture. What is this feeling that I have for the images. Why does it seem right?[14]

The idyllic family life that was denied to him became mythologized in the drawings and photographs that he made based on his father's prints and negatives. Through that process he reconstructed the family pictured by his father. "Art as a metaphor for the concept of generations," he wrote in 1990, and continued: "Since my work deals with my father and my family and the issue of photo reproductions and the notion of the original . . . focus on portraits—faces . . . insert my identity into portrait tradition—read about portraiture."[15] His continuous engagement with art history were more than an aesthetic exercise; the notebooks' gathering his impressions of artworks often merge with personal observations, as this cryptic note from 1983 suggests: "depiction of mothers . . . relate my father's image[s] and mine of my mother to primitive artist image—in my work primitive or just from another culture."[16]

References to his mother in the notebooks are repeatedly conveyed in a heightened state of anxiety often related to his homosexuality, like in the retelling of a dream in the summer of 1986 in which painter Frank Moore is cast as his lover. In the dream, the mother figure is oppressive ("she tells me I will die tomorrow"), although at the end some measure of reconciliation is reached with the entire family and Frank Moore gathered in the kitchen around the stove while Ellis cries frantically. The narrative ends enigmatically in one short line: "my mother as god." The feeling of anxiety also characterizes many of the entries on his work process, the uniqueness of which he is sharply aware, and in those moments the presence of the mother is often conveyed even if obliquely: "Behind the anxiety I have about telling other artist[s] about using the left hand to draw is selfishness, a wish to keep it to myself. Like a child who doesn't share a toy he enjoys very much. This anxiety is irrational because this is only sharing a technique, no one can take away my art, vision and style."[17]

The toy analogy could as well be extended to his father's archive, given to him by his mother—a hypothesis that would validate his

[12] Darrel Ellis, Notebook 1990.1.
[13] Darrel Ellis, Notebook 1987.1.
[14] In his 1953 essay "The Function and Field of Speech and Language in Psychoanalysis," Jacques Lacan suggested that in the "name of the father" lies the basis of the "symbolic function, which, since the dawn of historical time, has identified his person with the figure of the law." See Jacques Lacan, *Écrits: The First Complete Edition in English*, trans. Bruce Fink in collaboration with Héloïse Fink and Russell Grigg (New York: W. W. Norton, 2006), 230. In 1974, Lacan returned to the same topic in Seminar XXI "Les non-dupes errent," playing with the sonority of the expression "le nom du père" ("le nom du père," and "les non-dupes errent") and thus emphasizing the concept as a play of language. In the latter text, Lacan also creates the portmanteau *troumatisme* (hole-trauma), adding that "nous inventons un truc pour combler le trou dans le Réel" (all of us invent something to fill up the hole in the Real). In a notebook entry from 1987, Ellis indicates some degree of awareness of the process of mediation between the real and the symbolic order when he writes: "In using my father's photographs as a basis for drawing and painting studies questions concerning reality and the nature of reality are brought up. It is important that I work from my father's photographs because they have been impressed, and reflect his will and concept of reality. They are charged, already set apart from reality like paintings."
[15] Darrel Ellis, Notebook 1990.2.
[16] Darrel Ellis, Notebook 1983.2.
[17] Darrel Ellis, Notebook 1985.1.

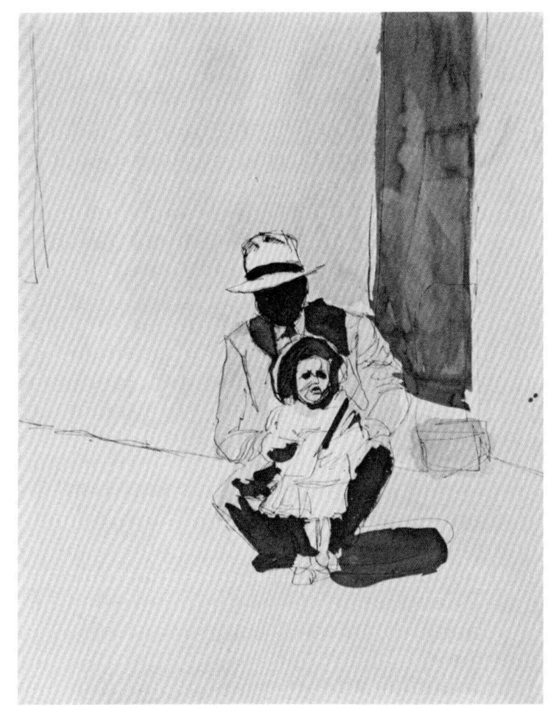

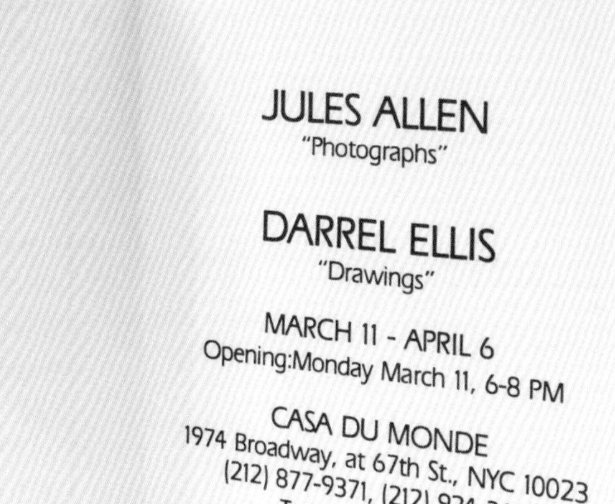


Invitation card for *Jules Allen, Darrel Ellis* at Casa du Monde Gallery, 1985
Collection of Liora Mondlak

mythologizing of family. Another entry from 1986 about his astrological chart stresses a feeling of guilt and repression ("a sense that I'm not good enough"), and the mother figure is equated with the "overcritical side of [his] nature," to finally become mythologized as the Jungian *anima*: "The mother in nature—also signifies the receptive—the womb from which all things come." Constantly shifting from inward analysis to outward considerations on art, the page ends enigmatically: "The big idea—the unifying principle / The big picture—express consciousness."[18]

In pursuit of the big picture, Ellis adopted a personal blend of concepts and practices drawn from art history and theory as well as notions related to Eastern philosophy, and in doing so he aligned his practice with the tail end of the countercultural movement. Whether relying on the mystic psychology of Carl Jung, astrology, the I Ching, or Hindu cosmology, Ellis's search for guidance was of a cosmological order, as this remarkable 1987 entry suggests:

> The way to go: lightness. Spirit as opposed to matter. Get the viewer to experience lightness—and immateriality. This is a very hard task upsets our notions about existence, and negates the reliance upon psychical perceptions, almost an impossibility. Material must be used we are matter, but we must use it to convey reality that which is beyond our present physical consciousness or limitations –
>
> Reinforce the nature lightness of the photographic image. Through contrast—the juxtaposition of a heavy material element.
>
> 2 – Increase the lightness of the image by the use of transparent plastic construction.
>
> Spirit comes into action after the end of a pralaya,[19] when it is passive—same there is no matter - Δ - these symbols for the spiritual and absolute truth come into existence with matter. They (spirit) are the reason for physical existence.[20]

In his search to create harmony ("unity in diversity," he scribbled in the same notebook), Ellis sees the blatant materialism that characterized the Reagan-Thatcher years as a barrier, a threat to art as a humanistic

[18] Ibid.
[19] *Pralaya*, from the Sanskrit, can be translated as "non-existence," "dissolution," or by extension "reabsorption, destruction, annihilation or death." In Hindu cosmology, *Pralaya* indicates periods of time during which a nonactivity situation persists. The source of this notion for Ellis is unclear.
[20] Darrel Ellis, Notebook 1987.1.

endeavor. He was keen to differentiate his formal explorations from the "anything goes attitude" of artists like Frank Stella that "reflects the impoverished content of contemporary art," but, he recognized, was "in line with the present state of man's development."[21]

As alternative, he offered a thoroughly worked-out system that aimed at reaching beyond the "looks and the reactions that come from our physical senses." Written in the late 1980s, these entries convey a complex understanding of the work he hoped to accomplish, incorporating both the early technical experiments with surfaces developed with Wentzy at PS1 and theoretical concerns gleaned perhaps during his participation in the Whitney Independent Studio Program. Perception becomes a central concern, like a node of feeling and reason that illuminates and gives meaning to the object and that is intrinsically connected to personal experience ("our feelings and ideas of the subject are colored by our past experiences and recollections of the person or event photographed"), and his views on the photographic process will follow along the same lines: "The present is made up of those things which our minds have taken from the past and are projected into the present—as a reference point, as a photograph is the visual record of a past event. So our feelings and ideas of the subject are colored by our past experiences and recollections of the person or event photographed. These perceptions aroused by the photo are not necessarily the ones that were present at the time of the making of the image, but are projected upon it."[22]

It is unclear, in his considerations on perception, whether he is responding to any specific philosophical text; and although the notebooks are punctuated with reminders to read Hegel, Barthes, Derrida, and Jung, it is difficult to fathom with whom he is in dialogue in notes such as in this excerpt: "The perception of object is distorted by the perceiver. Does the object have any existence outside from the function it has for the perceiver. It is a creation of the man: a total creation of the man its life is given by the perceiver. It has the form. . . . Matter is distorted through our process of perception—something must proceed [*sic*] the image as we perceive it."[23]

Toward the end of 1988, Ellis seemed heavily invested in the realm of the symbolic. The photographic process itself—with its interplay of black and white, positive and negative—becomes loaded of symbolic value, as he stated clumsily: "The nature of a photograph is B+W or positive and negative. Just as the nature of a painting from a formal perspective is 2-dimensionality."[24] And most poignantly, a few months later: "Light that by which we reflect on the past."[25] Overwhelmed by the very symbolism he created, he found himself entirely immersed in a process in which rephotographing his father's negatives had become a parallel reality, as hinted at in these fragmentary entries from 1988:

> I could say that the white spaces and the bending and distortions in the photographs are a metaphor for fire and heart.
>
> The geometric shape introduces the element of touch, feel—the basic element of photography.
>
> By re-photographing the photograph with an sculpture form [*sic*] I emphasize the materiality of physical reality. It emphasizes the feeling nature of photography and makes a connection between—physical touch—and emotional pshycic [*sic*] ~~touch~~ feelings.
>
> Draw a relationship between these abstract subjective elements and objective reality.
>
> A circle has no beginning and no end: like consciousness.
>
> Can't tell the figures for the shape—abstract element metaphor for family relationships: can't distinguish my feelings ○ about

[21] In a 1987 entry about Frank Stella's controversial exhibition at the Museum of Modern Art, he wrote: "It's a natural result of materialism. In this context Frank Stella's success is no surprise. Those responsible for his success are wealthy individuals and corporations all those who benefit from materialism and participate in the continuing the delusion caused by lack of true knowledge. And who themselves lack any spirituality. It would be quite different if in Stella's relief paintings there was a reason for relief areas the meaning changing with each relief – but we are denied this, all we get is purely abstract meaningless juxtaposition of form. Manipulation of substance, an 'anything goes attitude' is the motto which is reflected in our culture at large. What alternatives are left to the artist who strives to realize the higher qualities in man, and what means?" Darrel Ellis, Notebook 1987.1.

[22] Darrel Ellis, Notebook 1987.1.

[23] Ibid.

[24] Darrel Ellis, Notebook 1988.1.

[25] Darrel Ellis, Notebook 1989.1.

the situation, people, etc. for the reality of the subject.

It is from memory that we touch, feel and experience physical life.

I see a relationship between karma and the re-photographs. The distortions are caused by the way in which the image falls in a particular form or angle, much as our form is the result of karmic reactions, which gives the world its variety of forms.[26]

These entries indicate a point in his process where impasse could no longer be resolved by reason alone. Since early in 1983, he had frequently consulted the I Ching as a decision-making aid. But in contrast to John Cage, who employed the I Ching in the early 1950s for compositional purposes, Ellis's approach to the I Ching, hastily registered in his notebooks, conveys a frantic mind split between art ("where do I go from here in my work?"), material survival, and health concerns ("Do I have AIDS?").[27] The answer he came up with was a highly personal use of photography that incorporates elements of sculpture and drawing into a three-dimensional structure in which the real intersects with the symbolic, the present with the past, and that connects the photographer with the viewer.

Light or illumination comes from the distorting element—we look into the past. Distorting element: 3-dimensional geometrical figures—which describes our physical state at the moment we are looking back, our only means of relating the scene in the photograph. This is what causes the charge that my photographs give off. The relationship between the 2-D signified as the past, the floating quality of the image-scene and the 3-D quality of the geometrical form place within the photographic scene.

In the organic or round reliefs, I add the 3-dimensional quality [to] the image in order to give the image a heightened sense of life, so that it effects [*sic*] us in our present, physical state at that moment we are looking at them.

The 3-D geometrical shapes functions [*sic*] as a way to enter the 2-D of the photograph. We are 3-dimensional physically as we look at a photograph, but the photograph remains 2-dimensional, the two remain separate but in my photographs I try to make them relate.

The viewer is in the work. His role is incorporated into the work.
<u>Eternity in the transitory.</u>[28]

The subjective mind is infinite in its potential—the rephotos will be many in number to signify infinity—though the 3rd element the drawings will be more or less the different interpretation of the original photo.

These drawings come from a desire to show how the reading of an emotion in a picture can be expressed more forcibly by changing the context of the central emotion.[29]

The photographic image represents the public, generalization. The obliteration of the face in my photos could signify the erasure of individuality, impersonal. Drawing the polar opposite of this is completely personal for me.[30]

This structure is particularly evident in the series he produced based on a photograph of his sister Laure as an infant holding a toy rabbit. The original negative, shot by his father in Crotona Park in the South Bronx, was projected on a surface that obliterated Laure's face and rephotographed by Ellis in his studio. Ellis made at least six versions of this work, each featuring holes of different shapes or added color ink abstractions. The entire group of photographs, printed on 11-by-14 inches sheets, plays with notions of repetition and uniqueness. To complicate the series, he made works in different media: several pen-on-paper drawings of the photographs faithfully reproducing the distortions on the

[26] See p. 162. Darrel Ellis, Notebook 1988.1.
[27] See p. 160. Darrel Ellis, Notebook 1983.1.
[28] Darrel Ellis, Notebook 1989.1.
[29] Darrel Ellis, Notebook 1984.1.
[30] See p. 168. Darrel Ellis, Notebook 1989.1.

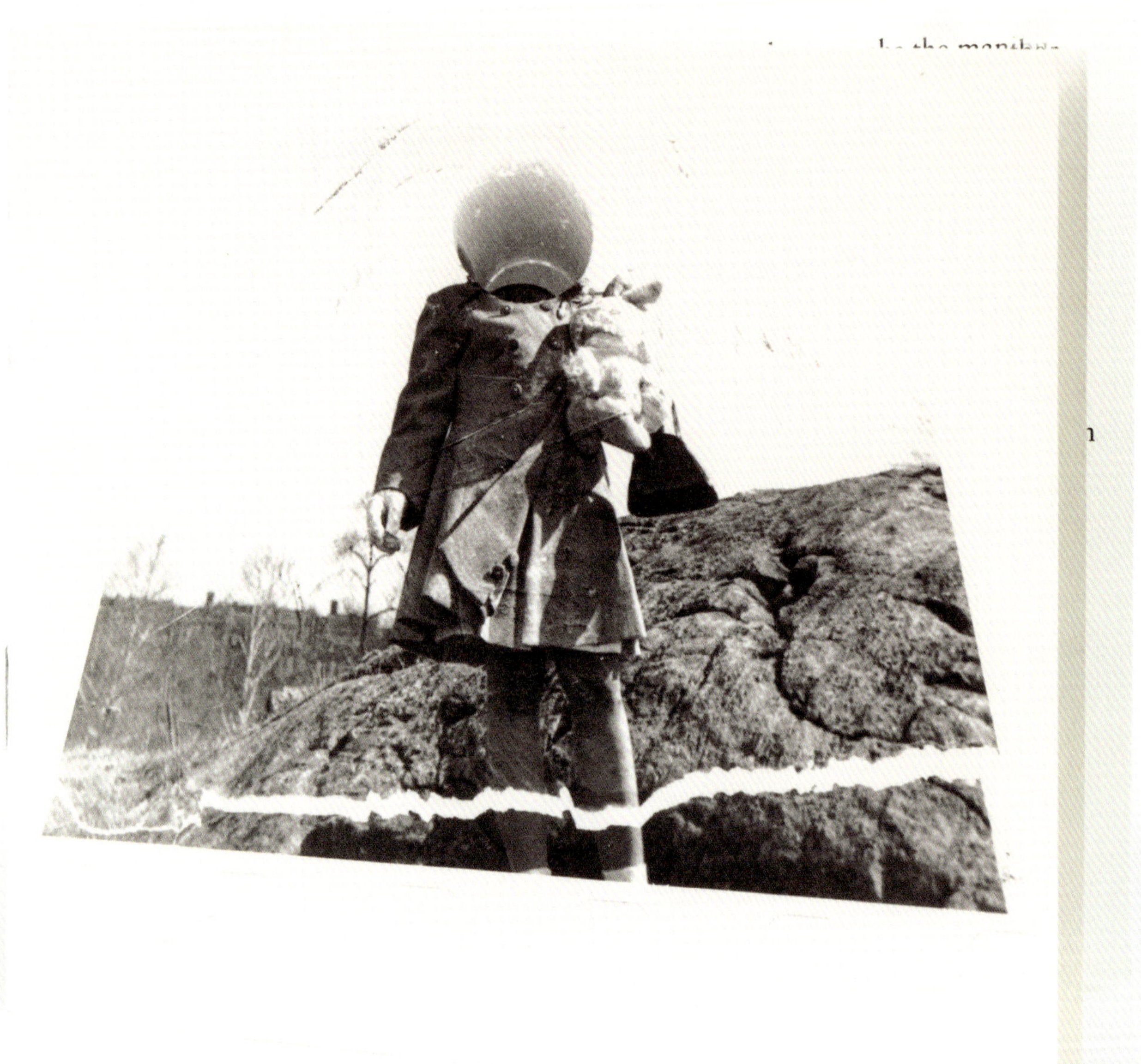

A small brochure produced
for the solo exhibition *Darrel Ellis*
at Baron/Boisanté in 1991
The Bronx Museum of the Arts,
New York

figure's face and an acrylic painting on a trapezoid shaped canvas of significantly larger scale in which the image of Laure is rendered through expressive, exacting brushstrokes. The picture of Laure seems to have exerted a powerful spell in Ellis's imagination, allowing him entry into a childhood experience different than his own. Most tellingly, this picture seems to have played a central part in Ellis's understanding of his work process, a system also employed in the extensive variations on his mother and other family members, like uncle Richard and his beautiful wife, Connie, and dapper uncle Joseph.

One of Ellis's pictures of Laure was featured on the cover of the micro catalogue produced for his exhibition at Baron/Boisanté in 1991. In an email exchange, Mark Baron remembered that "Darrel seemed very comfortable with his paintings, and uncomfortable with his photos," and that he only came around with the installation of his photographs after reading the catalogue's short essay by Joshua P. Smith. His photographs, Smith wrote, "shamanistically connect him to a time he never lived in and to a father he never knew. They also serve to expose, yet cauterize, the open wound inflicted by his father's perpetual absence."

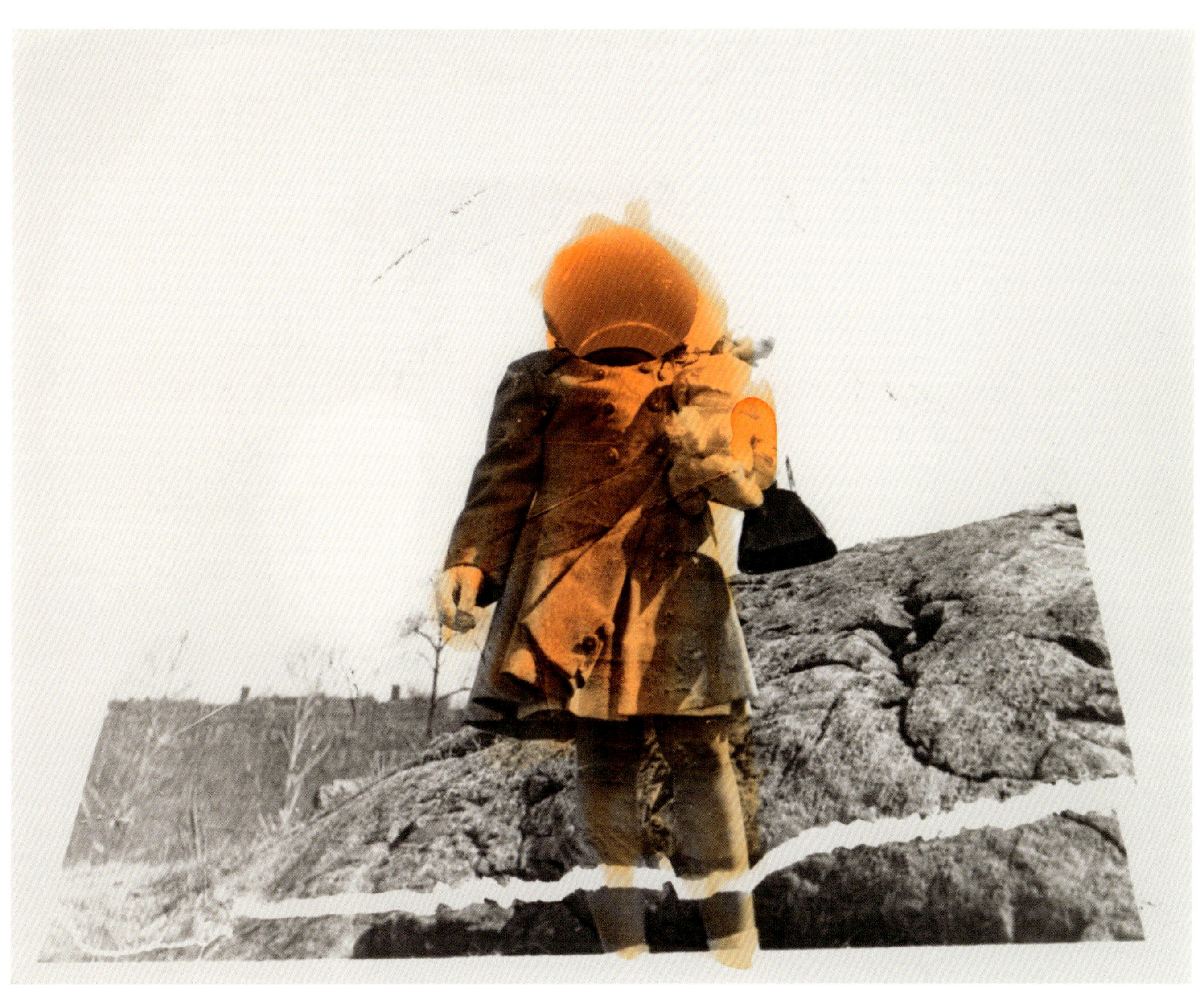

*Untitled (Laure on Easter Sunday)*, ca. 1989–91
Gelatin silver print with colored ink
10 ½ × 13 ½ in.

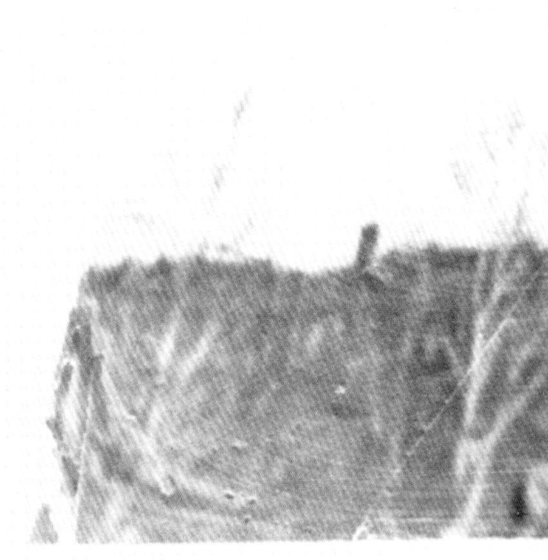

*Untitled (Laure on Easter Sunday)*, ca. 1989–91
Gelatin silver print with colored ink
11 × 14 in.

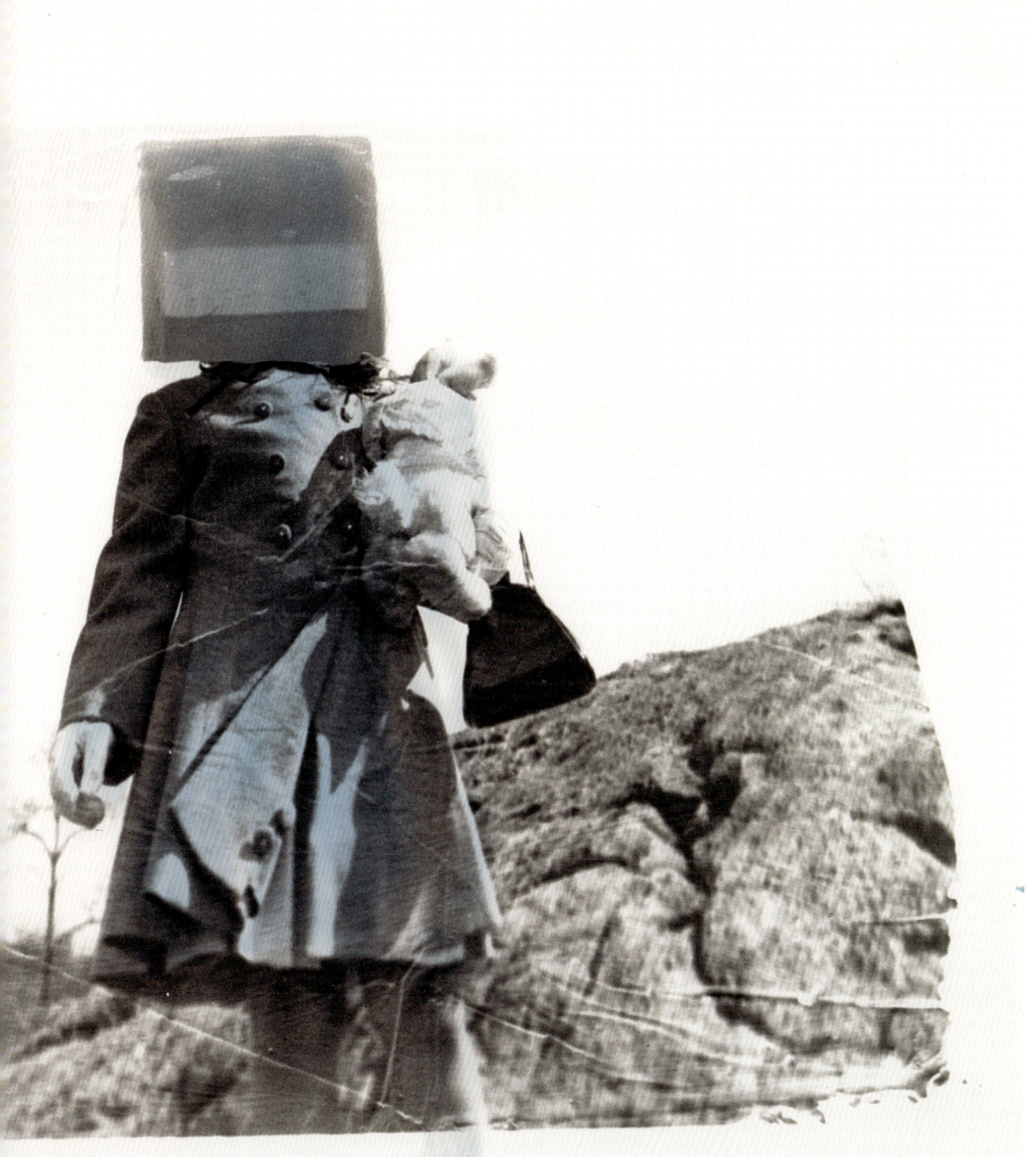

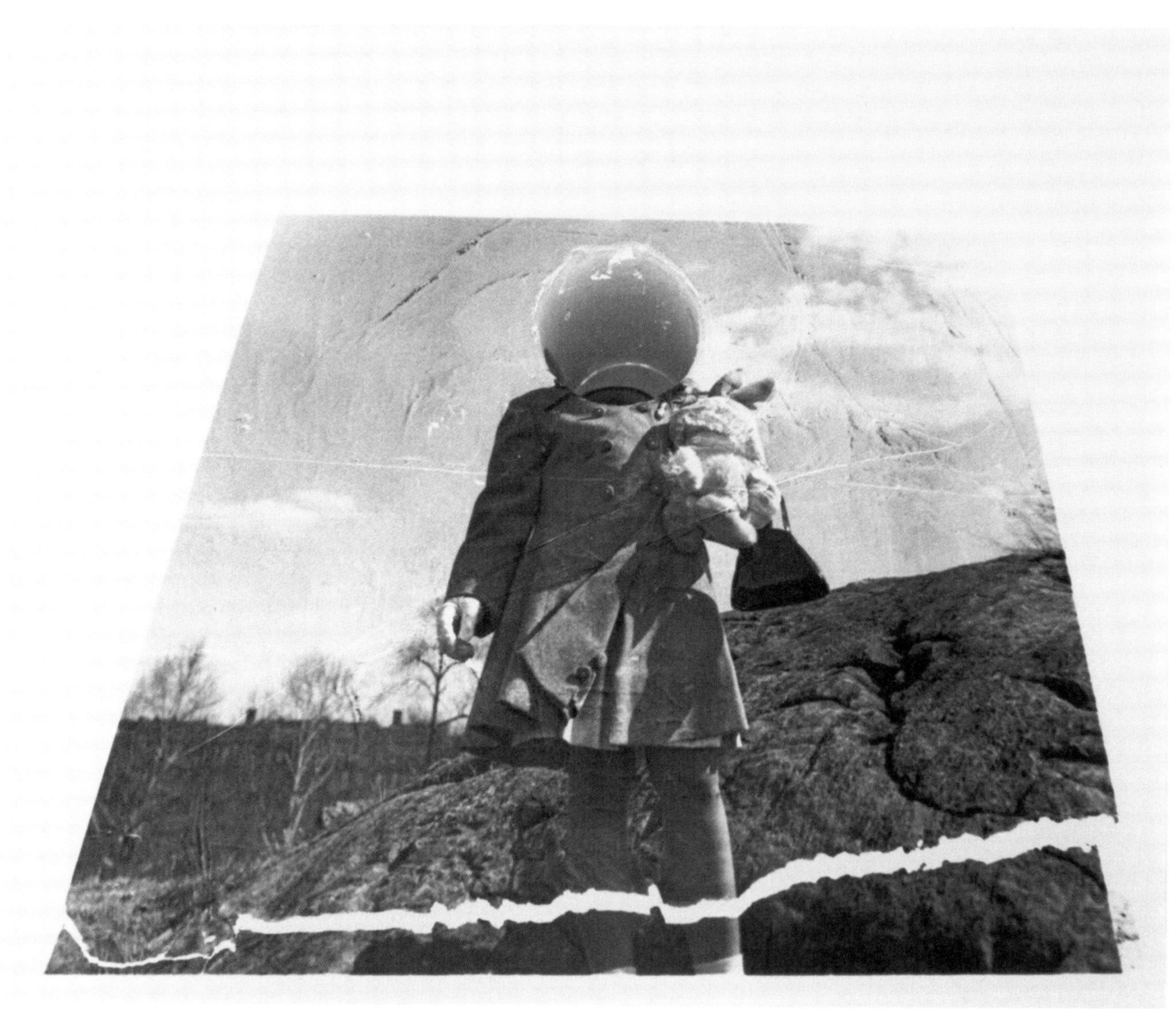

*Untitled (Laure on Easter Sunday)*, ca. 1989–91
Gelatin silver print
16 × 20 in.
The Bronx Museum of the Arts, New York
Gift of Joseph T. Baio

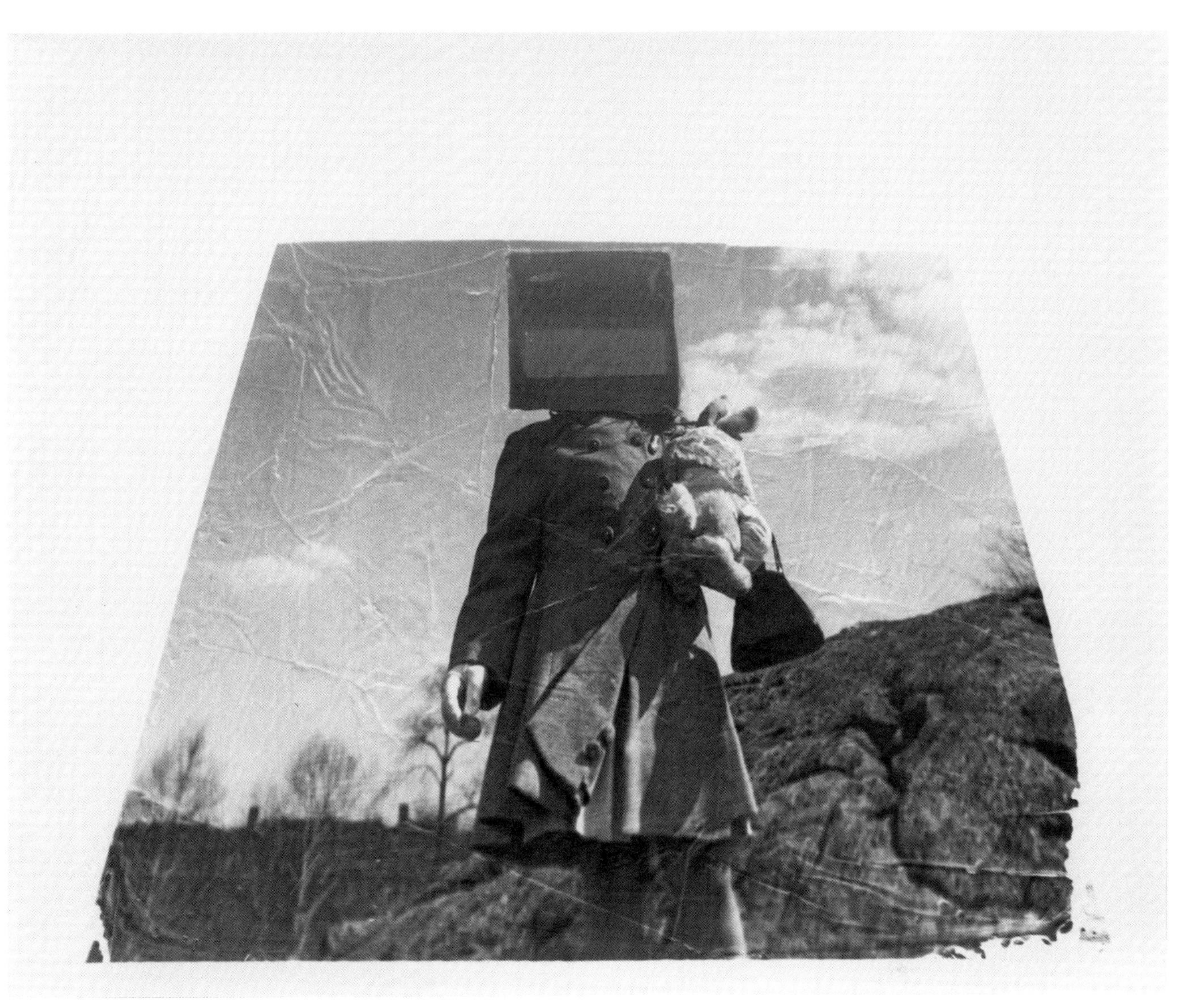

*Untitled (Laure on Easter Sunday)*, ca. 1989–91
Gelatin silver print
16 × 20 in.
The Bronx Museum of the Arts, New York
Gift of Scot and Julie Cohen

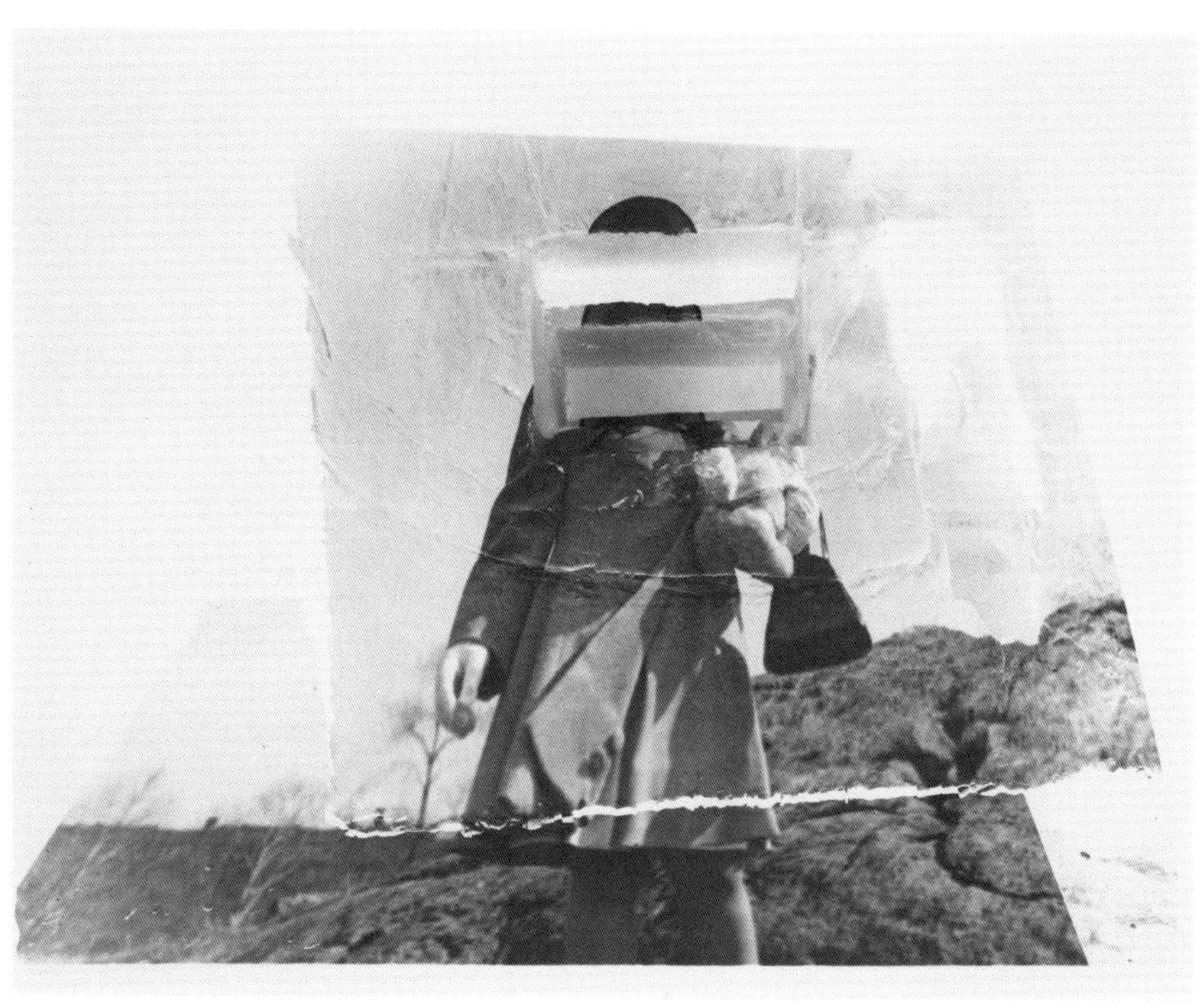

*Untitled (Laure on Easter Sunday)*, ca. 1989–91
Gelatin silver print
11 × 14 in.

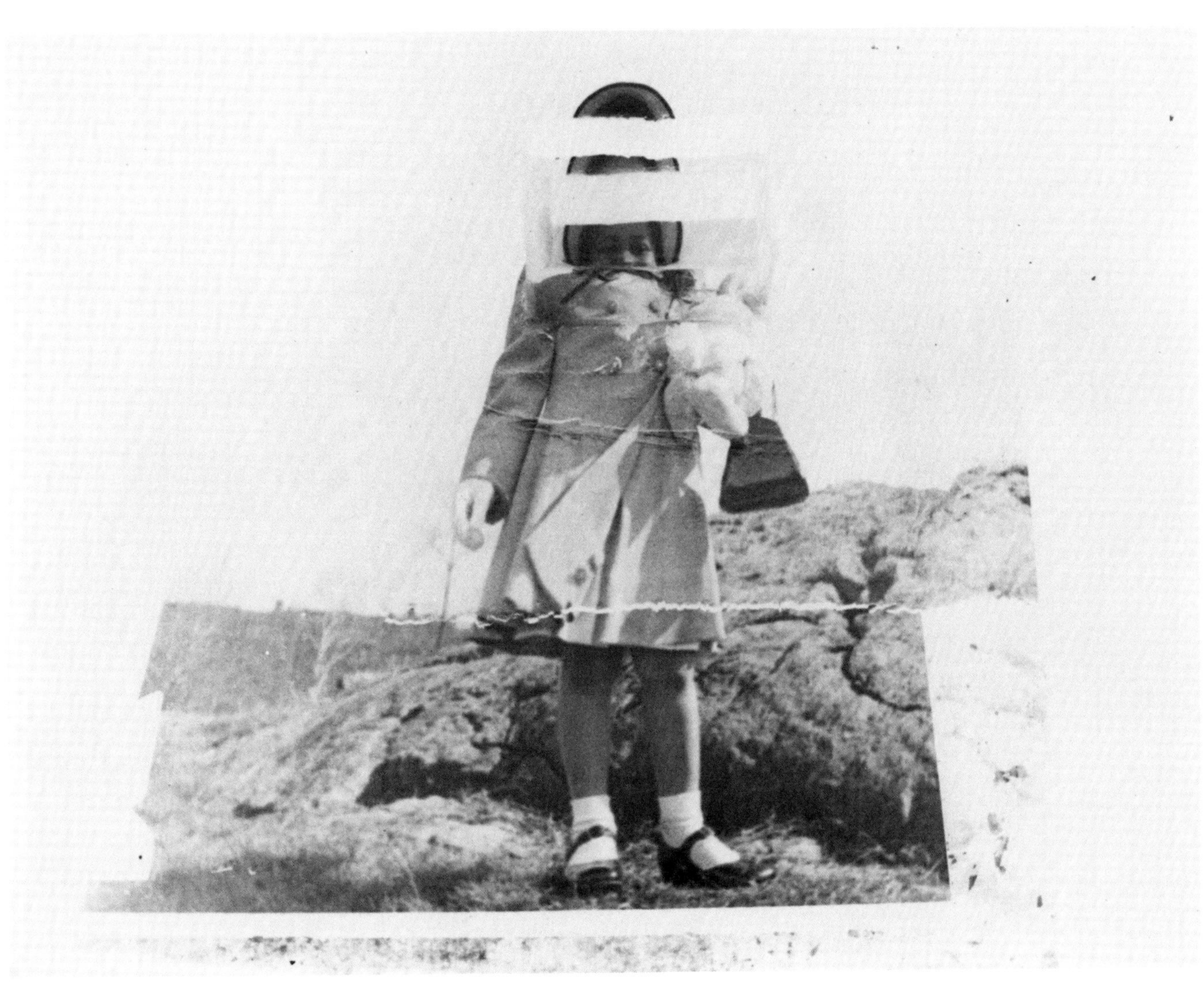

*Untitled (Laure on Easter Sunday)*, ca. 1989–91
Gelatin silver print
11 × 14 in.
Collection of Sebastian Daub

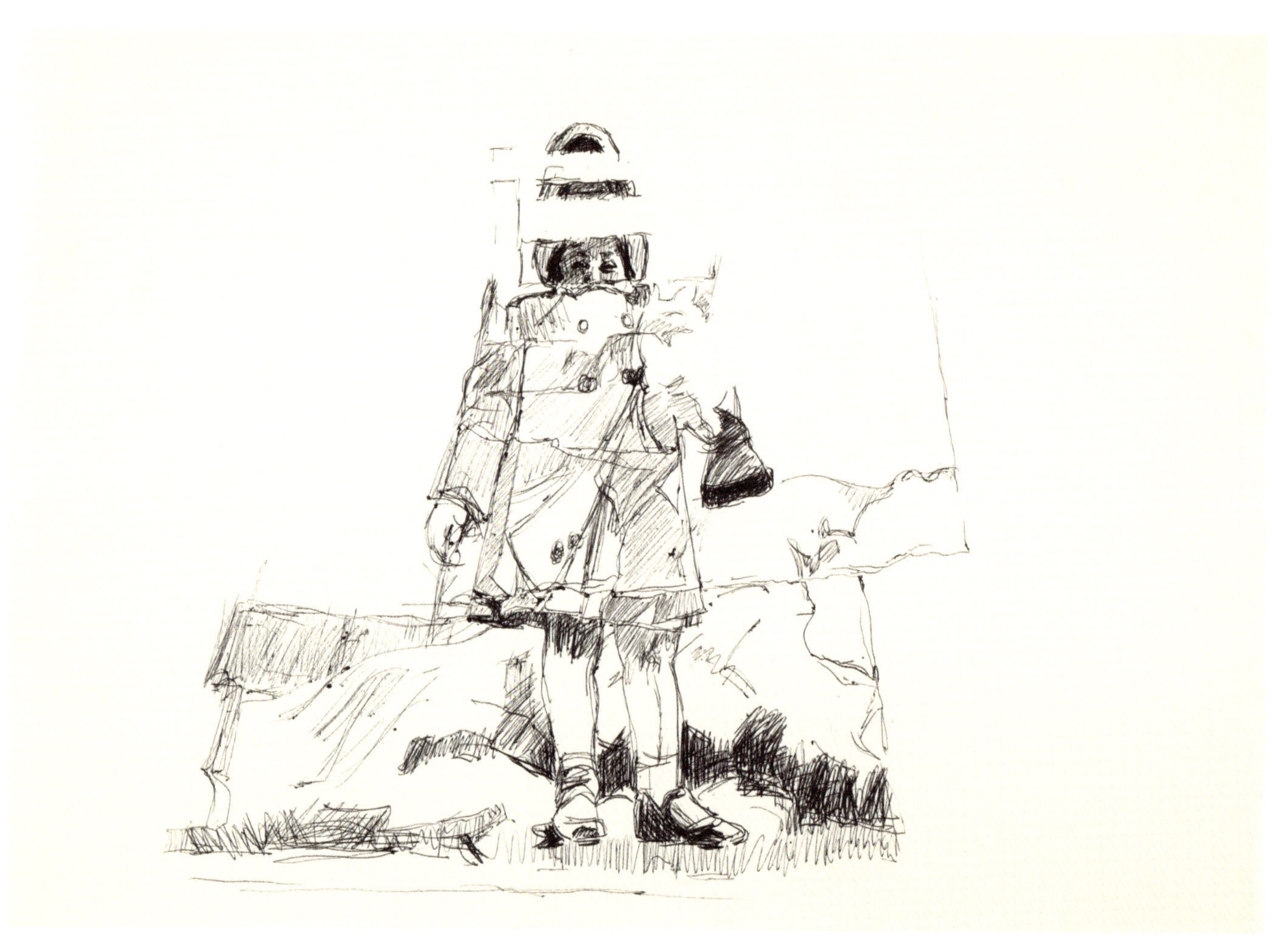

*Untitled (Laure on Easter Sunday)*, ca. 1989–91
Pen and black ink on paper
13 ¾ × 19 ¾ in.

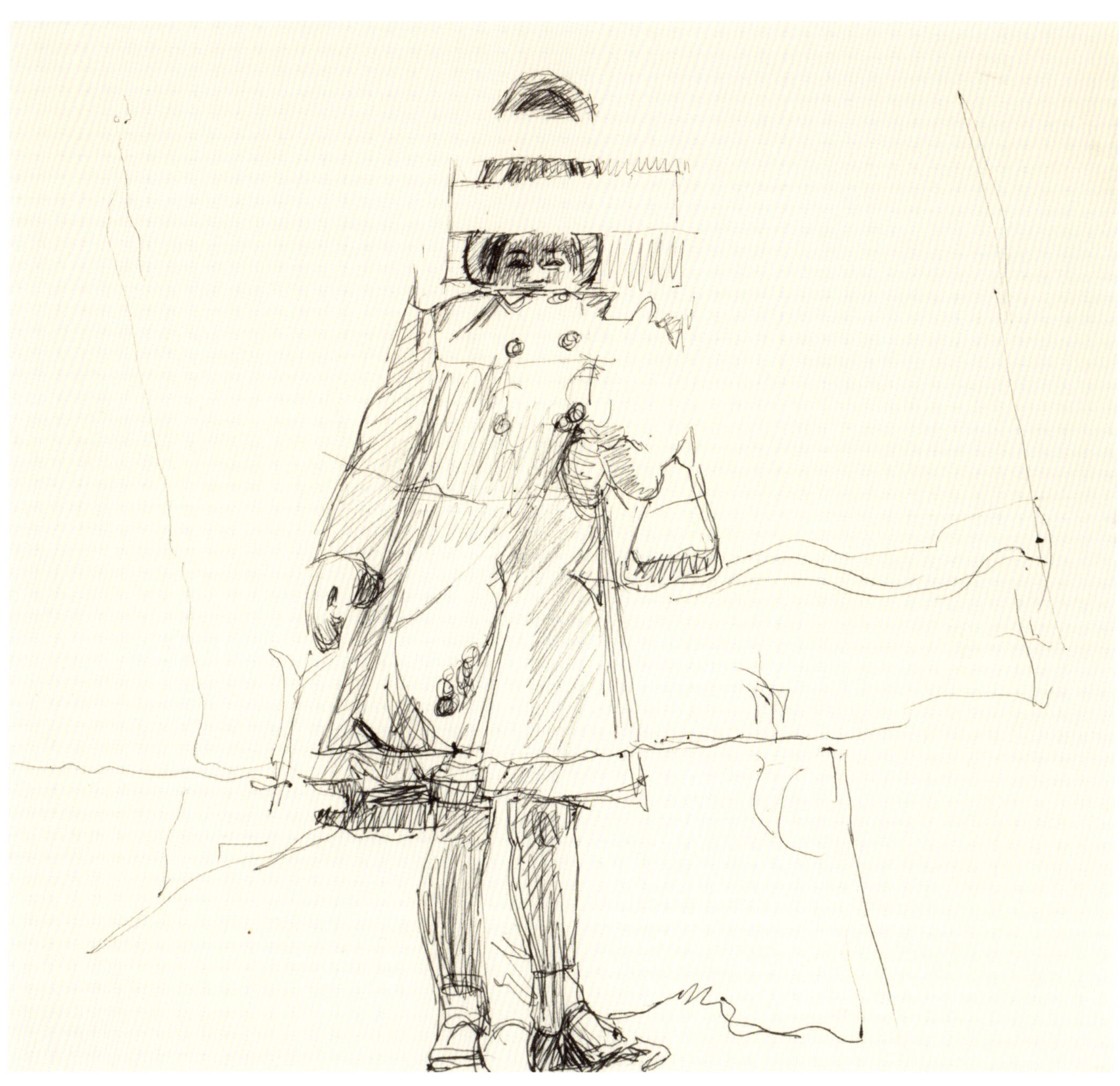

*Untitled (Laure on Easter Sunday)*, ca. 1989–91
Black roller ball pen
12 ¾ × 14 in.

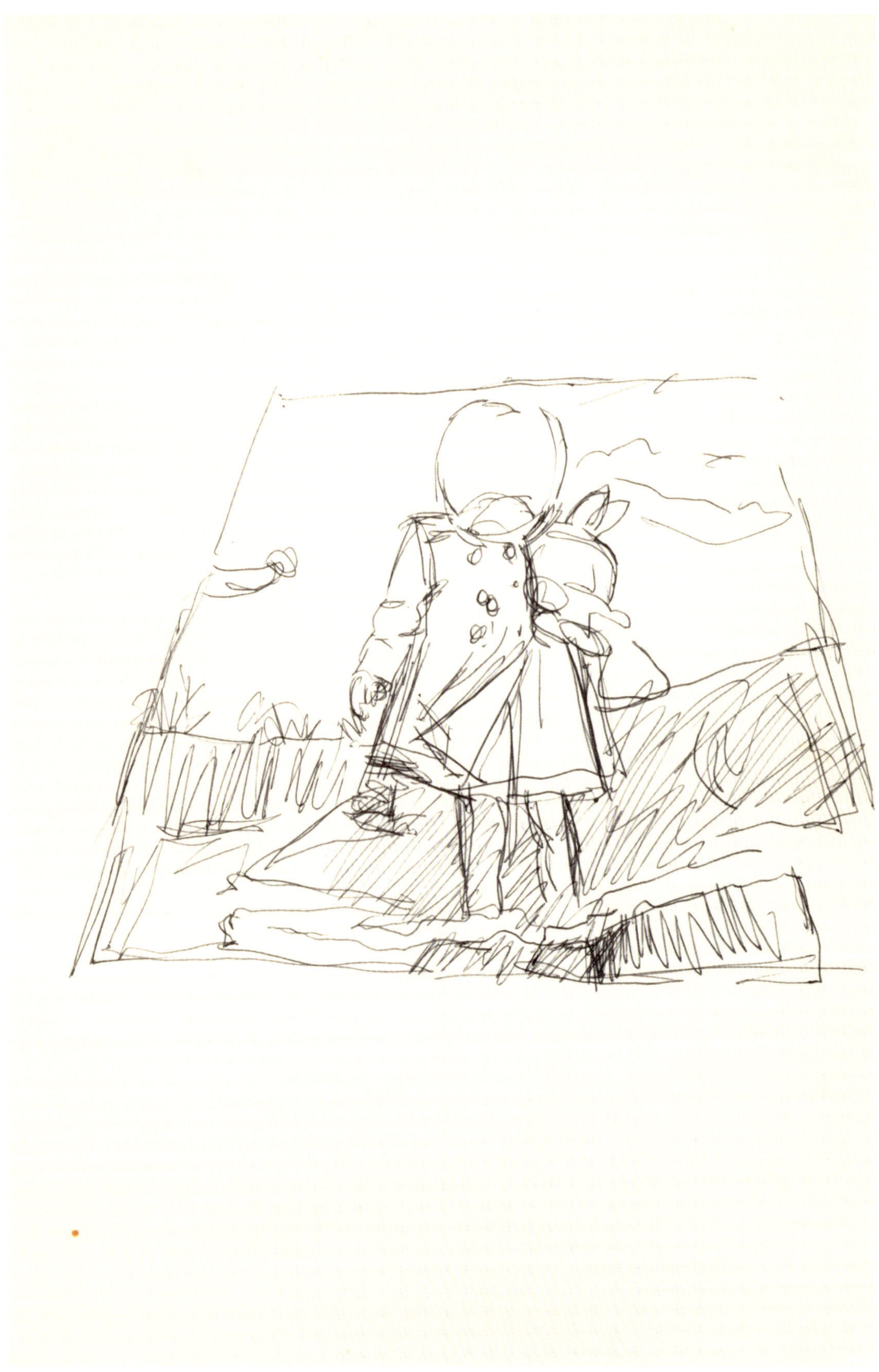

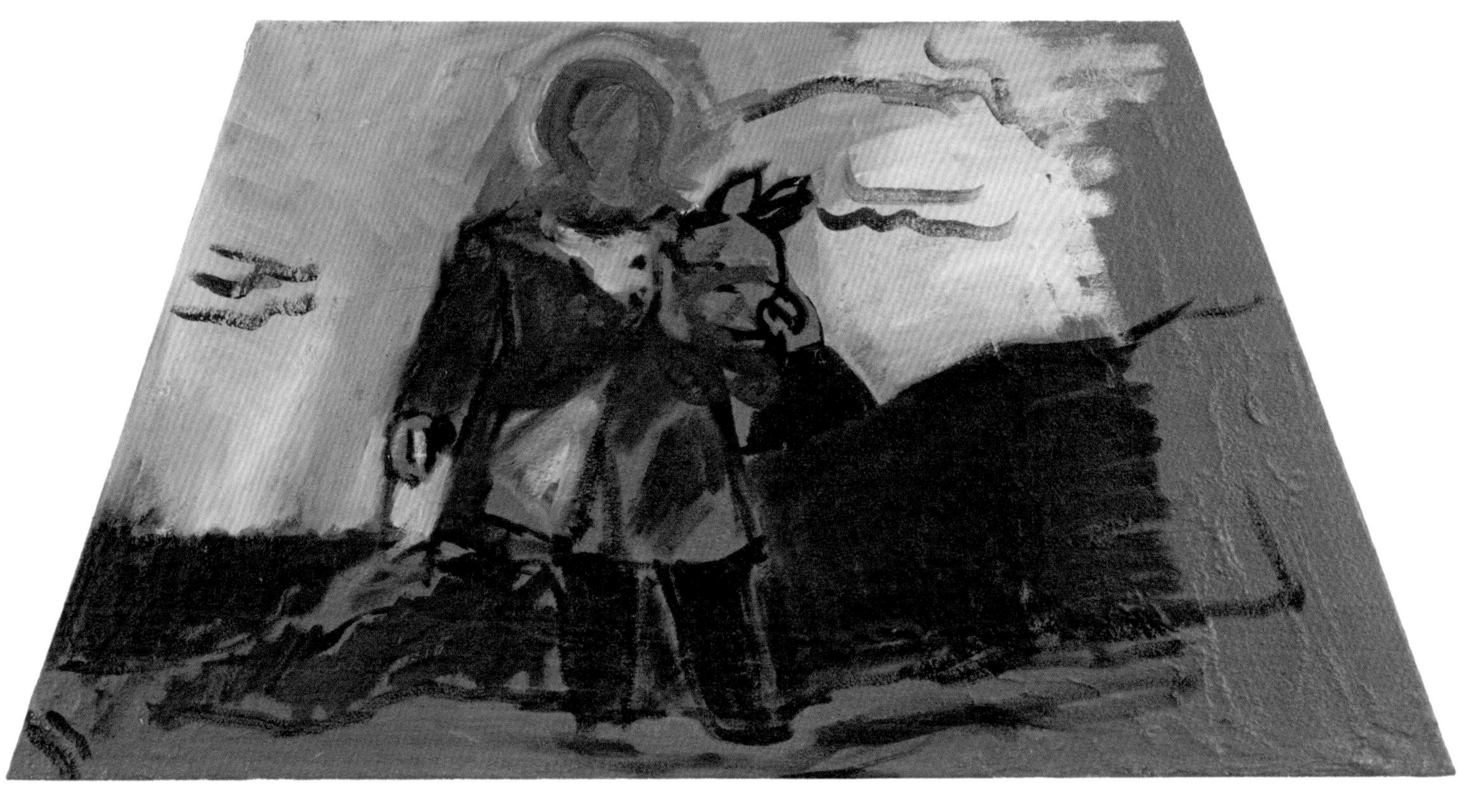

*Untitled (Laure on Easter Sunday)*, ca. 1989–91
Pen and black ink on paper
11 ½ × 7 ¾ in.

*Untitled (Laure on Easter Sunday)*, ca. 1989–91
Acrylic on canvas prepared with textured sand ground
21 ½ × 39 in.

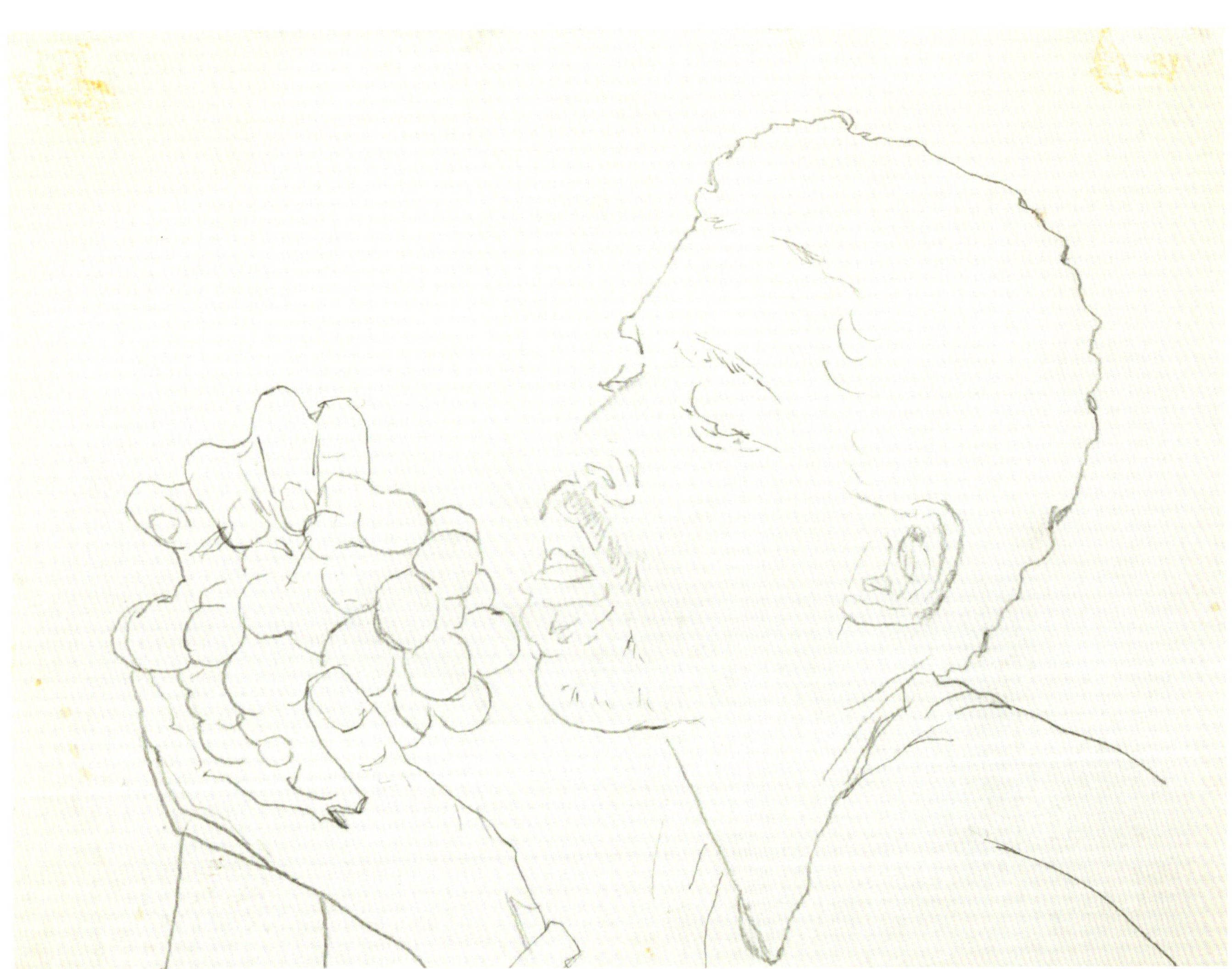

Allen Frame

# Uptown/Downtown: A Remembrance of Darrel Ellis

Already as an elementary school student in the South Bronx, Darrel Ellis was interested in drawing, copying from the Archie and Veronica comic books as a pastime. It was no surprise to his family that by high school he wanted to do fashion illustration and chose to go to High School of Fashion Industries downtown in Chelsea. According to his homeroom teacher, George Steinberg, the students there were almost all girls and Black. "There were so few boys that they stood out," he says. "Everyone knew who they were." He did some fashion illustrations throughout high school, but a teacher sent him and his classmate Miguel Ferrando to the Metropolitan Museum to sketch after the old masters.

At some point in those years, Darrel called his mother to tell her he was gay and that he had decided to leave home. His older sister Laure spoke to him and said she was neither surprised nor shocked, and that it was not a problem, so he moved back in. Darrel was seeing an older man around that time, a headmaster of a private school, who would sometimes send a car for him. "The man had money," Laure says, and Darrel had an account at Bloomingdale's. "He had Argyle sweaters and the socks to match." There's a two-page portrait of a bearded man with glasses in his book-lined apartment in one of the sketchbooks from this time, and on a page with his pencil self-portrait, Darrel wrote, "Dear Ken, I feel awful. I don't know why. Please love me. D." Around that time he started frequenting the 9th Circle, a gay bar on West 10th Street in Greenwich Village, always taking a sketchbook with him. Older men, like Metropolitan Museum curator Henry Geldzahler, whose name appears in one of the notebooks, and younger gays, some hustling, were part of the mix. There, in 1978, Darrel met photographer James Wentzy, who had come from South Dakota to apprentice with a film editor. James lived in a brownstone on Gates Avenue that had been renovated by an acquaintance who needed someone to take care of the property. It was an early instance of gentrification in Brooklyn and James, with his blonde hair and fair skin, says he "stuck out like a lit bulb at night." The A train felt so threatening that he found it safer to walk all the way across the Brooklyn Bridge to the West Village and back.

The following year, when Darrel was living with roommates on the Upper West Side and spending time exploring non-profit galleries in Lower Manhattan, he learned of a new studio program at PS1 in Long Island City. He and James decided to apply together, submitting a project related to rephotography and distortion. James used a large format camera to take a formal picture of Darrel sitting in his living room, which they projected over a mold, and captured the projection with a slide. The resulting work was sent together with their application. Darrel's roommate uptown at the time, dancer, and jazz musician Alan Bustweed, remembers the Eureka moment when Darrel came home, saying, "I've found it! I've found it!", holding a small piece of mesh covered with a lumpy surface of putty. He was going to project photos over it to fragment the image.

The PS1 studios were granted for a year, and there was a small monthly fee of about $45. In its second year, Darrel was the third Black artist to get a studio at PS1.

page 128
*Untitled (Self-Portrait)*, ca. 1989–91
Graphite on paper, 11 × 15 in.
Collection of Stephen Dull, Coral Gables, FL

James Wentzy in the attic of PS1,
ca. 1981. From a negative in the Estate
of Darrel Ellis

The selecting jury that year included curator Lowery Stokes Sims, the critic William Zimmer, and one of the artists in the program, Efrain de Jesús. The program was international, with artists from France, Spain, and Germany, who were supported by their governments. "I was shy," said James, "but Darrel was personable. He made friends with all the artists right away." Andrew Lyght, an artist from Guyana who had entered the program the previous year, remembers Darrel as "extremely reserved, and private, like myself . . . I think he was guarded about people seeing what he was doing. He was protecting his artistic secrets." Andrew was discreetly living there, as were about four others, and soon James and Darrel were living there too. They got permission to install a darkroom in a former nurse's room that had a bathroom, hiring a plumber to make the necessary retrofitting. James's father, like Darrel's, had also been a photographer and taught press photography in his hometown. In addition, James had studied still photography in high school, and later in college, and he felt confident enough to coach Darrel on camera and darkroom basics. Soon they started their proposed experiment of projecting images over sculptural forms. In one notable collaboration, Darrel helped James make a plaster cast of James's lower front torso and James projected a nude slide of one of his friends over it, then photographed the projected image.

Darrel and James applied for a year extension, justifying it by saying that too much time had been lost in building the darkroom and, what's more, that their interests now diverged. They were granted separate studios and James moved to an upper floor. Not a committed couple, their relationship was, according to James, "more like occasional randy companions." James remembers that Darrel was "easily amused," except for the time James threw a phone down the hallway at him because of an unpaid phone bill. "He wasn't quite so amused over that, but he earnestly said, 'I'll pay the bill! I'll pay the bill!'" During his second year at PS1, Darrel met the Colombian actor José Rafael Arango and moved into his East 4th Street apartment, on the same block as La MaMa Experimental Theatre Club, where José sometimes performed. The son of a plantation-owning family in Medellin, José was a striking actor with a strong temperament, and performed with important downtown playwrights and directors, such as Maria Irene Fornés and Charles Ludlam, while working during the day as a Spanish translator for court cases. Agosto Machado, the legendary performer who lived across the street, remembers that on a warm night with José's window open, you could hear their voices in heated arguments, José resorting to Spanish and Darrel yelling at him to speak English. Their tumultuous affair had ended by the fall of 1981 when I met Darrel at The Bar, on Second Avenue down the street. Formerly an Israeli café, The Bar had opened around 1978 and was a low-key destination for actors, artists, and writers who mingled around its pool table.

My apartment in the West Village was a fifth-floor walkup on Perry Street, with artworks from artist friends hanging everywhere, most impressively a large sculptural piece over the bed, lent to me by Ken Tisa. When Darrel entered my apartment, he looked around and asked, "Who are YOU?" I was amused because, like my roommate Butch Walker, also from Mississippi, I was supporting myself cleaning apartments, but I had curated one big show the year before at a hair salon in Tribeca called Jungle Red Studios that included the work of many friends, such as Tisa, Zamba Gomez, John Heys, Frank Moore, Nan Goldin, Jody Guralnick, Kenny Scharf, and Robert Gober. Darrel had just been accepted at the Whitney Program on Lower Broadway, and he wanted me to come and see his work. In his transition from PS1, Darrel arrived at the Whitney two months late, but his studio was already filled with paintings and drawings on the walls and photos spread out on the floor. He had

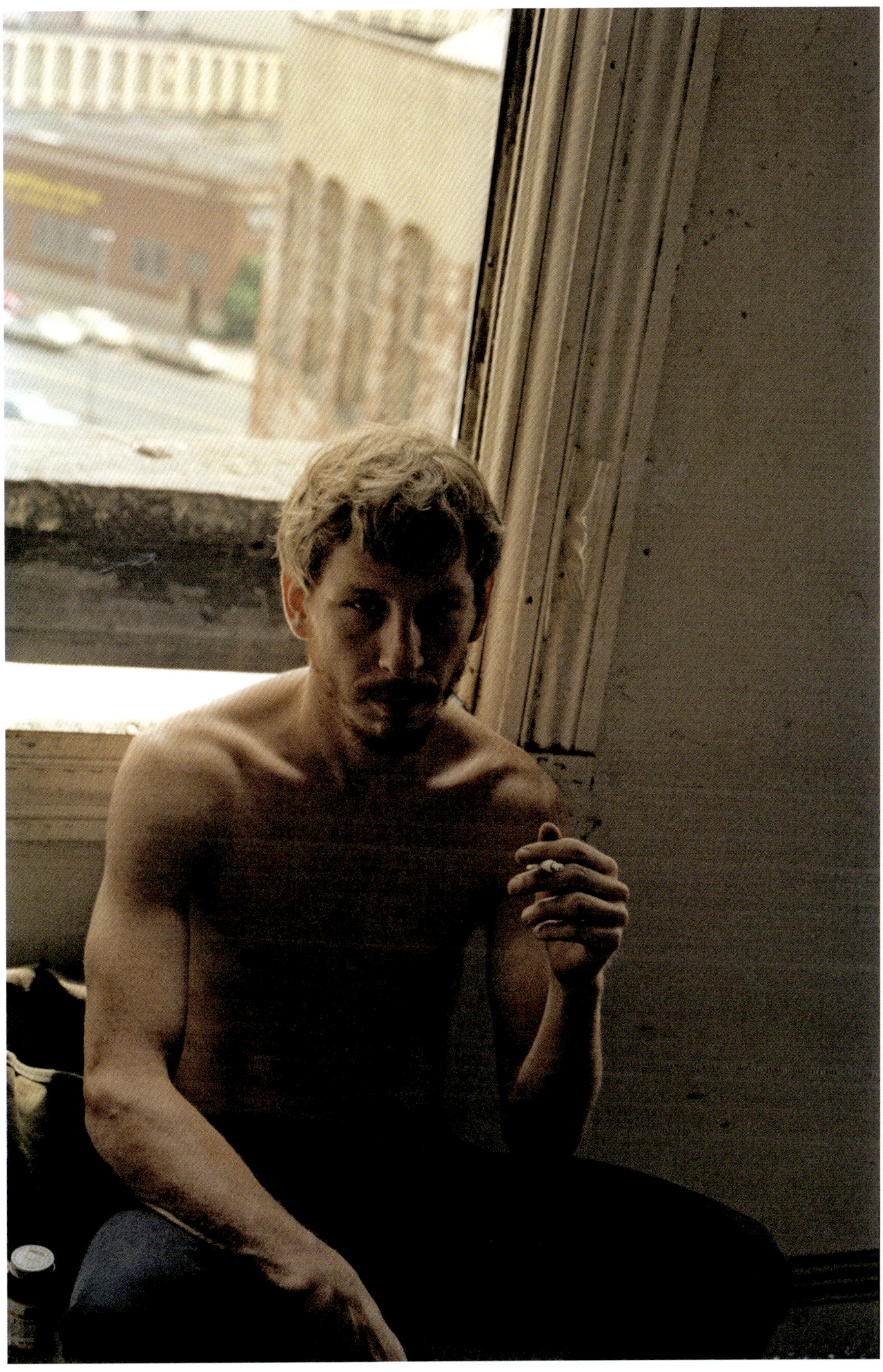

recently discovered a trove of negatives made in the 1950s by his father and was making contact sheets from them. Thomas Ellis had participated in Camera Club competitions, submitting still life and studio photographs, but his family portraiture looked more interesting both to me and Darrel: women posing at family parties, a group toasting at a wedding, a family picnic in the park, a brother-in-law passed out drunk on the bed—they were more dynamic and composed than the average family pictures.

Lauren Stringer and Darrel were the only figurative painters in the program at the time. Lauren remembers that when Darrel started, Ron Clark, the program director, told the group, "We have another artist coming, and I want you all to be really kind to him." He was probably thinking how hard it was to enter a small group like that after the initial bonding had occurred, in addition to the fact that Darrel was the only Black artist, and the only one who was openly gay. A sizeable space that had been used for supplies was cleared out for Darrel's studio, next to which was a darkroom. German artist Annebarbe Kau recalls that Darrel seemed awkward and shy, and that he was mostly in his studio working when he was there. In fact, there was not a lot of hanging out, in general, Lauren remembers; still, they exchanged frequent studio visits and had many conversations about their work and artists they were looking at. Lauren was experimenting with the use of text. "I had been doing figurative work with a lot of words, because of all the reading we were doing in the program. There were always words, large or small, passing through the heads of the figure, the faces, the bodies." There were weekly meetings where Ron Clark would lead discussions about heady readings he would hand out—from Lacan, Derrida, Barthes, Brecht, Freud, John Berger, Merleau-Ponty, Rosalind Krauss, Douglas Crimp, Benjamin Buchloh, and others—but Darrel did not come to them. He did show up for some of Yvonne Rainer's weekly seminars in which she talked about film noir, female directors, the femme fatale, and the female gaze. She would take them to screenings at Film Forum, which was doing a series that year on the Western.

At the time, Lauren was assisting painter Judy Rifka who was best friends with poet and influential art critic René Ricard, notorious for creating scandals in print as well as at gallery openings. In December 1981, his

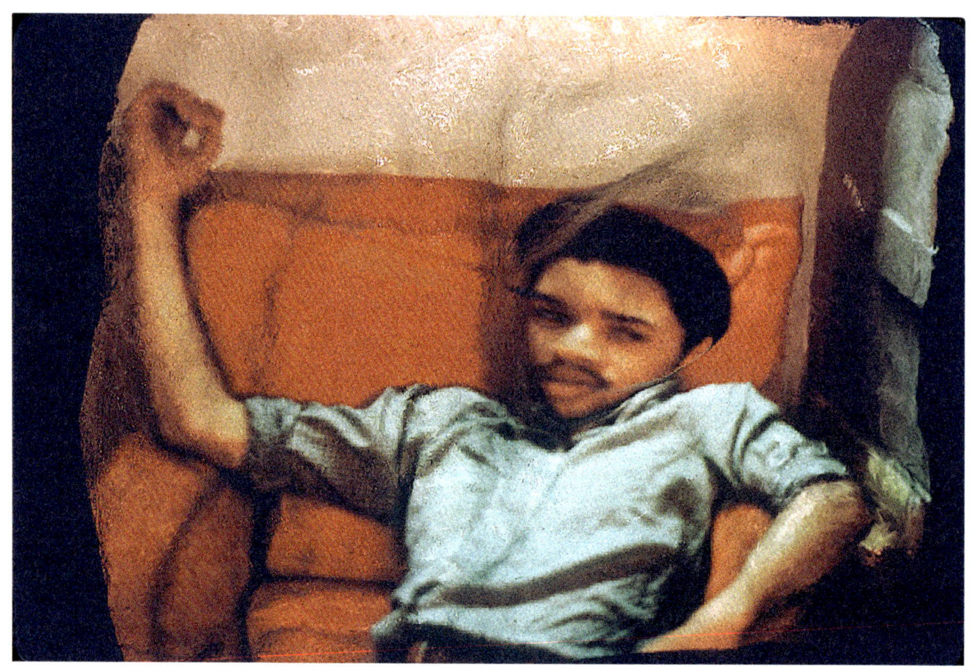

An early experiment with rephotography, produced collaboratively by Ellis and Wentzy for their residency application to PS1, 1979. From a Kodachrome slide in the archive of James Wentzy

career-making *Artforum* piece "Radiant Child" appeared, lavishing attention on Jean-Michel Basquiat, Judy Rifka, Keith Haring, and John Ahearn; Ahearn would become a close friend of Darrel's through Fashion Moda. Lauren would encounter Ricard at Rifka's frequently. "I would go in the morning and make coffee and the two of them would drag themselves out of bed," she remembers. "They always slept in the same bed. They weren't lovers; it was just, 'Oh, c'mon, let's just sleep together.' I would make them coffee, they would talk about whatever had happened the night before, and I'd be stretching canvases for Judy." When the Whitney group insisted on having an Open Studio at the end of the program, a first time because Ron Clark was opposed to it, Rifka and Ricard came, along with Colab artists like Kiki Smith and Tom Otterness who had just made a splash with their *Times Square Show* in 1980. "So, it was like a big to-do because there were all these 'big artists' that were coming," says Lauren, "and I do remember a lot of people gathering in Darrel's studio. Maybe it was because he had a lot of work up, and there was a lot to look at and talk about. I remember René Ricard was talking with him quite a bit."

Right after we met, Darrel got a bad cold, so we did not see each other for a few days. He was back at José's, and I offered to bring him chicken soup. When I got there, he asked me to sit down at a long table, and from the other end began to do my portrait in pen and ink. When he finished, he gave it to me and said he did not want to see me anymore. Our fling was over before it began. Darrel seemed irritated by my casual lack of ardor. I did not argue, and instead, we became friends. Butch and I would have brunches that were just an excuse for me to photograph everyone in daylight because I was shooting in color. Darrel came to them and met our friends—performer John Heys, writers Bill Jacobson, Jane Warrick, and Susan Heeger, and artists Coco Ugaz, Charlie Boone, Cady Noland, Frank Moore, Jody Guralnick, and Dan Mahoney—then, in turn, introduced me to his friends: Lauren Stringer, whom I met at their Whitney Open Studio, Miguel Ferrando, and the Swiss artist Not Vital, who had briefly hired Darrel as an assistant and became a lifelong friend. Not bought some of Darrel's early experimental photographs and introduced him to his friend Flurin von Albertini, who also bought Darrel's work throughout the decade.

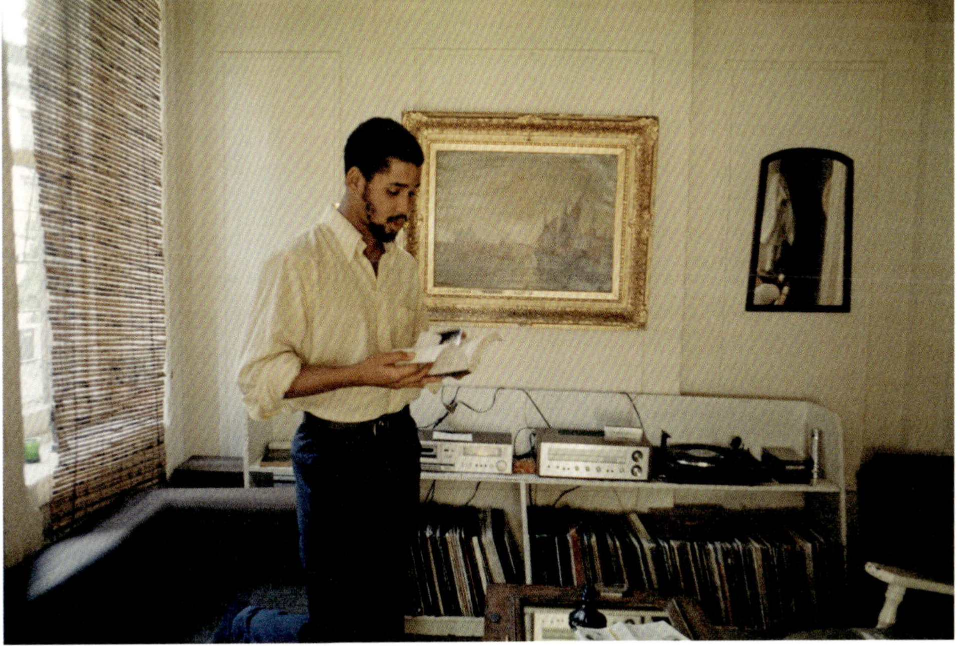

Allen Frame, *Darrel Ellis in José Rafael Arango's Apartment*, 1981
Chromogenic print, 11 × 14 in.
Collection of the artist

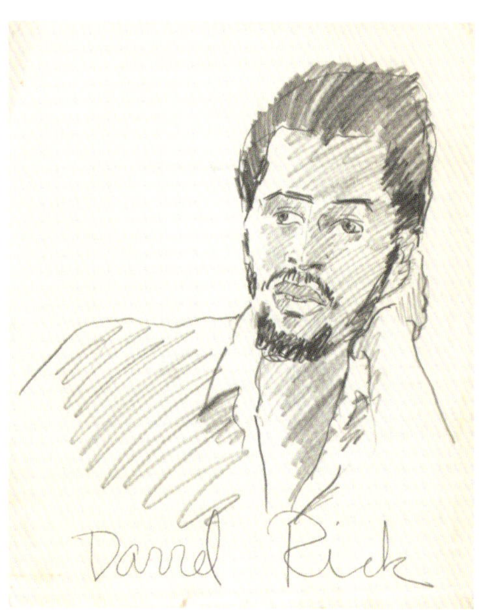


Richard Brintzenhofe, *Darrel Ellis*, ca. 1979
Graphite on paper, 17 × 14 in.
Estate of Darrel Ellis

Darrel had met Not through his friend Richard Brintzenhofe, who was assistant to Malcolm Morley. Rick was lovers with Miguel Ferrando and introduced both Miguel and Darrel to Morley, whom they assisted briefly. Rick, Miguel, and Darrel were all avid sketchers from life, as well as after the old masters, but Darrel was more figurative than Miguel and Rick, who were more prone to still life and landscape. Rick was close to Peter Hujar, and it was probably through him that Darrel met Hujar, who photographed him in the same weekend as Robert Mapplethorpe in 1980. Photographer Frank Franca remembers the impact Darrel made physically. "The thing that made him stunning," he says, "was the color of his eyes. From the moment you looked at him, there was something ethereal. His eyes were the color of honey, very luminous." In the meantime, Darrel had moved back to his mother's apartment in the Bronx, where his younger siblings Katrina and Kim still lived. His mother had separated from Joseph Stewart, her second husband, and she and Darrel were both single again, seeing people and comparing notes. "My mother loved Darrel," says Laure. "We could always sit down and talk with him. He was very unassuming and a lot of fun."

Darrel began to explore the South Bronx art scene that centered around Fashion Moda, the art space cofounded in 1978 by Stefan Eins and Joe Lewis in a former furniture store at 149th Street and Third Avenue. There he met John Ahearn and Wendell Headley, a street provocateur who would create flamboyant, carnivalesque outfits and wear them in public. Katrina remembers Wendell wearing his creations when he would come to their apartment, undaunted by the stares he would get. Wendell had grown up with middle-class foster parents in White Plains until he was ten, when his father got custody of him and brought him to the Bronx.

At Fashion Moda, Darrel also met Susan Spencer Crowe, who was volunteering for Eins and Lewis, but soon became director of the Lower East Side Printshop, which had been set up as a community-based workshop in 1968 and had a Minority Artists Workshop. There, Joe Lewis initiated a series of silkscreen books, for which Darrel produced a book of his own photographs of family members in the Bronx apartment—unposed portraits in the kitchen, living room, and bedrooms, as they went about their daily lives. According to Lewis, "[Darrel] was very specific about the work that he wanted to put into the book . . . it was kind of an homage, really, to the relationship he had with his mother, at that home." His father's photos had shown him how powerful family photos could be. He had also seen, in Nan Goldin's work and mine, the trend towards photographing the friends and lovers in one's own world, and years earlier, he had come to love the figurative interiors of Edouard Vuillard and Pierre Bonnard, before that kind of intimate, domestic imagery became significant in photography.

Now, through his connections to Germany (artists he met at PS1, at the Whitney Program, and at Fashion Moda), Darrel was invited to participate in a group show in Cologne. When the show traveled to a second venue in Brühl in 1986, he decided to go to Europe. By this time, at age twenty-seven, he had participated in three prestigious residencies, had been published in *Bomb* magazine twice, had had exhibitions at Fashion Moda in the Bronx and Christminster in the East Village (a gallery Butch Walker had become a partner in), and had met New York's most ambitious emerging artists. He thought it was time to leave New York for good, or at least for a long while. "I remember he bought a one-way ticket," says Laure. "He wasn't planning on coming back. He was determined that he was not going to stay here. Whatever he was looking for, it wasn't here."

Darrel came to London first. I had moved there in the fall of 1985 and was living with photographer Frank Franca in a basement sublet in Earl's Court. Darrel arrived with a young German named Thomas whom he had met on the plane, his blonde hair down to the middle of his back. They locked themselves in

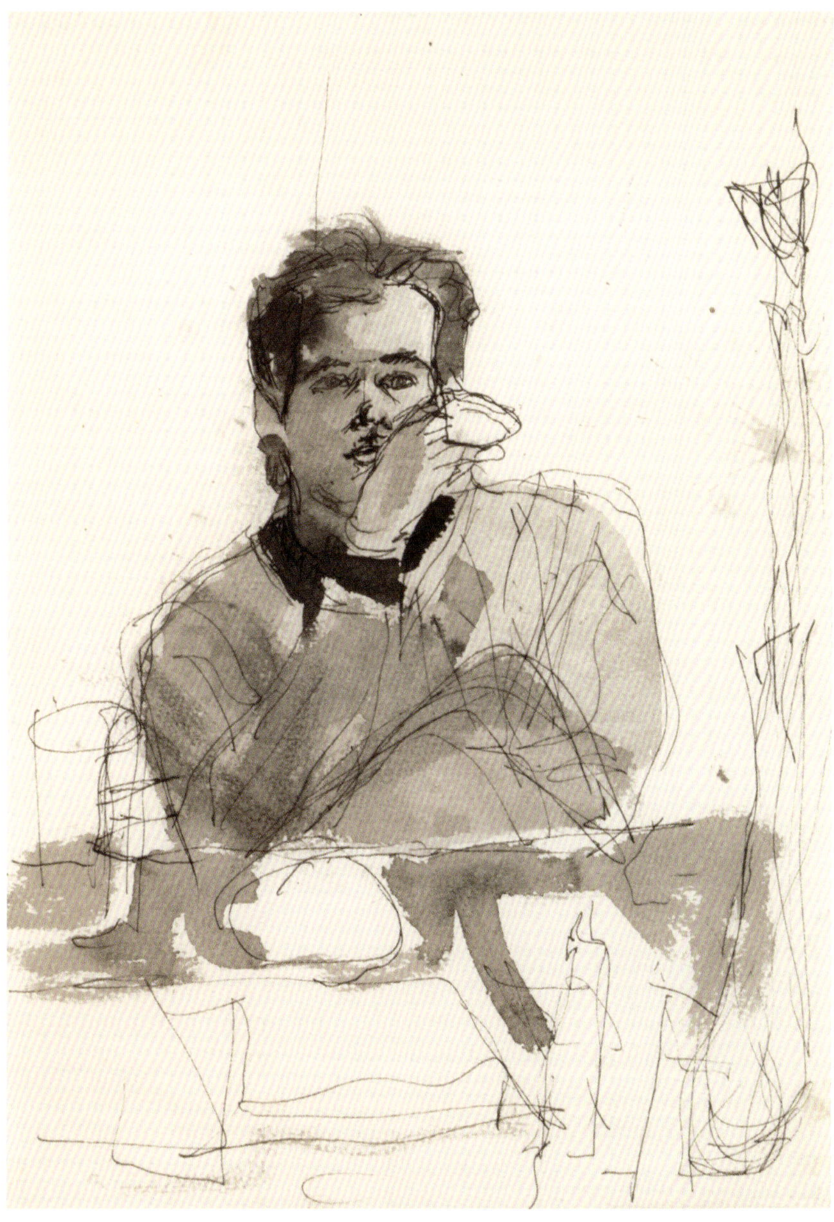

*Untitled (Allen Frame)*, 1981
Pen and brush and black ink and wash on paper, 14 × 9 ¾ in.
Collection of Allen Frame

a bedroom until Thomas was ready to leave for Cologne the next day. In the following two weeks Darrel met, and sketched, several of our friends: writer/actor Bertie Marshall; filmmaker Paulita Sedgwick (Edie Sedgwick's cousin); and theatrical lighting designer Paule Constable (a descendant of the painter John Constable). Brian Britton invited him to Streatham for a studio visit. "He was beaming with delight at this British ritual of sitting around a table to have tea and cakes in the late afternoon," recalls Brian. We went to museums and took a day trip to the coast in Cornwall. He stayed for two weeks, and then was off to Brühl, arriving early. He had planned to stay there until the exhibition opened, but the curator was nonplussed and sent him away, so he went to Berlin, where he met a cooperative of women who welcomed him into their squat.

From there Darrel visited his young lover Thomas and sent a postcard back to Miguel that said:

> I'm in Berlin now. Last week I was in a German city called Tubingen. There I saw a great Toulouse Lautrec show of drawings and paintings. I was staying with a 20-year-old German boy I met on the plane. He invited me to stay at his home with his mother and father. I've seen a lot of art in Koln. The new museum is fabulous and expensive and cost a lot to get in. I will go back to Koln later on. The young man's name is Thomas, and we sort of fell in love. Though I don't want to. I want to be alone without the dependence that comes from being "involved." I've been drawing a lot. Finished one of the sketchbooks. People like the drawings. I'm a little lonely. I don't speak German which is rough. Thomas is going to Nicaragua for two months, then returns. So things are cooking. Wish you were here. You'd love it.
> Darrel

Then a circled postscript: *Thomas was just one of those things.*

The show opened at the Orangerie in Brühl, but Darrel was broke and had to call his mother for money to come home. By then, she was about to move to Mount Vernon, New York, with Tony Fark, a corrections officer she had been seeing at the time. Before leaving, she helped Darrel get a smaller apartment in the same building. He had started working as a security guard at the Museum of Modern Art and could pay the rent; but his brother Kim, and then his

John Ahearn, *Darrel Ellis*, 1982
Graphite on paper, 8 ½ × 11 in.
Estate of Darrel Ellis

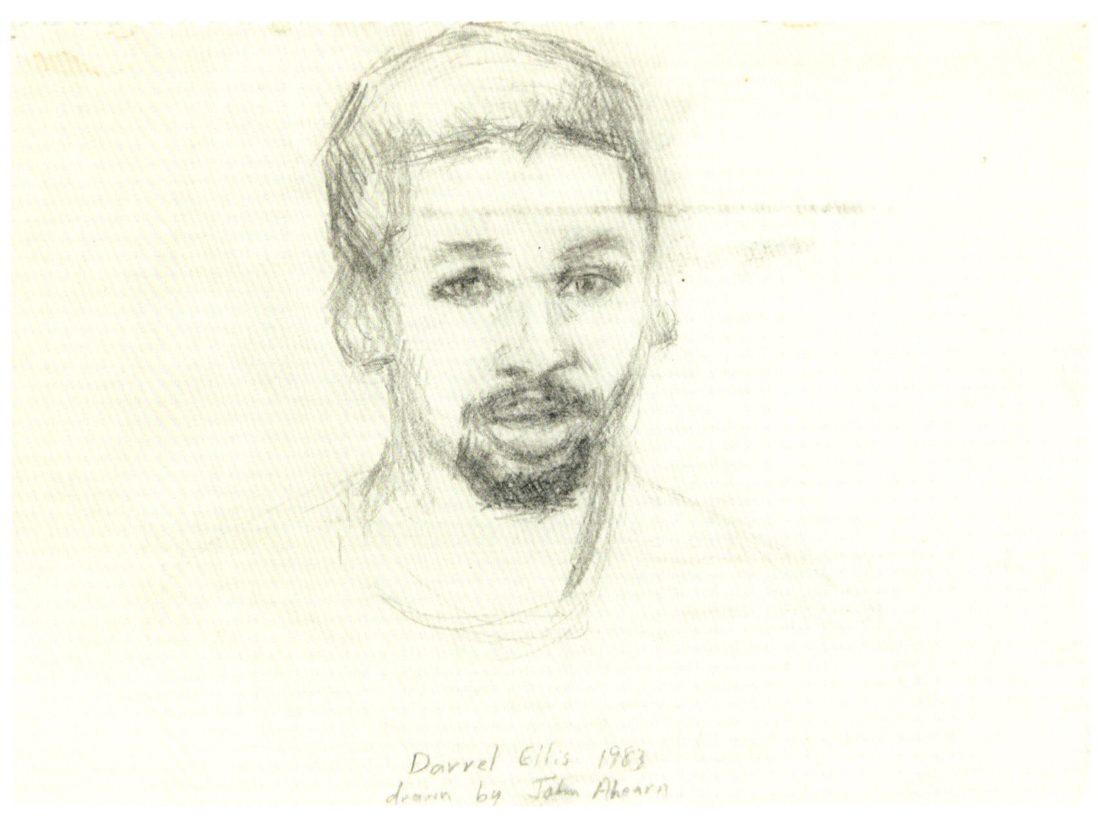


stepfather Joseph Stewart, also moved in, and Darrel realized he had to look for a place to himself. He found an apartment in Greenpoint, Brooklyn, through an artist he knew from PS1, Bruce Dow, who owned a building there. Darrel had gone back to experimenting with photographs, as he had done at PS1. This time they were ones that he had taken of his mother in her bedroom, lying on the bed watching television, or standing at the window. Katrina was sometimes depicted, too, with several friends. The fragmented compositions would then become the basis for subsequent drawings, prints, and paintings. Achieving a kind of conceptual abstraction with his own imagery, he then applied the same technique to his father's work, choosing a small selection of photographs to work from, repeating the imagery through a succession of variations and media. His new independence had led to a creative breakthrough and outpouring of work.

Bruce Dow's studio was in the storefront next door, and Susan Spencer Crowe lived down the street and had a studio nearby. "One night when I was going to my studio," she says, "Darrel stopped me and said, 'You can't go to your studio. You have to come over and see what I have.' . . . I went up and he had the photograph of the dog, the family pet. That's the first thing I saw when I walked in the apartment, and then he started showing me other things. And I said, 'This is really good work! You should be showing these.'" Peter Galassi, chief curator of photography at MoMA, made time to look at Darrel's work, and Darrel brought some of his father's photographs to show him as well. According to Susan, though, he was so mad after his visit that he came home in a huff. "He said Peter didn't even look at the work. I said, 'Darrel, it doesn't happen that quickly.' He was upset." Peter told Susan that when he met with him, Darrel spent most of the time showing him Thomas Ellis's work. "I certainly was very careful not to raise an artist's expectations about a show or an acquisition—anything, really—until I knew for certain I could deliver," says Peter. "I very much regret that I wasn't able to give Darrel some good news."

Around this time, Darrel learned that he was HIV-positive but did not tell anyone. In 1989, Nan Goldin invited us to be in the exhibition she was curating for Artists Space, *Witnesses: Against Our Vanishing*, for which she asked artist friends to respond to the AIDS pandemic. Darrel decided to work from the photographs that Mapplethorpe and Hujar had made of him in 1980. They had each given him a print, and he exhibited them in the show, above the paintings that he made from them. Stunning photographs, his mediation of them was poignant and confronting: the model talks back, pronounces his own truth. The sense of his own mortality was heightened by the fact that both photographers had recently died from AIDS-related causes, Hujar in 1987, and Mapplethorpe in 1989. There was a media storm around the show. The NEA had withdrawn funding from it because of an essay David Wojnarowicz had written for the catalogue, excoriating Senator Jesse Helms, and Cardinal John O'Connor for their irresponsible, homophobic positions on AIDS. When I dropped off my work at Artists Space, news anchors were waiting at the door, hoping to interview one of the participants, not understanding that the controversy was about the essay, not the works being shown. Darrel's painting of himself from the Mapplethorpe photograph was then widely used in the publicity for the show and was published in *The New York Times*.

The attention he received for these self-portraits led him to make others. He asked me to photograph him in Greenpoint to give him source material. He also made his own self-portrait photographs, role-playing as a militant, a beggar, a Caravaggesque hedonist, and posing in his MoMA security guard uniform. Just as he learned that he had won an artist's grant from the New York Foundation for the Arts in 1991, he was hospitalized with AIDS-related pneumonia and went into a coma, but came out of it, sharing his situation finally with family and close friends. He was too ill to keep working at MoMA but continued his prolific production at home. He had made enough photographs from his father's work to have a solo show at

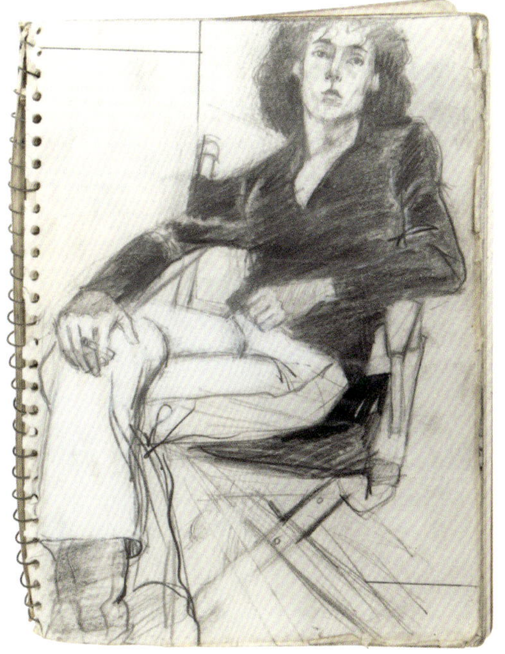

Sketch of Miguel Ferrando from a notebook of Darrel Ellis, 1976

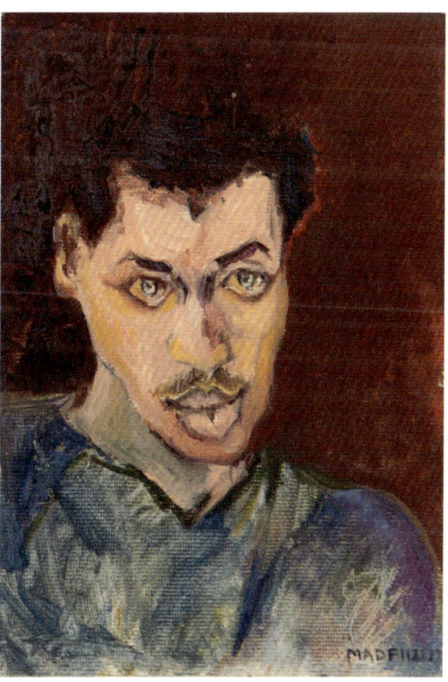

Miguel Ferrando, *Darrel Ellis*, 1977
Acrylic on canvas, 7 × 5 in.
Estate of Darrel Ellis

Baron/Boisanté, a gallery on 57th Street. And his mother, who had developed diabetes after getting married again, passed away in 1991.

Rick Brintzenhofe, who from 1980–85 lived mostly in Zurich, where most of his exhibitions happened, had moved to an apartment on Fourth Avenue in Brooklyn and was painting a group portrait of almost twenty of his gay friends, invoking the sense of despair we all lived with during the AIDS pandemic. Darrel, Frank Franca, and I went over to pose for it. It was a somber situation, but Rick was upbeat. So many of our friends and acquaintances had died, and here we were, sharing a collective identity around that loss and terror instead of feeling the bright future we had expected a decade earlier when we had met. When the finished painting was shown in Rick's exhibition *Voir* a year later at the Centre d'Art Contemporain, in Martigny, Switzerland, the critic Hélène Tauvel-Dorsaz wrote:

> One of the most striking canvases . . . includes a whole series of fragmented characters. Most often, only the face remains, but a face whose expression speaks volumes. Some have their eyes sadly lowered, as if they were already missing from life. Others feel in overwhelming distress, infinite fatigue . . . If we do not know what plague this canvas speaks the name of, we understand confusedly that it is terrible. In fact, Richard Brintzenhofe watched his best friends die of AIDS.

Rick died of AIDS-related causes in 1995, followed by Miguel, who died in 1996.

In April 1992, Susan and Bruce discovered Darrel at home in another coma and followed behind an ambulance to Wood Hull Hospital in Brooklyn. "When I got to the emergency room," remembers Susan, "I said, 'I'm not family, but they're on their way.' The orderly was really horrible to me. He said, 'You know he has AIDS? Is he your boyfriend?' He went on and on, and I said, 'I'm his neighbor and his friend. That's why I'm here.' So he cut it out. . . . There were people with guns in the place, and knives . . . and they were scuffling, too. It was a notorious hospital." He was soon transferred to Kings County Hospital in East Flatbush, a hospital that dated back to the

Allen Frame, *Darrel Ellis in Cornwall*, 1986
Gelatin silver print, 16 × 20 in.
Collection of the artist

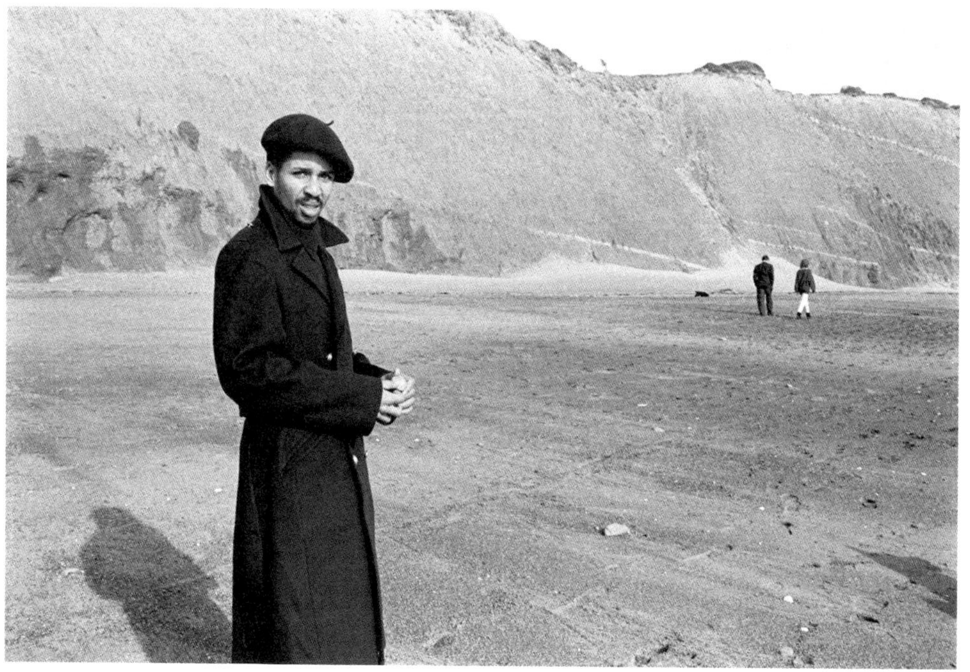

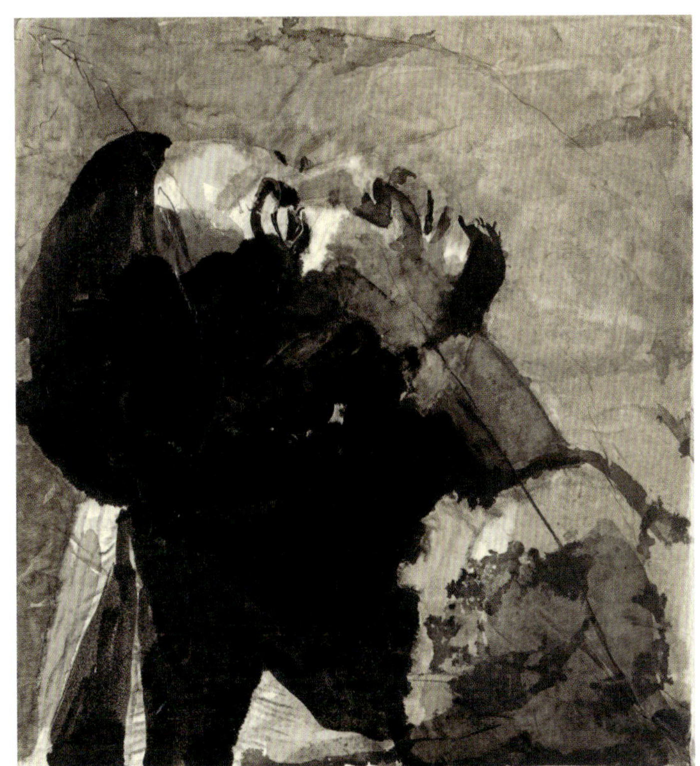

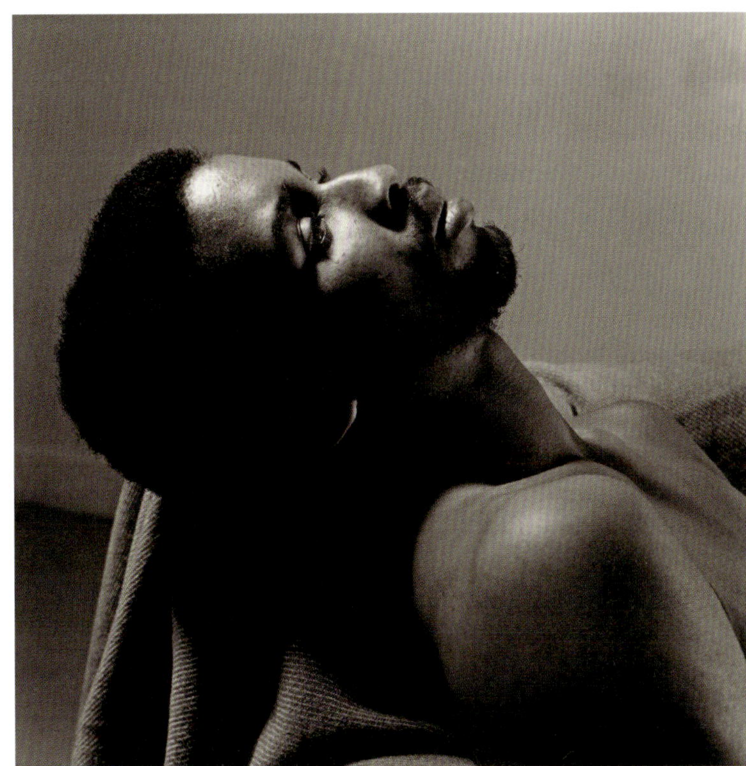

*Self-Portrait after Photograph by Peter Hujar*, 1989
Brush and black ink and wash over charcoal on Asian-fiber paper mounted on canvas, 24 × 22 × 1 in.
The Baltimore Museum of Art
Purchase with exchange funds from the Pearlstone Family Fund and partial gift of The Andy Warhol Foundation for the Visual Arts, Inc.

Peter Hujar, *Darrel Ellis (II)*, 1981
Gelatin silver print, 10 × 16 in.
Estate of Peter Hujar

1830s. He was in a huge, high-ceilinged room with about twenty other patients that reminded us of army hospitals we had seen in films. We knew that the previous time he had been hospitalized, he could actually hear us speaking to him through the coma. As Frank Franca, who also shot fashion at the time, remembers, "I would sit there and talk to him, and I would talk about fashion, among other things. He had been to a fashion high school and we had often related about fashion, what people were wearing, what was in style, and I remember that the medications they were giving him were making his hair straight, so I jokingly said. 'You've got to snap out of this so we can figure out which medication straightened your hair. I want to try it myself! We can make a killing!'" But Darrel never recovered. Later that year, Peter Galassi included his photographs posthumously in the exhibition *New Photography 8* at MoMA. The image used with *The New York Times* review of the show was of Darrel's mother, a rephotographed and abstracted Thomas Ellis photograph.

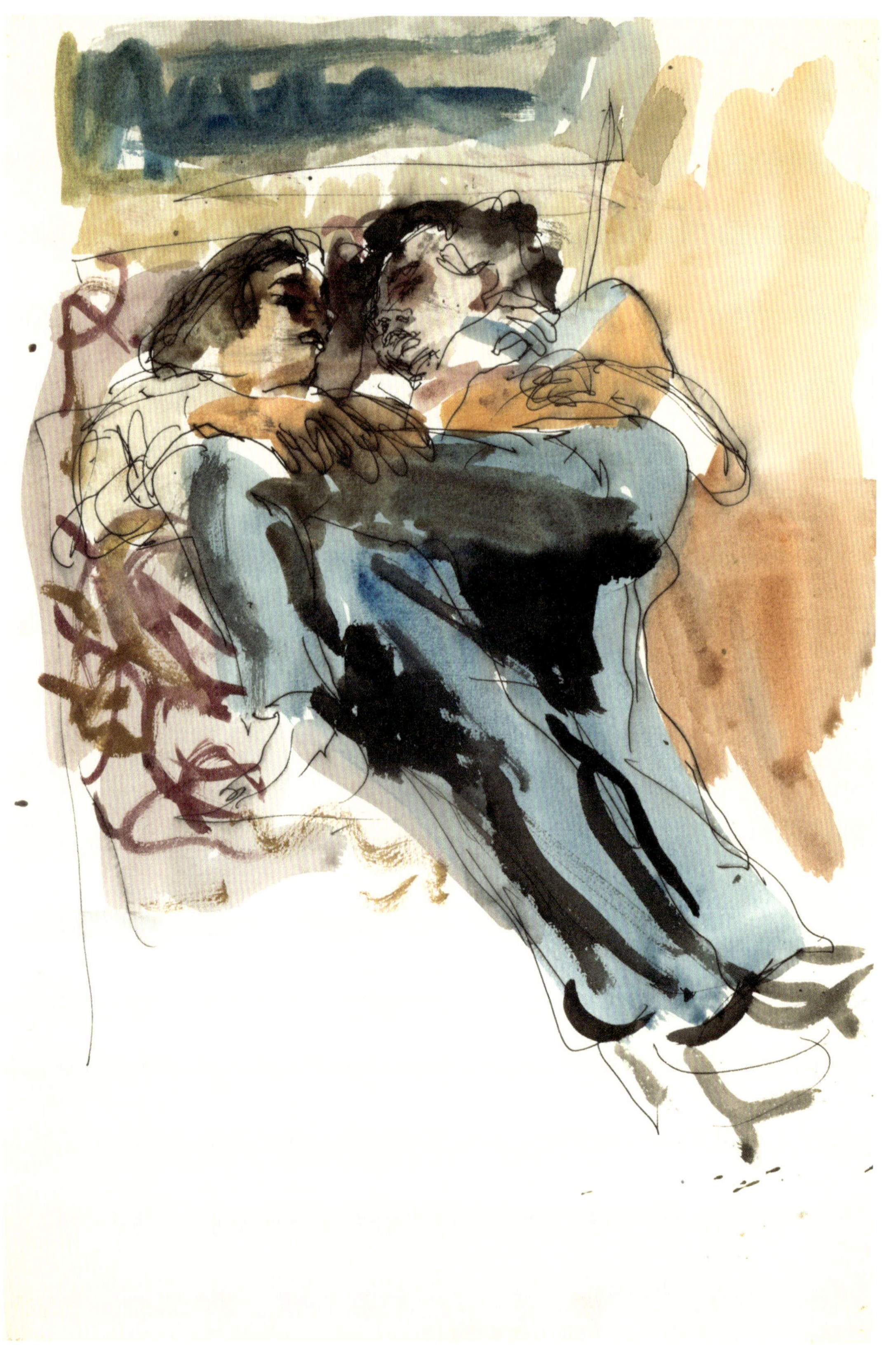

*Untitled (Couple Embracing)*, ca. 1980–83
Watercolor and black roller ball pen
on paper
18 × 12 in.

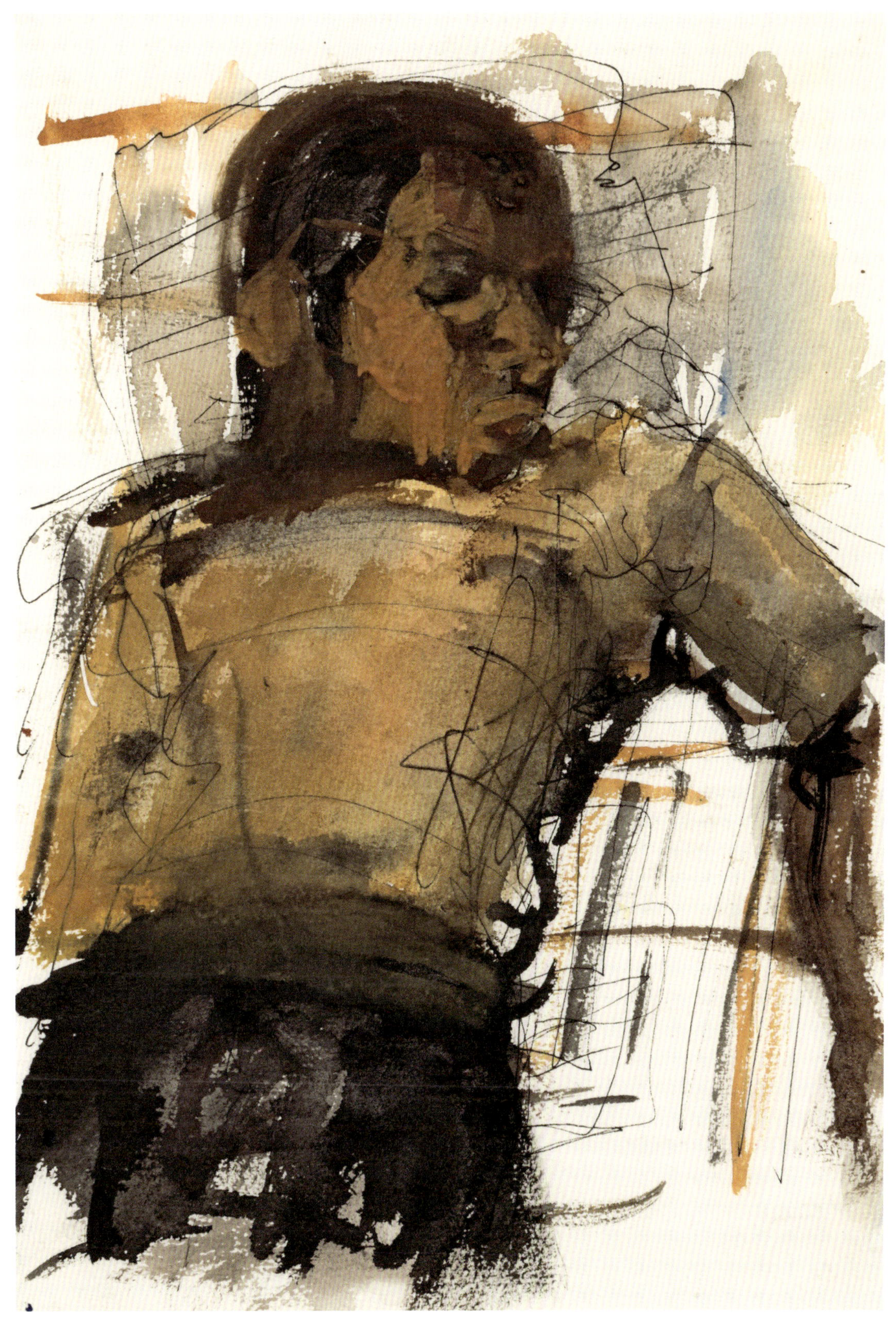

*David Resting*, 1981
Watercolor and pen and brush and black ink on paper
14 × 9 ¾ in.

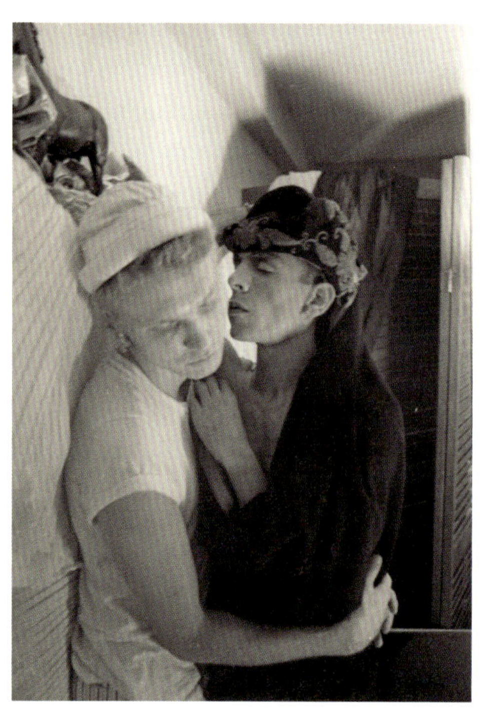

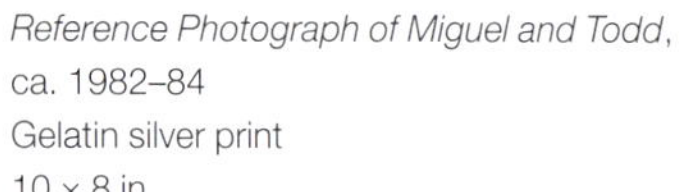

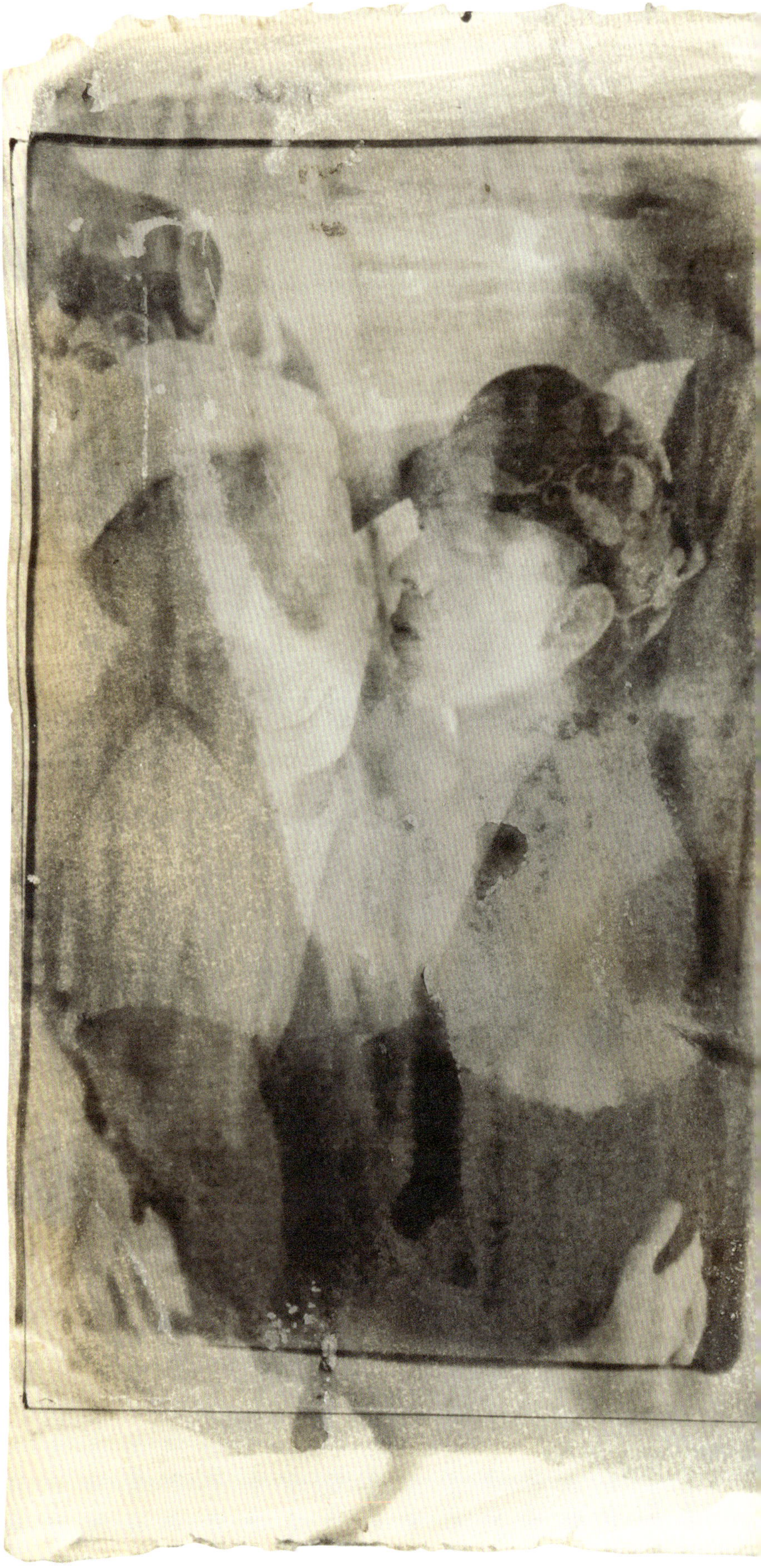

*Reference Photograph of Miguel and Todd*, ca. 1982–84
Gelatin silver print
10 × 8 in.

*Untitled (Miguel and Todd)*, ca. 1982–84
Photosensitive emulsion (Liquid Light), graphite, pen and black ink, opaque watercolor, and collage on paper
11 × 15 in.
Collection of Stephen Dull, Coral Gables, FL

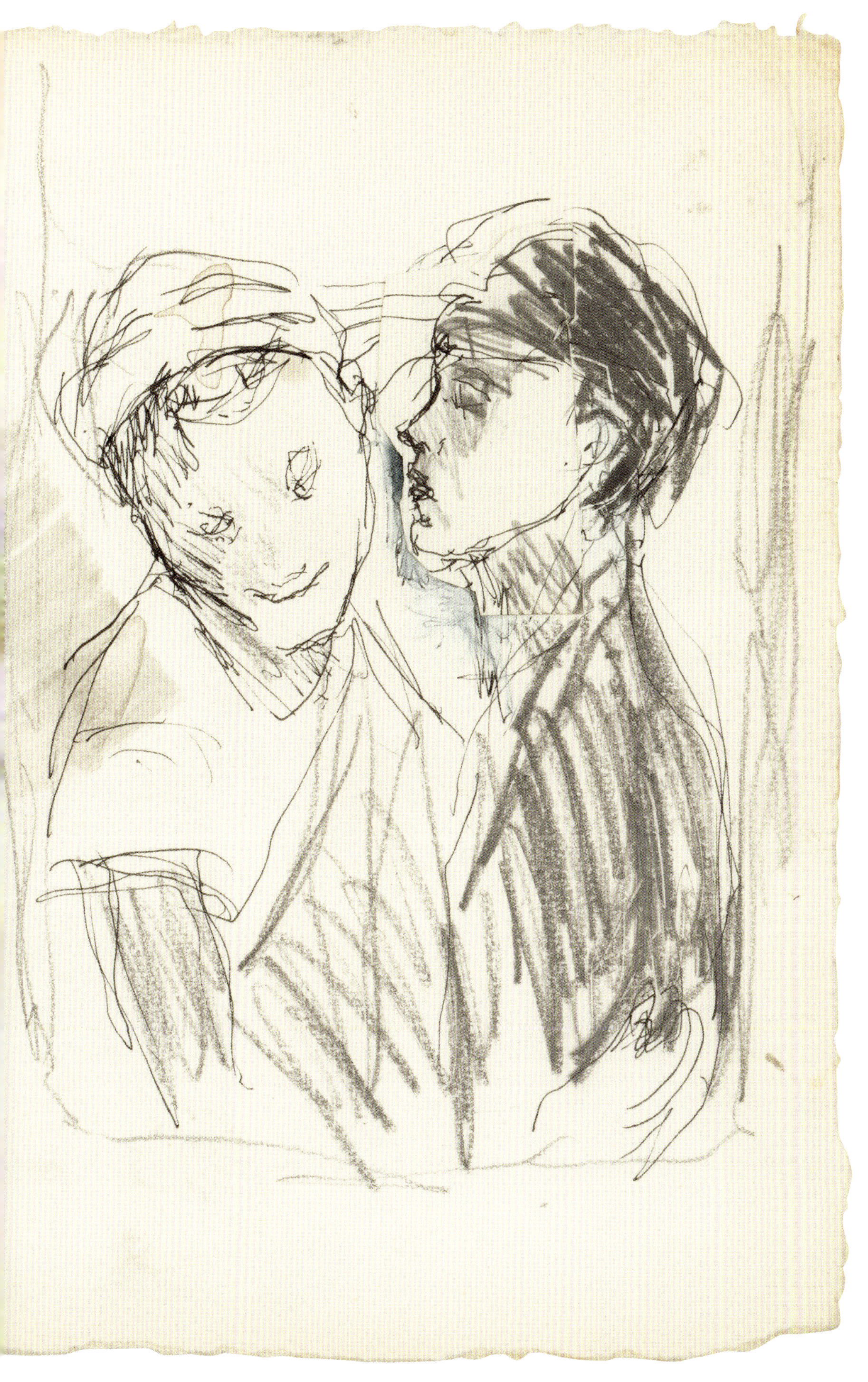

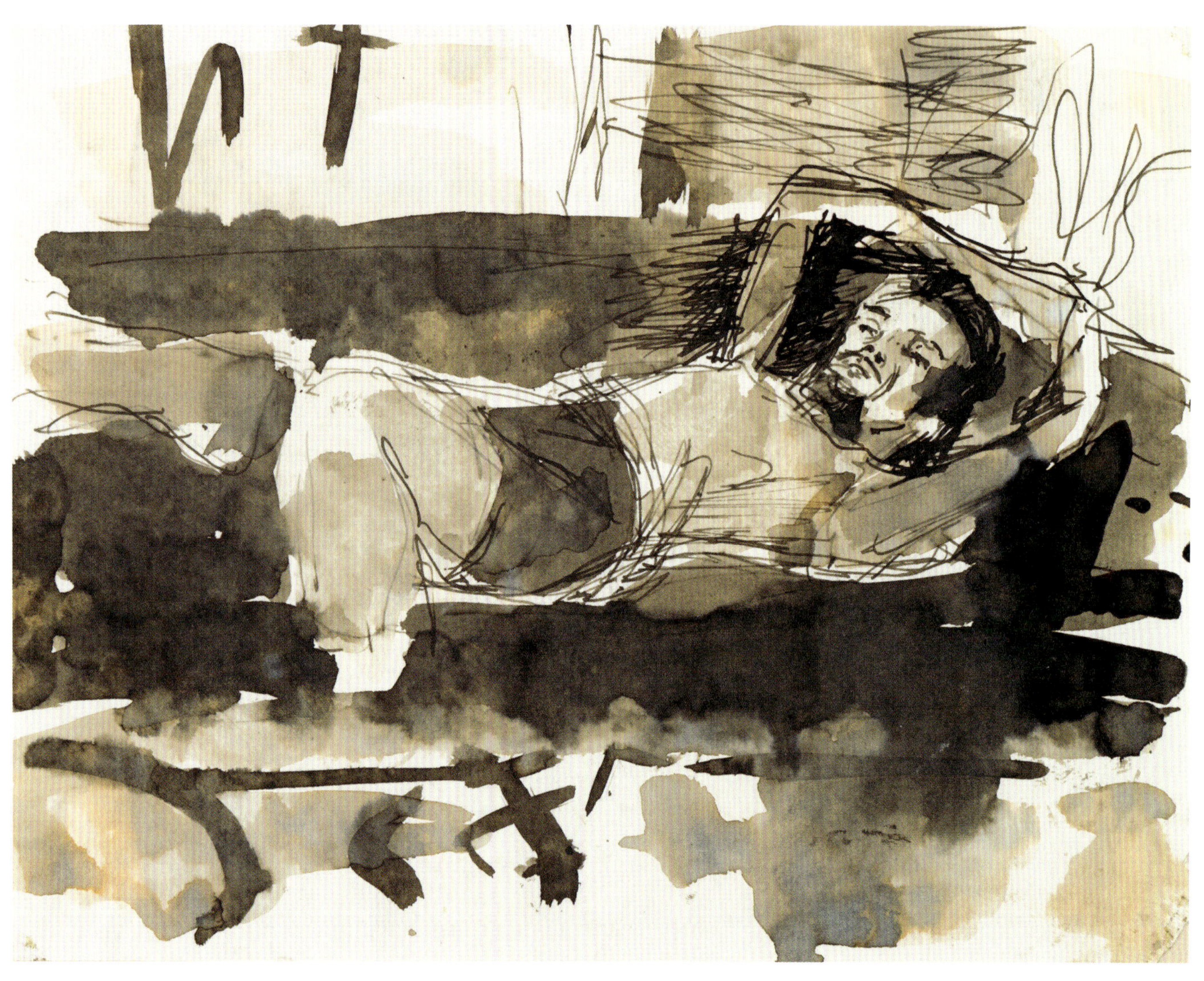

*Billy Laying Down*, 1981
Pen and brush and brown-black ink
and wash on paper
11 × 14 in.

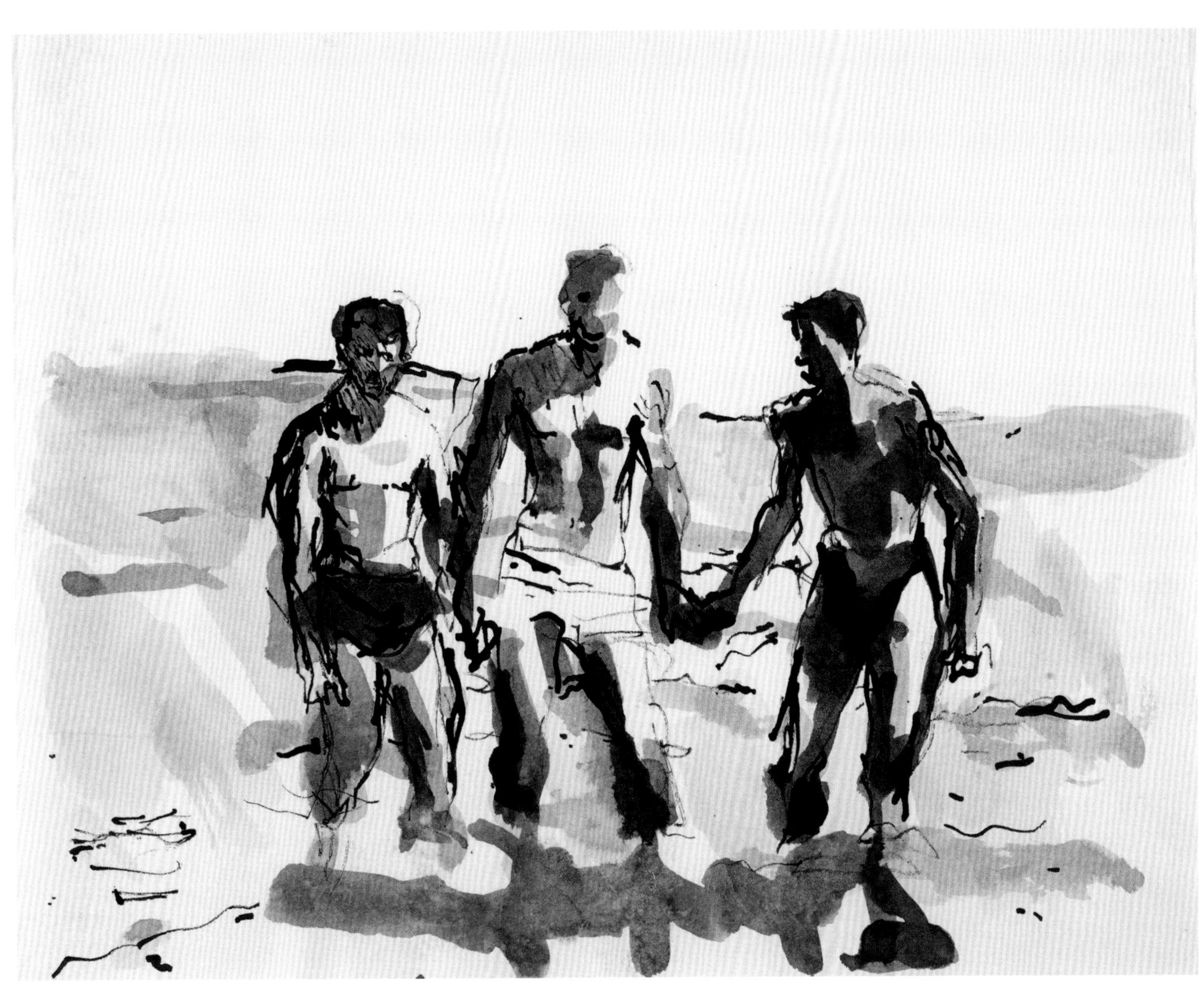

*Untitled (Bathers)*, ca. 1981–85
Pen and brush and black ink
and wash on paper
11 × 14 in.
Collection of Moez Kaba
and Bjorn Lundberg

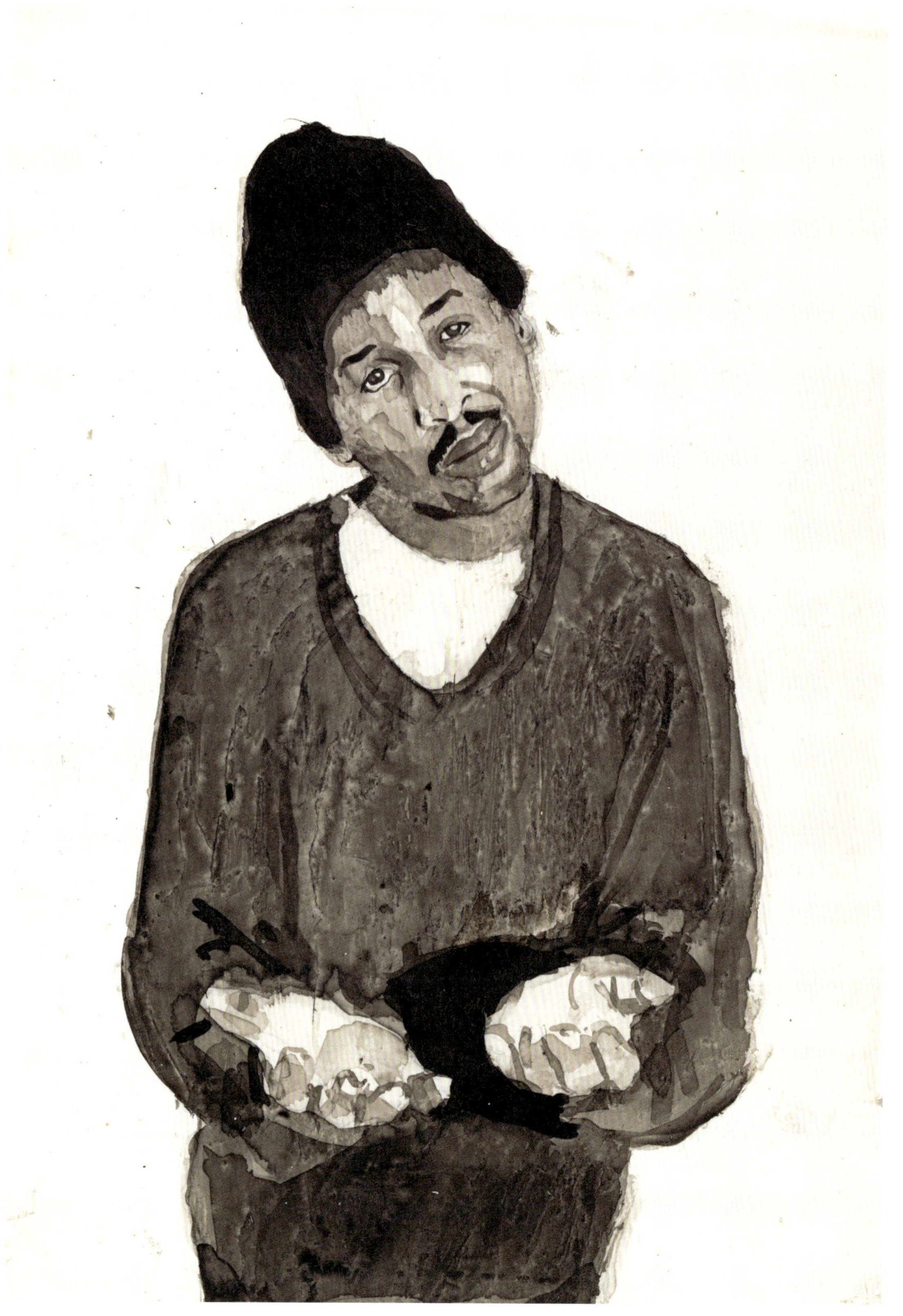

Linda Owen
and Scott Homolka

# Observations on Darrel Ellis's Materials and Process

While a resident at PS1, Darrel Ellis, working in collaboration with James Wentzy, developed an experimental process of projecting negatives onto hand-sculpted plaster reliefs and rephotographing the distorted projections. The resulting black and white prints typically appear inverted—with areas originally in shadow or darkness appearing as white and highlights as black—disorienting the viewer and obfuscating the artist's working process. Through this complicated process, Ellis aimed to recover his past and connect it to the present, by first exploding the picture plane of the two-dimensional projected image into a three-dimensional space, before collapsing it back again in the final photographic print. These prints served as inspiration for Ellis in other media, leading to many prints, drawings, and paintings based on his photography. A particularly evocative series based on his interior photography is discussed in this essay. The ultimate result is a body of work with iterations spanning photography, drawing, painting, collage, and printmaking, in which the artist explores additive and subtractive processes through the lens of personal history.

Ellis's process reveals itself through visual artifacts in the final prints, vestiges of physical features of the constructed reliefs that entice the viewer into deeper looking—and thinking—about the materiality behind their creation. For his experiments, he constructed two types of sculptural reliefs using plaster and other materials including Styrofoam, cardboard, and bandages: some reliefs mimic the organic, undulating forms of landscapes (with their textural, topographical surfaces creating rippled deformations of the images projected onto them); other constructed reliefs explore geometry (with rectangular, square, and cylindrical recessed cavities likely cast from small boxes, blocks, and canisters).[1] Other features such as air bubbles and creases imparted by plastic sheeting into which some of the paster surfaces were apparently cast are visible in specific works like *Untitled (Woman with Leopard Skin)* (see p. 102). Our study identified at least thirteen distinct geometric and organic reliefs, revealing the depth of the artist's commitment to his physical process.[2]

Ellis propped the reliefs at various angles and orientations to his photographic enlarger, a critical feature that allowed him to play with dramatic effects of shadow and volume as elements of the projected image disappeared into the sculpted cavities. The projections often extended onto adjacent surfaces, revealing details like the enlarger stand and other support materials, and illuminating key physical features of fabrication, including undulating contours, jagged edges, and gaps and fissures in the plaster surfaces. The projection was then photographed from a carefully chosen vantage point to exploit image distortion or to selectively conceal projected pictorial elements. One significant effect of this is a characteristic trapezoidal shape—created by perspective—in the final images.

The final step in Ellis's process usually entailed the creation of an internegative, so that the resulting photographic prints appear black-white inverted.[3] A handful of works examined for this study, such as *Untitled (Figures in Bedroom)* (see p. 96), appear to be printed directly from camera negatives onto chromogenic photographic paper without the

[1] The artist refers to these two types of reliefs as "organic" and "geometric" in his notebooks. See Darrel Ellis, Notebook 1989.1.

[2] Ellis's sketchbooks contain written entries and sketches documenting his explorations with plaster constructions going back to at least the early 1980s, with diagrams and notes showing the artist working through ideas of playing with negative/positive space, and casting objects into surfaces (see pp. 154–57). See Darrel Ellis, Notebook 1979.4 and 1980.1.

[3] He did not have a darkroom during this period and relied upon a commercial photography studio to process his film as well as produce internegatives and the final chromogenic and gelatin silver prints.

use of an internegative. These are identified by the lack of black-white inversion in the final print.[4] These images are valuable in deciphering Ellis's overall process, as we can directly visualize the studio setup much as the artist would have while working (with dark shadows surrounding a plaster relief upon which a negative is projected). With the exception of a small number of chromogenic prints, most images in the artist's archive are black and white gelatin silver prints. He selectively hand-colored many of these photographs.[5] Instrumental analysis of a small sample taken from one work, *Untitled (Mother's Bedroom)*, indicates a synthetic, organic colorant[6] consistent with a dye-based colored ink set, rather than an oil or watercolor paint, as has been speculated previously.[7]

Ellis's process lent itself to focusing on a single photographic image, which would then be explored as a series that underwent continued manipulations and spanned various media. Some series are relatively concise, with few permutations. Others are more extensive, such as the series depicting figures in the interior of his mother's bedroom captured by Ellis himself, which produced over twenty photographs, prints, drawings, and paintings from one negative. In this series, he used at least three different reliefs, and occasionally flipped the negative to reverse the orientation of the image,[8] further straining the relationship between copy and original at the heart of his artistic endeavor.

In this series, *Untitled (Mother's Bedroom)*, Ellis produced at least four main, second-generation photographic images from a single negative (opposite). In two of the images, the woman is positioned at the bottom of the void; their successive contracting shapes draw the eye in and concentrate its focus on her figure. In contrast, the seated man becomes lost or difficult to discern in the distortion caused by the recess. Thus the legibility and meaning of the image are impacted by the placement of the projection on the reliefs; the figures can be either highlighted or obscured, singled out or lost.

These second-generation photographs each serve as a departure point for further exploration in a variety of drawing, painting, and print media, creating additional branches of the series.

Constantly referring to the manipulated interior photographs, Ellis created third-generation drawings in both dry and wet media on a variety of paper supports. *Untitled (Mother's Bedroom)* (see p. 150, top) is executed in black and white fabricated chalks on a gray, moderately textured wove paper. In the detail, the slightly waxy binder of the crayon is evident in the flattened peaks of white media and in the striations from the strokes of the black crayon. Several works are executed on Asian paper, mounted to either canvas or wood panel, and reflect the artist's interest in the subtle textural and chromatic variation his materials produced.[9] In one work from the series, *Untitled (Mother's Bedroom)* (see p. 150, middle), Ellis laid out the composition with a minimal graphite underdrawing and brush and black ink on the Asian paper before mounting it to a linen canvas with a slightly yellow, glossy adhesive. Ellis continued to work the image with opaque white paint and ink.[10] This layering is seen in a detail from the work, where the black ink is selectively covered with white paint and then additional strokes of black ink extend over the white. The long fibers, characteristic of Asian papers, are also accentuated by the interaction between the white paint and black ink. Ellis often coated these and similar drawings with a varnish layer, identified as a polyvinyl acetate adhesive,[11] possibly mimicking the aged appearance of his father's photographs. Entries in the artist's sketchbooks document his fascination with and appreciation of aged surfaces.[12]

Ellis carefully replicated the physical imperfections in the plaster reliefs in these third-generation ink and opaque watercolor drawings. Diagonal elements in the foreground of many works derive from creases created during the plaster casting process. The undulating form and jagged

[4] Some chromogenic prints in Ellis's oeuvre were produced in a similar fashion to his typical black and white prints, appearing positive-negative inverted, for example, *Untitled (Picnic Scene)* and *Untitled (Boy with Bicycle)* on pp. 98–100.

[5] In Notebook 1989.1, Ellis states: "buy colored inks experiment," possibly referring to purchasing a colored ink set for hand-coloring photographic prints. The distinct use of colored inks in other categories of his work were not identified in this study of his material.

[6] The red colorant was identified using Raman spectrometry as a diazo β -naphthol dye, a type commonly used in water-soluble inks found in photo tinting kits, including those sold by Kodak, which are designed to be absorbed into the emulsion layers of photographic prints. For technical details on all instrumental analysis used for this study, see "Scientific Analysis of Fine Art, LLC," *Report 2187* (January 2022) on file at the Baltimore Museum of Art, Conservation Department.

[7] A small sample of the photographic structure from *Untitled (Mother's Bedroom)* (ELL226) was mounted in Bioplastic resin, prepared as a cross-section, and examined under magnification using a polarized light microscope in visible illumination. This revealed the diffuse red colorant absorbed into the paper fibers of the photographic support as well as in the gelatin emulsion layer.

[8] The three reliefs are a simple square void, a stepped, square recess with a triangular protrusion, and a rectangular stepped cavity. Ellis also experimented with the orientation of the rectangular void: the rectangular stepped relief was used in both a vertical and horizontal format in different works, greatly altering the composition and the legibility of the original image.

[9] Ellis lists types and sizes of Japanese paper in Notebook 1989.1, and then writes "buy paper and paper blotter from NY Central" a few pages later. NY Central was a specialty paper store in New York, NY, known for its extensive Japanese paper selection.

[10] This type of white paint is seen in many of his drawings. It is an opaque, water-based material also referred to as "gouache."

[11] Polyvinyl acetate is a homopolymer commonly found in the category of adhesives known as "white glues" such as the family of Jade adhesives. Ellis frequently mentioned buying Jade adhesive, specifically "Jade Glue . . . acid-free" in Notebook 1989.1. Samples of the material were analyzed using Fourier Transform Infrared Spectroscopy (FTIR).

[12] The artist mentions his appreciation of the "aged quality" of photographs in Notebook 1988.1.

page 146
*Untitled (Self-Portrait)*, ca. 1990–91
Brush and black ink, wash, graphite, acrylic modeling paste, and varnish on paper, 24 ½ × 17 in.
Green Family Art Foundation, Dallas

clockwise from top left
*Untitled (Mother's Bedroom)*, ca. 1987–91
Gelatin silver print, 16 × 20 in.

*Untitled (Mother's Bedroom)*, ca. 1987–91
Gelatin silver print, 11 × 14 in.

*Untitled (Mother's Bedroom)*, ca. 1987–91
Gelatin silver print, 16 × 20 in.

*Untitled (Mother's Bedroom)*, ca. 1987–91
Gelatin silver print, 16 × 20 in.
Collection of Stephen Dull, Coral Gables, FL

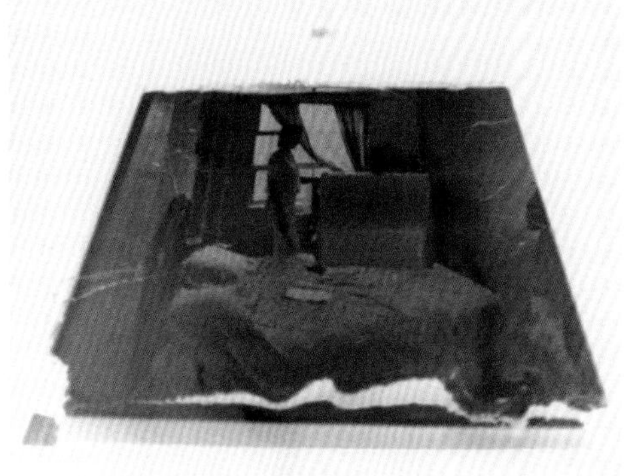

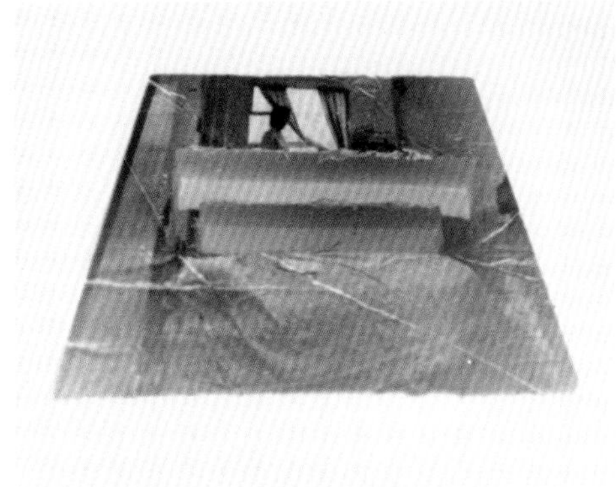

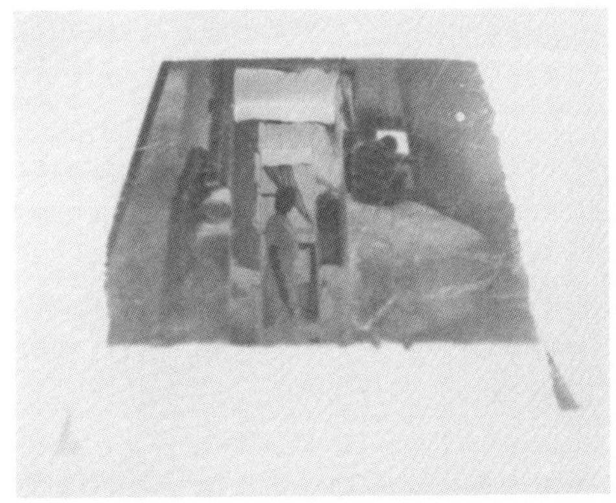

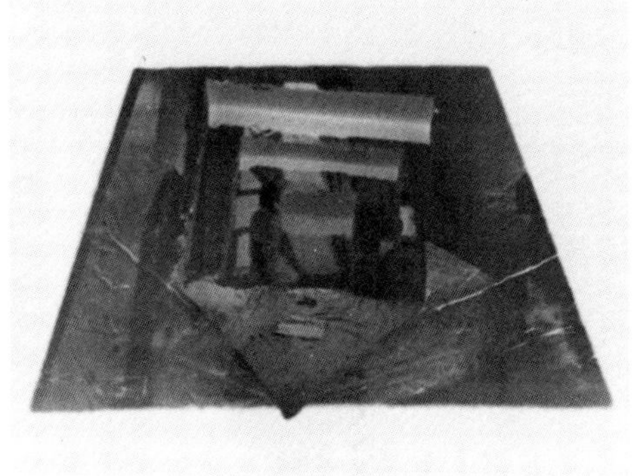

bottom edge of the plaster relief are also carried through the various iterations in different media (see p. 150, top). The trapezoidal shape of the rephotographed source image, a prominent remnant of the photographic process, floats within an empty border in certain paintings and drawings (see p. 150, middle).

Paintings in acrylic and oil on both linen and thin wood panel continue Ellis's exploration of the image in yet another medium. An unstretched work on linen from the period was intricately cut and contoured to replicate the undulating edge of the original plaster relief as well as the trapezoidal format, reflecting his continued interest in exploring the visual artifacts of his photographic process. Ellis sometimes brought a closer focus to the trapezoidal element by discarding the white, rectangular border of his photographs and drawings and creating shaped canvases, as seen in *Untitled (Mother's Bedroom)* (see p. 150, bottom). In these works, the linen canvas is stretched around angled strainers to fit the shape of the image, a process the artist had detailed in his writings.[13] Ellis also added sand to the gesso ground, visible in clumps embedded in drips of white gesso on the verso of the canvas, to create a prominently textured surface, a technique he describes in detail in a sketchbook.[14] Here the intentionally rough surface contrasts sharply with the smooth, glossy finish of his photographs.

While Ellis's interior scenes demonstrate the range of his technical innovation, the thick impasto layer the artist added to his portraits generate an additional layer of complexity. Past references to works such as *Untitled (Self-Portrait)* (see p. 146) include speculation about the use of wax or encaustic, or modeling paste.[15] Chemical analysis identified the impasto-like material, which was built-up underneath the figure in this work to create a sense of physical volume, as a white commercial priming gesso or modeling paste.[16] Ellis applied the thick paste in broad directional

[13] Ellis writes about the shaped canvases in Notebook 1988.1 (see p. 164).
[14] He records materials and processes potentially used to make textured ground in Notebook 1988.1, making lists that include "white gouache / gesso / sand / drop cloth."
[15] Ellis mentions encaustic in Notebook 1988.1 and even has encaustic on one of his shopping lists, which added to the uncertainty about the material used in the works.
[16] FTIR analysis identified an ethyl acrylate/methyl methacrylate copolymer resin containing calcium carbonate, but found no wax present.

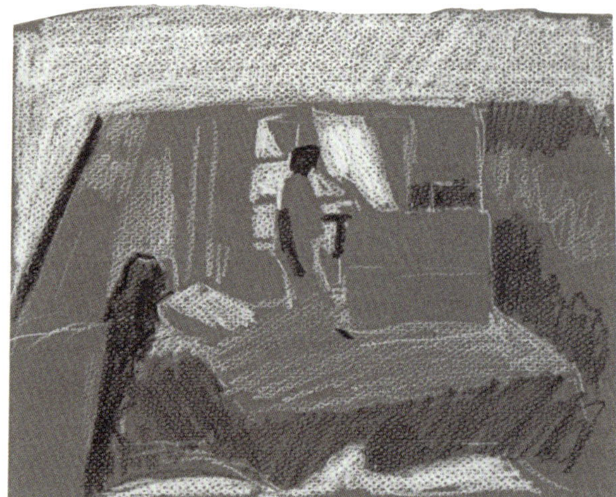

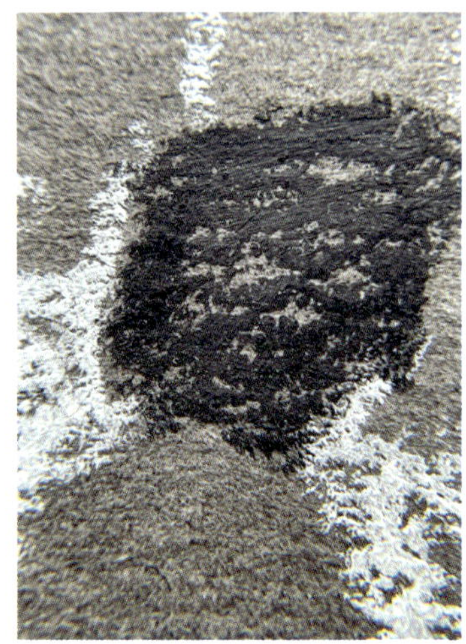

*Untitled (Mother's Bedroom)*, ca. 1987–91
Conte crayon on paper, 7 ¾ × 9 ½ in.

Detail revealing characteristics of Ellis's drawing materials, including striations in the black crayon from application

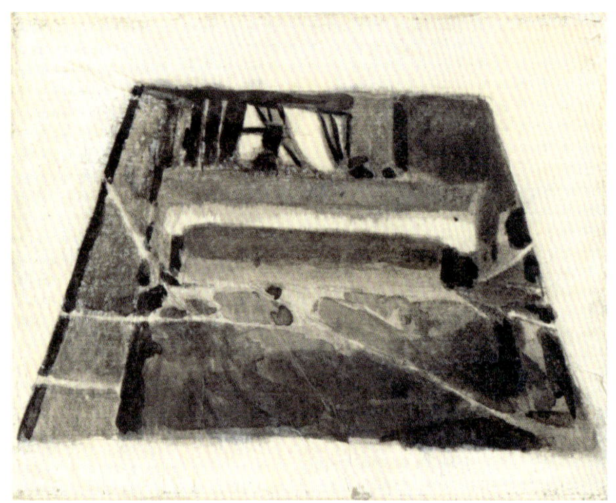

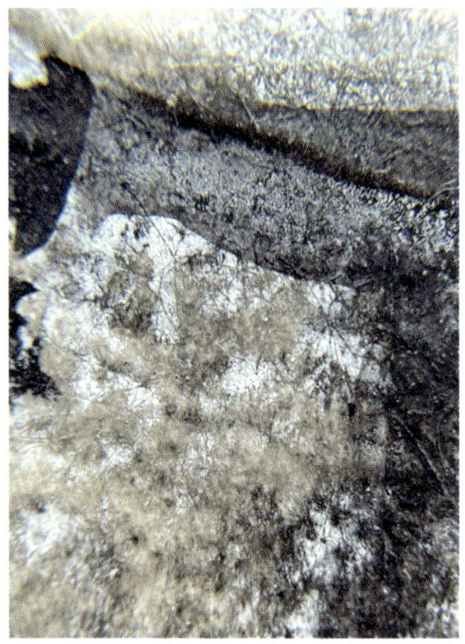

*Untitled (Mother's Bedroom)*, ca. 1987–91
Brush and black ink, opaque watercolor, and varnish on thin, Asian-fiber paper mounted to canvas, 8 × 10 ¼ in.

Detail showing Ellis's layering of black ink and white paint. The long fibers characteristic of Asian paper are also visible

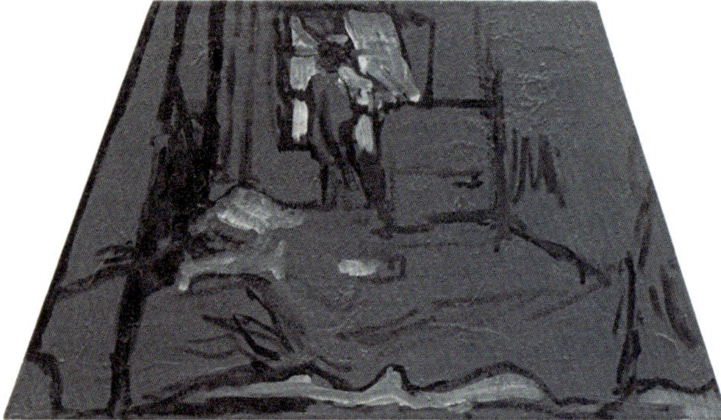

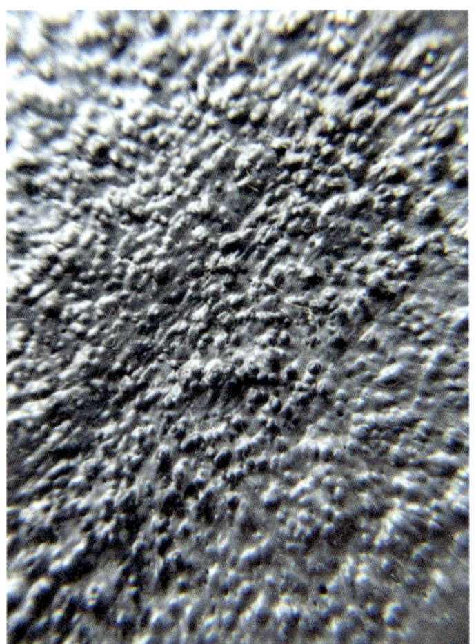

*Untitled (Mother's Bedroom)*, ca. 1987–91
Acrylic on canvas prepared with textured sand ground, 21 ½ × 36 ¼ in.

Details showing the prominent texture imparted in the painting (left) by Ellis mixing sand into his gesso ground

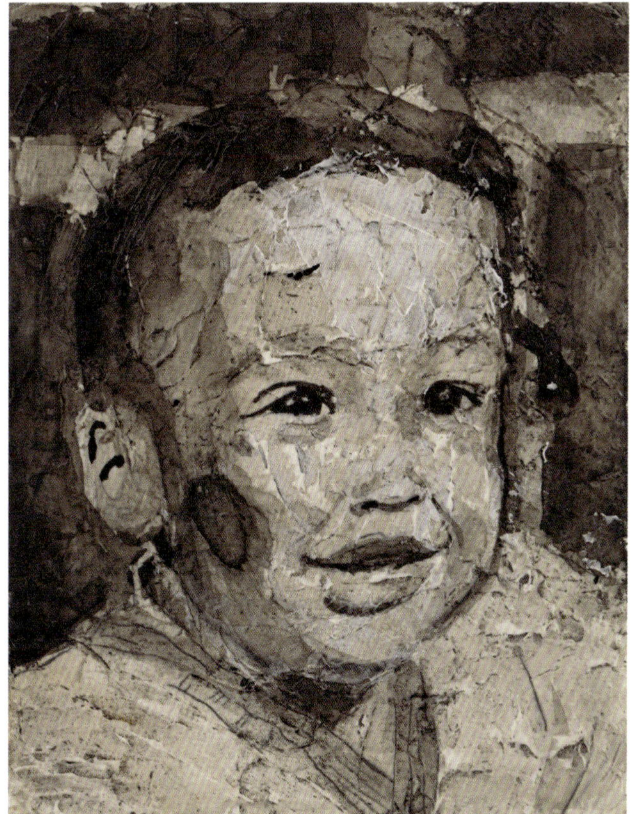

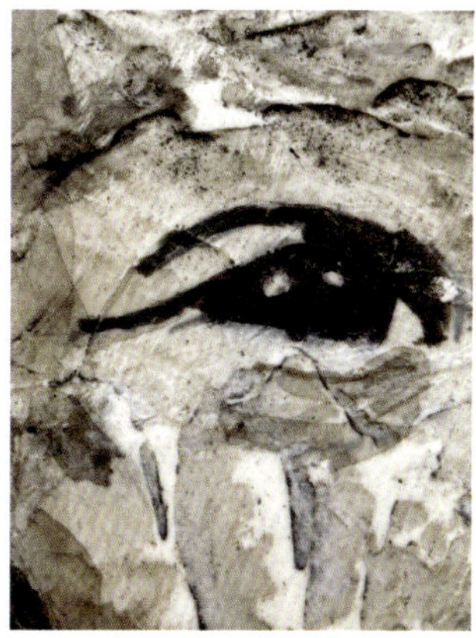

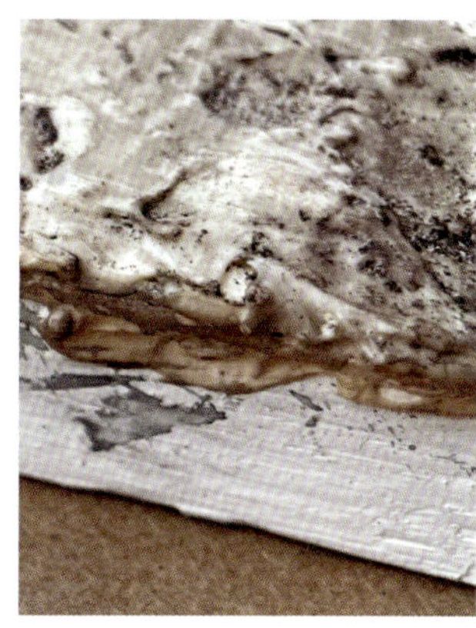

*Untitled (Baby)*, ca. 1990–91
Brush and black ink, graphite, acrylic modeling paste, and varnish on paper, 16 × 12 in.
Collection of Michael Sherman and Carrie Tivador

Details showing the dramatic impasto of Ellis's layered media in *Untitled (Baby)* (above), incorporating thick applications of acrylic modeling paste on a gesso-coated panel (below)

strokes, likely using a palette knife, which mimic the knit ribbing in the sitter's hat, and worked back into the paste with a blunt tool, such as the rounded end of a brush handle, to create deep furrows and ridges in the surface. He also selectively applied the same glossy polyvinyl acetate varnish, identified in the drawing described above, to areas of the surface. *Untitled (Baby)* is representative of a small group of works on gesso-coated wood panels where Ellis built up the entire surface in thick, impasto layers using this white medium, brush-applied black ink and wash, and graphite. He worked back into the composition with alternating layers of media including ink and graphite. Where in other drawings the graphite appears only as underdrawing, here Ellis uses graphite to bring emphasis to the contours of the face, along with lush passages of black ink that show through obscuring layers of opaque modeling paste in some areas, and pool on the surface in others. As a final step in the process, Ellis aggressively sanded back into the surface of the work (particularly visible though the center of the face), and the resulting fine particulate debris from the ink and modeling paste has settled into the crevices of the impasto.

Throughout his career, Ellis's complex working process involved obscuring and effacing one image in order to generate another—an irony that has made a detailed understanding of his practice particularly elusive. It is our hope that by examining the artist's methods and materials in greater detail, his explorations in photography and a range of diverse media are now more clearly accessible.

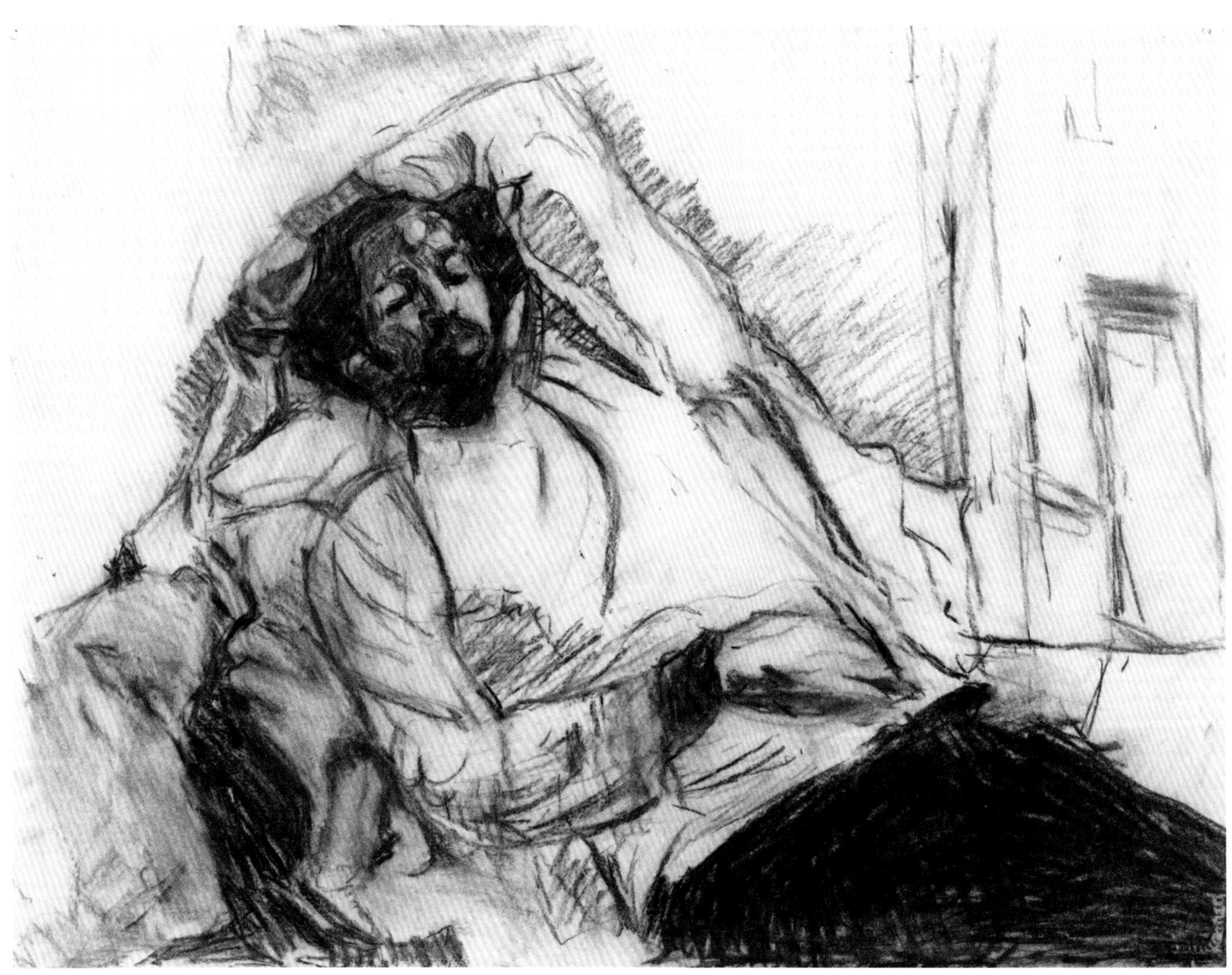

Kyle Croft

# The Notebooks of Darrel Ellis

Spanning from his senior year of high school in 1976 through the end of 1990, the fifty-two notebooks in the archive of Darrel Ellis's estate provide a singular perspective into the artist's aspirations, anxieties, and analyses. Reproduced in the following pages are a brief selection of pages from Ellis's notebooks that shed light on his re-photography process, from the creation of the sculptural reliefs to the symbolic meaning he invested into the resulting voids and holes.
About half of Ellis's notebooks date before 1980, providing a record of the young artist's development as a draftsman and reflecting his avid interest in art history. Many notebooks from this period are filled exclusively with sketches, often executed in the subway, at the Metropolitan Museum of Art, or in the domestic interiors of friends and family. His journal entries tend to reflect moments of anguish and anxiety—heartbreak and turmoil in his relationship with an older man named Kenneth, admonitions to himself about getting a job or quitting smoking—but there are also passages of unbridled excitement about painting, drawing, and claiming an identity as an artist.

Two of the densest notebooks relate to the time Ellis spent in residency at PS1 with James Wentzy, as the two embarked on a period of intense experimentation with photography and sculpture. Filled with notes, diagrams, and sketches, these notebooks demonstrate a shared fascination with perspective, dimensionality, and time that motivated this collaboration.

In the early 1980s, after receiving a trove of his father's photographs from his mother, Ellis began filling sketchbooks with drawings based on these images. Around the same time, he began recording I-Ching rolls in smaller notebooks, seeking guidance about what direction to take his art practice. (The I-Ching is an ancient Chinese divination text that can be consulted by flipping three coins six times, and reading the passage that corresponds to the resulting hexagram.) A 1983 notebook contains the only explicit references to AIDS in the artist's archive in two separate I-Ching queries. It is unclear when Ellis realized he was living with AIDS—the first HIV tests would not be available until two years after he wrote that line, but by 1984 his journals began to fill with notes on vitamins, supplements, and alternative medicines.

From the mid-1980s on, Ellis journaled less frequently and his writing focused increasingly on the meaning and direction of his art. As he dove deeper into his father's photographs and returned to his rephotography process, he reflected on his family history, the status of portraiture and representation, and the philosophical and spiritual implications of his artwork. Among these notes are numerous diagrams exploring how to exhibit his work, indicating Ellis's interest in displaying sequences based on a single source image: the original Thomas Ellis photograph, faithful renderings in ink or paint, rephotographed abstractions of the photograph, and drawings and paintings based on that abstraction.

At the time of publication, the notebooks remain in the artist's estate. Citations throughout this book refer to catalogue numbers given to the notebooks in 2022; none of the notebooks are paginated. All but fourteen have been dated, either through dated entries or through references to specific exhibitions or events.

doing whatever it is out of curiosi
He then learns. He then experiences
Why is Curious George a monkey
from africa?
Why is he a Curious Monkey?

Curious George absorbs light
more about Curious George

totally wrapped up in yourself

page 152
*Untitled (Reclining Self-Portrait)*, 1992
Charcoal on paper, 22 × 30 in.
Collection of Stephen Dull, Coral Gables, FL

Notebook 1980.1

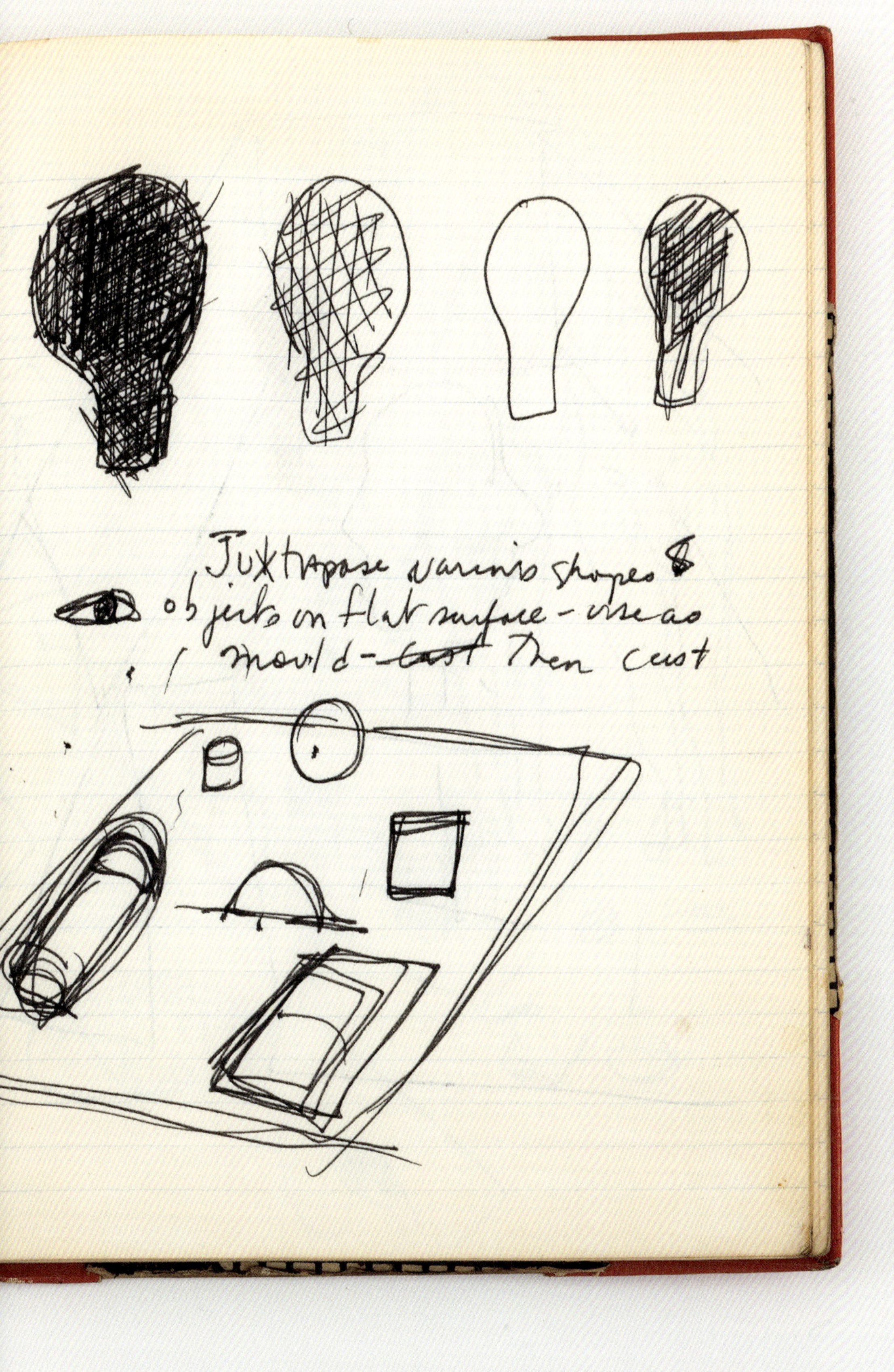
Juxtapose various shapes &
objects on flat surface - use as
mould - cast then cast

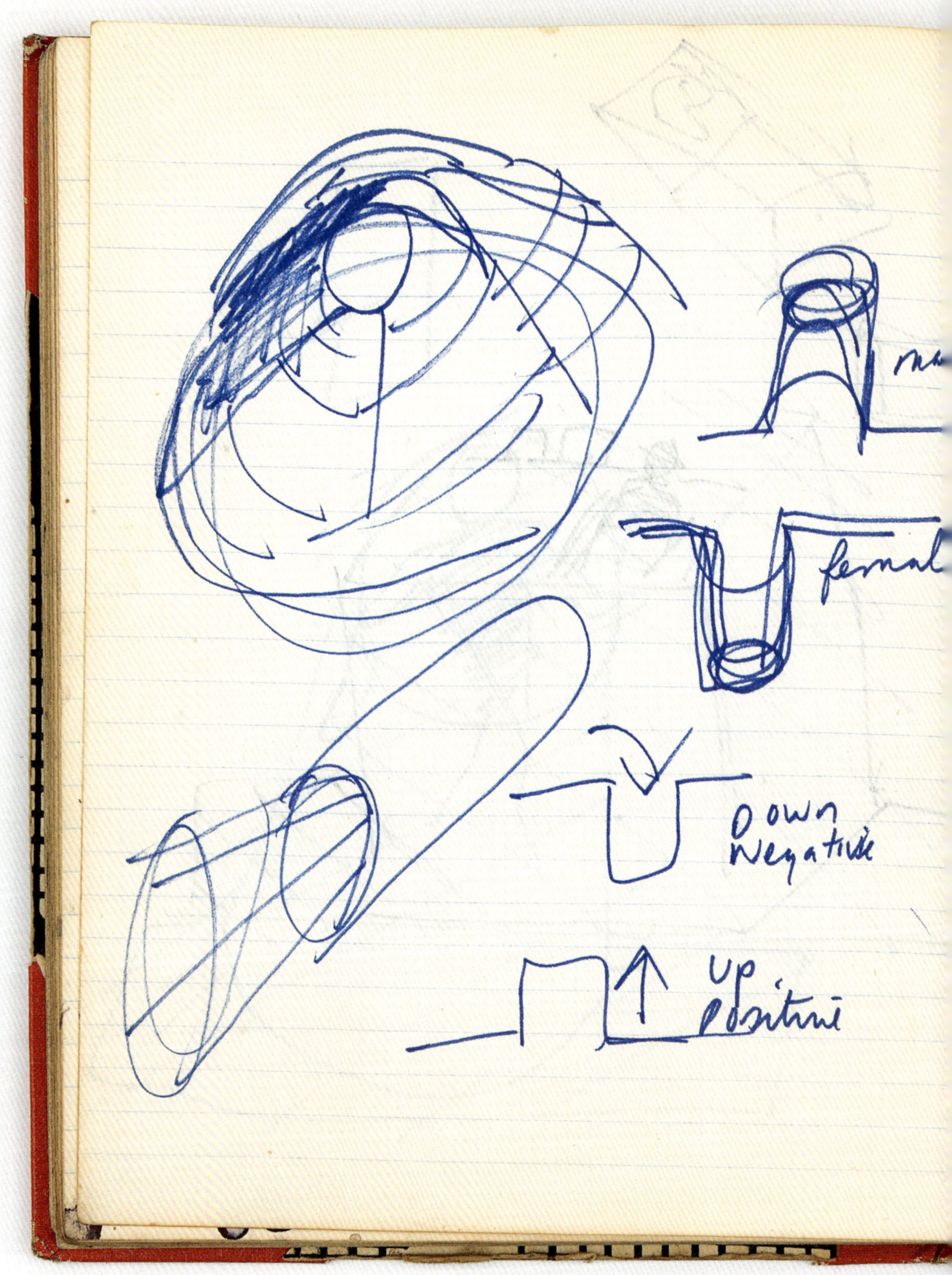


Notebook 1980.1

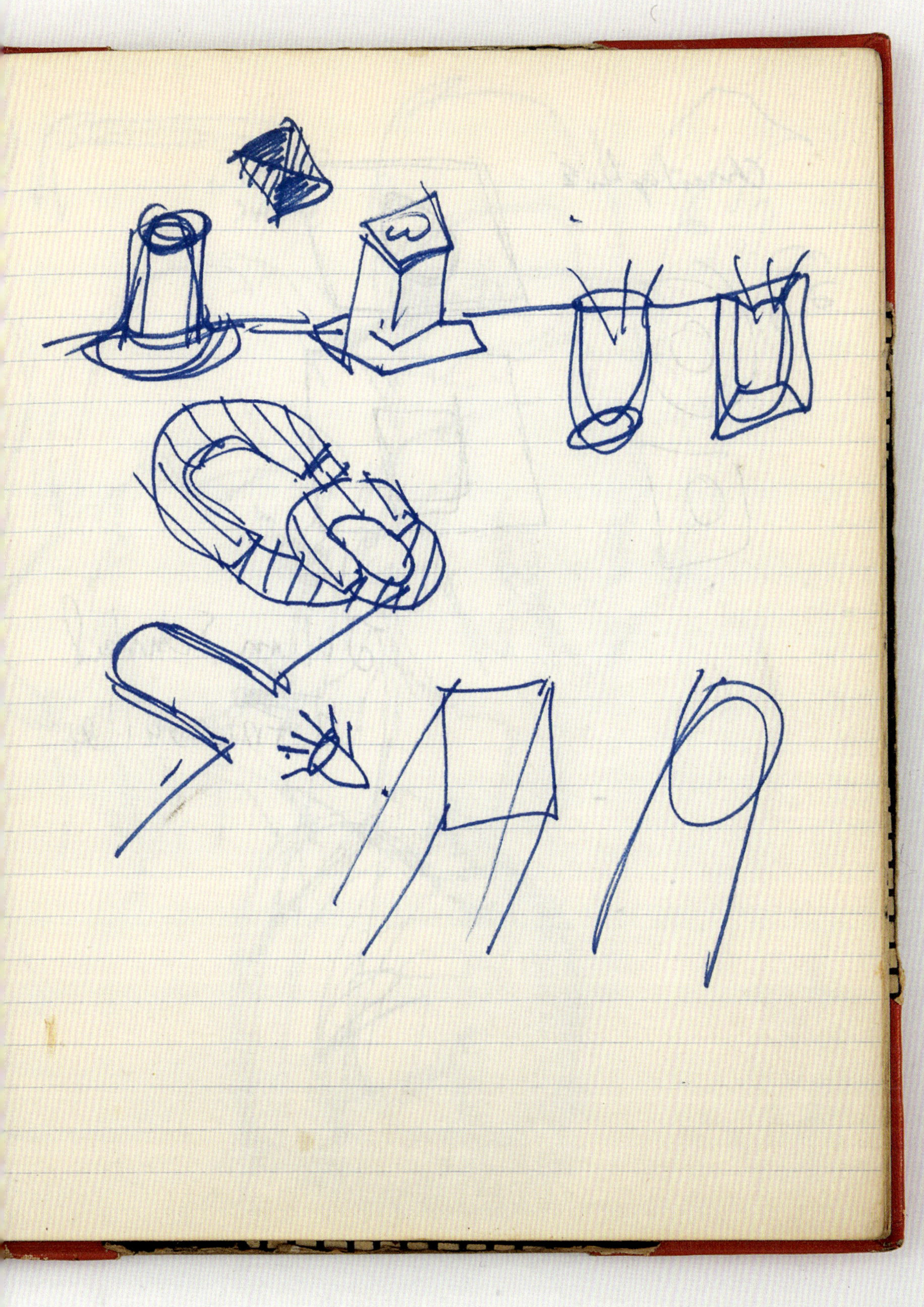

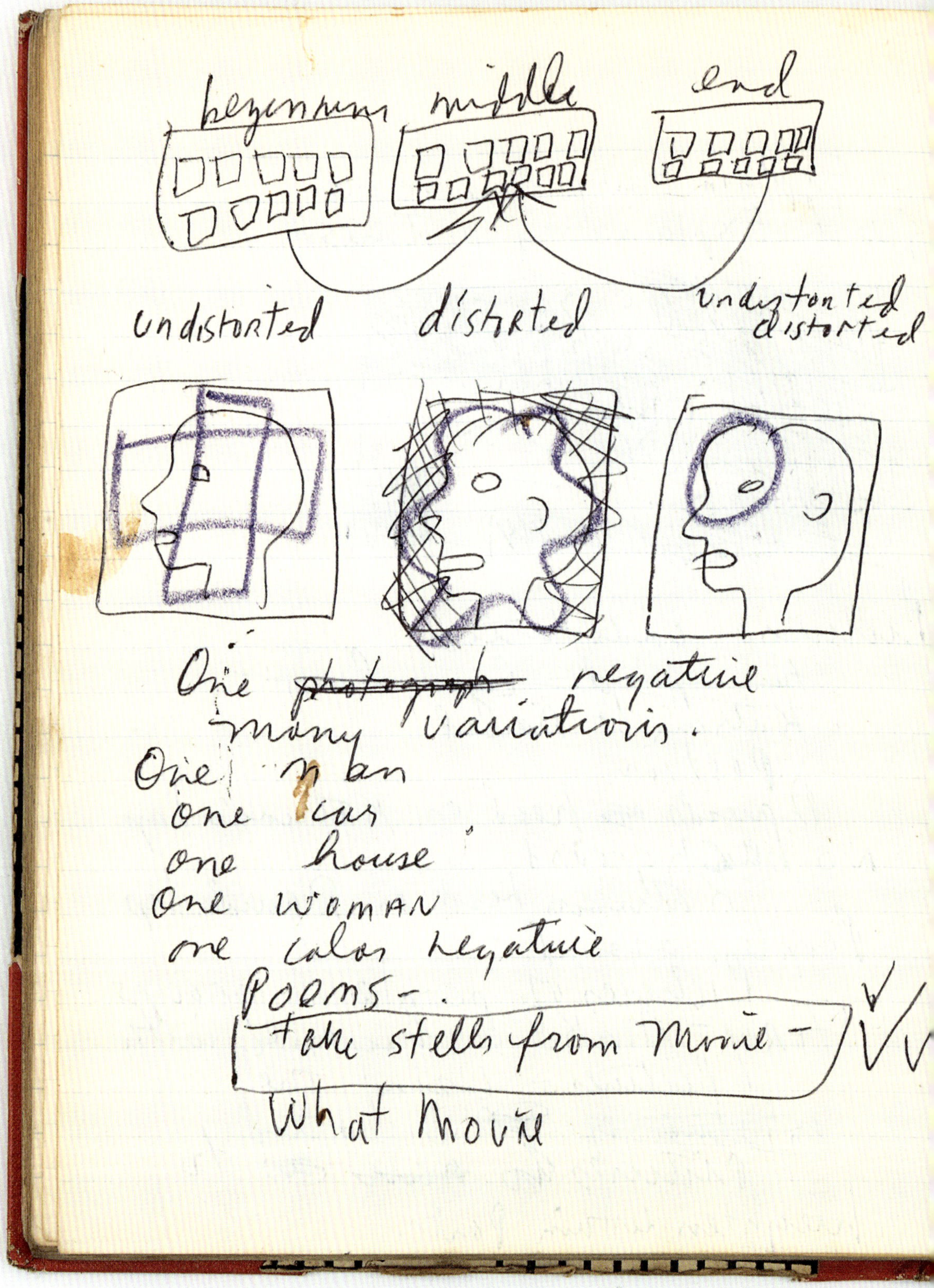

beginning middle end

undistorted distorted undistorted distorted

One ~~photograph~~ negative
many variations.
One man
one car
one house
One WOMAN
one color negative
POEMS –
take stills from Movie –
What Movie

Notebook 1980.1

Werner 741-1139

What Movie?
What films are available to me?
The Content - Subject matter
~~as I am working from the stills~~
Projector - Study the film:
use pictures in place of
words

what movies?
take stills from more then one
film -
to get negative ~~image~~ relief -
make positive relief

positive photo image
negative relief image
Before sculpture was 3-D
it was attached to architecture.
These photographs ~~can~~ use the

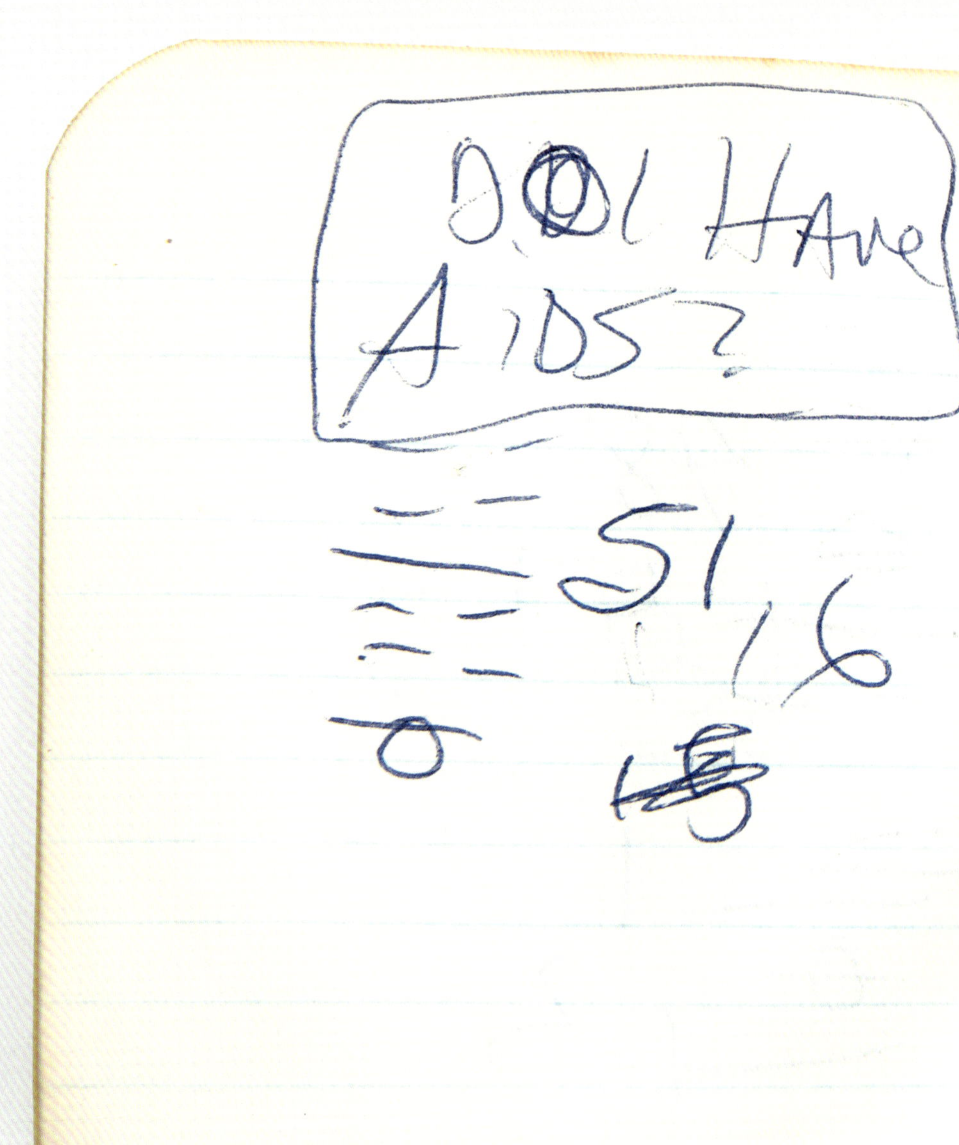


Notebook 1983.1

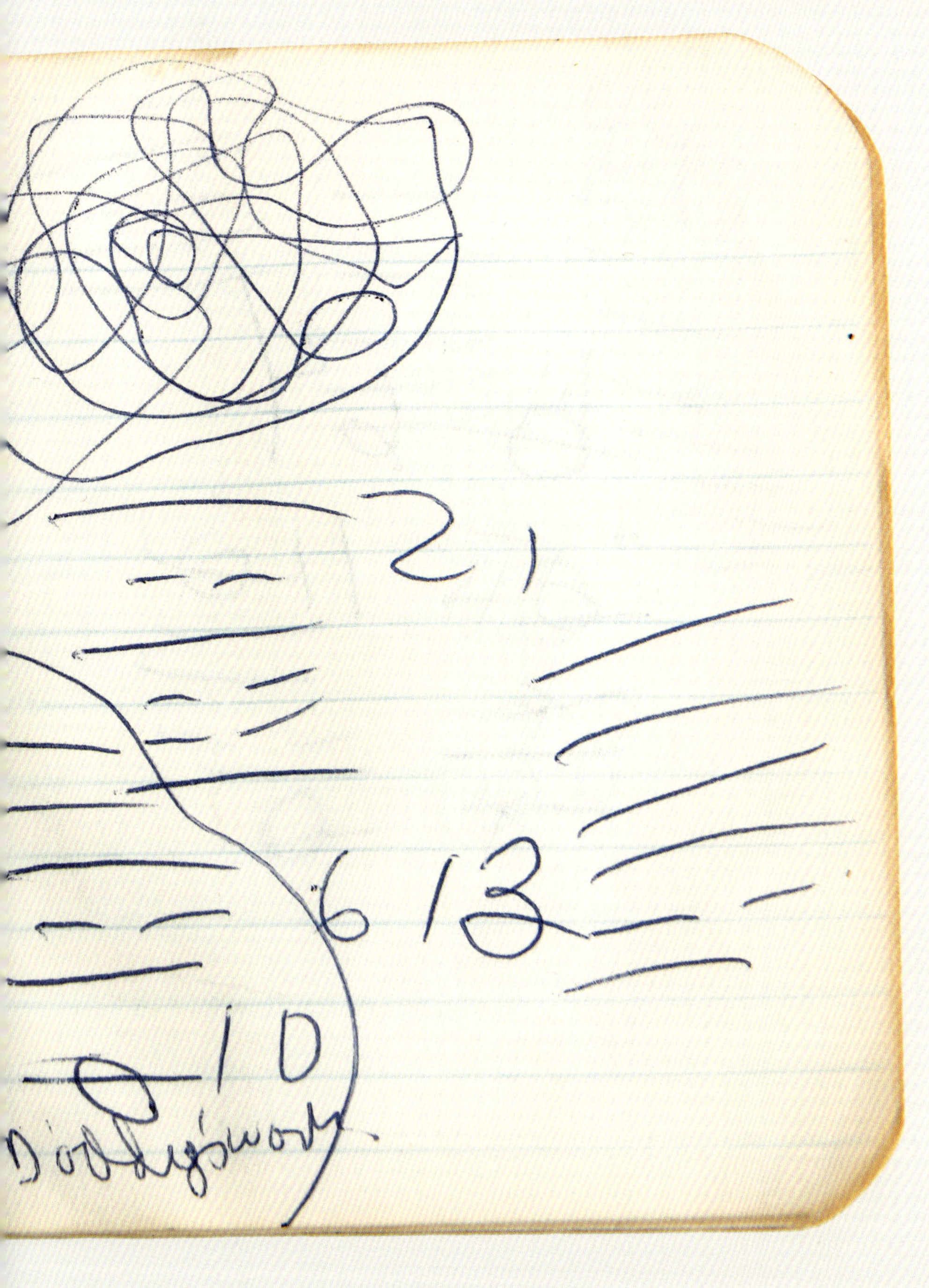
21
613
10

B on the re-photo's
Behind all immediate
experiences, are the
underlying, hidden
reality, or archetypal
reality - fluent posting
- Basic geometric or
elemental shapes
into the scene the
~~subjective~~ mood or
quality of the image is
heightened

The reason for 1

Notebook 1988.1

Wed –
1 – Bank
2 – Pay wed + gas bills
have prints made
Prod
4 – Ginseng

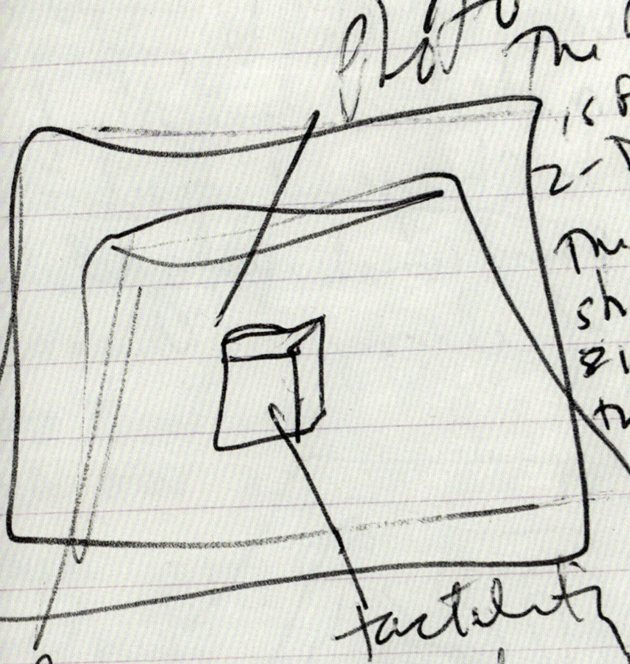

photo

The photograph
is flat
2 – D.

The geometric
shape
& introduces
the element
of touch.
Feel –
the basic
element
of ~~photo~~ photo-
graph

tactility

By ~~area~~ rephotographing
the photograph with a
Sculpture form I
emphasize the materiality

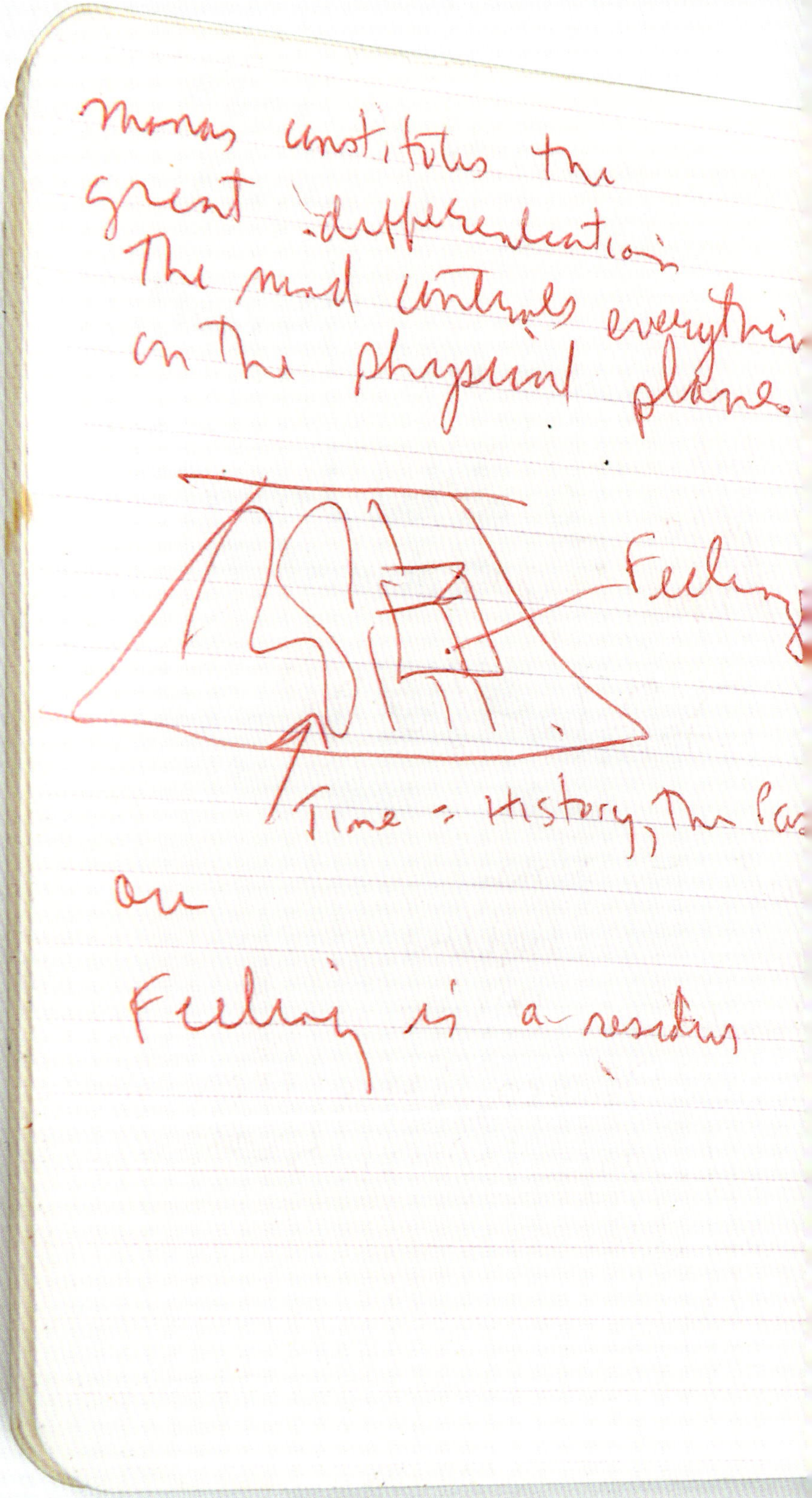

Manas constitutes the great differentiation
The mind contains everythin
on the physical plane.

Feeling

Time = History, The Pas

or

Feeling is a residue

Notebook 1988.1

The shape of the stretcher has itself a perspective

tonight I made what I hope will be interesting images –

lining up the image in a logical sequence so that it is readable

Notebook 1988.1

Perception

[s]itting on top of the sculpture and projection so I can get a straight [o]n view of the image [w]ith distortion, ~~to~~ perspective distortion.

should be interesting to see I thought about Bacon then Giacometti and how in order to see his sculptures like the man with the long pointed nose - you must stand directly in front of its [t]o correct the exaggerated [p]erspective of the nose length

The photographic image represent the public, generalities: The obliteration of the face in my photos – could signify the erasure of individuality, impersonal. Drawing the polar opposite of this is completely personal for me.

Notebook 1989.1

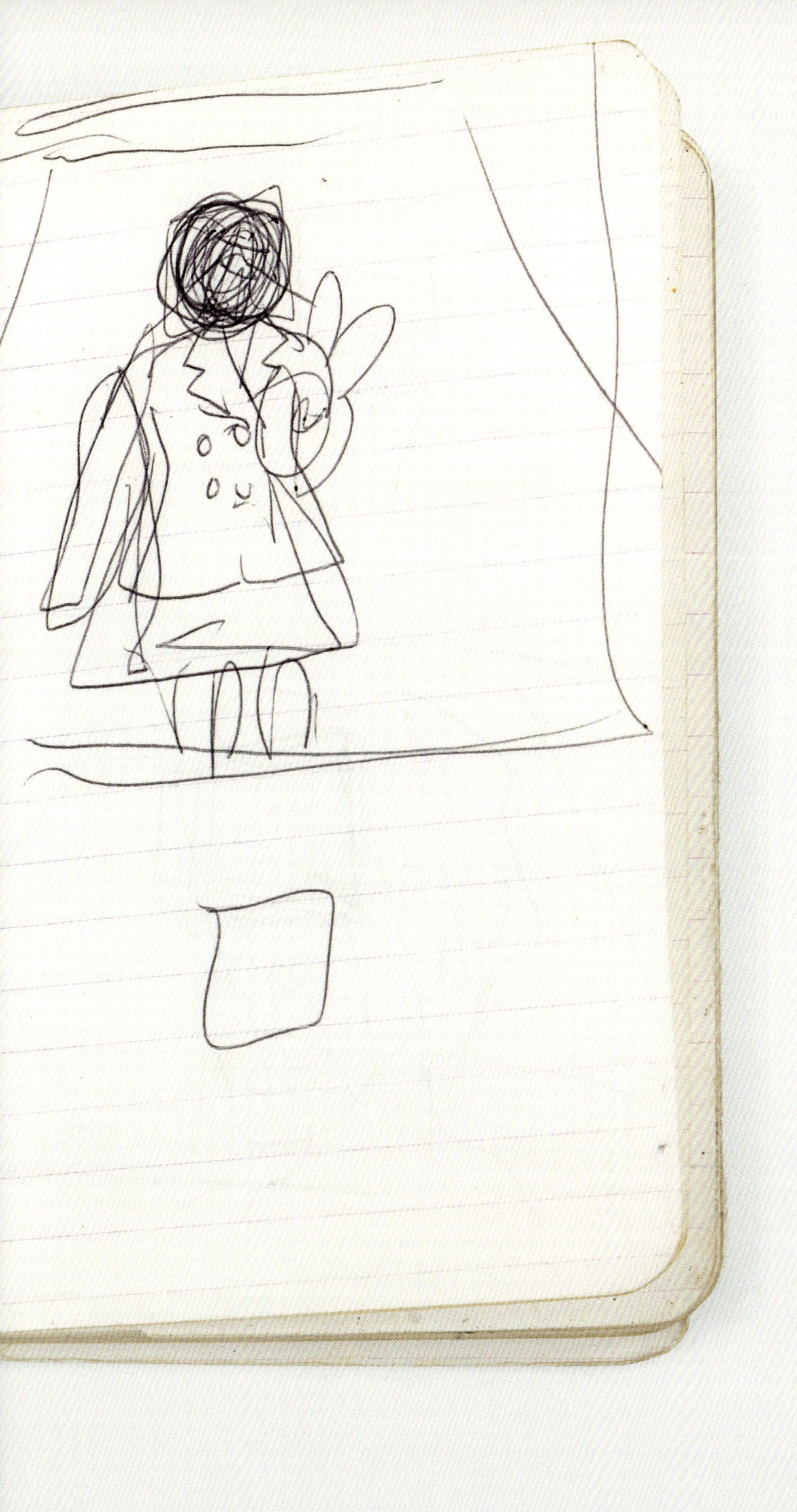

The works have to be larger -
1- Buy opaque projector
2- Stretch ① large canvas
982-7100 : DAVID DAVIS

1- almond Butter
2- BREAD, either Pumpernickel raisin
OR sprouted grain
3- millet, rice-cakes
4- cumin, coriander
5- olives, cheese
6- Soy Sauce -
Stretch smaller canvases like the size of the one I did at MoMA do non-linear, but larger than the ones I've done.

Notebook 1989.1

make lentil + okra · cauliflower soup
cook lentils, steamed veggies
combine
~~avocado + tomatoes~~, ~~watermelon~~ · ~~peaches~~
apple purée, Bottled water, parsley
lentil-veggie soup
soak lentils, cook - steam carrots cauliflower ~~...~~ parsley

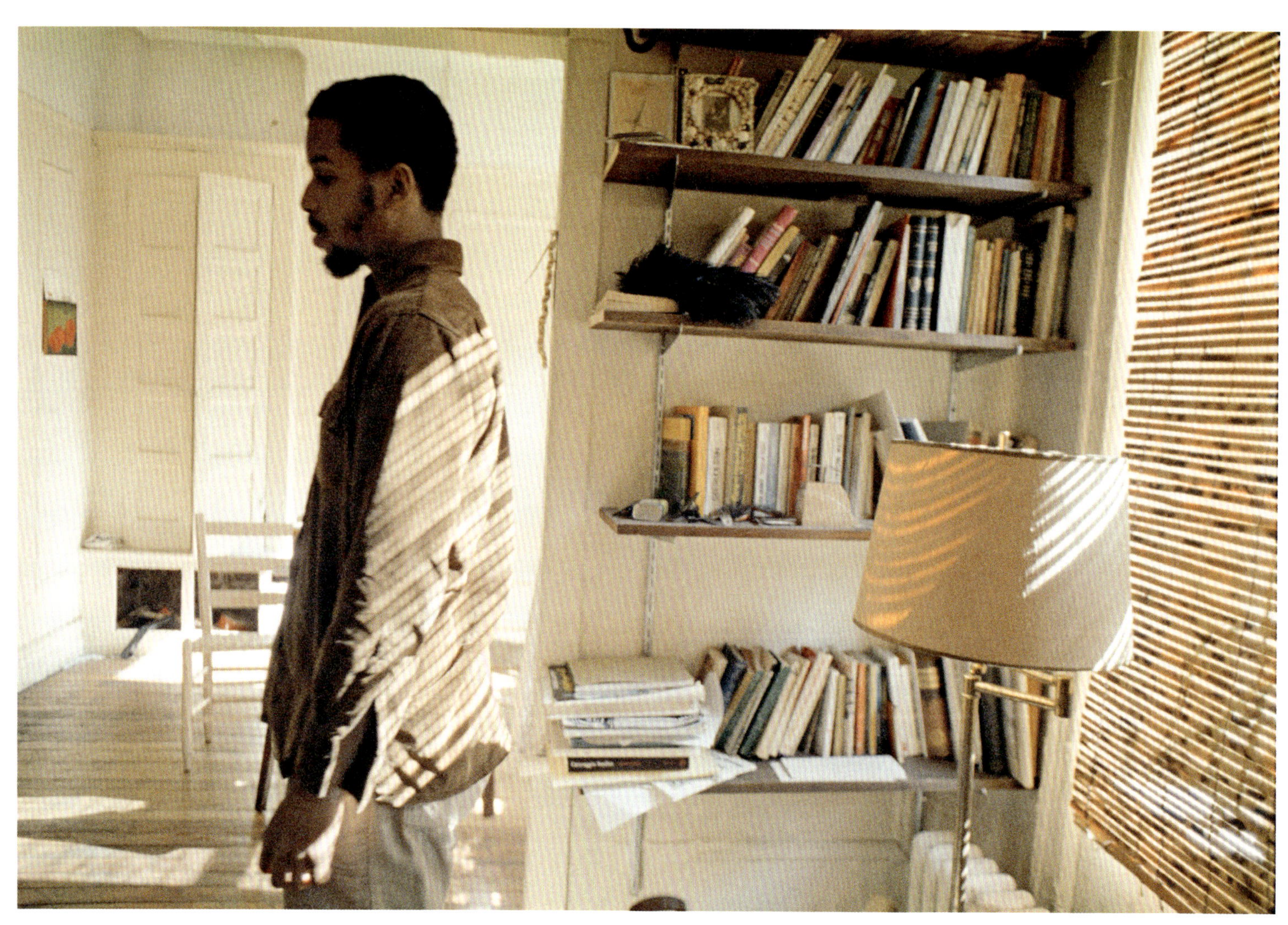

Allen Frame, *Darrel Ellis in José Rafael Arango's Apartment*, 1981
Chromogenic print, 11 × 14 in.
Collection of the artist

## Photo Credits

Unless otherwise indicated, all images courtesy of the Estate of Darrel Ellis and Candice Madey and photographed by Adam Reich.

front cover, pp. 1, 4, 16, 33–36, 38, 40, 42, 44, 49, 50, 56, 57, 59, 64–67, 70–72, 73 (bottom), 75, 78, 85, 86, 88, 91, 96, 98, 102, 109, 117, 118, 122, 123, 128, 145, 146, 149 (bottom left), 150 (top left), 151, 152, 176, 184, 185, 188–90: courtesy of the Estate of Darrel Ellis, Candice Madey, and Visual AIDS, photo by Christopher Burke Studios

p. 22 (left): digital image courtesy of Getty's Open Content Program
p. 22 (right): courtesy of the Metropolitan Museum of Art
p. 23 (left): © 2006 RMN-Grand Palais (musée du Louvre), photo by Thierry Le Mage
p. 24: digital image © The Museum of Modern Art, licensed by SCALA / Art Resource, NY
p. 25: © 2022 Artists Rights Society (ARS), New York / ADAGP, Paris
p. 26 (left): © RMN-Grand Palais / Art Resource, NY
p. 29: © James Van Der Zee Archive, The Metropolitan Museum of Art
p. 30: Henry Ossawa Tanner papers, 1860s-1978. Archives of American Art, Smithsonian Institution
p. 45: © The Robert Heinecken Trust
p. 46: © Estate of Nathan Lyons, courtesy of the George Eastman Museum
p. 48: courtesy of Women's Studio Workshop, photo by Alec Logan Smith
p. 54: Photographs and Prints Division. Schomburg Center for Research in Black Culture. The New York Public Library, Astor, Lenox and Tilden Foundations. Photograph © Morgan and Marvin Smith.
back cover, pp. 92, 139 (left): courtesy of the Baltimore Museum of Art
pp. 106, 107: courtesy of White Columns
p. 108: © James Welling, courtesy the artist and David Zwirner
p. 111: courtesy of Liora Mondlak, photo by Adam Reich
pp. 114, 120, 121: courtesy of the Bronx Museum of the Arts, photo by Adam Reich
p. 124: courtesy of Galerie Crone, Berlin
pp. 131, 133, 138, 172: courtesy of Allen Frame
p. 132: courtesy of James Wentzy
p. 139 (right): © 2022 The Peter Hujar Archive / Artists Rights Society (ARS), New York
pp. 142, 143: courtesy of the Estate of Darrel Ellis and Candice Madey, photo by Kunning Huang
pp. 150, 151 (details): photos by Linda Owen

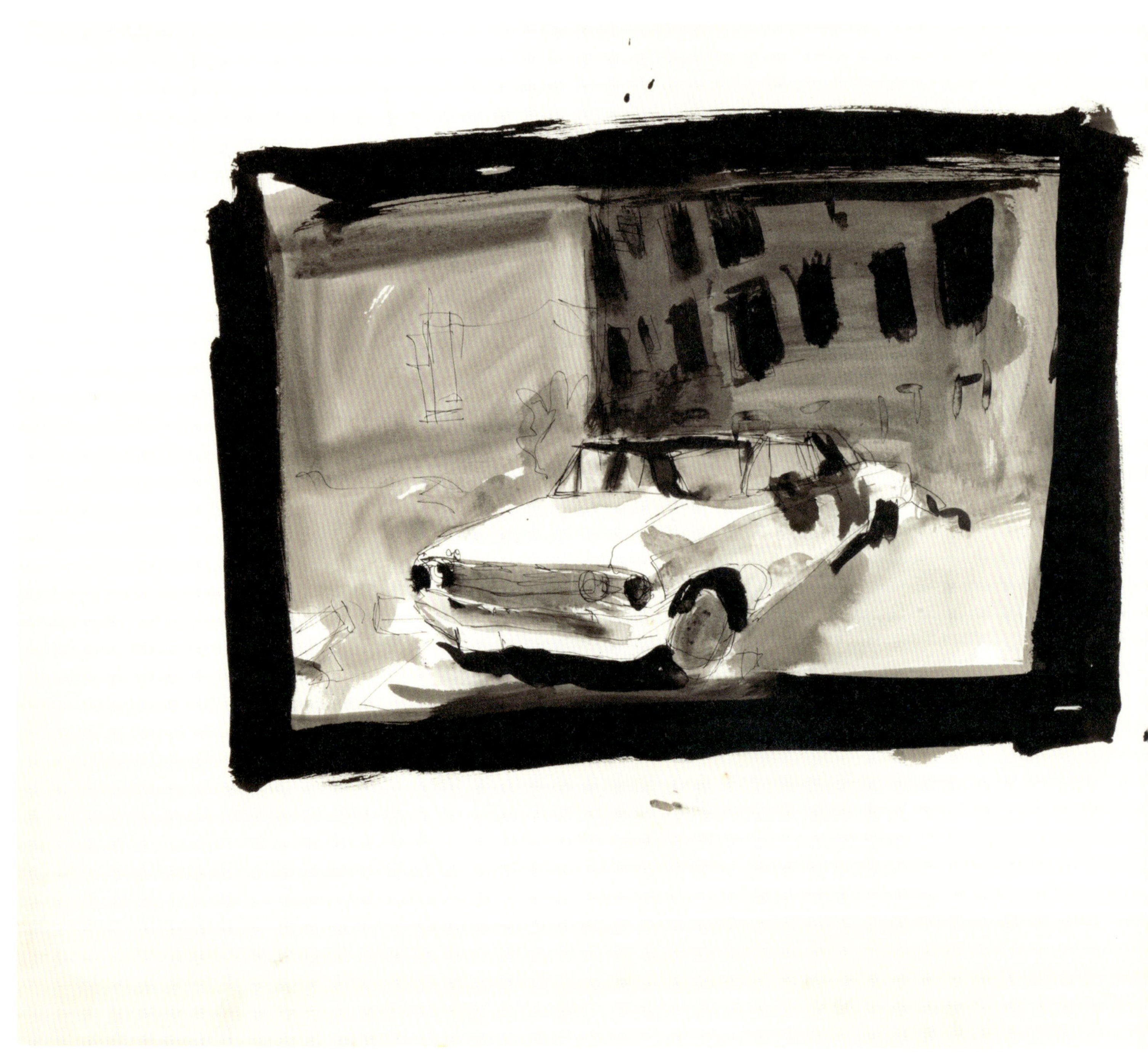

*Untitled (Car in Street)*, ca. 1988–91
Brush and black ink, wash,
and graphite on paper
28 × 40 in.

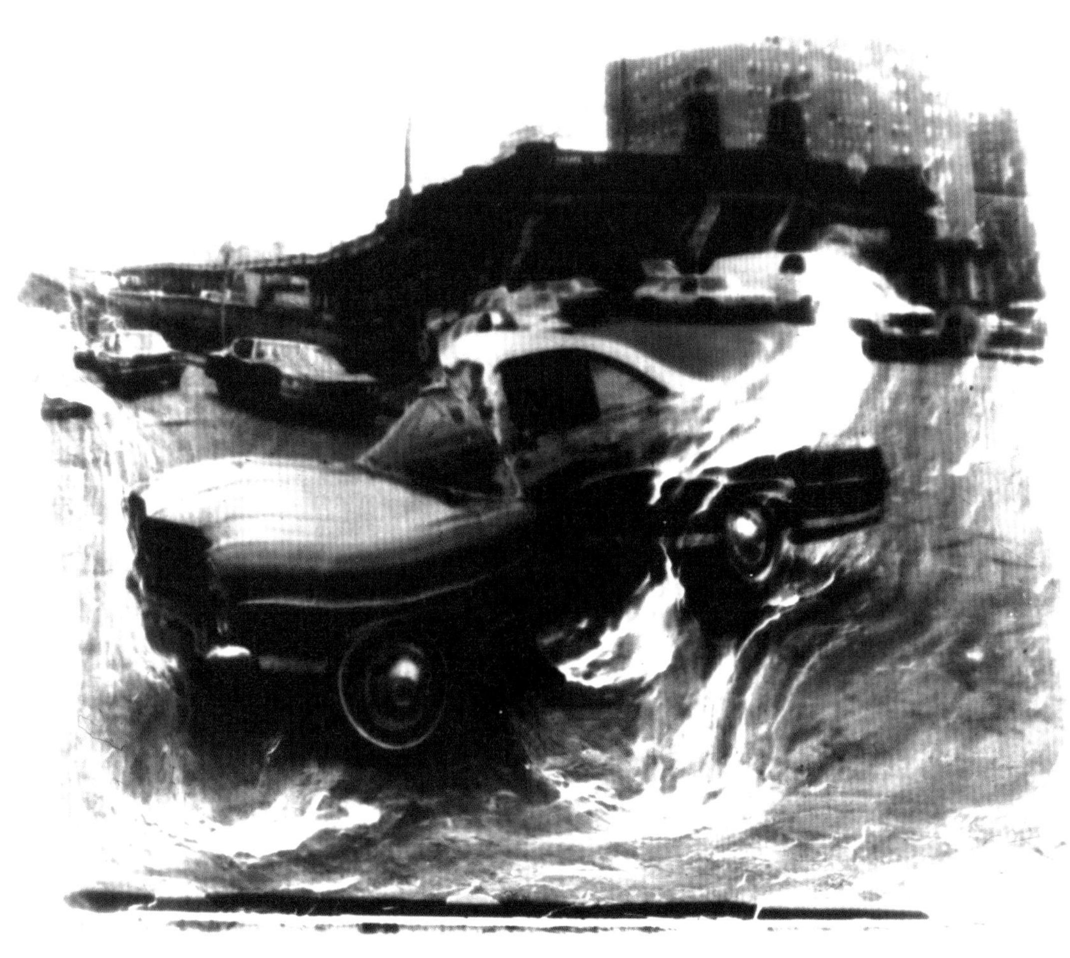

*Untitled (Car in Street)*, ca. 1988–91
Gelatin silver print
11 × 14 in.

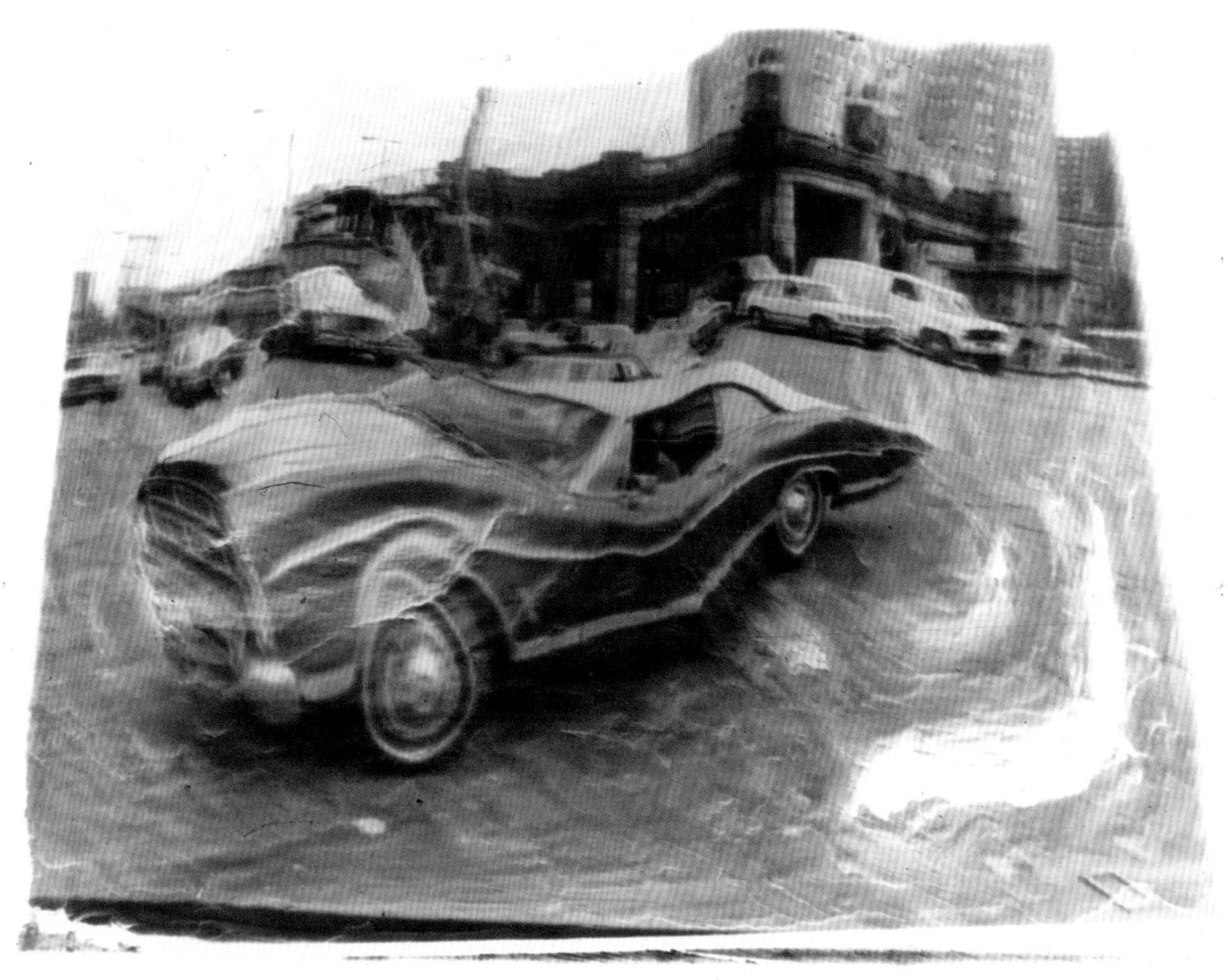

*Untitled (Car in Street)*, ca. 1988–91
Gelatin silver print
11 × 14 in.

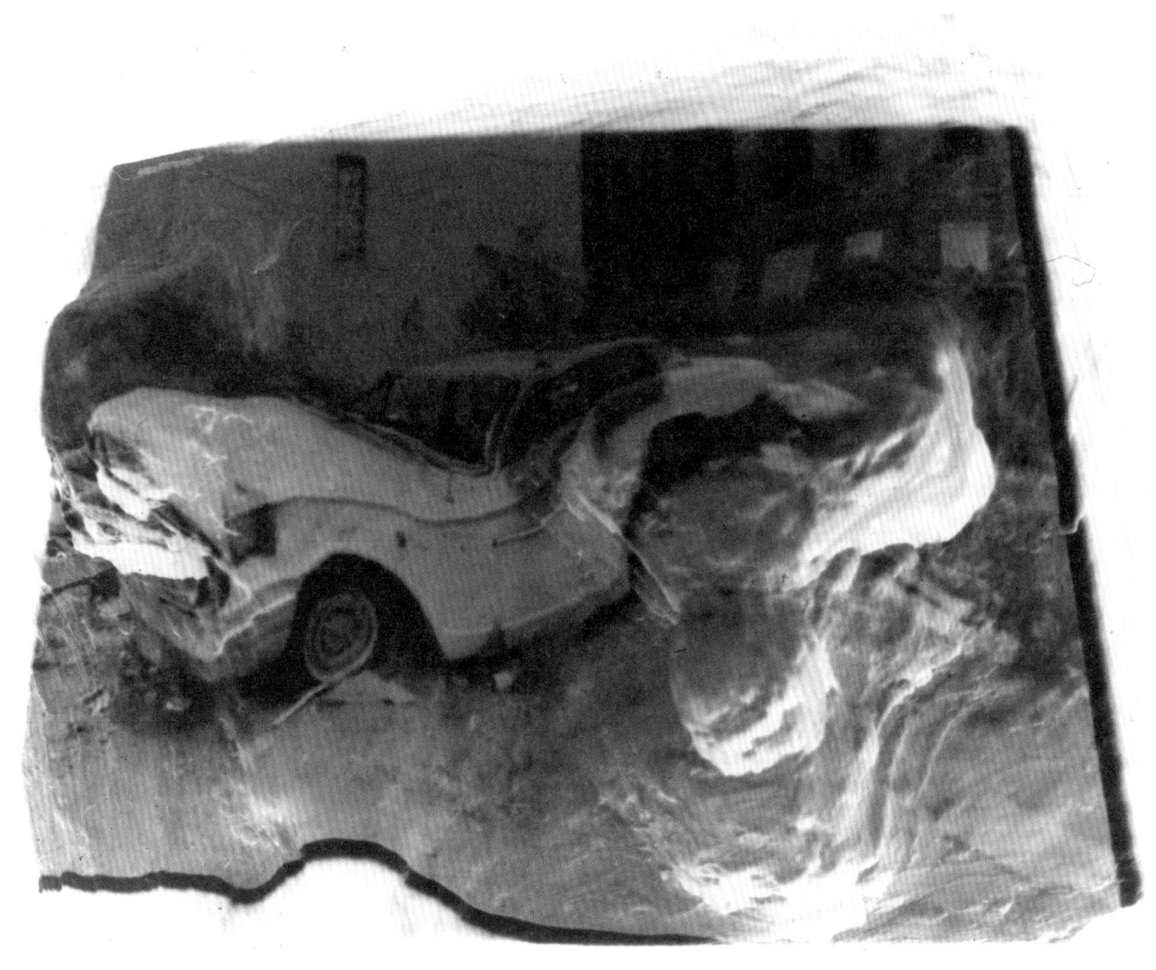

*Untitled (Car in Street)*, ca. 1988–91
Gelatin silver print
11 × 14 in.

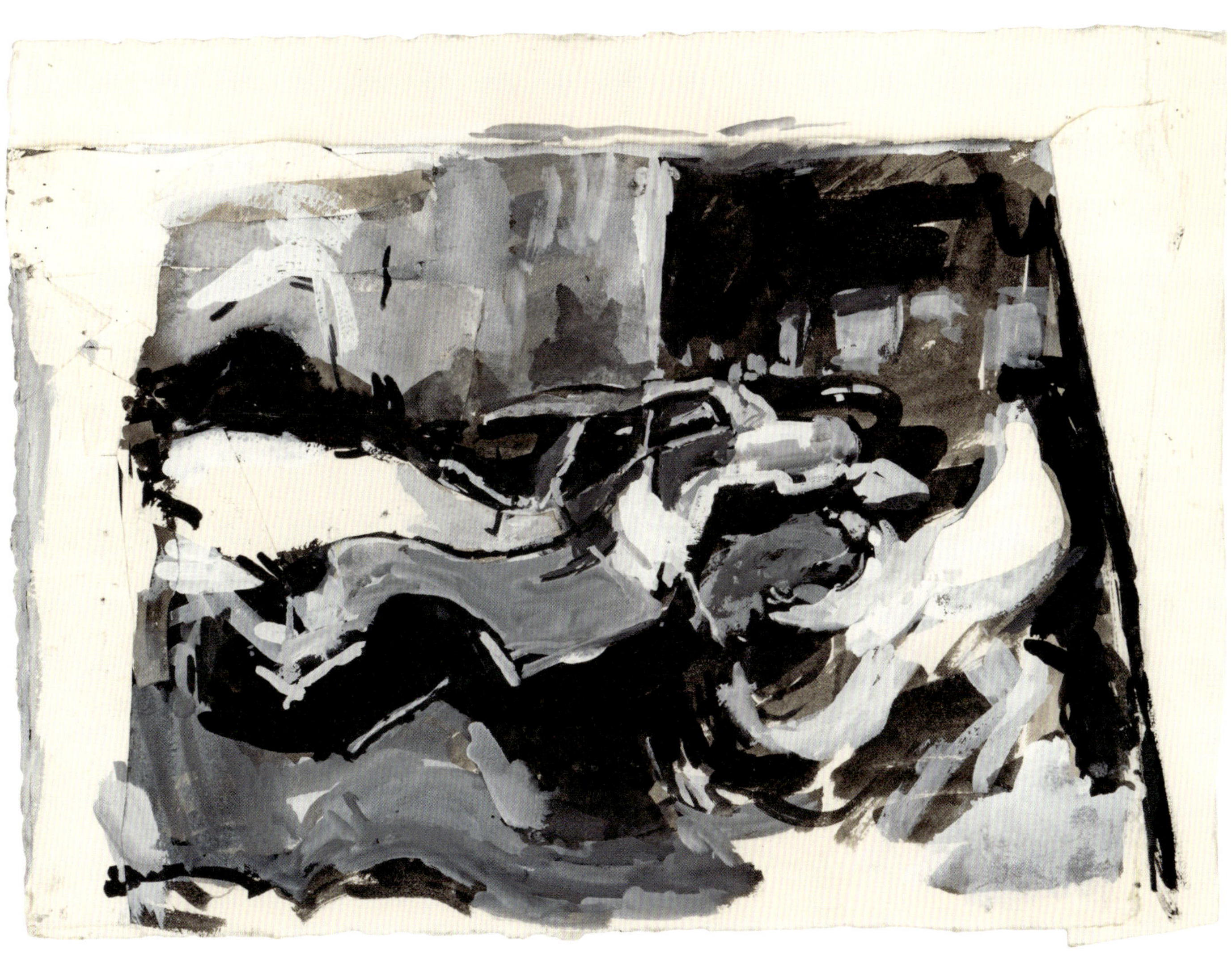

*Untitled (Car in Street)*, ca. 1988–91
Acrylic on paper
17 ½ × 24 in.

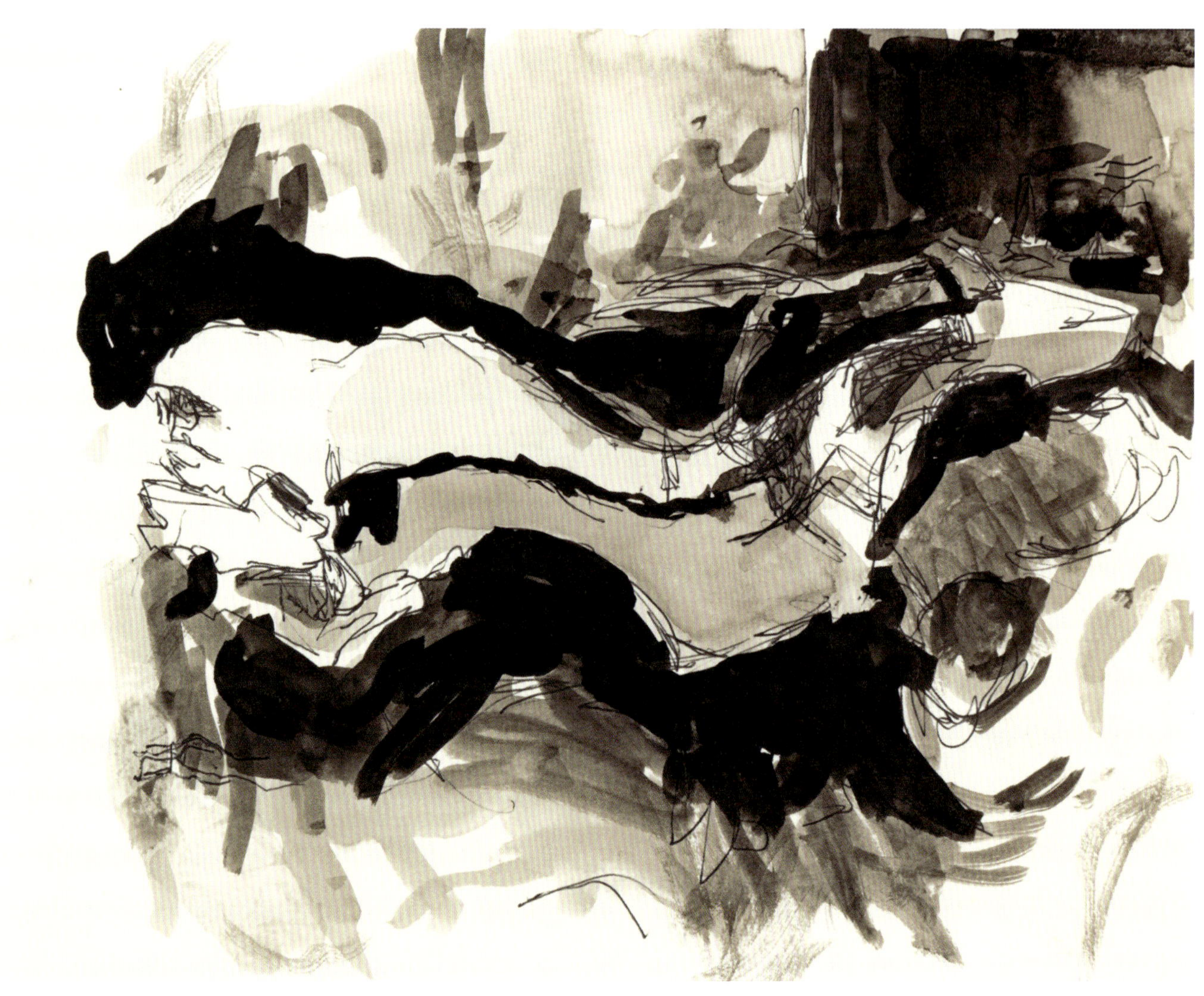

*Untitled (Car in Street)*, ca. 1988–91
Brush and black ink and wash on paper
9 × 12 in.

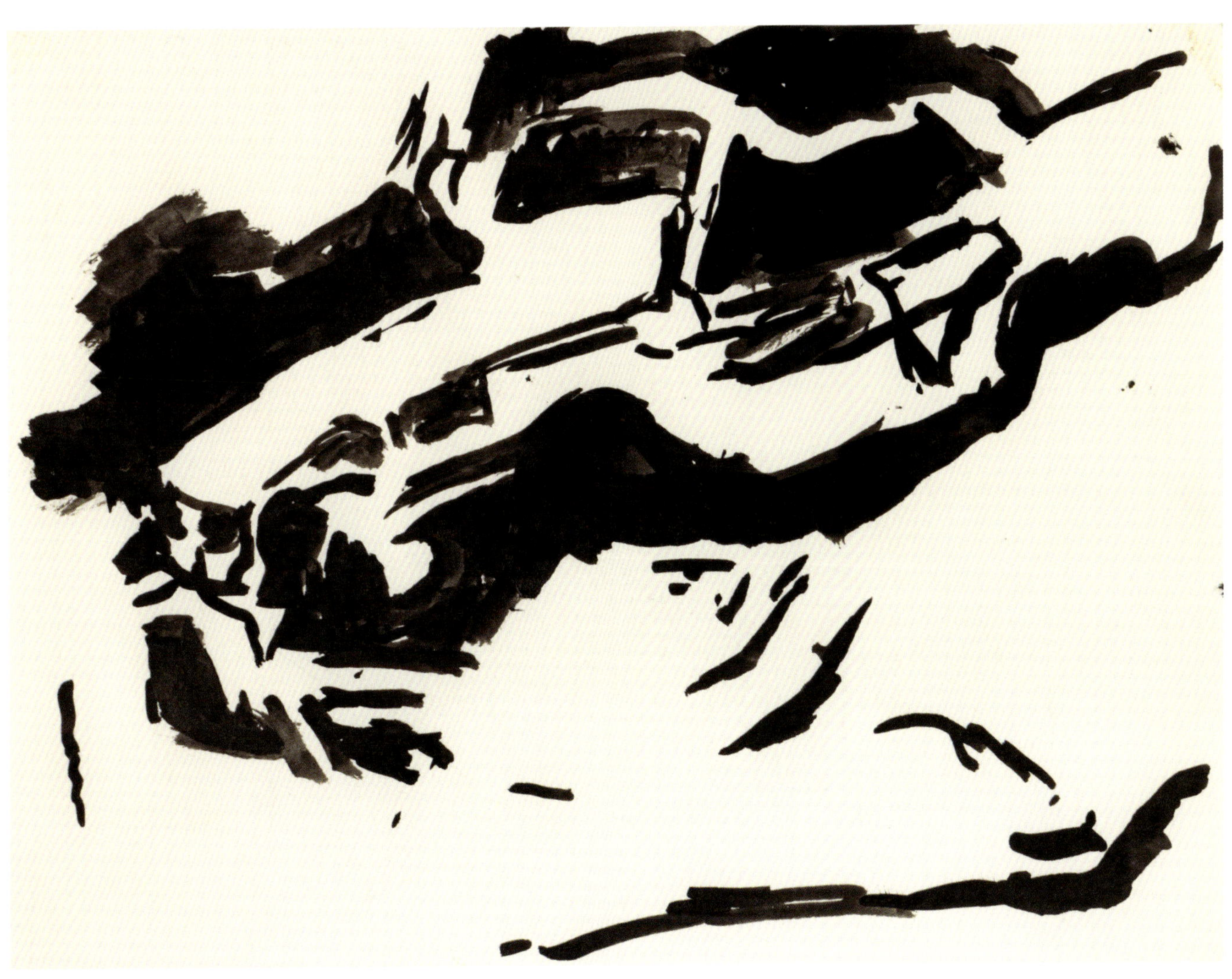

*Untitled (Car in Street)*, ca. 1988–91
Brush and black ink on paper
9 × 12 in.

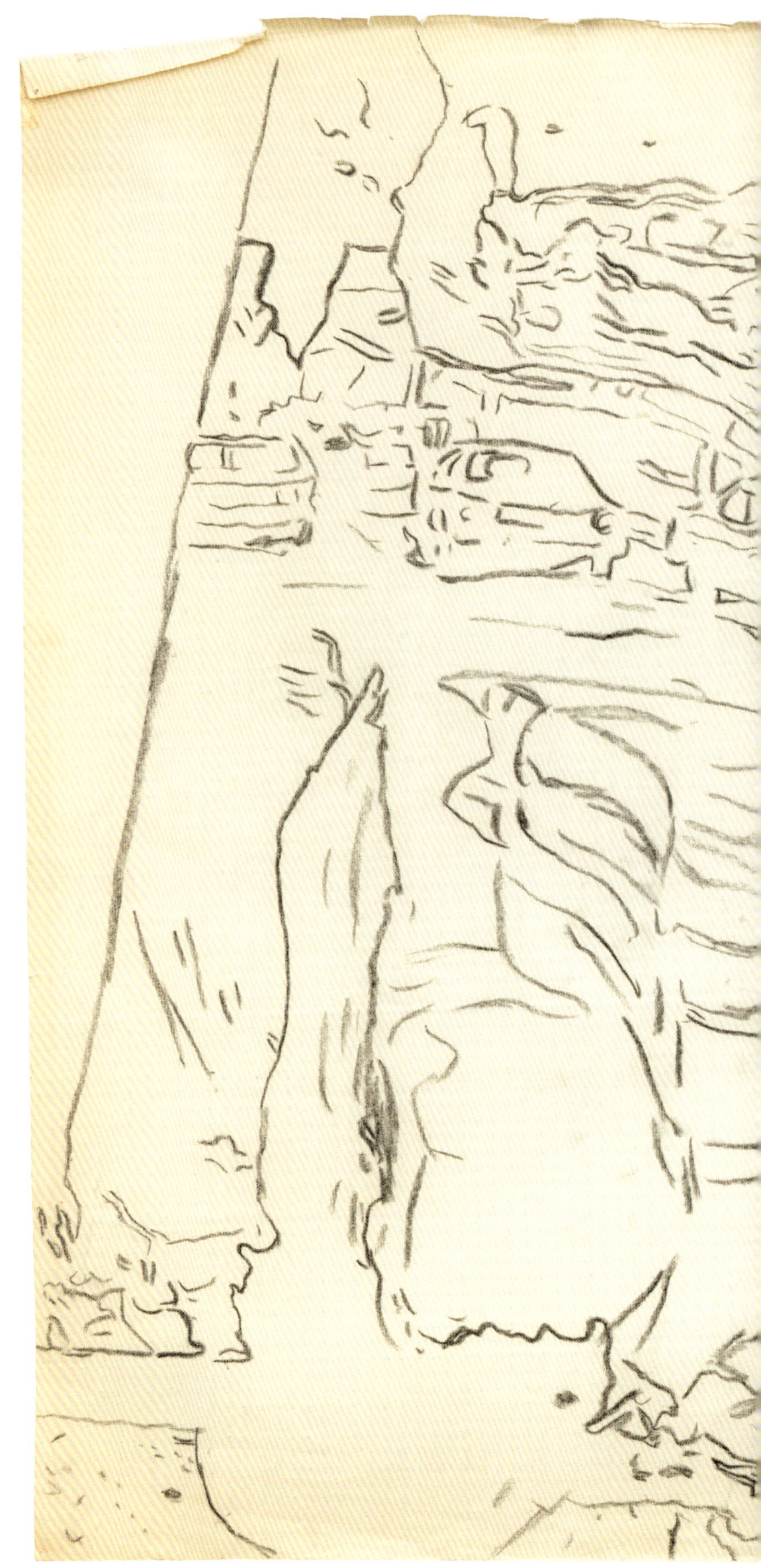

*Untitled (Car in Street)*, ca. 1988–91
Charcoal on paper
27 ½ × 39 ½ in.

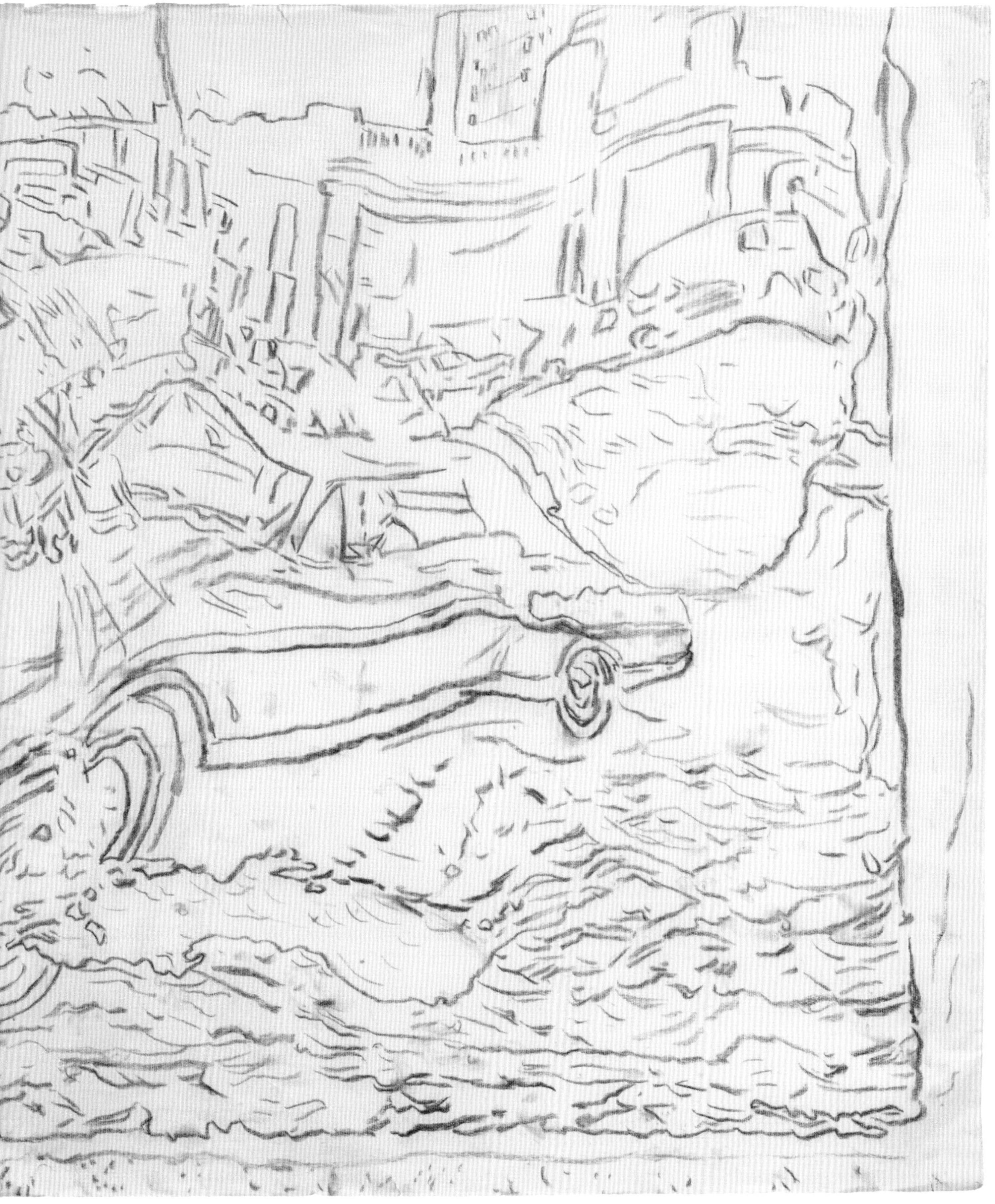

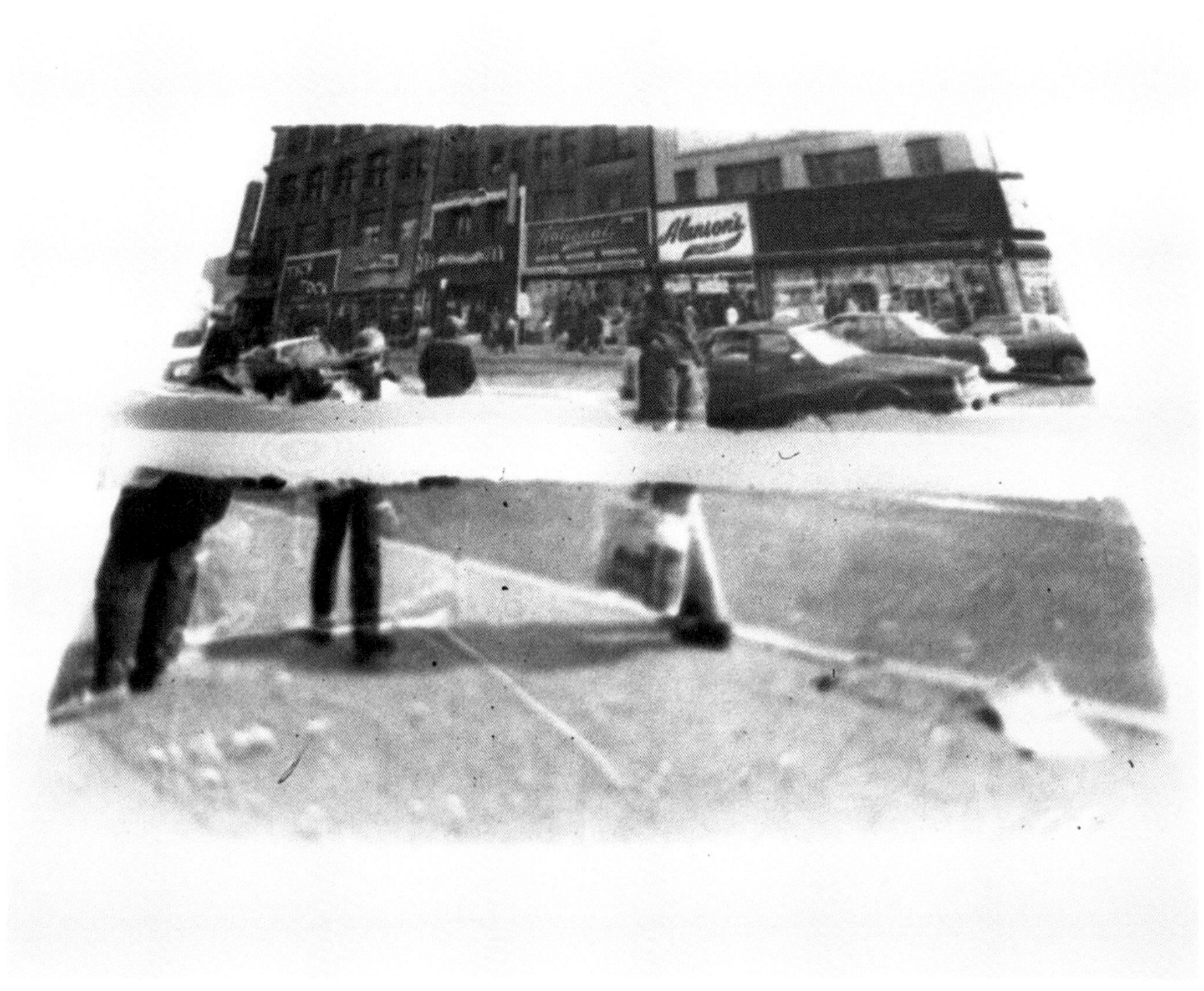

*Untitled (Street Scene)*, 1987
Gelatin silver print
11 × 14 in.

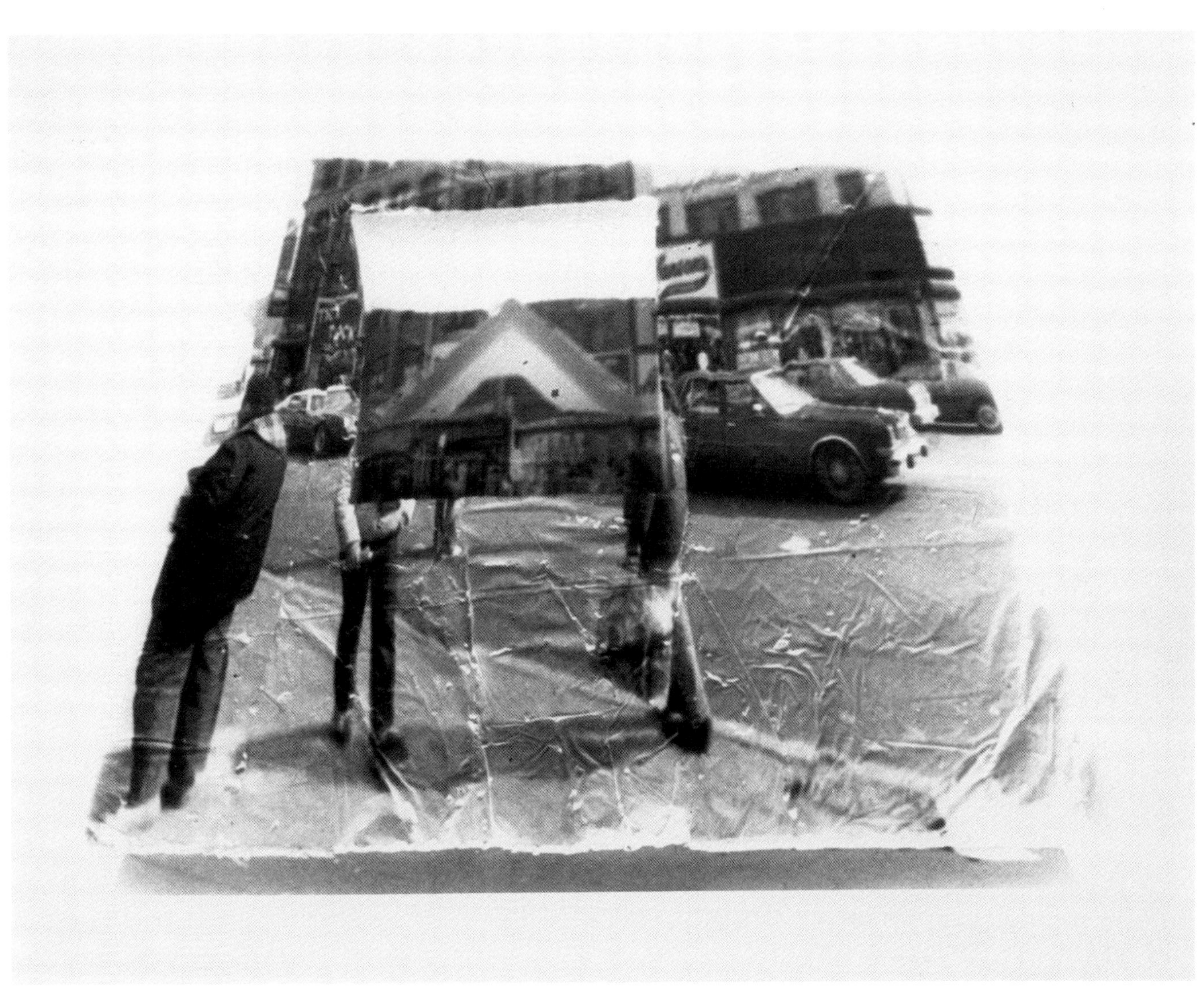

*Untitled (Street Scene)*, 1987
Gelatin silver print
11 × 14 in.
Whitney Museum of American Art

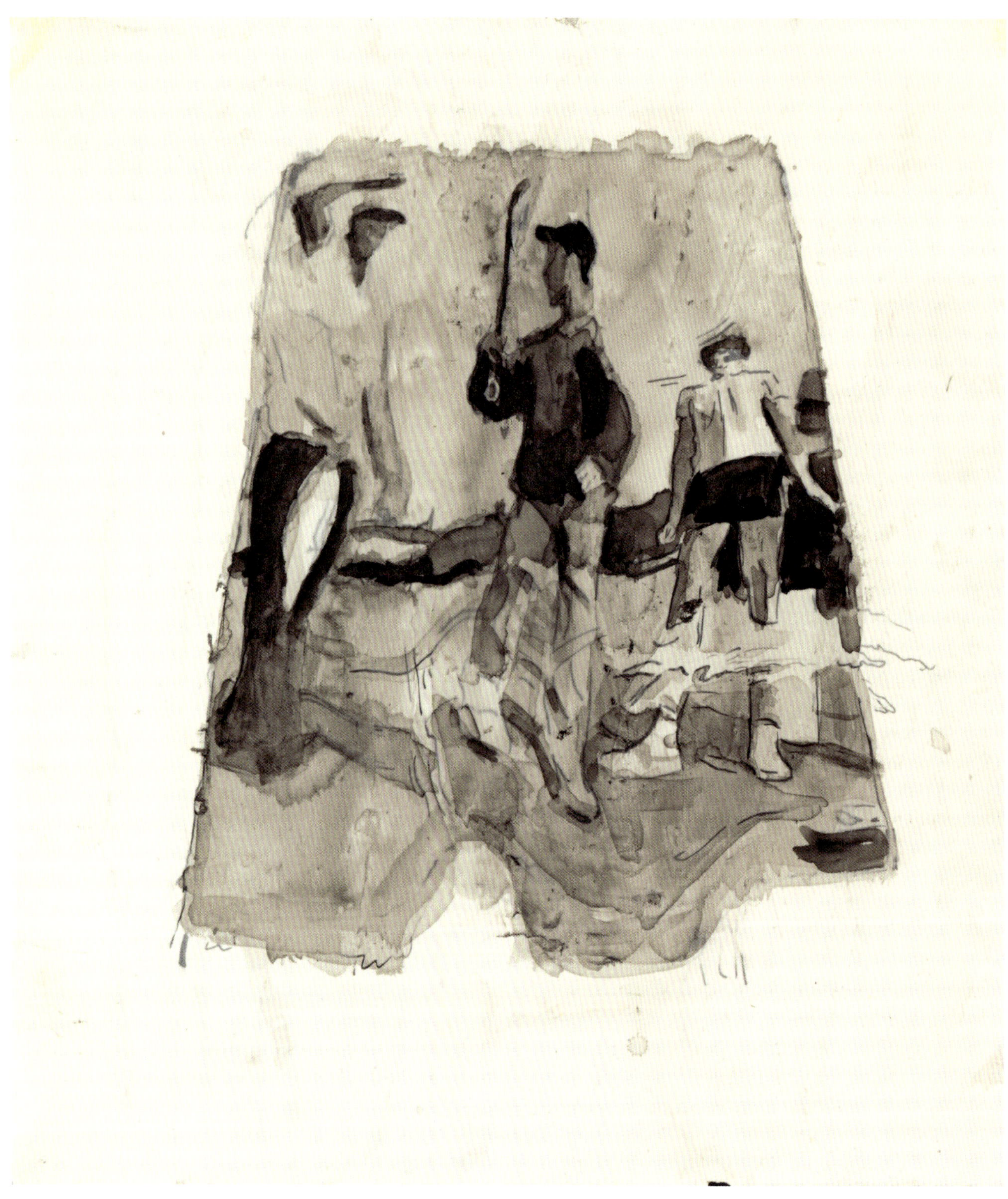

*Untitled (Figure at Greenpoint Pier)*, 1991
Pen and brush and black ink and wash
on paper
13 × 12 in.

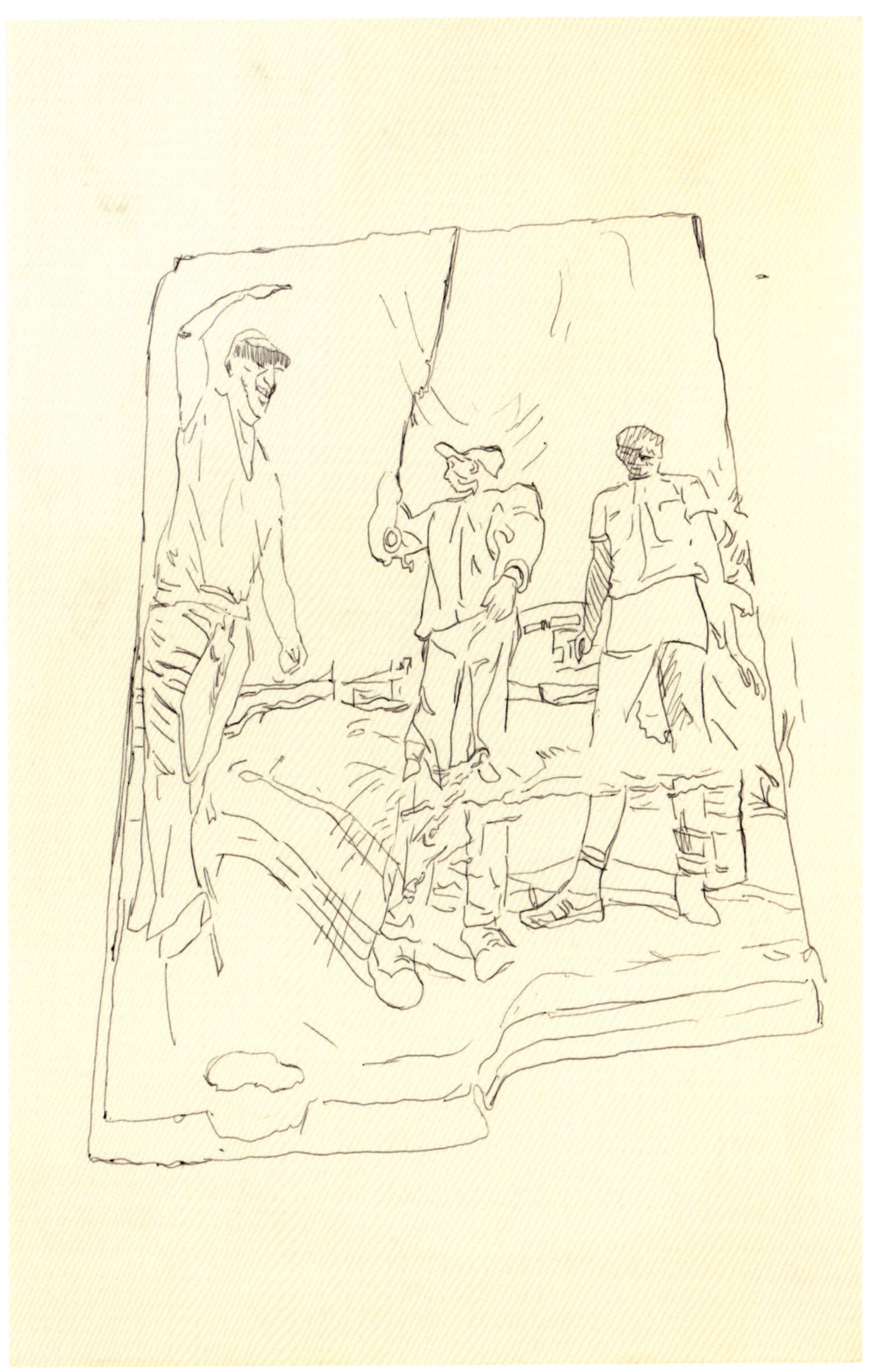

*Untitled (Figure at Greenpoint Pier)*, 1991
Pen and black ink on paper
18 × 12 ½ in.

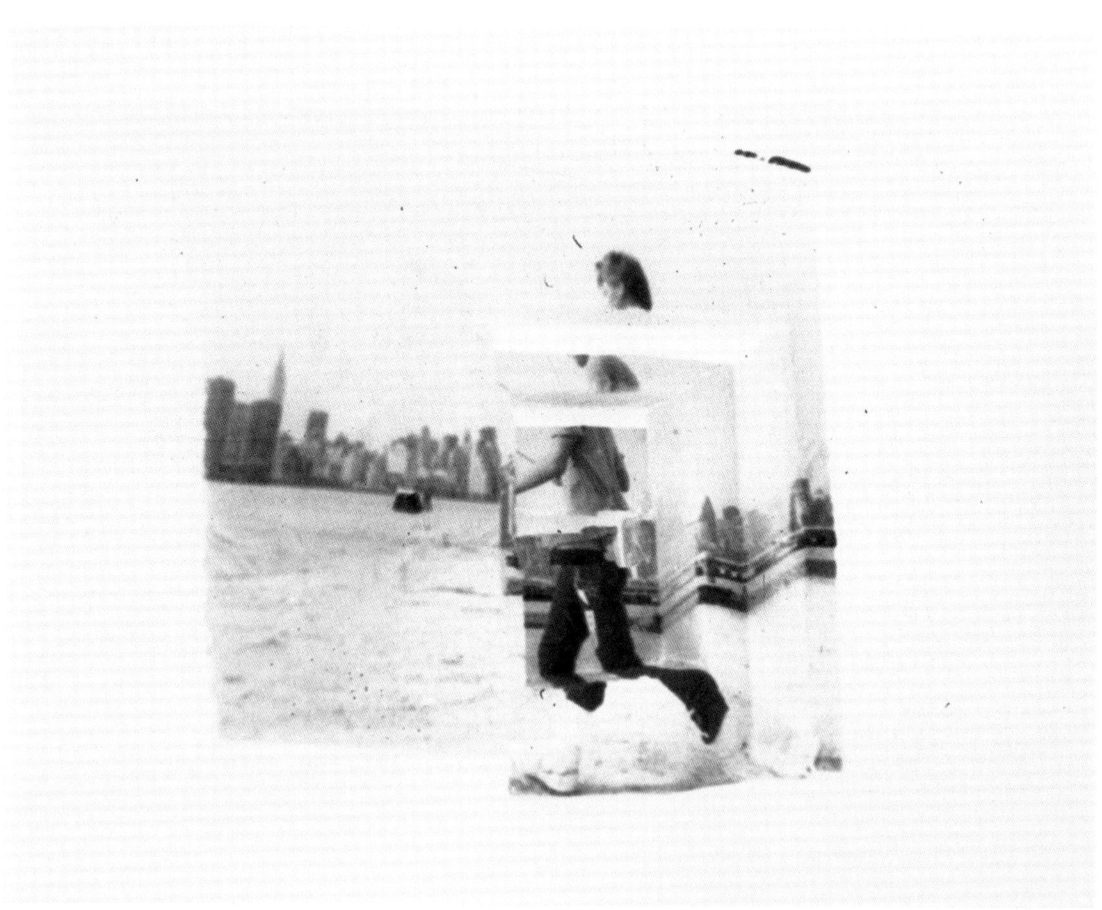

*Untitled (Figure at Greenpoint Pier)*, 1991
Gelatin silver print
11 × 14 in.

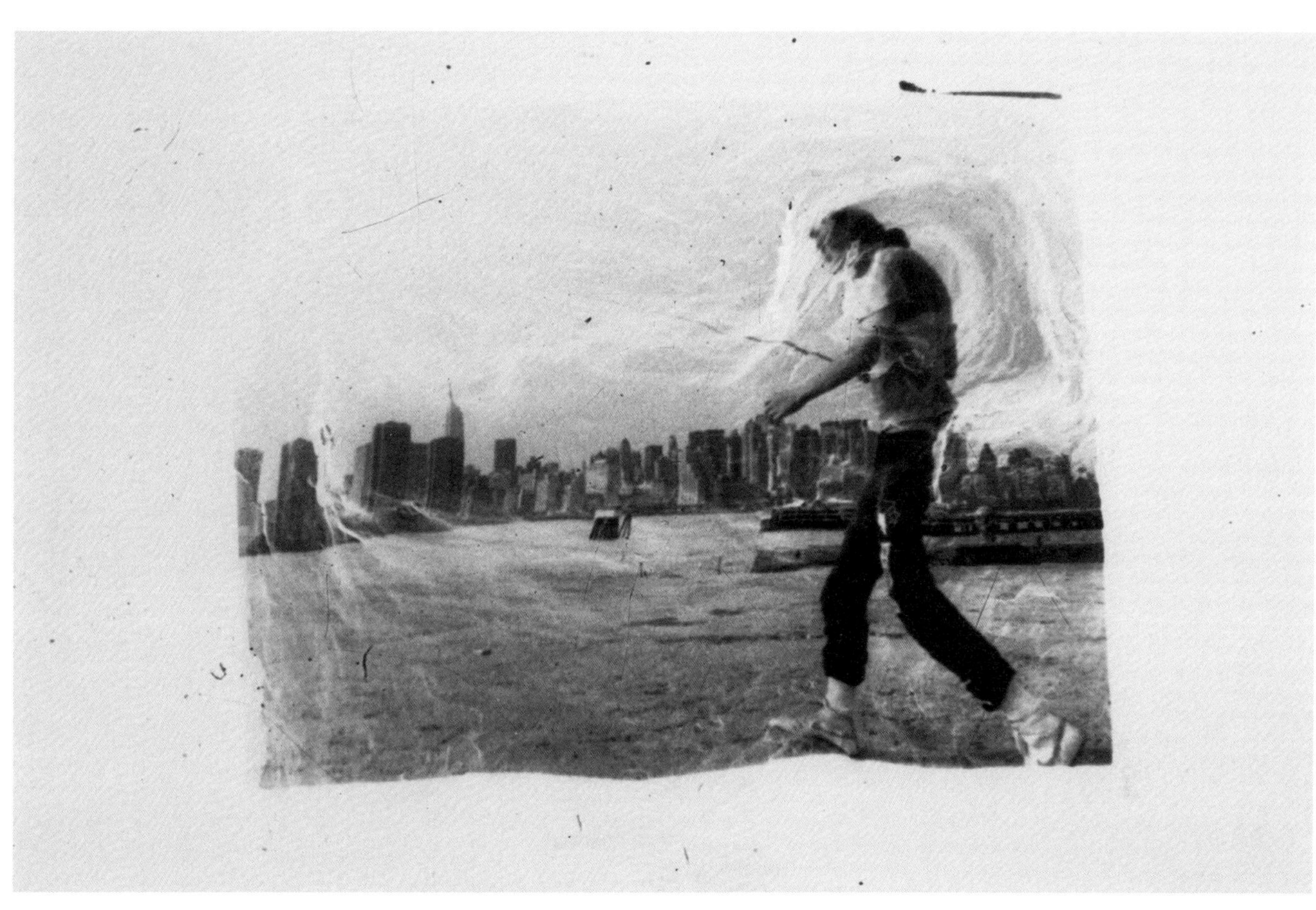

*Untitled (Figure at Greenpoint Pier)*, 1991
Gelatin silver print
9 × 13 in.
Collection of Luca Cipelletti

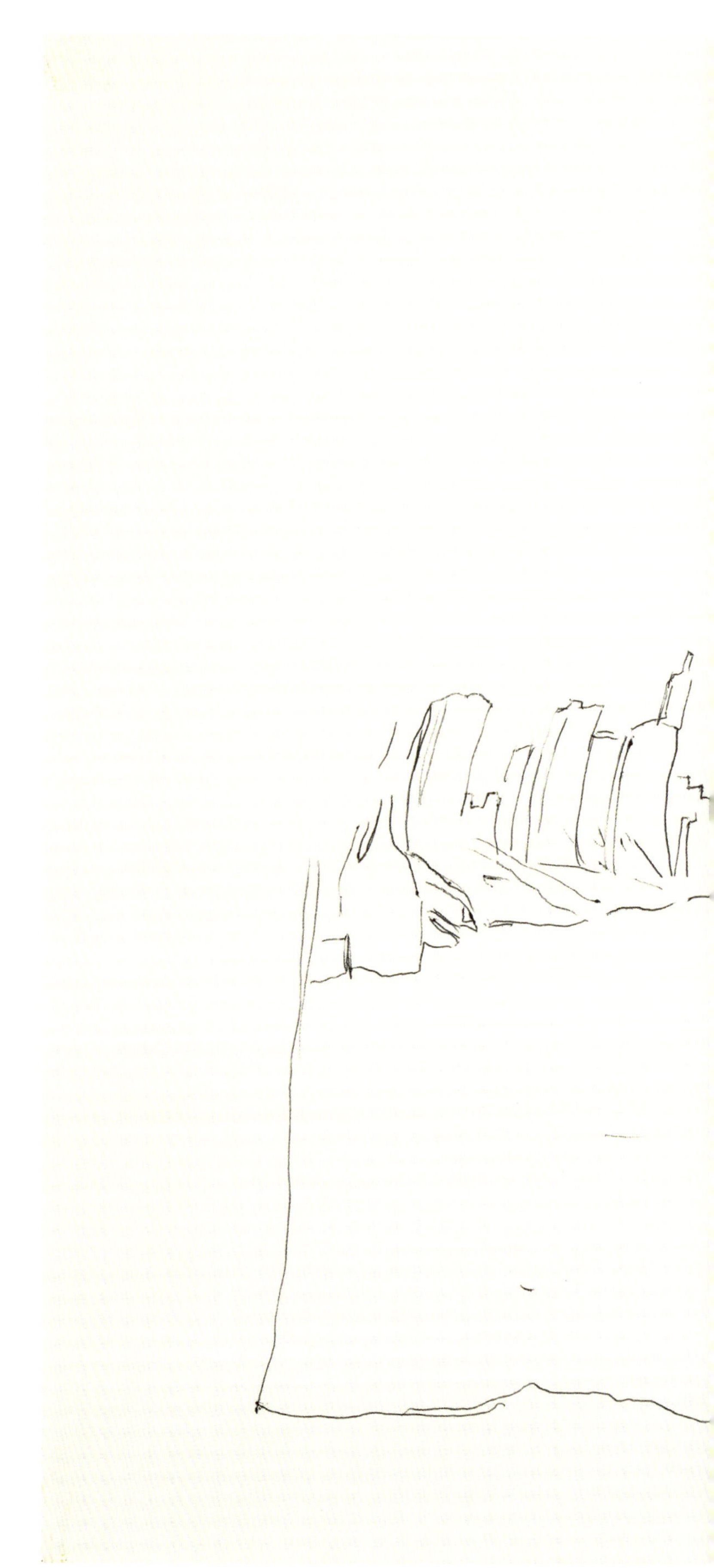

*Untitled (Figure at Greenpoint Pier)*, 1991
Pen and black ink on paper
19 ½ × 27 in.

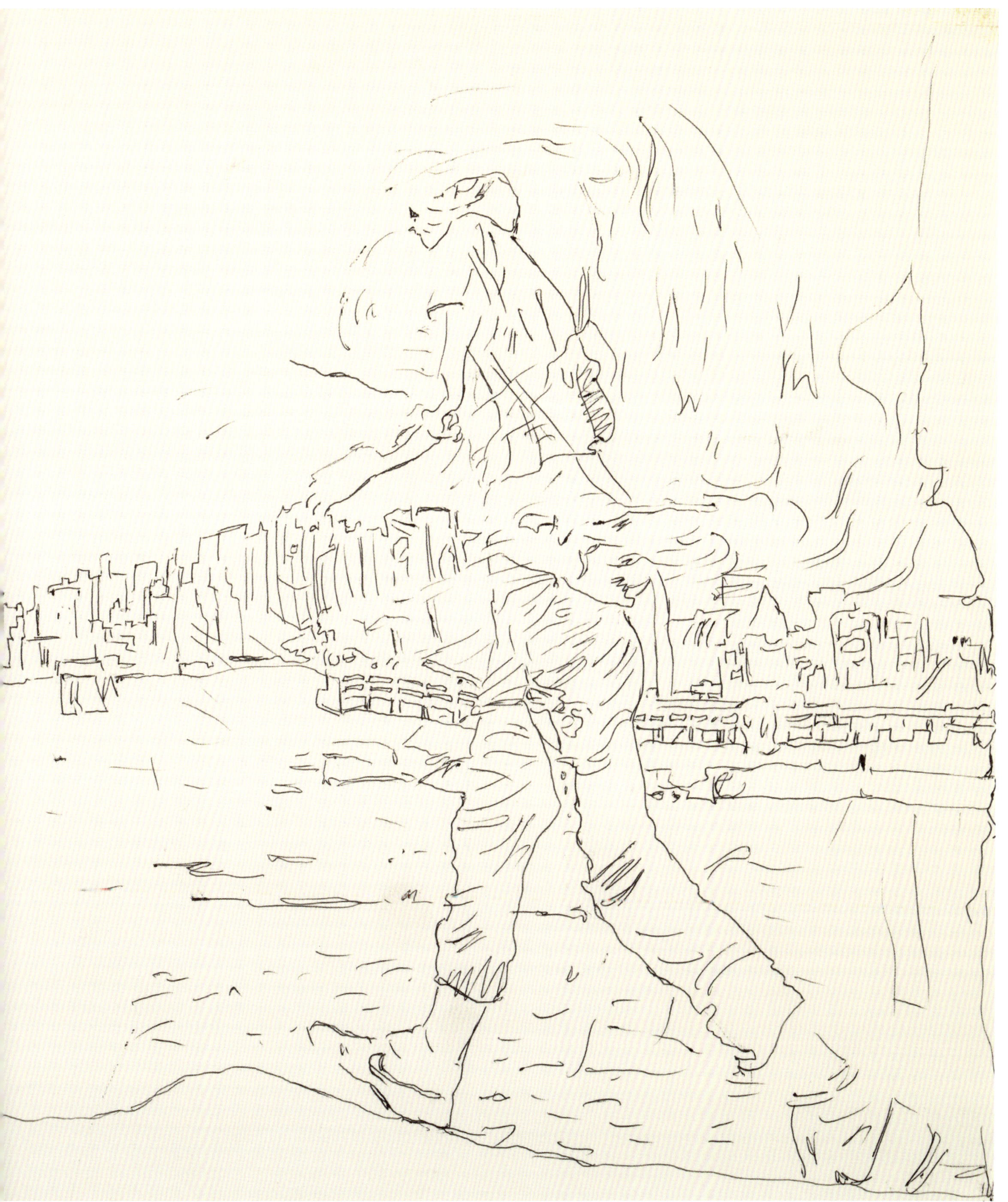